P9-DYY-657

Cambridge Studies in American Literature and Culture

Writing the South

Cambridge Studies in American Literature and Culture

Editor

Albert Gelpi, Stanford University

Advisory Board

Nina Baym, University of Illinois, Champaign-Urbana
Sacvan Bercovitch, Harvard University
Richard Bridgman, University of California, Berkeley
David Levin, University of Virginia
Joel Porte, Harvard University
Mike Weaver, Oxford University

Other books in the series

Robert Zaller: *The Cliffs of Solitude*
Peter Conn: *The Divided Mind*
Patricia Caldwell: *The Puritan Conversion Narrative*
Stephen Fredman: *Poet's Prose*
Charles Altieri: *Self and Sensibility in Contemporary American Poetry*
John McWilliams: *Hawthorne, Melville, and the American Character*
Barton St. Armand: *Emily Dickinson and Her Culture*
Mitchell Robert Breitwieser: *Cotton Mather and Benjamin Franklin*
Albert von Frank: *The Sacred Game*
Beth McKinsey: *Niagara Falls*
Marjorie Perloff: *The Dance of the Intellect*
Albert Gelpi: *Wallace Stevens*
Karen Rowe: *Saint and Singer*
Paul Giles: *Hart Crane*

Writing the South

Ideas of an American region

RICHARD GRAY

NEW HANOVER COUNTY
PUBLIC LIBRARY
201 CHESTNUT STREET
WILMINGTON, N. C. 28401

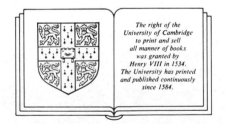

*The right of the
University of Cambridge
to print and sell
all manner of books
was granted by
Henry VIII in 1534.
The University has printed
and published continuously
since 1584.*

CAMBRIDGE UNIVERSITY PRESS

Cambridge
London   New York   New Rochelle
Melbourne   Sydney

Published by the Press Syndicate of the University of Cambridge
The Pitt Building, Trumpington Street, Cambridge CB2 1RP
32 East 57th Street, New York, NY 10022, USA
10 Stamford Road, Oakleigh, Melbourne 3166, Australia

© Cambridge University Press 1986

First published 1986

Printed in Great Britain at
the University Press, Cambridge

British Library cataloguing in publication data
Gray, Richard, 1944–
Writing the South: ideas of an American region.
– (Cambridge studies in American literature and
culture)
1. Regionalism – Southern States – History
2. Southern States – Civilization
I. Title
975   F209

Library of Congress cataloguing in publication data
Gray, Richard J.
Writing the South.
(Cambridge studies in American literature and culture)
1. Southern States – Civilisation. 2. Southern
States – Intellectual life. 3. American literature –
Southern States – History and criticism. I. Title.
II. Series.
F209.G724   1986   975'.0072   85-30945

ISBN 0 521 30687 6

SE

To
MY FATHER AND MOTHER
JOYCE, CATHARINE, BEN, AND JENNIFER

. . . his very body was an empty hall echoing with sonorous defeated names; he was not a being, an entity, he was a commonwealth. He was a barracks filled with stubborn back-looking ghosts . . .

William Faulkner, *Absalom, Absalom!*

Contents

Illustrations

SOURCES AND ACKNOWLEDGEMENTS

Nos. 1, 3, 4, 5–9, 10, 11 the American History Slide Collection, the American Studies Resource Centre, the Polytechnic of Central London; no. 2 Virginia Historical Society; no. 12 Atlanta News Agency.

Preface

Anyone who chooses to write about the American South is almost immediately confronted with a problem. *Is* there such a thing as the South, a coherent region and an identifiable culture that can be sharply differentiated from the rest of the United States? To be sure, W. J. Cash writing over forty years ago saw no such problem – or, at least, claimed not to. "There exists among us", he wrote in his prefatory remarks to *The Mind of the South*,

> . . . a profound conviction that the South is another land . . . Now and then
> . . . there have arisen people, usually journalists or professors, to tell us that it is
> all a figment of the imagination . . . Nobody, however, has ever taken them
> seriously. And rightly.[1]

But Cash's own approach was rather subtler – which is to say, more responsive to the difficulties clustering around the search for Southern identity – than these remarks suggest. And, since his book was published, the problem that he dismisses here with such breezy confidence has become ever less manoeuvrable, ever less easy to circumvent or surmount. This is the result, really, of two recent developments: the emergence of a sort of consensus among Southern historians about the relationship between region and nation, and the invasion of Southern historiography by various practitioners ("usually journalists or professors", Cash might say) of atomistic sociological techniques. On the one hand, increasingly more historians have argued that the South is not significantly different from the rest of the nation, offering at most a minor variation on the American norm. While, on the other, some sociologists, and many less academically inclined observers, have taken the quite different tack of concentrating their attention on particular localities and groups – the mountain communities of the Appalachians, say, the tourist areas along the Atlantic coast, or the urban cultures of

Atlanta, New Orleans or Nashville; in doing so, they have rendered the notion of a homogeneous place – "another land", to use Cash's phrase, complete and whole – less tenable or at least highly arguable. The *fact* of the South has been called into question, both by the nationalists and the localists. Consequently, attention has shifted in the past few years to the *idea* of the South, the study of the intellectual history of the region and the development of Southern myth.

The main aim of this book is to make some small contribution to this study of the Southern argument, the various ways in which people from below the Mason–Dixon line have tried to forge the uncreated conscience of their region. It is not, in any sense, a survey of Southern writing: anything along those lines would take several volumes, even supposing it were possible. Nor does it represent an attempt to sum up the mind of the South once and for all. If my intentions for it have been realised (which, of course, is a large 'if'), it offers no more than a series of notes towards a definition of the Southern idea. They are notes, it should be added, written in the belief that the South *is* primarily a concept, a matter of knowing even more than being, and as such part of the currency of our language and perception. Which is not at all to devalue it; quite the contrary, as I see it the vital importance of the Southern image springs from the fact that it represents what the poet Wallace Stevens would call an idea of order, a structuring principle – or perhaps it would be more accurate to say a set of structural possibilities, frames for composing and articulating experience. Generations of Southerners have, I believe, been engaged not so much in writing about the South as in writing the South; they have, whether they have known it or not (and, as a matter of fact, many have known it) been busy reimagining and remaking their place in the act of seeing and describing it. And in giving some account of this process, whereby a thing known has habitually become a thing reinvented, I have, wherever I have found it helpful, borrowed certain ideas from linguistics or literary theory; since such ideas offer, I think, a convenient and accurate way of beginning to understand the intense, cross-grained and yet extraordinarily creative relationship that can exist between a society, its people, and its writing.

All of this may sound intolerably abstract. I hope, though, that what I have to say avoids the dangers of abstraction by sticking always to particular moments, figures, and texts. Starting with the period of colonisation, and concentrating on certain crucial periods of transition, moments of crisis in the regional story, I have tried to discuss Southern thinking in terms of individual people, how they responded to crisis, and specific books, how they organise language and present arguments. Of course, I am well aware that to begin my discussion with the colonial period is in itself controversial, if only because many observers prefer to locate the beginnings of Southern legend in the late eighteenth or early nineteenth century: when, so they argue, the development of sectional interests – and certain more specific things like the rise of Abolitionism and the threat of slave insurrection – helped give birth to a regional self-consciousness. But it is my firm belief, which I shall try to substantiate, that the seeds of this self-consciousness were sown much earlier, by the colonisers and their friends and supporters, who were tempted to see the new world across the Atlantic under the compulsions of an old vocabulary. Prompted by feelings of dispossession and loss, they sought to figure the wilderness in terms that would not only help them to appropriate and subdue it but would also enable them to see it as redemptive. In the process, they drew up a sort of blueprint for the Southern argument; they became the first to give expression to those ideas of a distinct local identity, a peculiar character and a special destiny, that have underpinned so much that has been thought and said about the place ever since.

The details of that argument can be left until later, however; and the table of contents will, I hope, make it clear which periods and people I have chosen to discuss. For the moment, all that needs to be added is that the intended design of this book is incremental. Each chapter, while revealing how the business of writing the South was shaped and then reshaped by particular historical circumstances, is meant to contribute a few further clues to the discovery of the Southern image; it takes its place, or at least is supposed to, within a larger map of regional thinking. To be frank, the map as it is drawn here should really be called a preliminary chart; and emphasis should be placed on the distinction I am now trying to make between regional *thinking* (which implies, I believe, a continuous process, inviting conjecture and at most only partial, provisional disclosure) and the regional *mind* (a rather grander term, suggesting some solid, autonomous object that is available for complete explanation). I hope, nevertheless, that anyone interested in the area I have tried to navigate will find what I have to say of use, despite the many places in the Southern argument I leave uncharted. There seems to be no end to the questions that can be asked about the South, the problems and impediments to be negotiated, and no limit to the points at which the truthful cartographer must leave a blank. That is part of its fascination, though, one reason why it has intrigued so many people – and among them a number of foreigners such as myself. *Tell about the South*, asks a character in William Faulkner's *Absalom, Absalom!*,

> *What's it like there. What do they do there. Why do they live there. Why do they live at all.*[2]

It is an outsider, the Canadian Shreve, who asks these questions. As another outsider, an Englishman, I must admit that it was similar questions – together with related feelings of bewilderment, wonder, and a kind of incredulous admiration – that drew me to the South in the first place, nearly twenty years ago. They have drawn me ever since; and I have tried, as best I can, to begin answering them here.

I have incurred very many debts while writing this book: so many, in fact, that I can only mention a few of them. In the first place, I have drawn to some extent on essays I have written previously: in chapters 3 and 4 on "Kingdom and Exile: Mark Twain's Hannibal Books" and "From Oxford: The Novels of William Faulkner", in *American Fiction: New Readings* ed. Richard Gray (London: Vision Press, 1983), and in chapter 6 on "The Dream of Time Passing", in *The Times Higher Education Supplement*, June 25, 1982. Though the borrowings are relatively light, acknowledgements to these publishers are due. I would also like to thank the British Academy, the American Philosophical Society, and the International Communication Agency for their generous financial assistance, and the staff at the Inter-Library Loan section of the University of Essex Library for their unstinting help. On a more personal note, I owe special thanks to Tjebbe Westendorp for first giving me the idea of writing this book; Sylvia Sparrow for patiently typing the various drafts; Carter Martin, Dan Patterson, and Dan Young for their hospitality and expertise; Joe Allard, Chris Brookeman, and Mike Weaver for their invaluable advice about illustrations; Herbie Butterfield, George Dekker, Dennis Reid, Charles Swann, and Dudley Young for helping me to think about literature; and my family for just about everything. What is written here is, of course, my own responsibility: but I would never even have got started had it not been for the help, support, and encouragement of these and many other people – and, in the case of my family, without their tolerance and occasional moments of quietness.

RICHARD GRAY

Wivenhoe
March 1985

1

Virginia and the arguments for the South

REMEMBERING THE FUTURE: THE VIRGINIA PAMPHLETEERS

The colonisation of Virginia was primarily a business enterprise, financed by merchants and nobles who wanted a good return on their investment.[1] However, this did not exclude other less materialistic aims. Human motives are usually mixed; and if, in addition, one accepts the idea that English Protestantism helped to provide the mercantile capitalism of the Elizabethans with a spiritual and ethical base, then it goes almost without saying that the colonisers were interested in moral appropriation of the New World, theological conquest, as well as in economic gain. Nor did this go unrecognised by the colonisers themselves, or their contemporaries. For one of the most frequently cited aims of colonisation, as expressed in the Virginia Charter of 1606, was the "propagation of Christian religion" among those unfortunate enough to live "in darkness and miserable ignorance of true knowledge and worship of God"; and one of the most commonly expressed claims of those who sought to propagandise for the cause of emigration was that (as one of them put it) "the land is too narrow for us" and that consequently men had to "seek after such adventures whereby the . . . customs, . . . the honour and renown of our Nation" could be "spread . . . to the ends of the World".[2] Indeed, many contemporary observers were willing to go further even than that, and argue that the merchant adventurers of the Virginia Company of London were not merely helping to promote and extend a specifically English way of life – they were securing its preservation, ensuring its survival.

The reasons for this rather apocalyptic view of the New World are to be found, really, in certain radical changes that had taken place in the English economy, particularly the agricultural economy, and in people's

1

reactions to those changes. Since the time of the Black Death, the birth-rate had gradually been advancing over the death-rate. At the same time, prices rose at an unprecedented speed, working hardship on all those with fixed incomes – like farmers whose few acres were not quite self-sufficing, those dependent on customary rents, or wage-earners – and benefiting landlords who could rack-rent tenants, farmers producing for town markets, large-scale merchants, and the upper middle classes in general. To many contemporary observers, the population seemed to be growing beyond manageable proportions – which was to say, beyond the capacity of the land to sustain them – and everywhere they looked they found signs of "land hunger". "The people", declared one of them, "do swarm in the land, as young bees in a hive in June; insomuch that there is very hardly room for one man to live by another."[3]

Of course, people like the author of this remark did not fully understand what was happening. More specifically, they did not realise that the phenomena of competitive rents, prices, and wages – with their consequences in eviction, the decay of husbandry, the drift of the rural population to the towns, ruined villages, and vagabondage – were ultimately caused and aggravated by the fact that England was changing from a feudal, self-sufficing economy, based on custom, to one founded on individual enterprise. For all the limitations of their vision, however (limitations which, it need hardly be said, were not their fault), they did sense that older customs and values were being undermined; and so turned from attacking the abuses of the old system to defending its merits and criticising the new. Naturally, they focussed their attention on the most tangible evidence of change: the increase in enclosures and the corresponding increase in the number of "sturdy beggars". "If the King's honour standeth in the great multitude of his people", argued Hugh Latimer in a sermon preached before the King, "then these graziers, inclosers and rent-rearers, are hinderers of his honour."[4] His words were echoed and expanded upon by Philip Stubbes:

> . . . landlords make marchandize of theire poore tenants, racking their rentes, raising their fines and incomes, and settyng them so straight upon the tenter hookes, as no man can live on them. Besides that . . . they take in and inclose commons, where-out the poor commonalty were wont to have all their forage and feeding for their cattle, and (which is more) corn for themselves to live on . . .[5]

The decay of the countryside which, many observers felt, had been caused by the greed of a few wealthy men, was also a common subject of complaint – or, almost as frequently, of elegiac lamentation:

> The towns go down, the land decays,
> Off cornefeyldes, playne layes,

Gret men maketh now a dayes
A shepecott in the church.[6]

Economic and material deterioration was only one side of the story, though, and for many commentators much the less important side; far more crucial, in their eyes, were the symptoms of an inward, moral and spiritual decline. These symptoms, as they saw it, were two: the rise of a new class of landlords between whom and their tenants there was no personal tie, nothing except the cash nexus – and, even more disturbing, the disappearance of the small landowner and free tenant, the yeoman or husbandman. As far as the second of these deeper changes was concerned, the lament for the decline of the yeoman was more than a simple complaint against injustice, although it did involve this;[7] it was a protest, too, against the loss of something regarded as quintessentially English – against the destruction of someone who had traditionally been seen as the "backbone of England".

That the economic changes of the later sixteenth and early seventeenth centuries did, in fact, make for the decay of the yeomanry – as against the gentry –[8] is fairly clear. The progressive, rich yeoman during this period was absorbing the land of his poorer, less industrious or more scrupulous neighbour, with the result that the one rose into the ranks of the gentry while the other, less fortunate, sank down into the peasantry; with supreme irony, the forces of economic freedom and individualism that had brought the yeoman into prominence, when the manorial system began to collapse, were now contributing to his disappearance. As a result the yeoman was left complaining in something like the words that one contemporary writer, William Stafford, gave to him:

> Mary, for these Inclosures doe undoe us all, for they make us to pay dearer for our land that we occupy, and causes that we can have no land for our money to put to tyllage; all is taken up for Pasture . . .; in so much that I have knowne of late a dozen ploughes, within lesse compasse than sixe Myles about mee, layde downe within this seven yeares; and where three score persons or upward had their livings, now one man with his Cattell hath all . . .[9]

With the yeoman, it was argued, went not only a moment in English history, but also a mark of Englishness, an embodiment of the characteristically English virtues. Thomas Fuller, for example, insisted that the "good yeoman" provided "the surest landmark whence forreiners may take aim of ancient English customs; the gentry more floating after forrein fashions".[10] The essence of his condition, all agreed, was his ability to be self-subsistent – which permitted him the proud independence and love of personal freedom perhaps best expressed in lines like these from a contemporary ballad:

> My labour gives my heart content
> and I doe live in merriment:

He that true labour takes in hand
doth farre surpasse the Serving-man . . .[11]

Beyond that, his "fortunate condition, living in the temperate zone
betwixt greatness and want"[12] bred in him an almost paradoxical
combination of thrift and generosity, frugality and unstinting hospitality. His sons supplied the intellectual and spiritual leaders of the
kingdom; while he and his fellows provided the chief physical, as well as
the chief moral, defence of English customs and institutions. For as the
infantry was (to use Bacon's term) the "nerve of the army",[13] so the
yeomanry constituted by their numbers the bulk, and by their spirit the
strength, of that infantry.

It is, perhaps, as well to add a cautionary note here. For all the laments
and complaints, the condition of Elizabethan and early Stuart England –
and of the yeoman, in particular – was very probably not nearly as bad as
most contemporary writers claimed; quite apart from anything else, the
greater part of the land was still unenclosed at the beginning of the
seventeenth century. But there was evidence of unrest at all levels of
society, an unrest that was eventually to alter that society's entire
structure, its customs, values, and beliefs; and while there might have
been no excess of population in England as a whole, there certainly was
unequal distribution, as people wandering from decaying rural districts
invaded the highways, prisons, and rural slums. The remedies proposed
to solve these problems seem now pitifully inadequate. The most
immediately popular, of course, was government intervention to
prevent the further enclosure of lands and the growing inequality of
holdings. Another suggested solution was the transformation of moor,
forest, and waste land into more remunerative soil, by turning
purprestures, assarts, and intakes into arable, draining the fenlands, and
irrigating where water was needed.[14] The amount of land that could be
reclaimed in this way, though, was fairly small – ludicrously small, when
compared with the potential size of the problem – while little was done
or, it was felt, could be done by the state to halt economic forces already
well set in motion. So it was partly for want of a better solution, and
partly because God did seem to be offering a Providential means of
letting blood and so relieving the disease of over-population, that eyes
tended increasingly to turn westward.

The idea that America and, in particular, the land owned by the
Virginia Company of London might serve to resurrect the yeoman was
first tentatively broached by the Elizabethan colonial adventurers. To
begin with, it was a very tentative idea indeed. For example, the elder
Hakluyt merely proposed for the reader's consideration the argument
that "the poor and idle persons which now are ether burdensome or
hurtefull to this Realme at home may hereby become profyttable

members by ymploying theme . . . in those Contreyes";[15] while Sir
George Peckham, equally perfunctorily, simply mentioned in passing
that the "great number of men which doo now live ydely at home"
might "imploy [them] selves . . . in matters of husbandry"[16] across the
seas. Equally tentative, although in a different way, was the younger
Hakluyt, who in his *Discourse Concerning Western Planting* addressed to
Elizabeth I, gave more considered attention to the notion of using the
New World as a mode of release and revival. He began by citing the
example of other countries. This in itself was not a new device. Other
writers had suggested a parallel between the condition of England and
that, say, of ancient Rome before it became an imperial power:

> The Romans when the number of their people grewe so great,
> As neither warres could waste, nor Rome suffice them for a seate,
> They led them forth by swarming troops, to forreine lands amaine,
> And founded divers Colonies, unto the Roman raigne.
> Th' athenians us'de the like devise . . .[17]

But to this use of example Hakluyt added another element, the sense of
rivalry with the two great contemporary powers of exploration and
exploitation: "Portingale and Spain", he declared ". . . by their
discoveries, have founde such occasion of employmente, that this many
yere we have not herde scarcely of any pirate of these two nations."[18]
Insisting on the ineffectuality of statutory intervention, playing upon the
characteristically Elizabethan fear of internal dissension, rehearsing the
by now familiar themes of over-population, enclosure, eviction, and
poverty (". . . they can hardly lyve one by another, nay they are ready to
eat up one another"),[19] Hakluyt concluded his discourse by insisting that
the one practicable remedy for all England's ills, as well as the one best
means of asserting England's authority, was extensive colonisation of
Virginia. Colonisation, he argued, would have two important results. In
the first place, those who emigrated to the New World might find work
"in plantinge of sugar cane, in maynetenaunce and increasing of silk
wormes, . . . in gatherings of cotton . . . in tilling of the soil there for
grains, in dressing of vines". And, in the second, those who remained
might become "profitable members" of the community by helping in
the manufacture of "a thousand triflinge things"[20] which could then be
sold to the emigrants.

It is perhaps worth emphasising the fact that the arguments the
younger Hakluyt employed were almost entirely of an economic nature.
He was willing to exploit contemporary complaints concerning changes
in the land system, but largely to further his own aim: which was the
construction of a mercantile empire that might promote the wealth of
the nation as a whole and swell the coffers of investors in particular. His
concern, finally, was that people should be employed, not the specific

nature of their employment; there was no special value, for him, in the life of the small, independent farmer. Even allowing for all this, however, and allowing for the fact that most of his specific arguments had been anticipated elsewhere, there is no mistaking the seminal nature of his writings. For he was among the first to give coherent and reasoned expression to the idea that a possible solution for the land problem lay in mass emigration to Virginia; it lay with others to develop the implications of this for the "poor Yeoman".[21]

As early as 1617, the government accepted one of the younger Hakluyt's proposals: that of sending to the colonies the "surcharge" of "notorious and wicked offenders".[22] But it was in the pamphlets and sermons written to support the colonising enterprises of the London Company, rather than in any official document, that Virginia was first regarded, less as "a spleen to drain ill humours of the body", than as a providential refuge for the small farmer.[23] "God himselfe is the founder and favourer of this Plantation",[24] asserted the author of one of these pamphlets; and, in order to drive the point home, he and others like him tried to compare Virginia to the Promised Land and its potential yeoman immigrants to the Israelites. It became a commonplace to 'prove' the providential nature of the place by such things as the miraculous escape of Gates and Somers from shipwreck and their subsequent discovery of Bermuda, and equally commonplace to describe in detail the fertility and abundance of the countryside:

> Nor is the present wilderness of it [Virginia] without a particular beauty, being all over a natural Grove of Oaks, Pines, Cedars, Cypress, Mulberry, Chestnut, Laurel, Sassafras, Cherry, Plumtree, and Vines, all of so delectable an aspect, that the melancholiest eye in the World cannot look upon it without contentment or admiration. No shrubs or underwoods choke up your passage, and in its season your foot can hardly direct itself where it will not be dyed in the blood of large and delicious Strawberries.[25]

In effect, the pamphleteers claimed that this was "a land more like the garden of Eden, which the Lord planted, than any part else of the earth". A cross between Arcadia and that place "in which it pleased God himself to set the first man and most excellent creature Adam in his innocency", it inspired some to poetry – or, perhaps to be more accurate, a rather creaking form of verse:

> There is no fear of hunger here,
>   for Corne much store here growes,
> Much fish the gallant Rivers yield,
>   tis truth, without suppose.
>
> Great store of Fowle, of Venison,
>   of Grapes, and Mulberries,

Of Chestnuts, Walnuts, and such like,
   of fruits and Strawberries.

There is indeed no want at all . . .[26]

In this ideal atmosphere, it was argued, the "true labouring husband-
man, that sustaineth the prince" could once more flourish in the
occupation of "Adam . . . that most wholesome, profitable, and pleasant
work of planting". All he had to do was "but freely cast . . . corn into the
ground, and with patience wait for a blessing". The blessing would be as
much spiritual as material; for, working with a land that would "yield
much more fruit to . . . independent labours" than the tired, cramped
soil of England, the farmer would recover his independence, the means
and therefore the willingness to rely on nobody but himself. Returned to
conditions where "he maie have ground for nothing more than he can
manure", he would recover his other, ancient virtues too – his pride, his
thrift, and not least his neighbourliness, his generosity and hospitality:

> If any fall sick, and cannot compass to follow his crop which if not followed,
> will soon be lost, the adjoining neighbour will . . . join together and work on it
> by spells . . . and that gratis. Let any travel, it is without charge, and at every
> house is entertainment as in a hostelry, and with it a hearty welcome are
> stranger entertained.[27]

The avaricious gentleman, who "hath gotten most of the tillage in his
hand", would not prosper in this newer, freer climate, and the "slavish
penurious" farm-labourer as well as the "base" town-worker who could
"hardly keep himself from the alms box" would find it difficult to
survive unless they mended their ways. But the yeoman would find in
Virginia "a brave and ample theatre to make [his] merits and abilities
emergent, and a large field to sow and reap the fruit of all [his] honest,
industrious and public intentions".

It was upon such an ideal member of the commonwealth that William
Bullock, in particular, in what was perhaps the most remarkable of these
pamphlets, proposed that the entire social, economic, and political
system of Virginia should be based. In his pamphlet – which was entitled,
rather misleadingly, *Virginia Impartially Examined* – Bullock insisted that
the future inhabitants of Virginia should pursue a diversified agricultural
economy for the obvious purpose of promoting self-subsistence and for
the less obvious reason that in times of surplus the farmer could
participate at least a little in commercial farming. In addition, Bullock
argued, the "infinite trade by sea" that a diversified agriculture would
encourage would make emigration for the poorer folk easier and much
cheaper. Until such time as this was realised, however, it was still possible
for those dispossessed of their land and living to cross the seas at modest

expense – if, as Bullock suggested, they travelled on the ships headed for the Newfoundland fisheries. Not only was this inexpensive: it would also enable the emigrant, arriving in Virginia in the Spring, to "fall . . . into the ground" immediately and "before August . . . have a crop of Flax, Rice, Corn, Beans, and Peas".[28] So in no time at all he would become independent and self-reliant, and therefore ready to play his part in the new political economy.

It was at this point, in his description of the future political structure of Virginia, that Bullock pushed his argument further than most of the other pamphleteers. For the most part, they were quite content to leave that structure to the reader's inference and devote most of their attention to the prospective daily life of the farmer, portrayed in appropriately glowing terms. Bullock, however, was not content with hints and guesses. He clearly wanted to secure the pastoral ideal to some kind of political reality; and to this end he outlined an elaborate structure which gave ultimate power to the small farmer. Briefly summarised, what Bullock suggested was that Virginia should be composed of "Divisions", each consisting of forty to fifty small farms. In every one of these Divisions, the farmers would elect annually from among themselves six "Superintendents" who would be entirely responsible for local government – and who would meet once a year with other Superintendents from other Divisions in a General Assembly. On meeting, the General Assembly would deal with matters concerning the colony as a whole; and it would elect twelve from among its number to act as a Council administering the colony for the rest of the year. The only non-elected figure in this system would be the Governor: but even he would be more than nominally responsible to the freeholders he governed, since all laws would have to be approved by all three branches of the government, the General Assembly would act as the ultimate court of appeal, and the Governor could himself be examined and impeached by the Superintendents. Fundamental to the entire scheme, in fact, was the belief that "every man by law of Nature and Humanitie" had not only the "right of plantation" but the right also to secure himself against dispossession, the forces of the state and the market-place.[29]

Bullock's portrait of a new life in Virginia was an unusually elaborate and schematic one, certainly, but it would be a mistake to dwell for long on what makes it special, what distinguishes it from the portraits to be found in other promotional pamphlets. Complicated as it was, his plan was really only a more systematised expression of the idea common to many observers of the period: the idea that is, that the yeoman might become the "backbone" of the new world as he had once been, or seemed to have once been, of the old. Nor was that idea quite as absurdly optimistic as it might appear to be now. For while the Virginia Company of London was, it must be admitted, a predominantly mercantile enterprise – and originally a corporate one at that – it did have, as one of its principal aims, the eventual foundation of individual, not necessarily large land titles. The first experiment with independent ownership of small plots was, in fact, made by Governor Dale as early as 1614; while in 1618 a plan was formulated for giving every emigrant a stake in the country, even those who went initially as indentured servants.[30] Another way of putting it would be to say that the stockholders in the Virginia Company were eager to make their investment secure, as indeed all stockholders are; and the best means of achieving this, most of them felt, was to transfer the traditional English social structure to the wilderness. Where they eventually differed from someone like Bullock, however, was in their perception of this structure and their notion of its keystone. For whereas Bullock concentrated on the possibilities available to the "poor ploughman" and the "poor yeoman"[31] in the Eden across the sea, those who administered the Virginia Company ended by turning to forces quite different – and to a figure who was to dominate the life of the Old Dominion, in terms of influence if not numbers: the great landowner, running a large, one-crop plantation. As a result, the dream of a yeoman republic in the New World of Virginia was to remain just that, for over a century at least: a dream, dreamed by a few, now largely forgotten, pamphleteers and preachers.

DREAMS OF EXILE: THE FIRST FAMILIES OF COLONIAL VIRGINIA

In many ways, the figure to whom the ideal of the simple, self-reliant farmer eventually succumbed was also the stuff that dreams are made of; and the story of the process whereby the notion of the gentleman planter – himself a compound of gracious feudal patriarch and bluff English squire – was grafted on to the economic and political realities of colonial Virginia offers parallels with the one just told. For instance, this story, too, begins with a sense of loss, the feeling that there were few gentlemen left who were worthy of the name – capable, that is, of carrying out their moral and social responsibilities:

> Sometyme nobyll men levyed in the Contre
> And kepte grete householdis, pore men to sucowur;
> But now in the Courte they desyr for to be;
> With ladys to daly, thys ys ther pleasure.[32]

Given this feeling, it was perhaps not very surprising that many colonial adventurers saw Virginia as a place where the virtues of the old landed gentry could be conveniently recovered. What was surprising – although it is still a matter of controversy – was the extent to which this attempt at recovery was successful.

In 1578, the explorer and adventurer Sir Humphrey Gilbert was granted letters patent by the Crown to "Searche out" and settle "remote heathen and barbarous landes, countries and territories not actually possessed of any Christian prince or people".[33] The obvious object of his plans for colonisation was America and, in particular, that area later known as Virginia. After a series of abortive schemes, Gilbert formulated his last and most elaborate project in 1582 in a series of documents addressed to his fellow adventurers.[34] This provided, effectively, for the establishment of a feudal, hierarchical society over which he, Gilbert himself, would preside as both governor and landlord. Beneath him, the several classes of planters would be ranged according to the size of their holdings: at the top would be men with more than four thousand acres of land and more than ten "tenauntes-followers", while at the bottom would be those who had emigrated at the public expense, to whom were leased for a period of three lives sixty acres of land apiece. Each class, Gilbert suggested, would have to furnish arms and pay taxes for the "maynetenaunce of maymed souldiars, and of learnings, lectures, scholers, and other good and godly uses"[35] according to its station and means; and, as on a medieval manor, individual and corporate welfare were to be deemed inseparable. Apart from the governor, the keystone of this structure would be provided by the great landowners, from whom would be drawn the "Councellors for Marshall and mayne causes". They would constitute the cavalry in the new colonial army but they would also have to provide arms for every one of their "tenauntes-followers" – who, in this and other ways, broadly assumed the status of feudal retainers. Unlike the lesser landowners, they would be able to develop and control their holdings as they saw fit, and most of the responsibility for their tenants remained with them. Retaining a considerable degree of political, economic, social, and even legal and military power over those within their "seignories", they would in fact be like nothing so much as feudal barons, in appearance as well as authority.

It goes without saying, perhaps, that this ambitious scheme was never initiated. Like Bullock's idea for a yeoman republic, it never went beyond the planning stage; nobody even tried to put it to the test of experience. Equally with Bullock's ideas, however, it did express clearly, not to say schematically, a dream held in common by many of those who saw Virginia as a source of hope and a means of redemption. The difference in this case – and it is a significant one – is that those who saw Virginia in this way tended to be among the more affluent or enterprising emigrants and that their dream helped, at least to some extent, to shape their thoughts and behaviour. The "first families of Virginia" as they eventually became known – that is, those people who formed the ruling class by the end of the seventeenth century – were almost certainly not aristocratic by origin, or, if there were aristocrats among them, they were very few. Nevertheless, they tried quite deliberately to assume the prerogatives and manners of an aristocracy: to live, as one of them put it, "like . . . the patriarchs" (see Plate I).[36]

Precisely what the origins of most of those "first families" were is still unclear and a matter of controversy. The problem is all the greater because it is by now almost impossible to trace their English origins, and because in any event the social structure of the mother country, particularly during the early Stuart period, was much more fluid and indefinite than is sometimes assumed.[37] For all that, it seems highly probable that, as one contemporary historian Robert Beverley II suggested, the great majority of them were "of low Circumstances . . . such as were willing to seek their Fortunes in a Foreign Country", especially during the first years of colonisation. Admittedly Beverley adds a rider:

> . . . this way of Peopling the Colony was only at first; for after the Advantages of the Climate, and the Fruitfulness of the Soil were well known, and all the Dangers incident to Infant Settlements were over, People of better Condition retir'd thither with their families, either to increase their Estates . . ., or else to avoid being persecuted . . .[38]

In the light of the present evidence, though, even this seems something of an exaggeration, an attempt to bring the myth of the Cavalier emigrant in by the back door. Whatever the case, the real test of status in colonial Virginia remained always the extent of land owned, and this was a matter of initial capital and business acumen rather than birth.

Low their circumstances might have been, but this did not prevent the great landowners, who quickly assumed political as well as economic authority, from seeking to imitate the patriarchal model. That this was their source of inspiration was fairly obvious from the first from the whole character of their institutions, the intention of which seems to have been to make Virginia approximate to an idealised version of the Home Counties. An English religious system was established, consisting of parishes controlled by vestries, and an English legal system, with county and supreme courts; there was an English military organisation, relying principally upon the militia, and an English political structure, consisting of a single executive and an upper and lower legislative house. All the offices within this establishment were controlled by a fairly small group of families: with the result that the same person could be, and usually was, a Burgess and a Councillor, a vestryman, a county magistrate and a district commander of the militia. Political, legal, and social authority was very soon reinforced by economic supremacy; for during the course of the seventeenth century this same group acquired a tighter hold on the financial life of the colony. After 1660, in fact, such little health and wealth as the yeomanry had ever enjoyed gradually disappeared, as the profit margin on tobacco declined. Smaller profits made it necessary to cultivate larger tracts of land, if an adequate return was to be had on any investment; and, since hired help was painfully scarce, the more business-minded among the small farmers – who had already made what Bullock would have regarded as the mistake of committing themselves to commercial farming – felt required to become slave-holders in order to survive. The less enterprising, meanwhile, and those of stricter conscience were either reduced to comparative poverty or removed themselves to lands further west. The repercussions of these developments were profound. For as more and more land was engrossed by the great planter, and as the richer farmer moved into the class of slave-holders, the influence of the aristocracy grew and such distinctiveness as the yeomanry had ever had effectively vanished. The small landowner growing big allowed his social pretensions to become inflated as well, and his dependence on others even permitted him to adopt what one contemporary, Hugh Jones, called the gentleman's "easy way of living". In effect, he began to conform, in appearance at least, to that stereotype of aristocratic idleness which shaped so many people's perceptions of Virginia (and, later, the South), even those who visited it – like, for instance, this traveller from the mother country:

> The climate and external appearance of the country conspire to make them [Virginians] indolent, easy, and good-natured; extremely fond of society, and much given to convivial pleasures. In consequence of this, they seldom show any spirit of enterprise, or expose themselves willingly to fatigue.[39]

It cannot be emphasised too strongly, however, that this *was* a matter of appearance and stereotype rather than anything approaching empirical reality; the great landowners were almost never as idle as was commonly supposed. In point of fact, they were always primarily businessmen, concerned with the careful supervision and, whenever possible, the gradual expansion of their property. This was no small task, since as one of them, William Fitzhugh, put it,

> . . . without a constant care and diligent Eye, a well-made plantation will run to Ruin . . . without a constant care and continual residence thereupon, the labour and care of seven years is destroyed in as many hours.[40]

"'Tis no small satisfaction to me", wrote another great landowner Robert "King" Carter, "to have a pennyworth for my penny" and to this end he was painstaking in his supervision of his several plantations. This, for example, is part of a letter he wrote to a new steward in 1721 about the nature of his duties:

> You are first of all to acquaint yourself with the condition the several plantations are in and to use your utmost diligence and endeavour to get the crops all planted and to see that the overseers mind their business and keep their homes. You are to take an account as soon as you can of my goods at the several quarters . . . You must be careful and diligent in r[ea]ping and getting in the wheat as soon as it is ripe . . . As soon as conveniently you can you must get a particular account of my stocks of cattle and hogs, their ages and sorts.[41]

In a similar spirit, his grandson Robert Carter of Nomini Hall was continually experimenting with schemes for increasing his already extensive wealth. These included the manufacturing of agricultural implements, the production of salt, and the establishment of a textile factory and a flour mill. Nor were these men necessarily scrupulous in their business methods: both "King" Carter, for instance, and William Byrd of Westover used their position as agent for the proprietors of the Northern Neck of Virginia to acquire vast tracts of that area at a cheap rate.[42] In a very real sense, the great planters of the Old Dominion were the entrepreneurs of the period, with most of the usual entrepreneurial vices as well as the virtues.

Quite probably, it was the very depth of their commitment to business activities, as well as their often unremarkable origins, that made these great landowners anxious to assume the trappings of an aristocracy. William Byrd of Westover, for example, worked hard on all his properties, personally supervising them, arranging for the planting of crops, orchards, and gardens and attending to his duties within his own community and in the colony and the county. Yet he seems to have been intent, in his correspondence, on trying to convince his English friends that he was living a kind of Horatian idyll – as these brief passages from two separate letters amply testify:

> . . . we sit securely under our vines and fig trees without any danger to our property . . . Thus, my Lord, we are very happy in our Canaans if we could but forget the onions and fleshpots of Egypt . . .

> We that are banish't from those polite pleasures [of London] . . . take up with rural entertainments. A Library, a garden, a grove, and a purling stream are the innocent scenes that divert our leisure.[43]

The sense of anxiety that leads to the creation of a false image of the self seems to spring here from two, related things: a feeling of exile from the centres of cultural activity, and a desire to distance the spectres of provincialism and money-grubbing. In the case of a planter like William Fitzhugh, a third element is added: the fear that, unless one is very careful, people will discover that one has toiled mightily to assume an aristocratic status – rather, that is, than been born to it. A first-generation immigrant and the son of a woollen draper, Fitzhugh had to work hard to acquire land and wealth. Having done so, he immediately set about acquiring a coat of arms and all the paraphernalia of the gentleman. His sister was then invited to join him in the New World, but not before he had arranged for her to be "handsomely and genteelly and well clothed, with a maid to wait on her". "The method I have taken for your coming in", he informed her with evident unease, "I would advise you by all means to follow, which will give us both credit and reputation, without which it's uncomfortable living."[44] The message was plain: Fitzhugh had transformed himself from an ordinary person into an aristocrat and he now expected his relatives, if he was to acknowledge them, to accept a similar metamorphosis.

Still, the Virginian planters wanted more than just the appearance of aristocratic status. They wanted, first of all, to assimilate themselves to the rank once proposed for them by Sir Humphrey Gilbert: an aim that they pursued partly through their position as leaders of colonial society and partly as indisputable rulers of their own plantations. The fact that, as one contemporary observer put it, "the principal planters have nearly everything they can want on their own estates"[45] encouraged feelings of pride and independence – and a manner that was frequently equated, and perhaps was meant to be equated, with the arrogant self-will of the aristocrat. "Virginians", declared one traveller, ". . . are haughty and jealous of their liberties, impatient of restraint, and can scarcely bear the thought of being controlled by a superior power."[46] On his own holdings, the landowner could adopt the role and function of a feudal patriarch. Both William Byrd of Westover and Robert "King" Carter, for example, considered themselves the guardians of the moral and physical welfare of their slaves – whom they both referred to as their "people" – while another planter, Landon Carter, considered it an important part of his "social duty" to act as benevolent overlord to his: punishing the lazy "children", as he called them, rewarding the industrious, and having "all imaginable care" taken of such "poor creatures" as were sick.[47] In their social activities, too, these men sought to imitate their image of English nobility, indulging in the traditional sports of the rural gentry such as "gaming, hunting, and horse-racing"[48] – and even importing the red fox from England so as to perform the rituals of the hunt in the traditional manner. Before and after church-services and court-sessions, at dinners, balls, and "visits", they attempted valiantly to reproduce a pastoral atmosphere in what was still a remote and semi-primitive environment. The planters themselves did not, in fact, fail to recognise the "great wilderness" (to use William Byrd's phrase) of their environment; and very probably, their conviviality and hospitality was something of a conscious reaction against the loneliness that it imposed on them for most of the year. "Society that is good and ingenious", complained William Fitzhugh, "is very scarce, and seldom to be come at except in books":[49] a feeling that was given touching expression by those planters who had the road patrolled regularly by slaves, looking for strangers to invite home for a meal or even a visit.

Personal conduct, too, was important in accommodating oneself to the role of patriarch: something that the planters of Virginia implicitly acknowledged by acquiring at least some of the appropriate manuals of behaviour. No colonial library seems to have been complete without, for instance, Henry Peacham's *The Compleat Gentleman* and Richard Brathwaite's *The English Gentleman*.[50] From these, and similar, books they learned the traditional code of gentlemanly behaviour – and, in particular, the virtues of courtesy, fortitude, temperance, liberality, and hospitality. The problem here again, however, was the colony's lack of cultural resources, its "wilderness". Beyond a certain point, it was very difficult for those who wished to become gentlemen, or wanted their sons to become gentlemen, to find the appropriate training in the Old Dominions; and even after the foundation of William and Mary College, a considerably large number of great planters were sent across the Atlantic in their youth in order to study at English schools, universities, and inns of court. This was hardly conducive to the development of an indigenous culture – something that this "small number of virtuous and enlightened citizens" demonstrated on returning home. For they continued to read the works, not of native authors, but of English poets and essayists; they relied wholly on their factors in London to supply them with books, journals, and newspapers; they wore English clothes, little suited to the environment or to the activities of a planter in a semi-tropical climate; they ate food that was, as one of their own number admitted, "dressed, and serv'd up as . . . in London";[51] and they sat upon furniture made in England or imitated from English models. The architects, too, who designed their mansions (see Plate 2) and the artists who painted their portraits, concrete embodiments of their aristocratic pretensions, were almost invariably English. "The Habits, Life, Customs, Computations, etc., of the Virginians", declared a contemporary historian Hugh Jones, "are much the same as about London, which they esteem their home."[52] And this was true. William Byrd of Westover, who in any case spent much of his time in the mother country, never ceased to think of England as the proper place for him – a centre of culture, entertainment, and conversation as opposed to what he called "this silent country". His writings are full of references to the scenes and life of London, as if somehow language and more specifically metaphor could make up for what he lacked in life. For example, after finding some horses that had strayed near the misty, marshy region known as the Dismal Swamp, Byrd wrote: 'They were found standing indeed, but as motionless as the equestrian statues in Charing Cross."[53] The contrast here between the scene described and the mode of description – or, to use Saussure's terms, between the signified and the signifier – could hardly be more striking. On the one hand, the reader is confronted with a natural world of immense and even disturbing strangeness, while on the other he is presented with a cultural referent that is comfortingly familiar and known. In its own small way, in effect, this sentence seems to sum up the process of accommodation to which so many of the great planters committed themselves: their efforts, that is – and their immensely strained efforts, at that – to create a sense of connection between the new world and the old.

Speaking of Virginia in the early eighteenth century, three contemporary and on the whole sympathetic observers declared:

> When one considers the Wholesomeness of its Air, the fertility of its Soil, the Commodiousness of its Navigable Rivers and Creeks, . . . the Plenty of its Fish and Fowl, and wild Beasts . . .; in short, if it be look'd upon in all Respects as it came out of the Hand of God, it is certainly one of the best Countries in the world.

But, they added,

> if we enquire for well built Towns . . . for well educated Children, for an industrious and thriving People, or for an happy Government in Church and State, and in short, for all the other Advantages of human Improvements, it is certainly . . . one of the poorest, miserablest, and worst Countries in all America, that is inhabited by Christians.[54]

Rhetorical this may be, but it merely repeats in a different, more emphatic key the note of unease sounded by people like Byrd. The wilderness of a new world was an impossibly difficult place in which to build an aristocratic culture, and in their various ways many of the planters seem to have recognised that. Admittedly, their ways were not always like Byrd's; they too, though, seem to have been uncomfortably aware of the insecurity and, to some extent, the unreality of their position. Richard Lee II, for example, withdrew into his library of classical and Elizabethan literature where, ever more oblivious of the less civilised world about him, he came to resemble in his intellectual interests and social habits a learned gentleman of the late sixteenth or early seventeenth centuries rather than a planter living at the time of the Restoration.[55] Robert Beverley, too, dissociated himself from his fellow planters but in a more deliberate, self-conscious fashion, mocking their complacency and despising their dependence on the old world: "though their country be over-run with wood", he declared,

> yet they have all [their] wooden-ware from England . . . Thus they depend altogether upon the Liberality of Nature, without endeavouring to improve its Gifts by Art or Industry.[56]

Even William Fitzhugh, who had every reason to be grateful to Virginia for making him wealthy, thought of it as "a strange land"; and, having failed to establish himself as a lord of the manor – by offering absurdly generous terms to some Huguenot refugees if they agreed to become his tenants and dependants – dreamed of returning home to England. "My desires are now to breath my native air", he wrote to a neighbour, "and to enjoy the fruition of my native soil."[57] There, back home in the mother country, he believed, he could finally attain that "reputation and Credit", the distinguishing marks of a gentleman, which he had pursued in the colonies without success.

So the planters of the Old Dominion never managed, even in their own judgement, to create an indigenous aristocratic culture. The land that provided the economic basis of their claims to mastery – or to what Henry Peacham, in *The Compleat Gentleman*, called "sovereignity and transcendent predominance"[58] – was acquired and retained by means of a ruthlessness and frequent lack of scruple, as well as by a constant attention to business affairs, which naturally weakened those very claims. Such cultivation as they achieved was rather like the scheme of Sir Humphrey Gilbert, the result of a deliberate attempt to recover a largely imaginary English past (or, for those who never went back across the Atlantic, an imaginary English present); and, ironically, the more aware of the social graces they became, the more alienated they were likely to feel from the wilderness of their New World surroundings. Even their attempts to transfer wholesale to their new environment the political arrangements of an established rural gentry met, inevitably, with a certain amount of frustration. For example, the planters' desire to use the militia system to instil belief in a natural hierarchy, and habits of deference to authority, was vitiated by their fear of the populace. Unlike the English squire, they felt, they were not dealing with a known quantity, since many of the poorer folk were recent emigrants, consisting "for the most part of the worser sort of people of Europe". As one local politician suggested, might not those poor folk "rise upon and kill their superiors" if they were "fitted with arms" and given the chance of "meeting together by musters"?[59] Such misgivings were more than local and superficial, of course, since they betrayed the deep uneasiness many of the "first families" felt about the appropriateness of the aristocratic, hierarchical model – not only for themselves, not only for their environment, but also for the rest of the population, the tenants, servants, and traders with whom they had to deal. In sum, the gap between the planters' lives and their versions of those lives bred doubt and anxiety; and doubt and anxiety in turn encouraged an accelerated retreat into fantasy, an increasing dependence on certain admired aspects of life in the "home" country and bitter criticism of certain inadequacies in colonial society – inadequacies which were really only natural, in view of its youth.

But perhaps the last word on all this should be left with William Byrd of Westover: who was arguably the finest embodiment of the colonial Virginian intelligence. In his diaries, Byrd recounted the events of his everyday life, even the most trivial, and this, taken almost at random, is the entry for one, fairly typical day:

> I rose at 6 o'clock and read a chapter in Hebrew and two hundred verses in Homer's "Odyssey". I said my prayers and ate chocolate with Mr. Bland for breakfast. He went away this morning. I read law. Toney came to tell me all was well at Appomatox, and also that the hogs were ready. I ate nothing but hashed beef for dinner. In the evening I walked around the plantation. I said my prayers. I had good health, good thoughts, and good humor, and good understanding this day, thanks be to God Almighty. Daniel came to let me know the sloop was almost loaded.[60]

Byrd was, of course, exceptional as far as the range of his interests was concerned, but not so exceptional that he cannot stand as an example here. As a planter, his life was not so very different from that of his neighbours: a life combining continuous business activity with at least some attempts to cultivate manners and knowledge. Like William Fitzhugh and the Carters, in fact, he tried to apply an inherited model of belief and behaviour to new historical circumstances. That model was in some ways inappropriate, and destructively so: but, in others, it did help at least to ameliorate the harshness of a strange new world – and, as this diary entry shows I think, to make life more manageable, more amenable, and quite simply, more human.

FROM REVOLUTION TO REACTION: THOMAS JEFFERSON, JOHN TAYLOR OF CAROLINE, AND JOHN RANDOLPH OF ROANOKE

During the struggle for American independence, a group of men rose to prominence in Virginia who, in their different ways, showed a more liberal approach to the political, economic, and social problems of the state. These men were influenced mainly by two things, the moral upheaval of revolution and the European intellectual movement known as the Enlightenment:[61] the first was clear enough from their willingness to examine the assumptions implicit in the structure of Virginian society, while the second became obvious from their appeal to reason and the doctrine of "natural rights" while conducting this examination. The story of the arguments they mustered and the debates they participated in is already well known, and no attempt will be made to rehearse it here. One aspect of those arguments and debates, however, is significant in the present context and deserves a little more attention; and this is the extent to which these men, or at least some of them, managed to reformulate, develop, and even implement certain ideas broached by the Virginia pamphleteers nearly two centuries earlier.

Among the men of this period, Thomas Jefferson (see Plate 3) is, of course, at once the representative and the dominant figure. A person of innumerable, eclectic interests – and thereby the inheritor of a tradition that had previously been best exemplified by William Byrd of Westover – Jefferson's very myriad-mindedness has led to quite contradictory interpretations of both his aims and his achievement. He has been seen, for instance, by different historians as a man of the frontier and a cultivated planter, an idealist and a utilitarian, as the advocate of the rights of all and as a spokesman for the farmer in particular.[62] But it is not just his myriad-mindedness that is responsible for this conflict. Another reason is that, very often, when Jefferson thought and talked of America he was thinking and talking specifically of Virginia.[63] More significantly, it was not the actual, historical Virginia that he was thinking and talking of, which he described once in a letter as consisting of

> aristocrats (the great planters), half-breeds (yeomen who had married into aristocratic families), pretenders (men of wealth not belonging to established families), a solid, independent yeomanry, looking askance at those above, yet not venturing to jostle them, and last and lowest, a seculum of beings called overseers.[64]

It was not this, but rather an ideal Virginia in which the primary political, economic, and social factor was the yeoman. "I know no condition happier than that of a Virginia farmer", wrote Jefferson to a friend:

> . . . His estate supplies a good table, clothes himself and his family with their ordinary apparel, furnishes a small surplus to buy salt, coffee, and a little finery for his wife and daughter, enables him to receive and to visit his friends and furnishes him pleasing and healthy occupation. To secure all this, he needs the one act of self-denial, to put off buying anything till he has the money to pay for it.[65]

In a curious way, it was to this ideal that Jefferson tried to assimilate himself, although he was of course distinctly wealthier than the ordinary farmer. Monticello, as described for instance by La Rochefoucauld-Liancourt, was largely self-subsistent:

> Comme il ne peut pas attendre de secours des deux petites villes voisines, tout se fait chez lui, ses nègres sont menuisiers, charpentiers, maçons, charrons, serruriers, etc. . . .[66]

Jefferson laboured throughout his life to make the estate completely self-reliant: through the promotion of domestic manufactures, through a more diversified agriculture, and more significantly, through avoiding unnecessary luxuries. Like the yeoman of tradition, he practised thrift and felt a hatred for any large capitalistic enterprise, whether it involved banking, speculation, or commercial manufactures. This alone would serve to differentiate him from figures like William Byrd or Robert "King" Carter; like them in material and cultural endowments, perhaps, he nevertheless cherished quite different myths.

Despite his frequent claim that he wished to make no "Gothic" appeals to "musty records", Jefferson did in fact try to find an historical basis for his ideal. "Our Saxon ancestors", he declared, "held their lands, as they did their personal property . . . in absolute dominion, disencumbered with any superior."[67] Like the Virginia pamphleteers, he tended to regard colonisation as an opportunity, courageously seized by many, to recapture the pride and independence of the traditional yeomanry, in this case the Saxon yeomanry of legal tradition. The Saxons, he argued, had "left their native wilds and woods in the North of Europe" and emigrated to Britain, where they established a system of individual ownership. Then, in turn, as conditions deteriorated and the "fictitious principle" of feudalism acquired ascendancy, "our ancestors" went "in quest of new habitations" where they could live according to the old Saxon precepts. "For themselves they fought", he continued, "for themselves they conquered, and for themselves alone they have right to hold."[68] Again, there had been a series of betrayals by the British Crown, a "long trend of abuses"; and it was against this, he insisted, that people like him had the right to revolt. For, "is it not better," he asked a correspondent,

> that we return at once into that happy system of our ancestors, the wisest and most perfect ever yet devised by the wit of man, as it stood before the eighth century?[69]

The question, put in this way, hardly required a response.

Effectively, what Jefferson was arguing in this piece of historical analysis – or perhaps it would be more accurate to say, this fragment of historical mythmaking – was that natural rights rested upon a personal conquest of the land. It followed, by implication, that the full exercise of those rights was reserved for those who had achieved this conquest – that is, that they belonged to the freeholder alone. And, indeed, Jefferson was not afraid to develop this implication: to suggest, in fact, that power in the new commonwealth should reside with those who laboured in the earth. In part, the reasons he mustered for this were the traditional ones. Since the freeholder relied on nobody but himself, Jefferson declared, he was less likely than the wage-earner to act from dishonourable motives or to be swayed by outside influences; while, because he had a stake in the land, he was always likely to serve the interests of law and order, that is the interests of property. "Cultivators of the earth", he told John Jay, "are the most valuable citizens":

> They are the most vigorous, the most independent, the most virtuous, and they
> are tied to their country, and wedded to its interests, by the most lasting
> bonds.[70]

Fortunately, in his opinion, America would remain for the foreseeable
future an agricultural country; small farmers would therefore remain
"the true representatives of the Great American interests" and the
progress and prosperity of the new republic was virtually assured.

Not that he was willing to leave everything to chance and hope: on the
contrary, over the years he formulated a quite elaborate series of
proposals that had one overriding purpose, to ensure that the yeoman
would prosper just as anticipated. On the negative side, he proposed that
the great planters should be gradually weakened through the use of
graduated taxation and the abolition of primogeniture and entail; while,
on the positive, he advocated a scheme of education that would both
instruct the electorate and promote the development of a series of leaders
from the ranks of the people. One-crop farming, and in particular
tobacco-culture, was to be discouraged; farmers would be induced to
concentrate on food-crops, the bulk to be used for subsistence, and the
surplus to be exported. Commerce and manufacturing were to be kept to
an absolute minimum; since the first would possibly involve the infant
republic in conflict with the merchant navies of other nations, while the
second would quite certainly encourage the growth of a servile urban
proletariat and an avaricious, amoral capitalist class. "Generally speaking", Jefferson asserted in *Notes on Virginia*,

> the proportion which the aggregate of the other classes of citizens bears in any
> state to that of its husbandmen, is the proportion of its unsound to its healthy
> parts.[71]

Given that assumption, his aim was to keep the body politic as healthy as
possible using incentives and, when necessary, threats and penalties as
well.

Jefferson's insistence that the freeholder should be the only real source
of political and economic power was, in his eyes, not nearly so restrictive
as it might now seem to us. For, like the Virginia pamphleteers, he
regarded America as offering unlimited resources to anyone with the
courage and energy to exploit them. Once established, he felt, his society
of independent, happy farmers would require the minimum of
government necessary for the preservation of life and property. In fact,
the only state interference he hoped for that went beyond this minimum
was largely that involved in some of his pet schemes to ensure a "stake in
the country" for every family. As early as 1776, acting on his own dictum
that "the small landowners are the most precious part of the land",[72] he
proposed in a draft constitution for Virginia that every man over

twenty-one should be granted fifty acres, provided that he used it to support himself. While later, in 1785, he even suggested a scheme of taxation of the wealthy and state assistance for the poor which would, he hoped, help to diminish "economic inequality" in land holdings. Admittedly, like William Bullock before and John Taylor of Caroline after him, Jefferson believed that complete equality was "impracticable"; nevertheless, he felt just as strongly that wealth had to be "considerably distributed, to sustain a democratic republic".[73]

In many respects, then, Jefferson went beyond the arguments of the Virginia pamphleteers. He laid, for instance, far greater emphasis than them on the specifically moral value of rural life; he was reluctant to credit the urban proletariat with sufficient intelligence even to exercise the right of suffrage; he was considerably more aware than they of the emerging conflict between agrarianism and capitalism;[74] and he attempted to find an older legal and historical foundation for the yeoman-farmer by shaping the Anglo-Saxon past into another Golden Age. For all that, though, his basic assumptions were the same as those of a series of writers, the first celebrants of Virginia, of whom quite probably he knew very little. Like them, he saw the yeoman-farmer as the new hope for a new land; like them he saw the yeoman as a political bulwark; like them, he felt that absolute virtue resided in a simple, self-subsistence economy; and like them, too, he believed that the yeoman as militiaman would provide most effectively for the state's defence.[75] Certainly, at least part of Jefferson's achievement derives from this relating of concepts that the Revolution and Enlightenment had made current to a tradition of thought that was part of his inheritance as a Virginian. And in this he was not alone. The position, for example, of another gentleman of the Revolution, George Mason, was just as symptomatic of the intellectual climate at this time, although less striking and impressive. A friend and political associate of Jefferson's and a landed gentleman of liberal sentiments, Mason placed his faith just as Jefferson did in what he called "the strict economy and frugality" of "the most respectable part of the people",[76] the farmers of the middle rank. To this class Mason considered that he belonged – although, again like Jefferson, more in terms of quality of life than quantity of holdings. Without it, he believed, the nation was doomed, given over to what his friend Richard Henry Lee had termed, in a letter to him, "The coalition of monarchy men, military men, aristocrats and . . . rapacious traders".[77]

That last remark of Lee's suggests an undercurrent of fear, a slight tremor of apprehension that Jefferson and many of those like him shared about the direction in which their society was going. "When I look around me for security", Jefferson declared to a friend, "I find it in the wide spread of our agricultural citizens",[78] and while he might assert that, as a result, he felt perfectly secure – because, as he saw it, agriculture would remain "our principal object" "for some considerable time" – nevertheless even he felt the occasional moment of doubt. Might not people, after all, be lured to the cities, as they had been in Europe, where they would be reduced to "eating one another"? And might not the economy be structured so as to create a "monied aristocracy"[79] and deny the yeoman farmer anything other than a marginal status? These were substantial questions, even though Jefferson tried to ask them of himself as infrequently as possible; and just how substantial was to be shown, on a local level at least, very early on in the nineteenth century – as Jefferson, Mason, Lee, and their friends saw their state go into a steep and apparently irreversible decline. The reasons why the Old Dominion never even began to live up to the hopes that these gentlemen of the Revolution had for it were a mixture of the political, the economic, and the social. The political importance of Virginia, for instance, was reduced by the fact that emigrants to America usually moved into the West or the East rather than the South, and by the fact that many Virginians themselves emigrated westwards. At the same time, its economic status was badly damaged by the impoverishment of its soil, the result of the ceaseless cultivation of tobacco and other improvident farming methods, by the growth of competition from the younger agricultural areas, and by the loss of special treatment in the markets of England. Along the tidewater, in particular, these economic factors contributed to the decline of the old ruling class, who very often continued to live extravagantly despite the altered conditions – and who were not replaced, as Jefferson had hoped, by a race of thrifty, enterprising, self-reliant farmers for the simple reason that anyone of any enterprise tended to leave for richer land elsewhere.[80]

The intellectual consequences of these briefly sketched changes were profound. For the Old Dominion was, in effect, unwillingly assuming a position later to be held by the South as a whole: that of a conscious and declining minority within a young and growing nation. People like Jefferson (as I have already suggested) had always tended to think of their country primarily in terms of Virginia; and when to the immediate evidence of decline was added a more general feeling that the nation as a whole was moving towards preferential treatment for the business entrepreneur and the industrialist, towards the corporate state and a capitalist economy, then many of Jefferson's intellectual heirs turned increasingly from aggressive hope to nervous and protective special pleading – and from an articulate analysis of different types of rural life to an eloquent but often rather muddled celebration of that life in any form. Jefferson had proposed a very particular notion of agrarianism, associated with the figure of the small farmer, in the name of which he had attacked such things as the patriarchal plantation. Those later Virginians, however, who claimed to be developing his argument tended to confuse the issue and sing the praises of any or all kinds of agrarianism while reserving their criticisms for the speculator, the factory-owner, and the urban proletariat.

A figure who registers something of this gradual transformation of agrarian thought in Virginia is John Taylor of Caroline, who borrowed many of his arguments from Jefferson but then applied them to agriculture in general rather than just the plain farmer. Like Jefferson, for example, he chose to view history in terms of the role played in different periods by the landowner, and thereafter built on this to claim that "the agricultural interest is. . . an umpire of the public good", "the mother of wealth", and the best architect of national policy. Apart from its historical basis, the claim was also given an economic dimension: landowners, Taylor argued, ultimately bore the burden of taxation and so were "incapable of the avarice and injustice of a factitious legal interest". "A mere exchange of money", he went on, ". . . creates nothing, and does not augment the national prosperity." The only genuine wealth is in the land. The landowner caring for his holdings is the true creator of prosperity, the one sure protector of private property, and the one genuine supplier of life-blood to the body politic; more specifically, Taylor insisted, he acts as a barrier against both "fraudulent and swindling laws" that incite "the few to plunder the many" and those "impracticable, dishonest, and ruinous" equalising laws of "political enthusiasts" that enable "the many to plunder the few".[81]

As far as the moral implications of his argument were concerned, Taylor again borrowed from Jefferson. Those who work the earth, he suggested, are inclined to be hard-working, honest, and thrifty because their own prosperity, and even survival, depends on the possession of exactly these qualities. And the rural life in general is at once good and useful because, as he put it:

> It bestows health and content. It is a pledge of virtue. It doubles our happiness by enabling us to blend with it the happiness of others. Its benefits reiterate and spread like the undulations of the waves.[82]

Taylor did go beyond Jefferson, however, by emphasising the importance of the agricultural life for the development of the whole human being and explaining exactly how this development comes about. His explanation is worth quoting at length because it anticipates the position of many later Southern agrarians – not least in its author's reluctance to say just what kind of life he has in mind: whether he is thinking, for instance, of subsistence farming or one of the kings of cotton.

> The capacity of agriculture for affording luxuries to the body, is not less conspicuous than its capacity for affording luxuries to the mind: it being a

science singularly possessing the double qualities of feeding with unbounded liberality, both the moral appetites of the one, and the physical wants of the other. It can even feed a morbid love of money, whilst it is habituating us to the practice of virtue; and whilst it provides for the wants of a philosopher, it affords him room for the most curious and yet useful researches. In short, by the exercise it gives to both the body and the mind, it secures health and vigour to both; and by combining a thorough knowledge of the real affairs of life, with a necessity for investigating the arcana of nature, and the strongest invitations to the practice of morality, it becomes the best architect of the complete man.[83]

Significantly, the means by which Taylor arrived at this conclusion was as ambiguous as the conclusion itself. Taylor was enough of an intellectual heir of Jefferson to pay lip service, at least, to the Jeffersonian doctrine of "natural rights" and the tools of reason and logic.[84] When it came down to it, however, he tended to appeal more to the test of experience. The teachings of history, the stored wisdom of the past and of our own brief lives: these were the principles on which he based, for example, his own definition of government, the contrast he drew between the political economies of the United States and Europe – and, perhaps most significant of all, his attack on equalitarianism and the "enthusiastic philosophers" who proclaimed it. Implicit, in fact, in Taylor's attack on theoretical, or as he preferred to put it "numerical", analyses of society – and in such sweeping declarations as "Names constitute nothing"[85] – was a denial of those very rationalistic criteria that elsewhere he claimed to be invoking. Together with this emphasis on experience and "specific practice" rather than theory, Taylor often relied when reaching an opinion not on reason but on an appeal to "moderation": as when, for example, he defended both the independent landholder and state governments in terms of his belief that they offered a "mean" between tyranny and anarchy, despotism and a kind of communism. Later Southerners, of course, defending slavery or taking their stand on the idea of a noble agrarian past, were to go much further than this, and jettison the notion of natural rights and rationalistic political theory altogether. But Taylor either could not or would not go as far as this. As a result, his lingering allegiance to rationalism tended to propel him towards a fairly democratic and populist notion of a rural society, peopled by happy farmers, while the appeal to experience and history set him off in a more conservative, patriarchal and hierarchical, direction.

There was an element of confusion and uncertainty, then, in both Taylor's argument and his conclusions; and his method of dealing with this, or rather of reducing the confusion to a minimum, was quite simple but profoundly significant. In the first place, he concentrated much of his energy on the negative side of his argument: the major purpose of his most important work for example, *An Inquiry into the Principles and Policy of the Government of the United States*, is not so much an account of agrarianism as a critique of capitalism. And, in the second place, he used language as a weapon of concealment: in the fashion of every good orator, in effect, he tried to divert attention from the potential weaknesses and contradictions of his own case by using a powerful barrage of words, evocative phrases and unsettling metaphors. Capitalism, for instance, is constantly associated in his writings with wild beasts, aggression and destruction: at different times, the speculator or financier is called a "crocodile", "an ugly cur", a "tiger" – and "a robber" and plunderer, who employs an "artillery" or "battery" of schemes, "an engine of power and oppression"[86] to oppress and destroy his victims. Apart from reinforcing the idea that the urban-industrial system is essentially exploitative, concerned only with "spoil and carnage", vocabulary of this kind offered Taylor a convenient contrast with the notion of agriculture as the only natural or humane vocation – a notion signalled, among other things, by Taylor's insistent use of metaphors of flowering, vegetation, and growth whenever called upon to describe or celebrate it. Rural society is "natural", "organic", and "real", that was Taylor's assumption; and this helped supply him with another series of images whenever he wished to list the iniquities of the capitalist state – images, that is, which served to associate that state with "dogma", "chimerical systems", and "artificial schemes". Here, Taylor was playing upon two ideas: in the first place, his firm belief that all property other than land was "artificial", and, in the second, his equally firm contention that capitalism represented an attempt to regulate society, to "force down" and "impose" on it a preconceived plan of operation. The connection between the apparently polar evils of capitalism and the idealism of "enthusiastic philosophers" was thus implicit but clear. Both, it was being suggested to the reader, were a violation of that "nature" that was hostile, in an even-handed way, to "equalising and accumulating laws". They were the twin evils of an acquisitive urban society; since equalitarianism, even while it attempted to remedy some of the problems created by capitalism, employed the same mistaken method of making the mechanisms of government rather than the gradual processes of nature the "distributor of wealth, and consequently power".[87]

The vocabulary Taylor employed and the assumptions he exploited had, of course, their own specific place and purpose in his general argument. However, as anyone who has read a fair amount of Southern writing will be aware, what he was doing among other things in talking of agrarianism and industrialism in these terms was offering one of the first significant examples of Southern rhetoric. He was not the first by any means to use this kind of language, even in his own region, and it is worth noting that he did talk of farm and city rather than South and North, let alone Virginian and outsider. But this should not be allowed to detract from his importance. Writing at a time of unnerving change for his state, Taylor responded by falling back on its heritage, using the past to belabour the present and, even more, the foreseeable future. And having fallen back on this heritage, he then did what many others were to do after him: he tried to find refuge from its inadequacies and contradictions in an idiom that tended to equate everything that was natural and noble with one, specifically rural, way of life and everything that was destructive and dogmatic with its opposite. He began, in fact, in however unconsidered a way, to draw primitive portraits of the Southerner and Yankee.[88]

Taylor, however, does not supply the last episode in this necessarily brief tale of transition in early republican Virginia: that is provided by a figure beside whom even he seems positively liberal and optimistic, John Randolph of Roanoke. "Bred up", as he described himself, "in the school of Hobbes and Boyle, and Shaftesbury and Bolingbroke, and Hume and Voltaire and Gibbon",[89] John Randolph felt himself to be distinctly at odds with the world he saw emerging around him. That world, he felt, had been corrupted by a number of different, but interlocking and equally pernicious, forces: the "monstrous tyranny" of "King Numbers"; "fanatical and preposterous theories about the rights of man"; "the puritanical jargon" and "high-strained Calvinistic theory" that had supplanted "the practice of Christianity, of moderation, kindness, and charity"; an economic system that enabled people, "goaded by avarice", to "buy only to sell and sell only to buy"; and, not least, that "whole bundle of theories (bottomed on a Utopian ideal of human excellence)" that was for him the American constitution.[90] In short, Randolph was a self-conscious reactionary. More specifically, he was a man reacting in defence of his own state: which, as he saw it, was becoming increasingly eclipsed by an industrialised North and a barbarous West. "I confess", he wrote to a friend, "that I have . . . an hereditary attachment to the state which gave me birth"; and he embroidered upon this, in a speech he gave in Congress, by asserting, "No Government, extending from the Atlantic to the Pacific, can be fit to govern me or those whom I represent."[91] "The good old Virginia planter – the man who lived by hard work, and who paid his debts" was his ideal; and in defence of him – or, rather, of such few examples of his type as remained – Randolph resurrected all the familiar conservative principles – the natural inequality of men, the organic nature of society, the importance of precedent and the dangers inherent in change of any kind.[92]

"I am an aristocrat", Randolph insisted once, perhaps a little superfluously, "I love liberty, I hate equality." More important, he was an aristocrat who felt that his time was past. It was typical of him, for instance, that he chose to mark this passage from one of Macaulay's *Essays* for special attention:

> It is difficult to conceive any situation more painful than that of a great man condemned to watch the lingering agony of an exhausted country . . . to see the signs of vitality disappear one by one, till nothing is left but coldness, darkness, and corruption.[93]

Unlike Jefferson, he had no future, he felt, to look forward to; unlike Taylor, he seemed to believe that it was futile to argue with the present because the eclipse of his beloved Virginia was a *fait accompli*; and so he turned to analysing the process of decline, celebrating the past, and seeking to defend as best he could the few vestiges of this past, including himself, that somehow remained. "There is something in fallen greatness", he argued, "to enlist the passions and feelings of men even against their reason"; and his task, as he saw it, was to celebrate the greatness of the planters of colonial Virginia and to explain, even if only for his own satisfaction, the reasons for their fall. Of course, these reasons had nothing to do with any faults or weaknesses in the planters themselves. In a manner characteristic of the elegiast, Randolph pinned the blame firmly on external forces and other people – "the politico-religious Quacks", "a privileged order of military and monied men", manufacturers who were "citizens of no place or any place", and those unfortunate "connections with low people" that were the inevitable result of Jefferson's "levelling system" and "political metaphysics". "New men . . . time servers, usurers, and money changers"[94] were all that Randolph professed to see about him; and it was to these people, and the system they represented, that he attributed the destruction of what he termed "the old families of Virginia".

And what of the old families themselves, and the greatness from which they had supposedly fallen? Randolph's strategy in describing them was to accept them on their own terms, to surrender to their own idealised image of themselves. "Before the Revolution", he declaimed,

> the lower country of Virginia . . . was inhabited by a race of planters of English descent, who dwelt on their principal estates on the borders of . . . noble streams. The proprietors were generally well educated – and some of them at the best schools of the mother country, the rest at William and Mary, then a seminary of learning, under able classical masters. Their habitations and establishments, . . . spacious and costly, in every instance displayed taste and elegance. They were seats of hospitality. The possessors were gentlemen – better bred men were not to be found in the British dominions. As yet party spirit was not. Every door was open to those who maintained the appearance of gentlemen.[95]

Like an English preacher of the Elizabethan or early Stuart period, Randolph lamented the replacement of such honest patriarchs by a different, more avaricious class of man, and the consequent decline in hospitality and gracious living. "They whose fathers rode in coaches", he complained, "and drank the choicest wines now ride on saddlebags, and drink grog, when they can get it." "Perhaps you may think of me a querulous old man", he wrote to his niece, "praising past manners and undervaluing the present." But "so is Tacitus", he went on, "who prefers the state of manners under the Commonwealth to that which prevailed under Tiberius and his successors".[96] And having dealt, as he felt he had, with potential criticism, thoroughly convinced that the planters of colonial Virginia were indeed a nobler race of men than the ordinary, he continued drawing a moral dividing line between past and present. The present, for him, was epitomised by "a gloomy spirit of Fanaticism, which . . . has overspread our land" – and which, in its political and economic as well as in its moral and religious phases, he associated in particular with New England. The past, on the other hand, found its best expression, he felt, in "the character of the old Virginia planter", "lively and hospitable", capable of "rational and manly piety", moderate, cultivated, and mannerly.[97]

"A new order of things is come", wrote Randolph gloomily, and continued in this vein elsewhere:

> The old gentry are gone and the *nouveaux riches*, where they have the inclination, do not know how to live . . . Poverty stalking the land . . . We hug our lousy cloaks around us, take another "chaw of tobbacker", float the room with nastiness, or ruin the grate and fireplace, where they happen not to be nasty, and try conclusions upon constitutional points.[98]

There is an element of romantic posturing in this, of course: quite apart from anything else, Randolph's own life was, in material terms at least, a reasonably comfortable one. Nevertheless, it suggests something of the despair many Virginians felt after the first flush of enthusiasm for the new republic had faded and the evidence of deterioration in the Old Dominion had become unmistakable. Beyond that, this brief remark of Randolph's – along with the assumptions on which it is based and the general argument from which it is drawn – helps to bring into focus an important turning-point in the development of agrarian thought in the state. For a second time in Virginian history, the yeoman of English literary and legal tradition had been celebrated as the hope for the future, the prospective basis of a new society. For a second time, however, that hope had remained unfulfilled, and a less equalitarian ideal grew more attractive. In the seventeenth and eighteenth centuries, of course, this was because of the predominance of a few ruling families; while in the early nineteenth century it was because those very same families declined, not to be replaced, and because at the same time the economic and political power of Virginia within the Union gradually wilted. In the earlier period, as I have tried to show, the great planters had adopted as a model for imitation a largely imaginary English aristocracy, rendered plausible by remoteness of time or place; and in the later the model was provided by the memory of the planters themselves, appropriately aggrandised and romanticised by the sense of loss. Hope gave way to nostalgia, an idea of the future to a sense of the past, the idyll of the good farmer to the dream of the fine gentleman: it was to provide a not unfamiliar story for those who attempted to speak for their Southern place – although the precise details of that story quite naturally varied and it would be dangerous to indulge in simplification. Even the story here should not be over-simplified: for instance, the image of the yeoman could continue to exercise a seductive influence long after the state had begun to decline, and even over those apparently unsympathetic to it. John Randolph, to take an extreme example, was not averse to talking of "the ruddy offspring of the honest yeoman" and comparing them favourably with "the ricketty and scrofulous little wretch who first sees light in the workhouse";[99] and all this while advocating measures that would have reduced that honest yeoman, not to speak of his ruddy offspring, to economic and political impotence. In its contradictions as well as its possibilities, its occasional perversities and rough edges, the intellectual legacy of the Virginians was a rich one. Most were, perhaps, preoccupied with their own, local or state, society. All the same, the concepts and beliefs that they attempted to develop in their writings and express in their lives provided a foundation for the defence of agrarianism in the South, during the period when that region was growing to consciousness of itself. The point could again be illustrated by the eccentric figure of John Randolph who, in his later years, turned from an hereditary attachment to the state which had given him birth to a passionate defence of what he termed "the country south of Mason and Dixon's line and east of the Allegheny mountains"[100] using the same arguments he had used before, the same hypnotic dreams, the same insults and moments of elegy. As Randolph seemed to anticipate, in fact, the later development of the agrarian argument belonged to more than just one state; what Virginia started, it was left to the South as a whole to finish.

2

Holding the line in the Old South

VERSIONS OF HOME: JOHN CALHOUN AND THE
CONSTITUTIONALISTS

What Virginia started – in terms of a series of complicated and very often
self-contradictory arguments for its own existence – had also been
started, even if in a rather less thoroughgoing manner, by most of the rest
of the colonial South. From their inception, places like Carolina and
Georgia reflected a similar impulse to recover the lost perfection of the
old world in the new: a similar need, apparently as profound as it was
irrational, to see the Southern colonies in terms of some prelapsarian idyll
– and, more specifically, to impose on them a model fashioned out of a
figment of national myth, some idealised notion of the English past. The
process of trying to domesticate the wilderness – of attempting to subdue
American nature by absorbing it into some familiar European cultural
forms, and interpreting it in terms of some equally familiar pastoral
fantasies – is illustrated very clearly by the early history of Carolina.
Carolina was chartered as a single colony in 1663, and then granted as a
proprietary province to a group of English noblemen. The lords
proprietors engaged John Locke to frame the Fundamental Constitutions; and Locke responded by concocting a plan that was just as
complicated, and quite as hierarchical, as the one drawn up for Virginia
by Sir Humphrey Gilbert. Briefly, Locke's plan was that the land, as
settled, would be divided into "counties" of twelve thousand acres, each
of them subdivided into forty squares of equal size. Of these squares,
eight would be retained as "seignories" for the proprietors, while a
further eight were to be held as "baronies" by an "hereditary nobility"
consisting of what Locke called "landgraves" and "caciques". In
addition, a sizeable amount of land – not less than three thousand and not
more than twelve thousand acres within one colony – could be granted

31

to manor lords who were to be known, Locke suggested, as "gentlemen commoners".[1]

Apart from a few farmers with fifty acres or more, all the lesser inhabitants in this feudal state were to be termed "leetmen" and would be "under the jurisdiction of the respective lords of the said seignories, baronies, or manors, without appeal from them".[2] In return for obedience, the lords had to fulfil a number of duties, such as the presentation of ten acres of land to any leetman about to be married; and they had the responsibility of governing the colony through an elaborate, hierarchical system of courts. In order that this nobility should remain a fixed number, they were not to be allowed to sell or otherwise "alienate" their land; and so that the ruling families should remain unchanged, Locke insisted that any "heir general" would have to assume the name and arms of his predecessor as a condition of receiving the land as his property. Nearly all the economic and political power was to be kept in the hands of a few families, indeed no one was to be allowed to participate actively in any branch of government unless he owned at least five hundred acres; and these families were also, whenever necessary, to enlist men for military duty and lead them into battle – every man in the colony between seventeen and sixty years of age being "bound to bear arms". The purpose of all these arrangements hardly needed explaining. Nevertheless, Locke introduced his plan by informing the lords proprietors that what he wished above all to do was to "avoid erecting a numerous democracy", which he saw as a threat to stability and even survival in the strange new world of America. In effect, he wanted to render the unknown safer by accommodating it to the known; to be more precise, he wanted to minimise the political challenges and natural dangers of a new environment by responding to it in terms of a comfortingly familiar, comfortingly stable legend.

By contrast, the "numerous democracy" that John Locke wished to avoid at all costs was not very far away from the thoughts of the Georgia Board of Trustees. In 1732, Georgia was made a trusteeship – that is, a colony held in trust by trustees who were not supposed to profit from the enterprise; and it was these men, twenty-one of them in all, who set about trying to raise money to pay the expenses of emigrants to Georgia and attempting to regulate the terms on which the emigrants lived once they arrived there. The bulk of the emigrants, the trustees insisted, should consist of those who were likely to "relieve themselves and strengthen Georgia by resorting thither":[3] for example, those unfortunates burdened by "numerous families of children" or those "of reputable families, and of liberal, or at least, easy education" who found themselves for one reason or another "in decayed circumstances".[4] Such people were to be given free passage, tools, agricultural implements, seeds, and full support until the crop was harvested. More important, perhaps, not one of them was to have more than fifty acres of land, and each was to enjoy all the "liberties, franchises, and immunities" proper to free-born Englishmen who supported themselves. The fifty acres were not, admittedly, to be granted in absolute ownership: but this was simply to prevent land being exchanged or sold and so accumulating in the hands of a few. Speculation in landed property was, in fact, made illegal, as was the offering or use of mortgages; and, in order to exclude the possibility of absentee ownership, all landholders had to clear at least ten acres of their grant within ten years of being granted it. Like William Bullock, in fact, what the Georgia Board of Trustees seemed to have hoped for in the new world was a kind of yeoman republic; and to this end, warned in part perhaps by the example of Virginia, they also prohibited the importation of slaves.

This brave experiment lasted only a very few years; the trustees soon ran into financial trouble, in any case they found it difficult to control their trusteeship in the way and to the extent they had hoped, and the charter was surrendered to the Crown in 1751. The dream was never, in effect, realised, and never even began to be, just as Locke's never was. Nevertheless, the two plans, the one for Carolina, the other for Georgia, show that the Virginians were not alone in the way they saw themselves and their "Virgin Countrey": not alone, that is, in seeing those things in terms of a series of inherited and in some senses irreconcilable mythologies – in trying to talk of the new world using an old vocabulary. In this respect, it is perhaps worth quoting something that the linguist Edward Sapir said. "Human beings do not live in the objective world alone", Sapir argued,

> ... but are very much at the mercy of the particular language which has become the medium of expression for their society. It is quite an illusion to imagine that one adjusts to reality essentially without the use of language and that language is merely an incidental means of solving specific problems of communication or reflection. The fact of the matter is that the "real world" is to a large extent built up on the language habits of the group. No two languages are ever sufficiently similar to be considered as representing the same social reality. The worlds in which different societies live are distinct worlds, not merely the same world with different labels attached . . . We see and hear and otherwise experience very largely as we do because the language habits of our community predispose certain choices of interpretation . . .[5]

It is not difficult, I think, to see a connection between what Sapir is describing here and what people like Bullock and Gilbert, Locke and the Georgia Board of Trustees were doing. The pastoral mythologies through the use of which they perceived the colonial South were in effect their language, their means of structuring and encoding it and, if Sapir is to be believed, their only means of coming to terms with its more rebarbative features. As another, later linguist, Benjamin Lee Whorf, put it:

> We cut nature up, organize into concepts, and ascribe significances as we do, largely because we are parties to an agreement to organize it in this way – an agreement that holds throughout our speech community and is codified in the patterns of our language. The agreement is, of course, an implicit and unstated one, BUT ITS TERMS ARE ABSOLUTELY OBLIGATORY; we cannot talk at all except by subscribing to the organization and classification of data which the agreement subscribes.[6]

Obligatory or not, these terms – the terms, that is, inherited from colonial times and in the longer view from the mother country – were those in which the Old South saw itself, during the period when it was acquiring self-consciousness. In their anomalies and (when taken as a whole) their contradictions, they were the terms in which, for example, John Caldwell Calhoun perceived his region as he leaped to its defence, prompted largely by the feeling that it was under siege. The feeling, although obviously melodramatic and exaggerated, did have its roots in some sort of historical reality: since, at the time when his political opinions were maturing, the South as a whole was rapidly approaching that sadly debilitated condition to which Virginia had already succumbed. Since the end of the 1812 war with England, the region had been suffering from a prolonged economic depression; while at the same time its proportion of representation in the central government was gradually decreasing and the powers actually appropriated by that government were steadily on the increase.[7] Naturally, Southern politicians were inclined to see a direct, causal connection between these phenomena. Calhoun himself, for example, never ceased complaining about what he termed "the unjust, the unconstitutional, the mistaken and pernicious means" that "the manufacturing interest" employed to further its interests, while Jefferson Davis, the future President of the Confederacy, declared in a speech in Congress:

> . . . the present condition of the Southern states has served to impress more deeply on my own mind the grievous oppression of a system by which the wealth of the country is drained off to be expended elsewhere . . . The fruits of our labour are drawn from us to enrich other and more favoured sections of the Union; while, with one of the finest climates and richest products in the world . . . we exhibit the extraordinary, the wonderful, and painful spectacle of a country enriched by the bounty of God, but blasted by the cruel policy of man.[8]

That there was some relation between contemporary political developments and what one observer called the "non-progressiveness, . . . decay and desolation" of much of the South can now hardly be doubted.

However, it was not nearly as simple as some spokesmen for the region were inclined to imagine. A connection between the growth of urban-industrial life and the development of a central government strong in its ability to create and fund debts, to grant bounties and tariffs, and to confer perpetual charters, there certainly was and is. But it is doubtful whether this ever reached the scale of systematic exploitation imagined by people like Calhoun and Davis – and whether it was possible, in any case, for any group in a continent of vast resources with a rapidly growing population to prevent such a development.

Whatever the deeper reasons for these changes, though, it was in opposition to them that the South began to grow aware of itself as a separate, coherent and identifiable, interest. Already by the second decade of the nineteenth century sectionalism had become crucial to the Congressional debates over such matters as internal movements, public banks, the United States Bank, and the tariff; and over the next decade it began to spread into other, widely differing areas of activity – further encouraged, no doubt, by such unnerving events as the growth of Abolitionism and the Nat Turner rebellion. In religion, for instance, the growing conservative orthodoxy of the evangelical South offered a startling contrast to the liberalism of the North-East; while in education, the establishment of Southern colleges and theological seminaries fostered intellectual provincialism, and in literature regional novels, literary and religious journals began to multiply. So as it became increasingly obvious that the North – with its superior financial and population resources and its close ties with the markets of Europe – was outdistancing the South, the region responded by turning in upon itself and adopting what could perhaps best be described as a posture of belligerent defence.[9]

Which brings us back to Calhoun. "I am a Southern man",[10] declared Calhoun in one of his speeches in Congress; and it was to the defence of the South – that region from which he issued and which, as he saw it, he personally embodied – that he devoted a good deal of his life. His defence, however, and its theoretical infrastructure were not quite as seamless as Calhoun seems to have believed they were. For when one looks at what he said in any detail certain inconsistencies appear – or, to be frank, certain examples of flat, downright self-contradiction – that pull his argument, and evidently his allegiances as well, in at least two quite separate directions. The reason for this was quite simple: by the time Calhoun came to talk of the South, it had already been "codified" (to use Whorf's word), ascribed particular significances, and perceived in terms of certain inherited mythologies that in many ways conflicted with each other. There was, first and perhaps more obviously, that familiar dream of a feudal society – an organic, hierarchical order changing very slowly and only in response to urgent demands – which shaped much of Calhoun's constitutional argument. Government, Calhoun declared, is "of Divine ordination" and is rendered necessary by the selfish tendencies of human nature. Because of its divine origins, it is seldom to be tampered with or altered; as a rule, he insisted, "there is . . . more efficacy and wisdom in non-action than in action". Even when action has to be contemplated, the statesman should refer for guidance to experience: his own experience, certainly, but even more important the experience of his predecessors, since "the past is the parent of the present". This would be far better than attempting to shape things in accordance with some imaginary notion of the future, a strategy he associated with "that fanaticism, which . . . carried thousands of victims to the stake" and more specifically with movements like Abolitionism. As far as the American context went, what all this meant for Calhoun was that only such changes should be contemplated as would cure what he saw as the "political degeneracy" of his times, reassert the "old Whig doctrines of '98", and bring about "the thorough reformation of the Government, and the restoration of the Constitution to its original purity". "The most unceasing vigilance will be necessary", he declared,

> to restore the Constitution to its primitive purity, and reform the many and dangerous abuses which have crept into the administration of the Government. I trust, however, as great as is the difficulty, it will not be found insuperable . . . If there ever was a struggle calculated to call forth the highest energy of freemen, that struggle, particularly as far as the fate of this section is involved, is the present one.[11]

The very mention of the Constitution, however, suggests the curiously shaky, double-edged nature of Calhoun's argument. For side by side in Calhoun's mind with an organic, and for all practical purposes inegalitarian, notion of political society there existed a mechanical theory of social contract derived from a far more liberal tradition. The Constitution, as he saw it, consisted of an elaborate series of checks and balances by means of which each individual person and each of "the various and diversified interests of the community" could have an effective voice. This system, he emphasised, was the product, not of tradition and "growth" but of a specific "compact" drawn up by men who disregarded past example and the principle of cautious innovation in a manner that, elsewhere in his argument, he dismissed as "foreign", "french", and (worst of all) "ideal". The contradiction went further; since the terms in which Calhoun chose to describe the society that would undoubtedly issue from the restoration of the Constitution to its primitive purity were nothing short of Utopian. With the recovery of the original principles, he suggested,

there will be diffused throughout the whole community kind feelings . . .
instead of faction, strife, and struggle for party ascendancy there would be
patriotism, nationality, harmony, and a struggle for supremacy in promoting
the common good of the whole.[12]

Elaborating on this, using the optimistic (not to say, idealistic) terms
favoured by William Bullock and the Virginia pamphleteers, Calhoun
anticipated a day when "truth, justice, integrity, fidelity" would, by the
means he suggested, become the leading characteristics of both government and people, and economic and political advancement would be
assured. In this way, that obsession with progress which he often satirised
and that concern for the future which he delighted in attacking was
ironically illustrated by his own words and dreams.

To an extent, Calhoun was aware of a contradiction here, in his
discussions of "man . . . as a social being",[13] and he tried to resolve it by
talking of the "government" and the "constitution" as two quite
separate entities. The one was decreed by God, he argued, and was a
matter of Divine Necessity while the other was of strictly human
"ordination". However, this rather sophistical distinction only served to
emphasise the problem rather than solve it; since it seemed to rest on the
acceptance, at one and the same time, of an extreme and pessimistic
determinism and an equally extreme, implicitly optimistic belief in
human free will. Quite apart from anything else, Calhoun never
explained why God, having forced man to form a government in the
first place, should then, in His wisdom, leave him perfectly free to decide
what kind of government this should be. Nor did the contradictions stop
there. A cynical observer might say that Calhoun's entire, tortuous
theory of human society was formulated for the very particular and
pragmatic purpose of defending the interests of the South. Be that as it
may, it is clear that Calhoun regarded himself as a leading spokesman for
his region, a bulwark against Northern domination in both the political
and intellectual fields. But what sort of South, exactly, was Calhoun
speaking for? When one looks at his references to his region, it becomes
clear that Calhoun was just as confused here as he was in his constitutional
arguments, torn between the different structures of feeling, the
conflicting vocabularies he had inherited. For, on the one hand, he could
talk of "poor and honest" farmers as the backbone of the South and, on
the other, he could say this:

> The Southern States are an aggregation, in fact, of communities, not of
> individuals. Every plantation is a little community, with the master at its head,
> who concentrates in himself the united interests of capital and labour, of which
> he is the common representative . . . These small communities aggregated
> make the State in all, whose action, labour, and capital is equally represented
> and perfectly harmonized.[14]

Again, as in his constitutional arguments, Calhoun tried to solve the problem he had got himself into with casuistry. "I fearlessly assert", he declared during a speech on the Abolition Petitions, "that the existing relation between the two races in the South . . . forms the most solid and durable foundation on which to rear free and stable political institutions."[15] According to this theory – which was by no means peculiar to Calhoun, although he was one of its most effective popularisers – all Southern whites, being members of a privileged caste, were equals; they were all members of a "Greek" or "white democracy" that combined the finest features of an aristocratic structure – such as a patriarchal regime and a cultivated elite – with the better aspects of a democratic state. The theory was an odd one, to say the least; and it was later to be brilliantly satirised by Mark Twain in his portrait of Pap Finn – who, despite his perpetual drunkenness and squalor, is outraged at the notion that "a free nigger . . . from Ohio, . . . a p'fessor in a college"[16] should presume to have some of the same rights as him. Much of its oddity, as Twain perceived, stemmed from its inappropriateness, and from the fact that it did, somehow, give the poorer whites an absurdly exalted notion of their own status, an extreme form of false consciousness. For Twain, this extremity was comic: but for another observer, Frances Kemble, the gap between the high-flown theory of "white democracy" and the sordid practices of Southern society came very much closer to being tragic. "Labour being here the especial portion of the slaves", wrote Kemble in her *Journal*,

> it is thenceforth degraded, and considered unworthy of all but slaves. No white man, therefore, of any class puts hand to work . . . This is an exceedingly dignified way of proving their gentility for the lazy planters who prefer an idle life of semistarvation . . . to the degradation of doing anything themselves; but the effect on the poorer whites of the country is terrible . . . These wretched creatures will not, for they are whites, labour for their own subsistence. They are hardly protected from the weather by the rude shelter they frame for themselves . . . Their food is chiefly supplied by shooting the wildfowl and venison, and stealing from the cultivated patches of the planters nearest at hand. Their clothes hang about them in filthy tatters, and the combined squalor and fierceness of their appearance is really frightful.[17]

Of course, it could be argued that Kemble's perception of what she termed here – somewhat sardonically, perhaps – "the yeomanry of Georgia" was just as myopic and distorted as Calhoun's; if only because she tended to equate that yeomanry, such as it was, with the very poorest of the white population. But it can hardly be doubted, given the weight of contemporary observation, that the idea of a "white democracy" *was* totally inappropriate and, in so far as it influenced opinion, did nurture among Southerners a false image of themselves: so much so, in fact, that more than one traveller to the region likened it to a kind of dreamland.[18]

Also, it is difficult to see how the idea could even begin to be reconciled with Calhoun's frequent assertion that the "large, educated planters" were the natural source of authority for other whites as well as slaves – or how it could be squared, for that matter, with a simple statement of belief he made during a speech on the Oregon Bill. "Men are not born free", he declared with what was, even for him, uncustomary baldness, ". . . Nor is it less false that they are born 'equal'".[19]

The ambivalence of Calhoun's position often manifested itself in other, minor ways. For example, his notion of Southern society necessarily involved an idealisation of agriculture – which he termed "the first of pursuits". "I know nothing", he wrote to a relative, "by which our enlightened and wealthy citizens can more effectually place their country under obligation than by contributing to its improvement." And the contempt that he expressed for manufacturing and commerce was correspondingly powerful. "Of all the things in the world", he insisted, "I have the least taste for money-making, . . . and in particular the branch connected with stock, exchange, or banking, to which I have a peculiar aversion."[20] All that could result from business adventures, he declared, was the creation of an "artificial moneyed Aristocracy". Yet during the latter part of his life one of his main ambitions was to promote Southern business and industry, and so in effect build the very system he professed to despise. To further this particular ambition, he was even willing to employ the most ingenious casuistry. For instance, he insisted that the federal government could and should provide grants for the improvement of navigation on the Mississippi and its tributaries because it was not really a river but "for all practical purposes . . . an inland sea". Large land grants could and should also be given, he suggested, to those willing to build railways and new roads in the South: this despite the fact that the suggestion clearly violated one of the most fundamental of his general principles – the one, that is, that prohibited any subsidies or privileges being offered to a special interest. In the circumstances, it seems a nice irony that Calhoun should have been regarded as a stern, unbending man of logic by many of his contemporaries – "a great dialectician", to quote one of them – or that Calhoun should have said this of himself, anonymously, in a campaign biography:

> A philosophical observer of men and their affairs, he analyses and reduces all things to their original elements, and draws thence those general principles, which, with inconceivable rapidity and unnerving certainty, he applies on all occasions, and banishes the perplexity and doubt by which ordinary minds are overwhelmed and confused.[21]

The reason for concentrating on Calhoun here is that he did commit himself so wholeheartedly to the role of advocate for the South and, as a result, does illustrate so effectively that region's confused picture of itself. Perhaps it deserves re-emphasising, though, that a similar picture emerges when we look at the habits and customs of the ante-bellum era as a whole or at the statements and proclamations made by other Southerners. Contradiction, for instance, was a principal characteristic of the social structure of the region in the decades before the Civil War. Despite a supposed "democratic revolution" beginning in 1830, the great planter did not abdicate his role before 1861, that is, during the ante-bellum period – nor did the end of that period signal a change. True, under the leadership of the frontier counties of the lower South, state after state did break with the oligarchic model of government that had been entrenched since the seventeenth century; and in fact, by 1850 nine Southern states had governors popularly elected, universal manhood suffrage, and provisions for the periodic reapportionment of seats. For all the apparent democratisation, however, a large proportion of local and state leaders still continued to be drawn from a small, wealthy class of people, and in any case the economic and social structure remained essentially unchanged. As one Charleston editor put it, "We are perpetually aiming to square the maxims of an impracticable philosophy with the practice which nature and circumstances force upon us."[22] The tug between two different political vocabularies, two separate mythologies continued in Southern life as well as its thought, leading to what one observer, Frederick Law Olmsted, saw as "a succession of miserable compromises". "One year", Olmsted complained, "a little is yielded to the common people within the state; the next, an effort is made to bully the General or the democratic states into some retreat from Confederate principles."[23]

Quite apart from the ambivalent nature of Southern society at the time, the arguments for the region put forward by spokesmen other than Calhoun show the same uncertainty and self-contradiction. Jefferson Davis, for instance, could insist that the South was the only truly democratic society ("every mechanic", he told Northern Senators, "assumes among us the position which only a master workman holds among you")[24] and the only genuine aristocracy ("Speaking of the peculiarities of his people", a contemporary biographer reported, "Mr. Davis said they were essentially aristocratic, their aristocracy being based on birth and education").[25] James De Bow could do the same, claiming within the space of one book that "the poorest and humblest" in the South were on a par with "the wealthiest planter", and that:

> The Almighty has thought well to place . . . His creatures in certain fixed positions in this world of ours, for what cause He has not seen fit to make quite clear to our limited capacities.[26]

Like Calhoun, both Davis and De Bow tried to invoke the idea of a "white democracy" in order to minimise the conflict inherent in this argument. "Southern slaveholders", proclaimed De Bow,

> have always had English ideas of liberty, not French . . . They never favoured "abstract liberty" but have had from the beginning their own system . . . If they are "loud for democracy", it has been the democracy of the white man, and not the negro . . .[27]

De Bow, in particular, even imitated the curiously two-faced posture of Calhoun in his attitude towards the relative merits of agriculture and commerce. The book, for instance, by which he is principally remembered to-day is a compendious, three-volume work entitled *The Industrial Resources of the Southern and Western States*, which is devoted to detailing the advances made by manufacturing industry in the region and describing in glowing terms its future prospects. However, this did not prevent him from punctuating his argument with statements like the following:

> In every country the agricultural classes, or those who have an interest in the soil . . . who are removed far from the corruption of the cities . . . are the bulwarks of the commonwealth . . . Hardy independence, stern patriotism, enthusiastic devotion to liberty and love of the country, and all the noble propensities, will be found in the agricultural classes.[28]

The common denominator in all this, of course, was a desire to celebrate the South, however it should be conceived of at any particular moment. Aristocratic or democratic, patriarchal or populist, agrarian or industrial, sleepy or bustling with activity: whatever the code or model – and very often more than one code or model would be used at a time – the premise was that the South was virtually without blemish, and that the few blemishes it had were hardly its responsibility, "The Creator has beautified the face of this Union with sectional features", declared the South Carolina orator William Lowndes Yancey:

> Absorbing all minor sub-divisions, He has made the North and the South; the one the region of frost, ribbed in with ice and granite; the other baring its generous bosom to the sun and ever smiling under its influence. The climate, soil, and productions of these two grand divisions of the land, have made the character of their inhabitants. Those who occupy the one are cool, calculating, enterprising, selfish, and grasping; the inhabitants of the other are ardent, brave and magnanimous, more disposed to give than to accumulate, to enjoy ease rather than to labour.[29]

In effect, the Mason–Dixon line became a kind of moral demarcation, crossed only by the occasional contaminating influence. Even those aspects of slavery that spokesmen for the South admitted were not entirely pleasant – and there were not very many of them – were usually blamed on those from above this dividing line. Of slave-traders, for instance, Jefferson Davis declared, "I know the odium which exists against this class . . . I have grown up in a community which feels it, and I partake of it myself." Unlike the care of slaves, he insisted, the traffic in them was something that he and his neighbours deplored. But then, he added, it was nothing to do with them: for "traders . . . are usually northern men, who come among us but are not of us".[30]

Quite apart from his confused vision of the South, Calhoun's use of both the organic and the contractual conceptions of society to defend that vision found its echo among many other spokesmen for the region. The Constitution, identified, however erroneously, with "tradition", came to be regarded as a sacred document – almost on a par with the Bible – whose word, literally interpreted, was law. Alexander Stephens of Georgia, for example, the future Vice-President of the Confederacy, described it in almost religious terms, as an embodiment of those "principles" that supplied the only adequate defence against human error and corruption. "Parties may rise and fall", Stephens proclaimed,

> but principles with me are the pole-star of my existence. What is the matter now with the country is that a class of men are in power who have no loyalty to principle . . . they are out for nothing but to undermine the most glorious structure ever devised by man.[31]

By a curious twist of logic, then, the specific contract that was the Constitution came to be described in terms of those universal and unalterable truths which organicists claim to defend. It should never be tampered with, the implication was, never be subjected to the whim for "innovation", because it represented that series of absolute necessities which Calhoun – taking a slightly different tack – associated with his notion of "government". Nevertheless, when power began to pass into the hands of the industrial North-East and the expanding West through entirely constitutional means, these same spokesmen for the South suddenly turned their argument on its head, and began to indulge in the very tampering with the sacred document that, in other circumstances, they roundly condemned. On January 11, 1861, for instance, R. M. J. Hunter of Virginia introduced into Congress an elaborate plan for the construction of "a new Government" and "a new Union",[32] including a scheme for a dual executive – to represent the conflicting interests of North and South – and a thoroughly reorganised Supreme Court. Nor was he alone in making such radical proposals: most of his specific recommendations had been anticipated by other representatives from Virginia, Tennessee, and Missouri.

Traveller after traveller in the Old South noted the existence of these and similar contradictions in its beliefs and behaviour: a "singular contrast", as one of them put it, between what Southerners said or did at one moment and what they said or did at the next. The inconsistencies inherent in the defence of slavery were especially noticeable, and particularly remarked upon by contemporary observers. Some of these will be discussed later, but perhaps it is worth pointing out something that Frederick Law Olmsted noticed in *A Journey in the Back Country*. "It is difficult to handle simply as property", Olmsted remarked,

> a creature possessing human passions and human feelings . . .; while, on the other hand, the absolute necessity of dealing with property, as a thing, greatly embarrasses a man in any attempt to treat it as a person. And it is the natural result of this complicated state of things, that the system of slave-management, is irregular, ambiguous, and contradictory – that it is neither consistently humane or consistently economical.[33]

Expanding on Olmsted here, we could say that the irregularities he noted stemmed directly from the familiar conflict between the patriarchal and populist structures of feeling. Within the patriarchal structure, the Negro slave could be granted at least a subordinate place, and could therefore be regarded as a human being – one with "a low order of intellect", perhaps, "of another and inferior race"[34] but capable, nevertheless, of being educated to a degree and taught the blessings of civilisation (see Plate 4). Within the populist structure, however, he had no specifically human role to play; for a system predicated on a belief in the independence and self-reliance of its every member had, by definition, to exclude slaves and reduce them to the status of goods and chattels. Naturally, these two ways of viewing the slave – or, to use Whorf's term again, these two codes for explaining his presence and function – led to conflicts of practice and, indeed, contradictions in principle. According to the laws of many Southern states, for instance, if a slave committed murder he was responsible as a human being for his act and could suffer the death penalty as a result. As property, though, his death by execution would involve loss for his master – who was therefore entitled to claim compensation.

Perhaps all conflicts of this kind could have been prevented if – setting aside, for a moment, the shame and problem of slavery – Southerners had been willing to accept that theirs was a fluid and amorphous society, so eclectic and incomplete that no particular figure could be said to embody it wholly: neither those very few planters who, as one traveller put it, "live like little sovereigns on their estates", nor those very many plainer folk who, as another traveller commented, "are daily taught the habit of self-reliance". But this was something that no leading political spokesman for the South, and least of all Calhoun, was willing to do. For people like Calhoun the language of the patriarchal and populist traditions held equal sway, and the figures of the fine gentleman and the simple yeoman possessed a similar fascination. Two images very popular at the time suggest something of the poles between which their minds moved. These were the images of the Virginia planter and the Kentucky farmer, used by numerous writers, publicists for the region, and other commentators to explain just what was special, in their opinion, what was "Southern" about the South:

> Eminently social and hospitable, kind, humane, and generous is the Virginian . . . By means of these social traits, they necessarily become well-mannered, honourable, spirited, and careful of reputation, desirous of pleasing and skilled in the accomplishments which please . . . of good intelligence, family, education, and breeding.

> The Kentucky farmer . . . putting forth the thew and sinew of a giant, to benefit posterity; his only present recompense the possession of rude independence . . . his relaxation an occasional frolic . . . these men seek wealth from the soil to return it back to the soil, with the addition of the sweat of their brows . . . their pride does not consist in fine houses, costly services of plate . . . they live in humble dwellings of wood, wear the coarsest habits and live on the plainest fare. It is their pride to have planted an additional acre of cane-brake, to have won a few feet from the river, or cleared a thousand trees from the forest.[35]

One or two things might be said about these two passages, by way of bringing this brief discussion of Calhoun and his associates to a conclusion. In the first place, it is worth emphasising the fact that the notions of Virginia and Kentucky exploited here were, like those of the planter and the farmer, part of the regional code. The real-life equivalents of "the Virginian" and "the Kentucky farmer" – or perhaps it would be more accurate to say, the actual people on to whom these imaginative versions of rural life were projected – could be found almost anywhere in the Old South; "Virginia" and "Kentucky" were, consequently, as much a matter of idiom as of fact, a way of ascribing significance with the help of a map – by drawing coordinates in space as well as time. In the second, it needs mentioning that one of these passages was written by a 'foreigner', that is to say a person born and raised outside the South: which only goes to show just how seductive the region's habits of language and perception could be, not merely for itself but for those, too, who came to visit.[36] And, in the third place and finally, the fact that these are two quite separate passages from two different books suggests, possibly, that not all those who sought to explain or justify the South were torn in the way Calhoun was. Many, outsiders as well as Southerners, chose to identify the world they described with one or other of those versions of it inherited from colonial days. This saved them from self-contradiction and casuistry, of course, but it necessarily involved them in acts of exclusion. Filtering everything through one particular sieve, interpreting everything they saw according to either the patriarchal or populist model, they gained in coherence, perhaps – but not, as we shall see, without losses of other kinds.

TO SPEAK OF ARCADIA: WILLIAM GILMORE SIMMS AND SOME PLANTATION NOVELISTS

At the time when people like Calhoun, Davis, and Stephens were attempting a political defence of their region, another group of men were responding in a rather different (if analogous) way to the South's search for an identity. Being storytellers, they did not pretend that the people they talked about actually existed somewhere. But being serious storytellers, they did presume on a kind of imaginative truth; that is to say, they did believe they were exposing and examining something of the character of their place and time. Were they correct in this belief? Hardly, since they tended to use either the patriarchal or the populist model as their means of understanding their chosen world; experience was mediated for them by the vocabularies of feudal plantation or simple, self-subsistent farm. As a result, it was not so much the lineaments of their region they exposed as its mind, or at least some significant aspect of it, its mental and mythical structures – and, to the extent that they participated in and endorsed those structures, their own minds, the shape of their own beliefs and means of perception too. In this, quite possibly, they had no choice. For, as Dorothy Lee observes,

> A member of a given society – who, of course, codifies experienced reality through the use of the specific language and other patterned behaviour characteristic of his culture – can actually grasp reality only as it is presented to him in this code. The assumption is not that reality itself is relative, but that it is differently punctuated and categorized by participants of different cultures, or that different aspects of it are noticed by, or presented to, them.[37]

What these writers and storytellers did, in effect, was largely accept their locality on its own terms, and then try to use those terms as a way of explaining its strengths and deficiencies. The punctuation marks, the systems of patterning they used were the ones supplied for the region, in the first instance, by the pamphleteers or the first families of Virginia; and they began by accepting them, assuming that the ante-bellum South did more or less reproduce the society imagined by William Bullock, say, or William Byrd. The interest their work holds is, as a result, nicely double-edged; since, however tough their specific, local criticisms of Southern life may be, that criticism is subverted by their original willingness to accept some part of the South's own image of itself.

Of those writers who used the patriarchal model in an effort to understand and occasionally criticise the South, none embarked upon the task with more enthusiasm or more energy than William Gilmore

Simms. Simms's personal background was modest, in some senses even deprived. "My immediate ancestors were poor", he wrote once in a letter to a friend. "My father was unfortunate in business. My mother died while I was an infant in the arms of a nurse." Brought up in Charleston, South Carolina by his grandmother, Simms attempted for most of his adult life to earn a living from his pen: something that was not helped, he felt, by the blithe indifference of the South, and more specifically Charleston, to his work. "Here", he complained,

> I am nothing and can be and do nothing. The South don't care a d—n for literature or art. Your best neighbour and kindred never think to buy books. They will borrow from you & beg, but the same man who will always have his wine, has no idea of a library. You will write for & defend their institutions in vain. They will not pay the expense of printing your essays.[38]

However, that is to tell only one part of the story. Although Simms's father failed in business, he was not ruined: when he left Charleston, without his son, to seek a new life in Mississippi he still owned over five hundred acres of land, while in Mississippi he acquired a plantation and slaves. And Simms's mother left her son a not inconsiderable inheritance, consisting of two houses and about twenty-five slaves – an inheritance that Simms then proceeded to lose trying to establish a newspaper in Charleston. This was enough, perhaps, to predispose him towards the landholding and slave-owning class: despite his feeling, expressed more than once, that "there never will be a literature worth the name in the Southern States, so long as their aristocracy remains based on so many heads of negroes and so many bales of cotton". And the predisposition was undoubtedly reinforced by Simms's second marriage, by virtue of which he became a member, of sorts, of the planter class. Thereafter, most of his life was to be spent at his wife's home, "Woodlands", an estate of nearly three thousand acres; and his life was to take on at least some of the characteristics of the country gentleman – a type that apparently he found it equally easy to defend and despise.

"To hunt, to ride, to lounge, and to sleep, – perhaps to read a few popular novels conducing to repose, – is the sum and substance of our country performances." This, from an essay entitled "Country Life Incompatible with Literary Labor",[39] is the voice of Simms the professional man of letters, forced to make his way in a world where he felt, as he put it once, like a "blooded horse locked up in the stable, and miles away from the Course": Simms the orphan and prickly *arriviste*, Simms the prophet without honour in his own country. But it was not by any means his only voice. Indeed, it could be argued that the very reluctance of the Southern ruling class, and that of Charleston in particular, to recognise and honour him drove him on all the more fiercely to assert its claims and defend its institutions: to adopt the voice –

especially in his fiction – not of dispossessed outsider but of defender of
the faith. It would not be the first time in literary history, after all, or
history of any kind, that a particular club found one of its stoutest
defenders in someone it chose to exclude – or, at least, to whom it offered
only the most restricted and temporary of membership cards. Be that as it
may, Simms was in the position – as he only too clearly and bitterly
realised – of being ignored or underestimated by the very region, and
more specifically the very interests, that he chose to describe, commemorate, and support. Consciously, he chose the path of sectionalism ("to be
national in literature", he once declared, "one needs be *sectional*") only to
find himself less popular and esteemed in his own section than in other
parts of the nation. "It is an old story", as his friend the poet Paul
Hamilton Hayne observed, "but not on that account the less
melancholy."[40]

During the course of his literary career, Simms published over eighty
books, including a series of long romances – written between 1834 and
1854 – that are based on the actual history of the South from its settlement
to the middle of the nineteenth century. Divided, in turn, into Colonial,
Revolutionary, and Border Romances, these show Simms trying to take
over the pattern first developed by Scott and later adapted by Cooper to
native American materials. It was a pattern which among other things
allowed him a good deal of imaginative latitude in the treatment of
historical fact: "the poet and romancer", he declared in one of his essays,

> are only strong where the historian is weak, and can alone walk boldly and
> with entire confidence in those dim and insecure avenues of time which all
> others tremble when they penetrate.[41]

And Simms used this latitude to incorporate legend and tradition into his
narratives. To be more precise, he used it to shape his raw historical
material as a whole in accordance with an overriding thesis, one central
organising principle: which was based on his belief in the patriarchal
model, a hierarchical system that found its summit and embodiment in
what he called "the Southern aristocrat – the true nobleman of that
region". This is seen most clearly and effectively in Simms's seven
Revolutionary Romances which are usually regarded as his best
imaginative work – and which taken together constitute, in the words of
one critic, "an exemplary epic story for the South".[42] For in them
Simms used the story of the American Revolution in South Carolina as a
kind of mirror for his own times: as a means of foregrounding
contemporary intersectional problems, celebrating current regional
achievements, and providing a standard for which, in his own opinion,
his fellow Southerners could and should fight.

In effect, Simms tended to regard the American Revolution as a
conflict between two fundamentally antagonistic social systems, an

anticipation of the conflict between North and South. So it is that, without exception, all his Revolutionary officers are depicted as young Carolinian cavaliers. This, for example, is the description of one such character, Colonel Walton in *The Partisan*, the first book in the Revolutionary series:

> Colonel Richard Walton was a gentleman in every sense of the word: simple, unpretending, unobtrusive, and always considerate, he was esteemed and beloved by all around him. Born to the possession of large estates, his mind had been exercised happily by education and travel; and at the beginning of the revolutionary struggle, he had been early found to advocate the claims of his native colony.[43]

Fighting, as this passage suggests, for their "native colony" rather than some larger, national or philosophical, abstraction, these gentlemen-officers were very often compared to knights of the Middle Ages – or, as Simms puts it in *Katharine Walton*, to the "masters" of "merry old England". In *The Forayers*, for instance, the penultimate novel in the series, a feast prepared by Simms's most famous character, Captain Porgy, for his fellow officers, is presented in terms of a medieval banquet. Never mind that the feast is held in a forest: Simms uses the long set piece of a dinner just as many later plantation novelists were to do – to celebrate Southern manners, the region's commitment to ceremony and ritual. With "the proper welcome for each as he drew nigh", the meal opens in state, with martial music accompanying the arrival of each guest. The guests "disposed . . . without confusion", a long and elaborate meal then follows, to be concluded with speeches and toasts, prayers for victory and battle hymns "worthy to be sung in the hall of Odin" (performed by Porgy's ensign, the "bard" of the regiment), and "with merry jest, jibe, and story, till the hours grew something smaller than the stars". A portrait in miniature of Southern order, the scene occurs towards the end of *The Forayers*; and it is surely no accident that *Eutaw*, the final Revolutionary Romance and a sequel to *The Forayers*, presents the reader, in its first chapter, with something very different – the dining customs or rather the lack of them, among the Tory irregulars:

> There was little talk among the party . . ., except such as took place with small groups . . . Words were spoken, as if not calling for an answer. Those who spoke, with the hope of amusing the company, or provoking response, were rarely successful . . . There was no song after supper.[44]

Simms's portrait of the civilians in sympathy with the Revolutionary movement helps to flesh out this idea of a proud nobility fighting for its independence. For nearly every young officer involved in the movement, for instance, there is a plantation belle, a focus for romantic interest who combines the domestic and the social virtues with an aristocratic appearance and graceful behaviour. Flora Middleton, in *The Kinsmen*, is a good example of the type:

> Flora Middleton . . . was a noble specimen of the Anglo-Saxon . . . She belonged to that wonderful race of Carolina women . . . who could minister, with equal propriety and success, at those altars for which their fathers, husbands, and brothers fought . . . She had her tastes, and might be considered by some persons as rather fastidious in them – but this fastidiousness was nothing more than method. Her love of order was one of her domestic virtues. But, though singularly methodical . . ., she had no hum-drum notions . . .[45]

And so on. The older officers, in turn, are matched (in terms of relationship or just sympathy) with some plantation matron, like a certain Mrs Singleton in *Katharine Walton*:

> This old lady was a woman of Roman character, worthy to be a mother of the Gracchi. She was sprung of the best Virginia stock . . . She was firmly devoted to the Revolutionary movement – a calm, frank, firm woman, who, without severity of tone or aspect, was never seen to smile.[46]

And, almost invariably, there on the periphery of the action are the lower levels in this essentially hierarchical system: the diverse body of merchants, artisans, farmers, and frontiersmen whose "blood" and training prevent them acting as leaders but who are more than willing to follow. At the very bottom, of course, are the slaves: who in Simms's perception are as devoted to the system and, more particularly, to those who embody it as any of the more privileged are. This, for example, is the response of Captain Porgy's Negro cook Tom when he is offered his freedom:

> "No! no! maussa", he cried, with a sly shake of his head, "I kain't t'ink ob letting you off dis way. Ef *I* doesn't b'long to *you*, *you* b'longs to *me* . . . and you nebber guine git *you* free paper from me as long as you lib."[47]

Precisely what old Tom is so reluctant to be free of is described in loving detail in those moments when Simms takes some time off from skirmishes, battles, intrigues, and hair-breadth escapes. As in many other plantation romances, the home of the gentleman-planter, for instance, is presented as an extension and material expression of its owner's nobility, an architectural emblem of his moral achievement. Thus, the description of Colonel Walton in *The Partisan* quoted earlier is preceded by this portrait of his house:

> . . . from a block-house station at first it had grown to be an elegant mansion, improved in European style, remarkable for its avenues of solemn oaks, its general grace of arrangement, and the lofty and considerate hospitality of its proprietors . . .[48]

Within these noble structures – some of them, we are told, "not ill planned for a palace" – an elegant social life is maintained despite the war.

The house of Mrs Singleton in *Katharine Walton*, for instance, is portrayed as "a favourite point of reunion among the patriots of both sexes". In propitious time, Simms adds, "the days were . . . consumed in 'fêtes champêtres' and the nights in lively reunions", while, at less favourable moments:

> Hither . . . came the Routledges, the Laurens, the Izards, and most of the well-known and famous families of the Low Country of Carolina, to consult as to the future.[49]

"Thousands of instances are recorded", says Simms in *The Partisan* talking of the Revolutionary forces, "of that individual gallantry . . . refined by courtesy which gives the only credentials of true chivalry." And it seems obvious that Simms regarded the partisans as chivalric principally because they devoted themselves to the defence of a patriarchal system – a system that, as he saw it, sustained and ennobled his own place and time. Not that the system was entirely inflexible: he could imagine some rising, like himself, as a result of natural merit and innate nobility. One of the characters in *The Forayers* seems to speak for him, in fact, when he declares:

> "No one, more highly than myself, esteems the claims of social caste. It is a natural condition, and rightly possesses authority; but God forbid! that I should sullenly and sternly reject the occasional individual, whose personal claims put him above his condition in society! He has received from nature his badges of nobility . . ."[50]

But, as this passage suggests, such people *were* to be regarded as exceptional; on the whole, the system remained unmoving, strictly hierarchical, and self-perpetuating.

It could hardly have escaped the notice of Simms's Southern readers, and especially those from his own state, that implicit in his Revolutionary Romances was a call to arms. South Carolina had fought once, the message was, to defend its institutions and should be prepared to do so again: not necessarily with sword and cannon, of course, but at all events with stern moral determination and resolute political action. The message was veiled in his fiction, perhaps partly because of his dependence on the Northern market, but in his private correspondence his tone became more and more openly defiant and secessionist ("I have long since regarded the separation as a now inevitable necessity", he wrote to a friend in 1850). And, when one thinks about it, the message was not as veiled as all that even in his fiction: for just as the Revolutionary forces embodied for him the virtues of the Southern system, so the Tories seemed to represent the worst features of the North. In simple terms, while Simms's partisan officers reproduced the familiar image of the gentleman, the feudal planter, the Tory officers and troops

were like nothing so much as the Yankee: that Southern stereotype of
Northern vices which, as W. R. Taylor has shown, was gradually
gaining ascendancy during the time when Simms was writing. The
Tories, we are informed in *The Partisan*, were mostly

> of the very lowest class, and just the sort of men to fight, according to the
> necessity of the case, on either side . . . Without leading principles and
> miserably poor – not recognised, except as mercenaries, in the social
> aristocracies which must always prevail in slave-holding nations – they had no
> sympathy with the more influential classes – those who were the first to resist
> the authority of England. The love of gain, the thirst for rapine, and that
> marauding and gipsy habit of life which was familiar to them, were all directly
> appealed to in the tory mode of warfare.[51]

"You're one of the bloody, proud, heathen harrystocrats", declares a
Tory soldier to one of his prisoners, in *The Forayers*,

> "that look upon a poor man, without edication, as no better than a sort of two-
> legged dog . . . But thar's a great change, thanks to the king's marcies! and the
> good time for the poor man's come at last! – and now, we've got a-top of the
> wheel! We've got the chance at the good things of this life; and we kin pay off
> old scores, wagon-whip and hickory, agin your nice goold-headed cane!"[52]

Speeches like this seem to focus all Simms's fears concerning the "great
change" he and many other Southerners saw occurring about them:
thanks to the North's exploitation of its numbers and its crafty way of
using democratic ideas to impose a colonial status on the region. And the
principal villains in most of these books tap the sources of these fears even
more powerfully, by uniting within themselves the complex vices of the
Yankee figure: cunning disguised by claims to philanthropy, greed
masquerading as democratic enthusiasm, abstract idealism linked in an
unholy alliance with very concrete forms of selfishness. Richard
Inglehardt, an important character in both *The Forayers* and *Eutaw* is one
of the most memorable examples of this type. The son of an overseer,
Inglehardt, Simms informs the reader,

> was a *new* man; an ambitious man, anxious to shake off old and inferior
> associations . . . He had abandoned his caste, an unforgivable offence, which
> moved the dislike of all its members; and he had not quite succeeded in forcing
> himself upon the affections . . . of that other circle which he sought to
> penetrate . . .[53]

Sharing in the legendary mobility of the Yankee figure, his separation
from and lack of sympathy for the strictly regulated class structure of the
South, Inglehardt also shares in that figure's coldness, manipulativeness
and rabid industry – his ruthless pursuit of whatever he desires. He is "a
cool, selfish politician", we are told, "subtle as a serpent", "wonderfully
shrewd and cunning", but knowing nothing of "generous affections . . .

glorious impulses . . . and noble frenzies". In fact, Simms's lengthy analyses of him are calculated to make him seem the mirror opposite of the partisans in nearly every respect. Here, by way of illustration, is just part of one of them:

> He had shown himself . . . cunning, but not wise; calculating, but not profound; able in the performance of ordinary duties, but not nobly adventurous. . . Talent he had; an adaptable capacity for the work before him; he was a shrewd judge of common men . . . but enthusiasm failed him; he could never comprehend the worth of impulse, generous self-sacrifice, ardent adventure, eager and impetuous zeal . . . He not only did not quite understand them, he did not believe in their existence . . .[54]

"Coldness of heart was the great and terrible infirmity of Richard Inglehardt", Simms declares; and combining this coldness with ruthlessness, while concealing both beneath the mask of a friend of the people, he presents an intimidating enemy for most of the course of the two narratives. True, like all villains in romances he is defeated in the end: but it is only occasionally that he is outfaced and humiliated as he is at the moment when he tries to make John Rutledge, the rebel governor of South Carolina, his prisoner. Rutledge's response is brief, and to the point: "You know neither me – nor yourself", he declares defiantly. "If you know either of us, sir, you would know that *I* am not to be taken prisoner by you!" And just for once, Simms makes Inglehardt aware of his moral blindness and consequently embarrassed by what he has attempted to do. "Inglehardt's cheek flushed", we are told:

> He could feel the sentiment of scorn. He, the son of the overseer and grazier, felt the sting of sarcasm from the born gentleman.[55]

The element of wish-fulfilment here, brought on by Simms's need both to allay his fears and whistle up some support, is so obvious as to be hardly worth mentioning. If only the aristocrat would stand up for himself, the implication is, and assert his superiority, his enemies would feel compelled to accept his case.

Not that Simms's presentation of that case was entirely uncritical. It frequently was, but in at least one of his Revolutionary Romances he allowed himself some reservations. This was *The Sword and the Distaff*, subsequently entitled *Woodcraft*, which is the best of the series and arguably Simms's finest novel. The principal character in the book is Captain Porgy, who is a Falstaffian figure in some ways, described in *The Partisan* as "one of the fat, beefy class, whose worship of the belly-god has given an unhappy distension to that . . . member". Porgy's physical appearance constitutes something of a departure from the normal run of Simms's gentlemen-officers ("His person was symmetry itself' is the opening phrase used of one of them), and it alerts the reader to the author's rather more mixed, critical assessment of the moral and mental qualities of at least *this* plantation hero. A "bon viveur" as well as a gentleman and a soldier, Porgy has deficiencies and, to some extent, is even aware of them. Even more important, Porgy is also aware that in this, his imperfections, he is by no means alone: "I was always one of that large class of planters", he admits at one point in the novel, "who reap thistles from their planting. I sowed wheat only to reap tares." In plain terms, Porgy is profligate: the reverse side of his dashingly romantic, aristocratic qualities – his bravery, his generosity, and his impulsiveness – is that he is hopelessly lacking in common sense, thrift, and those qualities of application and dogged industry that would enable him to achieve success in business – and farming, Simms suggests, *is*, at least to some extent, a business. At the beginning of the novel, in fact, Porgy is pictured returning home after the Revolution to an exhausted plantation and a dilapidated mansion. Some of the blame for this decay is placed on the war itself, but even more is laid at Porgy's door; the plantation had been declining even before the military conflict began, we are told, and ironically Porgy saw that conflict as a way of escaping from his financial problems – an opportunity to try his hand at something which he, "the most sprightly of cavaliers", *had* been trained to deal with. "Porgy . . . had never been taught the pains of acquisition", Simms explains, ". . . he had too soon and fatally learned the pleasures of dissipation"; and, having once gone into financial decline thanks to his carelessness, "he possessed no conscious resources, within himself, by which to restore his property, or even to acquire the means of life". The full pathos of his situation, and the principal reason for it, are beautifully caught in one of Porgy's many speeches (among other gentlemanly qualities, he enjoys "a liberal endowment of the gift of language") – when he tries to think of what to do now that, as it seems, his plantation is irretrievably lost:

> "The property? Yes! I suppose after a while, I shall have to surrender; but we'll make a d—d long fight of it, hence; and we'll get terms, conditions, when we give in – go off with our side arms, flag flying, and music playing . . ."[56]

Translating simple destitution into heroic military defeat, and disguising a failure of responsibility beneath a series of flamboyant gestures, Porgy demonstrates here that very romanticism, that evasion of ordinary day-to-day realities, that got him into trouble in the first place.

Eventually, Porgy manages to escape ruin. *The Sword and the Distaff* is, in fact, principally concerned with the process of restitution and recovery, the means by which what seemed to be inevitable turns out not to be. Not all of these means need concern us here, since they involve some fairly conventional intrigue and the unmasking of a pretty commonplace villain: but one of them, at least, is worthy of a little more attention. Porgy is persuaded to appoint his former corporal, a man named Millhouse, to be his overseer. Millhouse is a very different person from his old captain: a man of crassly limited vision, in some ways, who nevertheless knows how to work hard and drive a good bargain and who imposes a strict limit on Porgy's expenses. Two conversations between them, in particular, focus the difference. In the first, Millhouse argues that Captain Porgy does not need a pointer for hunting since he can shoot as many birds as he likes while they are still on the ground; and to Porgy's objection that this is not the way "a gentleman and a sportsman" hunts, he replies simply and forcibly:

> "Look you, Captain, them's all notions; and when a man's wanting flesh for the pot . . . it's not reasonable that he should be a sportsman and a gentleman. That's the sort of extravagance that's not becoming to a free white man, when he's under bonds to the Sheriff."[57]

The second conversation, or rather argument, develops along similar lines, and includes one of Millhouse's most powerful speeches. This is part of it; it is, of course, addressed to Porgy:

> "You don't know what's useful in the world. You only know what's pleasant, and amusing, and ridiculous, and what belongs to music and poetry and the soul; and not about the wisdom that makes the crops grow, and drives a keen bargain, and swells the money-box . . . Now, I reckon, you'd always git the worst of it at a horse-swap . . . Now, if there's wisdom in the world – that is raal wisdom – it is in making a crop, driving a bargain, getting the whip hand in a trade . . . As for music and po'try and them things, it's all flummery. They don't make the pot bile . . . ef there's one music in the world that's more sweet than another to the ears of a man of sense, it's the music that keeps tune to the money coming in."[58]

The interest of this speech lies in the fact that, while some of it – like the closing remarks concerning "music" – is clearly intended to reveal the limitations of Millhouse's vision, his lack of taste, imagination, and refinement, other parts of it have a colloquial power, an earthy poetry that makes much of Porgy's own idiom seem fragile, evasive, and even ridiculous. The point is not, of course, that in the long run Millhouse seems superior to Porgy, more accomplished or of better understanding. It is simply that, for once in his work, Simms admits a more critical look at the patriarchal mode and even admits a different language, a separate verbal perspective, in order to give that criticism some bite.

Nor does Porgy's return to his former prosperity at the end of the novel brush this criticism away entirely. "Freed of anxiety", we are told, "Porgy resumed his ancient spirit" and his estate "became a sort of centre for parish civilisation". This is all very heartening, but the reader is not likely to forget that the credit for much of this recovery must go to Millhouse – in other words, that Porgy's charm and refinement depend for their exercise on his overseer's not very charming and totally unrefined approach to things. Of man, Millhouse says, at one point in the novel:

> "He's to go on gitting, and gitting, and gitting to the end of the season, untill Death gits him. As he gits, he kin increase his comforts – git better bread . . . git wine, git better clothing, hev' his horse to ride; perhaps his carriage, and just make himself a sort of king . . ."[59]

And this recognition of the strictly utilitarian base on which culture rests – with its implicit criticism of those romantic cavaliers like Porgy who deny that base – is confirmed rather than contradicted by what eventually happens. Simms's other Revolutionary Romances may well have expressed unwavering confidence in the superiority and strength of the Southern position. In *The Sword and the Distaff*, however, he permitted himself a note of uncertainty and anxiety – even, of warning. The threat to the patriarchal system, he seemed to be saying, did not come just from outside.

Several writers other than Simms were aware of the problems of deterioration and decay that he explored in the story of Captain Porgy. Like him – like, for that matter, Calhoun and the constitutionalists – they were disturbed and unnerved by the feeling that the South was in a potentially terminal state of decline. Their feelings were summed up by the Virginian writer, William Alexander Caruthers, writing of his home state but thinking, obviously, of other states besides his own:

> There are the dilapidated houses, and overgrown fields, and all the evidence of a desperate struggle with circumstances far beyond . . . control . . . Poor, exhausted Virginia! she is in her dotage.[60]

Building upon this, they tried just as Simms did to find the reasons for this decay: distancing their enquiry sometimes, as in *The Sword and the Distaff*, by setting it in the past but at others concentrating on the immediate present or even the future. Nor did they stop there: diagnosis was frequently accompanied by the tentative formulation of some remedies, suggestions for the projected revival of the South and its people. And all this was done, perhaps it should be repeated, in the same way as Simms had conducted his defence and occasional criticism of his region – in terms, that is, of the patriarchal model, by first accepting and then exploring one of the South's own images of itself.

No specific cure for the decline of the seaboard South had greater appeal than that of westward emigration. The qualities of energy, enterprise, and daring that characterised the very first settlers might, it was felt, reappear in their effete descendants, if those descendants were called upon to settle and civilise another New World; culture might be revived by means of a renewed contact with nature. This was the central assumption of, for example, *Westward Ho!*, a first novel by James Kirke Paulding, a Northerner who managed, like many converts, to become more fervent than many of those born into the regional faith. *Westward Ho!* is set among what Paulding calls "the ancient gentry of old Virginia" in colonial times but it is fairly clear, from his description of that gentry, that like Simms what he has principally in mind are contemporary plights and problems; as in *The Sword and the Distaff*, the past is being used as a mirror, a warning, and an example to the present. The action begins on a decaying plantation the owner of which, "Colonel" Cuthbert Dangerfield, is presented as the sad remnant of a "high-spirited" race – one of many who seem to have forgotten that they are planters as well as gentlemen and have consequently ruined themselves. "Plenty, nay profusion, reigned all around" these people, Paulding declares,

> yet many lived, as it were, by anticipation. They were almost always beforehand with their means, and the crops of the ensuing year were for the most part mortgaged to supply the demand of the present . . . they have almost all disappeared from their ancient possessions . . .[61]

As with many others, Paulding argues, Dangerfield's own carelessness and extravagance have impoverished him. He has exhausted his land using improvident agricultural methods and dissipated his capital by maintaining an "open house" for "all comers, rich and poor"; and when called upon to pay his debts his reaction, characteristically, is to challenge the creditor to a duel. Again, his response when advised to exercise prudence is seen as typical: "Prudence!" he declares, "Prudence is a beggarly virtue."

It is for want of this "beggarly virtue", however, that Dangerfield is compelled to sell his plantation – he has no Millhouse to save him – and then, together with his wife and faithful slaves, move westward to Kentucky. Curiously, from the moment Dangerfield sets down in his new homeplace a miraculous transformation occurs: a transformation that the reader is, for the most part, asked to take on trust. "Our intention", Paulding loftily proclaims,

> is not to detail the particulars of that struggle which . . . takes place between the patient industry of man and her [nature's] wild luxuriance . . . Suffice it to say, that the traveller who, some ten years after the sound of the first axe was heard in the woods, chanced to visit it, would have been charmed with the little settlement of Dangerfieldville, its rural beauties, and its air of rustic opulence.[62]

Certainly, Paulding suggests that a change of environment helps to explain the change of personality: the character of the old colonel, we are told, "rose with the exigencies of the occasion", responded to the demands of a new paradise awaiting civilisation, and revealed a "native sagacity and vigour which wealth, indulgence and above all, idleness, had lulled to sleep". But, on the whole, Paulding concentrates attention on the effects rather than the process of recovery: the effects on the colonel, that is, and on his even more spirited daughter and even more energetic and enterprising son. As a result, *Westward Ho!* reads less like a creative inquiry into the region's ills and their possible cures than a simple fantasy, in which a sense of decay and death engenders the dream of resurrection.

In a romance that appeared a few years after *Westward Ho!*, *The Cavaliers of Virginia* by William Alexander Caruthers, the qualities of adventurousness and industry were again seen as the prerequisites of revival. In Caruthers's book, however, the actual process of transformation involved not so much a change of place as a change of opinion: a confrontation with and partial absorption of, not nature, but another and alien culture. Caruthers was very much a nationalist in his allegiances; indeed, in one of his novels he had a character argue that "Every southern should visit New York. It would allay provincial prejudices, and calm his excitement against his northern countrymen."[63] And his suggestion in *The Cavaliers of Virginia* was quite simply that "the aristocracy which prevails . . . to this day" would be improved if it were to adopt some of the characteristics traditionally associated with the Northerner. Like Paulding, Caruthers set the action of his romance in colonial Virginia: to be more exact, in the late seventeenth century, at the time of "Bacon's Rebellion". Like Paulding, too, and for that matter Simms, he clearly had contemporary issues in mind and, more particularly, the worrying state of at least some parts of the South. Unlike Paulding, however, he seems to have been somewhat less than totally impressed by the potential of "that generous, fox-hunting, wine-drinking and reckless race of men"[64] he chose as his subject: less than impressed by them, that is, when taken in isolation and considered specifically in terms of their capacity for hard work. This comes out notably in his portrait of Sir William Berkeley, the Governor of the colony, and his retinue, whom Caruthers adjudges "the first founders" of the Southern ruling class on the grounds of both genealogy and style. Berkeley and his companions demonstrate all the familiar attributes of an old, honourable but decaying, gentry. Naturally, Caruthers allows them their merits. They are, we are informed, gallant and courteous, showing "the most courtly and deferential humility" in their meetings with equals or superiors and "refined and polished" manners when dealing with those whom they consider to be socially beneath them. But there is no doubting his fairly severe judgement of their limitations, weaknesses, and faults: their "turbulent and impetuous temperament", their occasionally "cold, haughty, and sneering" behaviour, their excessive "pomp and formality", their stiff pride and indolence. Far from idealising his "Cavaliers", Caruthers shows them warts and all and, in the process, calls into question the adequacy of the aristocratic mode.

Set against Berkeley and his companions are the Puritan members of the colony, forerunners of the conventional Yankee figure. Of these, the most notable is a character called "the Recluse", a Cromwellian in hiding, whose detachment, enthusiasm, and self-control are suggested by, respectively, his "exile" from ordinary society, his "half-puritanical, half-military" costume, and the indications of "sensuality . . . tempered . . . by some other fierce and controlling passion" in his features. The Puritans are seen as everything that the Cavaliers are not: forceful, intellectual, energetic – but also contentious, ungenerous, and hypocritical. Something of their less attractive side is suggested by one Cromwellian veteran, Ananias Proudfit, who when he speaks often sounds like a crudely satirical anticipation of an Abolitionist:

> "Here am I", said . . . Ananias Proudfit, "whom the Lord hath commissioned . . . to take away the wicked from the land, and to root out the Amadekite, and the Jebusite, and the Perrizite, and the Hittite . . .[65]

Inclined, as one character puts it, "to pervert the word of God" to their "unholy and murderous purposes", they are seen to be no more capable than their enemies are of providing an appropriate model, an adequate design for living.

Of course, there is a character who provides this model; and of course, since this is a romance, it is the hero, Nathaniel Bacon. *The Cavaliers of Virginia* is not simply a romance, however; and, although Bacon bears many resemblances to the run-of-the-mill hero of romantic fiction, he bears even more to the wavering hero in the Scott tradition. He is, in fact, an example – however crudely drawn, at times – of the figure that tends to occupy centre stage in what Georg Lukács has called "the classical form of the historical novel". It is the task of such a figure, Lukács argues,

> to bring the extremes whose struggle fills the novel, whose clash expresses artistically a great crisis in society into contact with one another. Through the plot, at whose centre stands this hero, a neutral ground is sought and found upon which the extreme, opposing social forces can be brought into a human relationship with one another.[66]

Towards the beginning of the story, Caruthers actually refers to Bacon as a man occupying "a neutral position", and the point is underlined by his personal and familial associations. While he is attached to the family of Gideon Fairfax, a Cavalier and a friend of the Governor, there are rumours that he has leanings towards the other side and of a "connexion with the Recluse". At one point, the Recluse even believes Bacon to be his son. Finally, it is revealed that Bacon does indeed have a mixed heritage; since his father was, he learns, an officer in the Commonwealth army and his mother was an English lady. What is more, the mixture has turned out to be a blessing. For from his mother, Caruthers suggests, he has inherited refinement, and a sense of honour so highly developed that it even seduces him into a duel; while to his father he owes his "prompt and decisive" character and a self-discipline that enables him to surrender power, once he has seized it by force of arms, to a convention of the people. At one moment of crisis, Bacon is given a long speech in which he attacks "fratricidal conflict" and asks:

> "Who can tell how far to the mighty west the tide of civilization and emigration would have rolled their swelling waves, but for the scenes of personal rivalry and contention like the present, which have disgraced our annals?"[67]

And at the end of the novel, this spokesman for reconciliation begins to answer his own question. Jamestown, associated with the torpor and corruption of the old regime, is left behind in ruins; and Bacon goes forth to help found a new society "at Middle Plantations". As Caruthers must have realised, the name is an appropriate one, since this new society – set in the past but clearly intended to provide a signpost for the future – seems to have achieved a perfect accommodation between South and North, the generous-hearted but lazy gentleman and the energetic but uncultivated entrepreneur. In the traditional manner of the classic historical novel, in fact, conflict between extremes leads, not to a *débâcle*, but to a fresh, hopeful order of things; thesis and antithesis are followed by synthesis.

But not all Southern writers felt, like Caruthers, that the Southerner would benefit from the acquisition of certain supposedly Northern characteristics. Some even felt the opposite to be true: that the South could only be saved by an act of complete political, economic, and moral separation from the North. This was, for instance, the clear belief of the Virginian Nathaniel Beverley Tucker: who gave it imaginative expression in *The Partisan Leader*, a novel published shortly after *The Cavaliers of Virginia*. Of the Union, Tucker once said:

> I will never give rest to my eyes nor slumber to my eyelids until it is shattered into fragments . . . there is now no escape from the many-headed despotism of numbers, but by a strong and bold stand on the banks of the Potomac.[68]

And, in true Utopian fashion, Tucker begins his story in the future with most of the South already separated from the rest of the United States – having been driven to this, we are informed, by "the fierce attacks of rapacity and fanaticism", the "usurpations" and "oppressions of the northern faction". As a result of this separation (accomplished without conflict, Tucker explains) the South has become "once more the most flourishing and prosperous country on earth". For the leaders of the region, "men . . . of cool heads, long views, and stout hearts", have established free trade with Great Britain, to the advantage of both parties.

Meanwhile, the South's "envious rival in the North" has seen its "artificial prosperity engendered by the . . . plunder of the southern states"[69] vanish, evidently for ever. The only Southern state that has not so far seceded is Virginia; and it is with that state's gradual movement towards secession, and the military conflict which follows, that the action of the novel is mainly concerned.

Using a device that was to become a familiar one in novels of the Civil War, that of a family divided by civil conflict, Tucker paints a large historical canvas – or perhaps it would be more accurate to say, a broad-brushed portrait of two opposing legends. On the one side, there are the forces of the North led by Van Buren who, we are told, has exercised more or less absolute power ever since the retirement of Jackson. Van Buren himself, referred to sardonically as "King Martin the First", is presented as an effete, corrupt, and above all effeminate monarch. "He was daintily dressed", Tucker says,

> his whole costume being adapted to his diminutive and dapper person . . . the place of hair was supplied by powder . . . he seemed, too, not wholly unconscious of something worthy of admiration in a foot, the beauty of which was displayed to best advantage by the tight fit and high finish of a delicate slipper . . .[70]

"When a people become corrupt", one character observes, "they must learn to be fastidious, and invent safeguards to prevent vice, and blinds to conceal it when it is indulged." This is the case, we are led to believe, with Van Buren's "kingdom", where the effeminacy and prissiness of the "palace" (as the White House is now called), and even more important its "prurience" and self-deceiving moral nicety, have been diffused "through all grades and ranks". The result is a society steeped in hypocrisy and cant: one in which, apparently, people say they are going to "retire" rather than use the word "bed", and in which children are used like animals in factories while being kept strictly segregated according to sex. And, for Tucker, the epitome of such a society is not so much the businessman as sexually ambiguous figures like Van Buren – or, more simply, what is referred to, at more than one point in the novel, as "our Yankee school-mistresses".

In drawing this portrait of the Northern states, Tucker seems to be playing on a contrast made by many Southern politicians: between what they saw as the essentially "feminine" notions of the North and the more "masculine" principles of their region. It was, of course, a contrast full of irony in a culture that claimed to revere women; the reverence, it turned out, had severely restricted limits. Just how severe they were was nicely illustrated by one politician from Mississippi who – in the course of a speech denouncing Abolitionism and notions of equality between white and black – asked rhetorically,

> if it be true that all men in a republican Government must help to wield its
> power, and be equal in rights, I beg leave to ask . . . – and why not all the
> *women*?[71]

The assumption, of course, was that this gentle enquiry was so manifestly
absurd that it left the entire Abolitionist argument in ruins. Tucker is not
quite as direct and crude about things as this, but a similar bias is at work
in *The Partisan Leader*: prompting him to present the North as a culture
dominated by "female" notions and, sometimes more literally, by the
sort of women who (we are told) "write books; patronize abolitionist
societies; or keep a boarding-school".[72] Sentimental, hypocritical,
utilitarian, and self-righteous: Van Buren's kingdom, as Tucker describes
it, is a misogynist's nightmare – a matriarchal world perceived with, and
distorted by, a mixture of humour, hatred, and fear.

It goes without saying, perhaps, that the Southerners in Tucker's
romance, and more specifically the Virginians, are defined in terms of
opposition to all this. "If Virginians can be fooled into identifying
themselves with the Yankees", one character declares,

> " – a fixed tax-paying minority with a fixed tax-receiving majority – . . . they
> will continue to hold a distinguished place among [those] . . . that have been
> gulled into their own ruin ever since the world began."[73]

And the political and economic irreconcilability is sustained, Tucker
insists, on the level of character: a point nowhere more forcibly shown
than in the portrait of the men who eventually feel compelled to fight for
Virginia against the Union. A "noble" force in which, "every man is an
officer", the army of Virginia consists principally of those driven by
"outrage to the laws, outrage to the freedom of election, outrage to those
respected and beloved" to defend their principles, their "independence",
and their land against the oppressor. It is perhaps worth emphasising that,
like many spokesmen for the region before and after him, Tucker
chooses to associate the struggle for Southern "liberty" and "rights"
with the American Revolution. At the end of the book, the battle for
Virginia is not yet over. But, Tucker insists, leaving us in little doubt as to
the eventual outcome,

> old Virginia would yet show itself in the descendants of the men who had
> defied Cromwell, in the plenitude of his power, and cast off the yoke of George
> the Third, without waiting for the co-operation of the other colonies . . .[74]

It is difficult to think of two proposals for regional recovery more
drastically opposed than those of Caruthers and Tucker. Opposed as they
were, however, they shared with each other and with the imaginative
arguments of Paulding and Simms one crucial and seminal impulse: a
willingness to accept the patriarchal model as an adequate explanation of
the South – a readiness to believe that there was such a thing as "the

Southerner", recognisably different from other Americans, and that this
difference could be defined almost entirely in terms of the South's
feudalism, its commitment to an antique, gentlemanly way of life. The
Southerner *was* an aristocrat: that was the initial assumption. Some
writers, like Tucker, might then go on to see him as the sum total of
aristocratic virtues, while others, like Simms, Paulding, and Caruthers
might choose to see in him a few of the aristocratic weaknesses and vices
as well. But there could be no doubts entertained about the assumption
itself: Southerners, it was felt, could be accommodated quite comfortably within it – in their deficiencies as well as their merits, their strengths
and their weaknesses, their former prosperity and foreseeable decline. In
this, of course, they were not alone. Even Abolitionist writers like
Harrier Beecher Stowe tended to start by accepting the feudal
explanation of things and then tried to adjust their criticisms to fit it; even
foreign novelists like G. P. R. James were willing to take the South on its
own terms, regardless of whether they had been there or not.[75] Nor was
this entirely unfortunate. After all, it enabled people like Simms, and to a
lesser extent Paulding and Caruthers, to offer some searching criticisms
of the region without creating too much disturbance – at a time, that is,
when disturbance was only too easy to create. And it allowed a writer
like Tucker to offer a version of the enemy that was not absolutely
wrong, not totally unconvincing – that possessed, in fact, some of the
persuasive power of legend. It was not entirely unfortunate, then: but it
did mean that all these writers were saddled from the first with a partial
and debilitating idiom, a mythic vocabulary that did not meet all of their
needs. For, in effect, people like Simms, Paulding, Caruthers, and
Tucker tried to perceive and know the Old South using tools that
necessarily distorted perception and that could block knowledge just as
much as facilitate it: tools, it should be added, that the Old South, as
courteous, obliging, and insidious as ever, had been only too ready to
provide.

CHAINING THE ROUGH BEAST: THE SOUTHWESTERN HUMORISTS

At the same time as writers like Simms were interpreting Southern
society in terms of the plantation patriarch, another group were using a
quite different model to register what they saw as the distinctive qualities
of their region. This was the group later to be known as the
"Southwestern humorists": a motley assortment of lawyers, doctors,
newspapermen and others who were drawn by their professions into the
rawer states of the interior – such as Missouri, Mississippi, Alabama, and
Arkansas – and who, in travelling there, came upon a world that up until

then was largely unknown to American letters. It was a world largely
unknown to them as well: characterised, as they saw it, by "vulgarity –
ignorance – . . . unmitigated rowdyism . . . bullying insolence" and
"swindling . . . raised to the dignity of the fine arts".[76] Violent, rowdy,
and anarchic, in many respects a frontier society, it clearly frightened
these gentlemen of the professions, who were used to a more stable
culture with habits of deference and respect. So, in an eminently
understandable way, they attempted to distance their surroundings, to
place them in a framework that would make them manageable and
known. They tried, in effect, to "encode" them. One technique they
used for doing this was, of course, humour. As critics have observed time
and again, the classic humorist tale consists of a narrator, identifiable as
superior in class and education, setting up the scene and bringing on the
rustic characters, putting them through their violent routines complete
with comic dialect, and then returning us at the end of the story to his
own stable, secure world and standard English.[77] By this means,
viciousness is transformed into play, social anarchy into comic spectacle,
and fear and anxiety into mild amusement. But another technique, less
commented upon, was just as important, just as vital to the humorists'
purpose of translating the unknown into the known; and this was their
use of the populist model. What they did was quite simple: consciously
or otherwise, they tried to identify the rough, rude world they saw
around them with a familiar rural type, associated with the region since
its first settlement – the plain farmer, with his straightforward approach
to things, his raw integrity and earthy language, and above all his
muscular self-reliance. In this way, violence could be interpreted as an
excess of high spirits and honest energy; apparent moral anarchy was
metamorphosed into a reassertion of conventional principles; and the
disruption of established social patterns could be regarded as a crucial step
on the road to the recovery of a traditional, populist social structure.
Strangeness was minimised, horror was turned into pleasure or, at least,
into a reassuring sense that not all was lost; because, by using the populist
vocabulary, these writers felt that they understood what they saw.

One writer who illustrates this process of accommodation fairly
clearly is Joseph Glover Baldwin. Baldwin was a Virginian, and some of
his sketches are directed primarily to Virginian readers. This includes a
sketch in his book *The Flush Times of Alabama and Mississippi*, that is
mainly concerned with the misfortunes of Virginia planters in the South-
West, particularly during the financial panic of 1837. Entitled "How the
Times Served the Virginians", it begins with a warm and sympathetic
portrait of the old Virginian in the new country, part of which was
quoted earlier on in this chapter; and it then goes on to describe how this
figure failed to adjust to his altered circumstances – a failure which,

Baldwin argues, was the direct product of his fineness and generosity of temper. All the habits of the Virginian's life, we are told,

> his taste, his associations, his education – everything – the trustingness of his disposition – his want of business qualifications, his sanguine temperament – all that was Virginian in him, made him the prey, if not of imposture, at least of unfortunate speculations . . . He knew nothing of the elaborate machinery of ingenious chicane . . .[78]

Still, Baldwin concludes, even in failure the "jolly Virginian" behaved "like a gentleman"; and as an illustration of his point he describes at length the plight of "Old Major Willis Wormley" who "belonged to the old school of Virginians" and who was reduced, after moving to Alabama, to selling his plantation and keeping a tavern. The Major is described with affection, his decline is seen as pathetic and no fault of his own; and, all in all, Baldwin's portrait of what he terms "this fast country" is disturbing. There is a note of anxiety sounded here, in fact: a sense that a particular quality of life associated with the Old Dominion is under threat, with the accompanying feeling that Virginians – and that included Baldwin and many of his readers as well as "Old Major Willis Wormley" – ought to look to their defences.

The defence to which Baldwin looked was essentially a verbal and psychological one. He managed to convince himself that what he perceived was a vigorous yeoman republic, an example of democratic ideas in action. This comes out again and again in *Flush Times* – in, for instance, this passage taken from a fairly long descriptive piece towards the end of the book:

> A man of great parts may miss his way to greatness by frittering away his powers upon non-essentials – upon the style and finish of a thing rather than upon its strength and utility . . . above all things, success more depends upon self-confidence than anything else . . . And where can a man get this self-reliance so well as in a new country, where he is thrown upon his own resources; where his only friends are his talents; where he sees energy at once leap into prominence . . .; where there is no "prestige" of rank, or ancestry, or wealth, or past reputation . . . Unquestionably, there is something in the atmosphere of a new people that refreshes, vivifies, and vitalizes thought, and gives freedom, range, and energy to action . . .[79]

This is a far cry from the elegy for the world of old Virginia: a world that is now dismissed as one dominated by "influence, prejudice, custom, opinion" – by what Baldwin refers to in this passage, rather contemptuously, as the " 'prestige' of rank . . . or past reputation". The patriarchal model exists here only in negative, as it were, as something to which its populist counterpart can be favourably compared; what the writer is now asking us to admire, in fact, is not the "style and finish" of a rural nobility but the "strength and utility", the energy and self-reliance, of a

simple, rural republic. In doing this, he is not being entirely disingenuous, any more than he was when he described Virginians (including, by
implication, himself) in terms of the gentlemanliness "of the old school";
clearly, he has been impressed by what he has seen and the people he has
met, and, to some extent, he wants his readers to be impressed too. But it
is worth emphasising the point that what Baldwin says here directly
contradicts what he says elsewhere: there is no mention now, for
example, of "ingenious chicane" and "imposture", everything is said to
depend on freedom, application, and energy. And it is worth adding that
by this act of contradiction – or, if one wants to be more charitable,
exclusion – he is turning a discomfitingly three-dimensional world into a
comfortingly familiar but disappointingly flat heroic portrait.

Of course, heroism was not always to the fore in the humorists'
portraits of the old South-West. Unlike the Virginia pamphleteers and
the Jeffersonians, they could hardly ignore the cruder aspects of rural life,
using comedy, as I have said, to contain and control those aspects – to
make them palatable, not least to themselves. This is particularly
noticeable in the stories of two humorists: Johnson Jones Hooper and
George Washington Harris. In Hooper's tales, one character in particular, called Captain Simon Suggs, becomes an imaginative projection of
what his creator clearly felt was the restlessness, the unnerving mobility
and unintelligibility of the "new world" and its "new people". Suggs's
motto defines his character and vocation: "It is good to be shifty in a new
country". He is a confidence-man, a rural trickster of the kind descended
ultimately from ancient legend: a person who uses lies, disguises, and all
possible forms of jugglery and deception to dupe, among others, his own
father, the congregation at a camp meeting, Indians, land-speculators,
bankers, and politicians. "Human natur' and the human family is my
books", declares Suggs proudly in one of Hooper's stories, "and I've
never seed any but what I could hold my own with."[80] Quite apart from
the comfort provided by the comedy – by turning "ingenious chicane"
and "imposture" into an amusing game – there is the further
containment offered by this equating of the amorphousness of a frontier
culture with the shiftlessness and playfulness of a familiar literary type.
Uneasiness about imposture is consequently dissolved into a pleasurable
interest in those tricks of the trade, the different but uniformly elaborate
forms that that imposture assumes. And, at the same time, nervousness
about the threats posed by an alien land and a new kind of people is given
boundaries of a sort by identifying those threats with a very particularised
form of low comic cunning. The relevant comparison here, really, is
with Melville's *The Confidence Man*. For whereas the disconcerting fact
about Melville's trickster is that nobody, not even he, knows who he is, it
is only too clear who Suggs is and what, in any specific instance, he wants.

To equate the strangeness and mystery of an unknown space with a known quantity, a recognisable figure, is precisely what Melville does not want to do and Hooper does: which is to say that Melville is aware of the problem of encoding, of ascribing names to things, and Hooper is not.

With Harris, the comedy is different, partly because the gap between him and his subject is much narrower than it is in either Baldwin's tales or Hooper's, and partly because his principal character, Sut Lovingood, is quite unlike Simon Suggs. Both points are illustrated by this brief passage from one of *Sut Lovingood's Yarns*, where Sut is describing his attitude towards "book-larnin'":

> ". . . what I think ove plannin an' studdyin: hit am ginerly no count. All pends, et las' on what yu dus an' how yu kerries yursef *at the moment of acushum* . . . Long studyin' am like preparin a supply ove warter intu a wum hole barril, tu put out fire: when the fire dus cum, durn'd ef yu don't hev tu hustil roun pow'ful fas', an' git more warter, fur thar's nun in the barril."[81]

It is not difficult to see here an anticipation of Huck Finn's lack of interest in Biblical stories – "I don't take no stock in dead people" – or, indeed, of Whitman's dismissive reference to "the spectres in books". For all Sut's protestation, "I haint got nara a soul, nuffin but a whisky proof gizzard, sorter like the wurst half ove a ole par ove saddil bags", he does seem to contain within himself the shadowy presence of a more heroic figure, the independent countryman who thinks and speaks on his own account. His crudity of appearance, in fact, and his earthiness of speech are seen to be aspects of a basic, rough simplicity: a quality that leads him to dislike hypocrisy above everything else – and to detest, in particular, the self-righteousness of evangelists, the pompous rhetoric of politicians, the cunning and duplicity of Yankee pedlars.

Admittedly, this Adamic element in Sut's character is as much a matter of potential as anything else; since Harris does not underestimate the squalid conditions in which his main character lives, and the degree to which those conditions have warped him. He even bears the marks of his environment on his body, which is stunted, distorted, and grotesque: Sut, we are told when he first appears, is "a queer-looking, long legged, short bodied, small headed, white haired, hog eyed, funny sort of a genius". But, clearly, this is intended as a comment on the world in which he is placed as well as on him: a world that has evidently deprived him of his full potential. Nor does it prevent him from speaking with authority (an authority founded partly on the fact that his narrator often uses him as a mouthpiece) and responding to experience in an authentic and open way. This, for instance, is his description of a storm:

> "I'se hearn in the mountains a fust rate fourth proof smash ove thunder cum onexpected, an' shake the yeath, bringin along a string ove litenin es long es a

quarter track, an' es bright as a weldin heat, a-racin down a big pine tree, tarin hit into broom-slits, an' toof pickers, an' a raisin a cloud ove dus', an' bar, an' a army ove lim's wif a smell sorter like the devil were about, an' the long darnin needil leaves fallin roon wif a tif-tif-quiet sorter soun, an' then a quiverin on the yeath as littil snake die, an I felt quar in my in'ards, sorter ha'f cumfurt, wif a little glad an' rite smart ove sorry mix'd wif hit."[82]

The power of this description depends on its immediacy and apparent sincerity: Sut seems to be searching for the appropriate, homely image in an often quite tentative manner, and moving the description slowly forward as he tries to recall the minute particulars of each moment. The rambling sentence – a curious anticipation of Twain and Hemingway – adds a further touch of intimacy; it is as if the experience is too involving, and too striking in its every detail to permit careful arrangement or an elaborate syntactical pattern. Of course, all this is a matter of premeditation: the use of the vernacular here is just as much of a literary strategy as are the more obviously rhetorical arrangements of some of the other humorists. But it is a definite symptom of Harris's desire to endow his protagonist with something of the clear-sightedness and clarity of the populist hero: Sut can, apparently, see things stripped of their "style and finish" (to use Baldwin's phrase again) and then render them with simplicity and truth.

A more straightforward, but nevertheless interesting, version of the populist hero is to be found in the stories of another humorist, William Tappan Thompson. In the Preface to one of his books, *The Chronicles of Pineville*, Thompson declared that his major purpose as a writer was to capture the "manners and language" of "the American backwoodsman". Precisely what his attitude was towards these backwoodsmen, and more especially the Georgia variety, was suggested by what he then went on to say about them, by way of a preparatory character-sketch: "as a class", he insisted, "they are brave, generous, honest, and industrious, and withal, possessed of a sturdy patriotism".[83] As Thompson saw them, in fact, they were an early nineteenth-century regional variation on the traditional figure of the yeoman. Some of this comes out in Thompson's descriptions of the society of Pineville, a fictional community of small farmers situated around the country town that gives one of his books its name. It is, Thompson informs us, a friendly, leisurely community that preserves, as far as possible, its simple traditions of work and play and depends, for its amusements, upon the interchange of hospitality, "Crismus Dinners", the rituals accompanying birth, marriage, and death, quarter-races, and the occasional election or muster day. But it comes out with particular force in Thompson's portrait of his most famous character, Major Joseph Jones, the hero of two of his books. A substantial farmer, who owns one or two slaves, Major Jones is presented as kindly and naïve: unlike Sut Lovingood and Simon Suggs, he tends to be the butt of jokes and tricks rather than their perpetrator. He is not, however, a fool; indeed, he tends to be a butt precisely because of his virtues – his simplicity, his integrity, his transparency of character, and not least his touching belief that people say what they mean. Fitting his own magnanimous description of a political adversary, he is in effect depicted as "coarse, strong, and honest, without tinsel or false gloss":[84] a man who, being a plain farmer and republican – and therefore the backbone of the nation, according to Jefferson – feels that he is entitled to meet the President of the day, simply by knocking at the door of the White House and introducing himself.

Just how much Thompson admires Jones is evident from the principal comic device that he employs in these stories. The Major may sometimes be the butt of the joke or trick; more often than not, however, the humour derives from his own observations, as he describes some "fool quality notion" of someone he meets in Pineville or, it may be, in the course of his travels. The Major Jones stories are written in the epistolary form, without the mediation of a genteel narrator, which necessarily closes down the gap between author and character; and this is further narrowed by the fact that Thompson – being, like most of the humorists, a Whig – uses his protagonists as a medium for Whig propaganda and satire. Jones's yeoman qualities make him useful in this respect: honest, simple in his tastes, completely without guile or cunning, he functions as both an innocent eye and a foil, especially in *Major Jones's Travels* where he is allowed to travel northwards and observe city life. "There was among 'em some of the most outlandish specimens of human nater I ever met with", says Jones of the inhabitants of one large city; and his comments on some servant girls he sees cleaning the steps of a big house in the same town suggest the direction and source of nearly all his, and his creator's, criticisms. "I couldn't help feelin' sorry", Jones declares,

> to see such butiful, rosy-cheeked white galls down in the dirt and slop in the streets, doin' work that is only fit for niggers . . . whatever they is, they is my own colour, and a few dollars would make 'em as good as ther mistresses, in the estimation of them that turns up ther noses at 'em now.[85]

We are back here with the idea of a "white democracy" discussed earlier in this chapter, and with the populist belief that the freedom, equality, and even the humanity of every white person finds its guarantee and proof in the enslavement of black people, and their exclusion from the human community. Thompson's satire is in fact directed not just at contemporary fashions in behaviour and dress, such as long whiskers and large bustles, but at the oppressions and hypocrisy of an emergent urban culture – a culture that (to take the example offered in this passage) claims to have abolished slavery but retains it in all but name. And the source, in turn, of that satire is to be found, not in the gentlemanly background of the Southern section of the Whig party, but in the populist notion of things. There is an intriguing parallel with the 1840 Presidential election here; when the Whigs swept to victory on the slogan, "Log Cabin and Hard Cider" – applied somewhat disingenuously to their candidate, a courtly, dignified man who had had very little experience of either.[86] Playing his own variation on this strategy, Thompson uses the image of the yeoman, not only, like other humorists, as a means of making the backwoods acceptable, but as a weapon for belabouring the opposition. Major Jones may not live in a log cabin, but he issues from the same compelling myth of rural self-sufficiency and simplicity. And in literary terms he performs a similar function to the Whig party's slogan and its accompaniments: which is to say, he enables his creator both to conceal his own doubts and uncertainties and to launch a vigorous attack on one thing he is quite certain about – the ideas and people he dislikes.

A comparable strategy was often employed by Augustus Baldwin Longstreet, whose *Georgia Scenes* stands at the beginning of Southwestern humour. All of Longstreet's stories use the frame mentioned earlier, that enables the genteel narrator to maintain a discreet distance between himself and the routines and incidents he describes. Naturally, the reader, too, is kept at a distance by this device. Any violence that may be described – and these stories do contain a good deal of it – is consequently mitigated, its edges softened; and any anxiety or nervousness that violence may arouse is, at the same time, suppressed, soothed away by the comforting tones of the storyteller. Typical, in this respect, is the closing paragraph of one tale, "The Fight", which, as its title suggests, describes "a hard-fought battle" between two simple countrymen, and does so in fairly gruesome detail. Longstreet's final remarks take us away from what he calls "a hideous spectacle" and are clearly meant to provide us with reassurance, the feeling that his and our bland lives need not be unduly disturbed by what we have just witnessed:

> Thanks to the Christian religion, to schools, colleges, and benevolent associations, such scenes of barbarism and cruelty as that which I have been just describing are now of rare occurrence, though they may still be occasionally met with in some of the new counties. Wherever they prevail, they are a disgrace to that community. The peace-officers who countenance them deserve a place in the Penitentiary.[87]

This is, of course, an ancient device, a sort of literary equivalent of slumming. Having visited the poor folk, and been titillated by the raw nature of their lives, we can now scurry back to our own rather more salubrious district, with any guilt or horror that we may feel safely contained by two things – our reassertion of the appropriate moral attitude (a mixture of disapproval and condescension) and the consoling thought that the conditions we have witnessed are on the mend anyway.

But Longstreet does not always use the narrative frame in this way. On occasion, taking a quite different tack, the gentlemanly visitor to the backwoods positively admires the world he is visiting, and explains in detail the reasons for his admiration. This is the case with, for instance, "The Dance", an account by a gentleman from the city of a trip he once made to a frontier county, to see a local farmer. The dance that gives the story its title is held at the farmer's house, and Longstreet's main purpose is fairly evident from the beginning: to contrast the pretensions and hypocrisies of the gentleman's own urban background – pretensions and hypocrisies which the gentleman himself is well aware of, and despises – with the plainness, simplicity, and honesty of his hosts. So we are informed that the farmer's daughters knew nothing of "the refinements of the present day in female dress"; clothed "in neat but plain habiliments of their own manufacture", they

> used no artificial means of spreading their frock tails . . . They had no boards laced to their breasts, nor any corsets laced to their sides; consequently, they looked, for all the world, like human beings . . . Their movements were as free and active as nature would permit them to be.[88]

The terms used here, in praise and blame, alert the reader to the fact that this is more than just a question of fashion. It is a matter of fundamental principles and assumptions, which find their expression in a particular way of dressing, speaking, and acting, a certain style of life. The life of the farmer, the narrator suggests, is "plain", "human", and "natural" – just as, for example, John Taylor of Caroline claimed it was – while the urban world is a network of artifice, divorced from everything that is real. And the point, having been made, is then underlined by the narrator's description of each stage of the dance. Thus, we are told that on arrival the guests greeted each other not, as in town, with a kiss, "the custom of the French and . . . Judas", but with "something much less equivocal: a hearty shake of the hand and smiling countenances". There were, too,

> no formal introductions to be given, no drawing for places and partners, no parade of managers, no ceremonies. It was perfectly understood that all were invited *to dance*, and that none were invited who were unworthy to be danced with . . .[89]

In this community of equals, the type of dance favoured by these "industrious, honest, and sensible farmers" is also deemed worthy of comment: the "good old republican six reel". "I had been thrown among 'fashionables' so long", the narrator admits, "that I had almost forgotten my native dance." Nevertheless, he tells us, he managed to relearn its steps – to recover, as it were, the patterns and lively rituals of simple country living – and to work up an appetite for the "plain fare", offered on "rough planks" but with "perfect frankness" and "good humour", that concluded the evening.

Other stories in *Georgia Scenes* make this comparison between country life and the fashionable ways of the town even more explicit. In "The 'Charming Creature' as a Wife", for instance, we are told how the son of "a plain, practical, sensible farmer" was ruined by marriage to the only child of a wealthy cotton merchant: a creature infected by what the narrator terms "town dignity" – which is to say, an inordinate sense of her own worth, a preference for the glittering social world in which she was brought up, and an accompanying failure to appreciate the "order, neatness, and cleanness" of her husband's home and community. It is worth noting, perhaps, that one of the faults of this "charming creature", according to her husband, is her tendency to be "more respectful to negroes than whites" – that is, to whites of the backwoods – behaviour that she defends by declaring, "Negroes treat me with more respect than some whites."[90] This is a neat and incisive dramatisation of the difference between the feudal and populist attitudes towards slaves. The woman treats them with politeness and respect, because instinctively she sees them as part of the human community, linked to her, in however humble a way, within the patriarchal system; while the man, with equally sure instinct, is horrified by the demotion this implies for at least some whites – including the plainer, poorer folk whom he numbers among his blood kin and friends. There is no doubt where the narrator's sympathies lie in all this: on every possible occasion, he criticises or makes fun of the pretensions of the "charming creature", her idleness and "irregular hours", and her longing to return to the fashionable world of town. Eventually, she gets her way; the couple leave the simple, rural world she detests, and in their new urban surroundings the husband is described, somewhat melodramatically, sinking into debt, drunkenness, illness, and an early grave. The story then ends with the narrator pointing the moral of his tale: which, not surprisingly, has to do not only with the pretensions but with the dangers of all those known as "charming creatures".

There is no avoiding the fact, really, that the message of stories like "The 'Charming Creature'" and "The Dance" flatly contradicts the message of such tales as "The Fight". In "The Fight" all that the nineteenth century associated with the word "culture" – taste of a certain genteel kind, "schools, colleges, and benevolent associations" – is held up for our approval; it provides the summit, the convenient vantage-point from which we look down and shake our heads over the "barbarism and cruelty" of natural man.[91] In "The Dance" and "The 'Charming Creature'", however, that very same culture is mocked and ridiculed – words like "refinement" and "fashionable" become terms of abuse – and the idea of the natural becomes our touchstone. The life of the plain farmer as Longstreet presents it in these stories is, of course, no more natural than any other way of life is; it, too, is founded on certain assumptions and codes – linked, in this case, inexorably to the populist vision of things. But this is merely by the way. Whatever terms one wishes to use to describe the conflict – whether one chooses to talk about the "cultural" versus the "natural", or whether one employs slightly less misleading terms like the "patriarchal" versus the "populist" or the "gentleman" versus the "yeoman" – the point is that Longstreet saw that conflict from two diametrically opposed points of view. The reasons for this, when one looks at it, are quite simple. Different as these two versions of backwoods life are, when one reads them on the page, they were shaped by the same impulses, the same leading motives. In both cases, Longstreet manipulated his material so as to put it at some remove from himself and dissolve any threat it might offer. The anarchy of the backwoods is contained in both kinds of tales: in the one, because Longstreet acknowledges it as anarchy but then places it in a narrative cage, to be viewed only sometimes and from a distance, and in the other, because both it and the backwoods are changed utterly by the idiom Longstreet adopts, caught safely within the timeless framework of pastoralism. As amusing barbarian or as yeoman, the new man ceases to be a source of anxiety, a rough beast slouching towards the frontier to be born; he becomes the shape of things past rather than the shape of things to come, and that is exactly how Longstreet wanted to see him.

The technique of contrast exploited by Thompson and Longstreet among others was employed by many of the other, less well-known humorists as well. There are, for instance, several stories that use some member of "the honest yeomanry" (as one of these storytellers terms them) as an innocent eye or satirical commentator on the deficiencies of town life; and many more in which a similar figure is cheated of what is rightfully his by a preacher, townsman, Yankee pedlar or some other character more "ingenious in chicane" than himself. In either case, the traditional virtues of the populist hero act as a foil to what one humorist calls:

> The dishonesty of "them Gimblit fellers" [cotton-brokers], the extortions of hotel-keepers, the singular failure of warehouse steelyards to make cotton-bales weigh as much in Augusta as at home.[92]

The plain farmer's strengths could in this way also be seen as his weaknesses: which was, of course, another means of patronising him while seeming to admire him. He could be praised for qualities that, even while he was praised for them, rendered him an easy prey to those more cunning and street-wise than himself. He could be celebrated or criticised, the storyteller could laugh with or at him: whatever, he was effectively placed – even seen, sometimes, as a charming anachronism or a fond memory of yesteryear – chuckled over and carefully contained. The use by other, minor humorists of the trickster motif, along the lines developed by Hooper, had a similar effect of turning peril into sport. It is, perhaps, no accident that a major outlet for the humorists' work was a sporting magazine, called *The Spirit of the Times*. For one of the main purposes of these stories – instinctive, rather than intentional – seems to have been to render the backwoods comprehensible, to encode it, by turning it into a giant playing-field, with rules that were rough and ready, it might be, but still rules.

Not that the editor of *The Spirit of the Times* ever saw it in this way. On the contrary, when he came to edit the first of two anthologies of stories from his magazine, what he emphasised was their historical accuracy. The tales he had collected in *The Big Bear of Arkansas* were, he insisted, all concerned with "a hardy indomitable race whose sons and daughters are now enjoying a green old age". And in this claim to authenticity he was not alone. In his Preface to *Georgia Scenes*, for example, Longstreet insisted that his tales consisted "of nothing more than fanciful *combinations* of *real* incidents and characters". "Some of the scenes", he declared, "are as literally true as the frailties of memory would allow them to be." Frequently irritated by the suggestion that he was a "mere" humorist, he even went so far, in later life, as to suggest that he was a kind of historian. "The book", Longstreet said (talking, of course, of *Georgia Scenes*),

> has been invariably received as a mere collection of fancy sketches, with no higher object than the entertainment of the reader, whereas the aim of the author was to supply a chasm in history which has always been overlooked . . .[93]

Similarly, Baldwin considered himself a reporter of "that halcyon period . . . that golden era, when skin-plasters were the sole currency", rather than an imaginative writer; and Thompson and Hooper believed that they were rendering a living world, doubtless with a little comic exaggeration for entertainment's sake – that they were, to quote Thompson in the Preface to *The Chronicles of Pineville*, capturing "manners living as they rise". In this, they were not entirely wrong, of course: they had visited the places they described, encountered a culture and people quite unlike the one with which they were familiar, and they tried to capture something of the strangeness of that culture and (as they saw it) the oddity of these people in their sketches and stories. Trying to capture all this, however, they went much further, altered things much more radically, than the simple exigencies of humour required. For, in the first place, they used various devices such as a genteel narrative voice or the literary conventions of the trickster to impose a rigid frame on their material, to exercise some sort of dominion over the squirming facts and often unpleasant details of backwoods life. And, in the second, they permitted that life to be mediated for them by the populist model: the frequent roughness and crudeness of the back country could thereby be seen in soft focus – perceived as a hearty love of independence and a noble propensity for truth-telling – while, at the same time, the writer's own fears for the future could be metamorphosed into nostalgia, or at least a smiling acknowledgement that old folkways still persisted. It is no wonder, really, that Longstreet and the other humorists insisted on their accuracy, their reliability as historians or reporters; since it was precisely their aim to persuade their readers and themselves that – with all due allowances made for slips of memory and the play of fancy – things as they saw them equalled things as they actually were. As they instinctively recognised, if this were not the case, if the backwoodsman were other than they described him, then clearly their language had failed them, and they themselves, their language, and the culture that had supplied that language were all under threat; the rough beast was still there, in fact, behind the smiling face of the yeoman or the amusing mask of the trickster, still biding his time – still waiting for the right moment to be born.

3

The New South, the lost cause, and the recovered dream

A few months after Lee surrendered to Grant at Appomatox, a Georgia girl wrote this in her diary:

> I hate the Yankees more and more, every time I look at one of their horrid newspapers and read the lies they tell about us, while we have our mouths closed and padlocked. The world will not hear our story, and we must figure just as our enemies choose to paint us.[1]

The feelings expressed here were, as it happened, widely shared. Southerners had experienced a comprehensive defeat after a genuinely heroic struggle (see Plate 5), and they were suffering further deprivation even though the war was over. That, in itself, was bad enough. But to this was added their sense that "the Yankees" were proclaiming their military defeat as a moral one, and offering their now unquestioned political and economic ascendancy as proof positive of the justice of their original case. How correct Southerners were in believing this is not at issue here – although, if Northerners did celebrate their victory in moral terms, they would not have been the first victors in history to have done so; it is an eminently understandable reaction and, given at least some of the issues over which the war was fought, not a wholly unjustified one at that. What does concern us is that Southerners, like this Georgia girl, did believe it and were, as a result, troubled by feelings of bitterness and resentment – a nagging sense that, having been defeated, they were now being humiliated as well. Their response to this, given the evidence of previous behaviour, was perhaps predictable: defensiveness turned gradually into defiance and a proud determination to tell *their* story, *their* side of things. One form this reaction took will be discussed a little later: which was the tendency to look back with regret at the good old days before the war and celebrate the civilisation which, it was felt, the barbarian hordes from the North had effectively swept away. Another form, however, was just as important and has received relatively little attention;[2] and that was the impulse felt by many Southerners to retell the story of the war itself – to define the region in terms of the one, crucial moment in its history when it tried to defend its culture and its identity by simple force of arms.

"All over this land of ours," declared one magniloquent Southerner,

> there are men . . . sleeping upon merits that are as holy as death, and who, amid all reproach, appeal to the future, and to the tribunal of History, when she shall render her final verdict in reference to the struggle closed, for the vindication of the people . . .[3]

And his ringing words were echoed and expanded upon by the ex-Confederate general, Wade Hampton. "Can any higher incentive to exertion be held out", Hampton asked,

> than those which call upon us to rescue our country from the unjust obloquy that has been heaped upon her; to justify our actions in the eyes of our contemporaries; to secure a verdict of acquittal from posterity, and to do honour to the memory of our dead? . . . As it was the duty of every man to devote himself to the service of his country in that great struggle which has ended so disastrously . . . so, now, when that country is prostrate in the dust, . . . every patriotic impulse should urge her surviving children to vindicate the great principles for which she fought . . . to show the unexampled triumphs of her heroic armies, and to place on eternal record an appeal from the distorted and vindictive judgement of her enemies, to the impartial tribunal of history . . .[4]

Through a retelling of Southern history, it was felt, and more specifically through a retelling of the war, respect could be paid to the past, vindication could be achieved for the present, and an example established for future generations. "The greatest boon that can be bestowed upon a people", insisted one Southern historian, "is the adequate setting forth of the history of their illustrious men";[5] and bearing this in mind, many Southerners, including among them a large number of ex-members of the Confederate army, set about the task of setting that history forth. The Southern Historical Society was organised in 1869 by a group of prominent Confederate veterans; periodicals such as *The Southern Review* were founded for the purpose of defending and promulgating the regional cause; and books, essays, and speeches poured forth dealing with the conflict as experienced by both observers and active combatants. The avowed purpose was to set the records straight, to counter Yankee duplicity and lies; what emerged from all this activity, however, was not so much a recovery as a reinvention of the past and a reassertion of established regional codes. Translated into the Confederate officer and the humble trooper, both the patriarchal and the populist models reappeared, dressed for conflict now but trailing the familiar associations.

Just how much the Southern portrait of the war involved a recreation of myth, an encoding of times past, is suggested by the accounts offered of the Confederate generals. Apart from Lee, each general was usually taken to illustrate some particular aspect of the patriarchal ideal, some facet of the aristocratic model; so that, together, the Confederate high command formed a kind of tableau, a detailed and comprehensive portrait of "the ancient chivalry" of the region and all its equally glamorous, uniformly flattering possibilities. J. E. B. Stuart, for example, was normally presented as the "beau ideal of the Cavalier". "Everything stirring, brilliant, and picturesque, seemed to centre in him", declared one commentator:

> There was about the man a flower of chivalry and adventure which made him more like a knight of the middle age than a soldier of the prosaic nineteenth century.[6]

To use W. R. Taylor's useful term, Stuart was seen in fact as a plantation Hotspur. His dress, with its dazzling buttons, gold braid, silk sash, black ostrich feathers, and golden spurs, was described in admiring detail; invariably, he was pictured laughing and singing, both before and during battle; and, almost equally invariably, he was likened to Prince Rupert who, it was claimed, was one of his ancestors. "Gallant, knightly, proud, gay . . . indomitable", he was also said to number among his spiritual forefathers Robin Hood, Don Quixote, and other heroes of "old romance"; for, like them, this "model countryman and gentleman" managed to enjoy battle as if it were a "pageant" or a "frolic". War to Stuart, we are told,

> seemed a splendid and exciting game, in which his blood coursed joyously, and his immensely strong physical organization found an arena for the display of all its faculties . . . Stuart loved . . . adventure . . . The romance and poetry of the hard trade of arms seemed first to be inaugurated when this joyous cavalier . . . appeared upon the great arena of the war in Virginia.[7]

The sporting metaphors, and the references to careless chivalry tended to disappear when Wade Hampton was the subject; since Hampton, it was felt, was more the sober squire than the dashing cavalier, and an idiom suggestive of substance, solidity and reliability was considered rather more appropriate for him. As with Stuart, however, Hampton's civilian life was regarded as inseparable from his military activities. For just as Stuart's life as a cavalier of the Old South had prepared him for "the glitter of arms" so, it was argued, Hampton's experience as a planter had prepared him for the burden of leadership in war. "A man capable of managing a large plantation", one Southern historian declared, "has advanced far in the qualities necessary to make a good Colonel"; and, he went on:

> It was in that school that Wade Hampton of South Carolina was eminently educated – a school which taught him not only the act of command, but which . . . produced an aristocracy . . . singularly pure, circumspect, and aspiring.[8]

Natural, unassuming, dignified, grave: these were the terms used most often in connection with Hampton. "He was evidently an honest gentleman", one commentator said,

> who disdained all pretence or artifice. It was plain that he thought nothing of personal decorations and military show, and never dreamed of "producing an impression" upon any one. This was revealed by that bearing full of proud modesty; neither stiff nor insinuating – simple.[9]

Looking forward to the Nashville Agrarians and *I'll Take My Stand*, we might say that the difference between the versions of the aristocratic type offered by Stuart and Hampton corresponds to the difference between, say, Stark Young's version of Southern life and John Crowe Ransom's: on the one hand, a vision of aristocratic flair and *bravura* and, on the other, a rather less obviously heroic portrait of squirearchical comfort, stability, and benign ease. The two versions are potentially compatible with each other, of course; indeed, they formed complementary aspects of the patriarchal model from the first days of the region's settlement. But they do involve two slightly contrasting variations on the regional idiom, two quite separate perspectives on the myth of the plantation.

Other perspectives were offered by the portraits of other generals. Jackson, for instance, was depicted as a simpler type of the gentleman-planter than Wade Hampton; simpler in his tastes, that is, and rather more frugal, laconic, and stoical – "opposed", as one historian put it, "to self-display". This fitted in, it was felt, with his Scotch-Irish origins and his background in western Virginia; and it did not prevent commentators from describing him as "punctiliously courteous and dignified", or from ascribing his qualities of leadership, as with Hampton, to his training as a planter. "The people of the Confederate States", the reader was told, "will cheerfully consent that this holy man . . . may stand forth to the world as their exemplar";[10] and the enthusiasm – as well as, on occasion, the implicit exclusiveness – of this remark was echoed in the descriptions of people like Beauregard, Ashby, Joseph Johnston, Polk, and Nathan Bedford Forrest. Nearly always, one particular characteristic was singled out to act as a key or catalyst, one fragment of the gentlemanly image. With Beauregard, for example, it tended to be his courteous demeanour, while with Ashby it was something more clearly romantic – his status as "the glass of chivalry" and spiritual descendant of

Hampden and Sidney. Joseph Johnston was usually praised for his empirical wisdom and restraint; Leonidas Polk was honoured in the belief that "as a man, he was unrivalled for the graces of culture"; and Forrest in turn was celebrated for the many ways in which, so it was felt, he embodied all that was finest about the old South-West – in his bravery, commonsense, feeling for kin, and not least in his innate gallantry.[11] With only one Confederate general was this quest for singularity, the search for a particular defining characteristic, ever abandoned, and that because he was thought to project every facet of the ideal. That general, unsurprisingly, was Robert E. Lee: who was described by one historian – in a not unprecedented or untypical flight of rhetoric – as "the finest gentleman of the South, the most perfect and beautiful model of manhood in the war".[12]

In effect, Lee was taken to contain within himself all the best qualities of the patriarchal model; he was seen, to quote one of his many biographers and celebrants, as "a type of the race from which he sprang". Even the background of this "Cavalier of the Old Dominion" was apparently impeccable. For, being "of an ancient and distinguished stock", his ancestry could be "clearly traced from the Norman conquest" on both sides of the family. And the mansion in which he was born and which he eventually inherited was presented in almost precisely the same terms as the homes of William Gilmore Simms's plantation heroes. This passage, for instance, is typical – as much for its rhetorical inversions, pastoral imagery, and dependence on a long-established tradition of idealised landscapes, as for its use of all the familiar aristocratic positives:

> Crowning the green slopes of the Virginian hills that overlook the Potomac, and embowered in stately trees, stood the venerable mansion of Arlington . . . Its broad porch and wide-spread wings held out open arms . . . to welcome the coming guest. Its simple Doric columns graced domestic comfort with a classic air. Its halls and chambers were adorned with the portraits of patriots and heroes . . . And within and without, history and tradition seemed to breathe their legends upon a canvas as soft as a dream of peace.[13]

What is especially noticeable about a passage like this – and its equivalent can be found in most of the books of the period dealing with Lee – is not its conventionality but its self-consciousness: the author's glimmering awareness that he is working with a prepared code. Everything in the landscape is disposed according to precedent – hills, curling river, and mansion overlooking all; and all the appropriate notes are touched, from the use of trigger-words like "stately", and "venerable" in the opening sentence, through the references to hospitality and Greek architecture in the middle section, to the coupling of "history and tradition" towards the end. Hovering over everything is a sense of arrangement, contrivance, artifice: a sense that is caught most noticeably in the four final nouns – "legends", "canvas", "dream", "peace". As he vaguely senses, the author of this verbal portrait is not just remembering a man, he is recreating a legend; he is not just describing a scene, he is trying to put a dream on canvas; he is not just a historian, he is something of a mythmaker, attempting to recover a sense of order and peace. He is reinventing the past, and part of him knows it, in however dim or uncertain a way, and knows too why the reinvention is necessary.

Which is all by way of saying that the heroic portrait of Lee fashioned by so many Southerners after the war was part of the South's *conscious* attempt at moral rehabilitation. "Will not history consent", asked one commentator,

> when we still uphold our principles as right, our cause as just . . . when those principles had for disciple, that cause for defender, Robert Lee?[14]

Quite deliberately, spokesmen for the region set out to portray Lee, not just as a perfect gentle knight – that in itself was too limiting – but as a combination of gallant knight and sober squire, romantic cavalier and Christian gentleman (see Plate 6). As "the representative of this Southland", he could be allowed no blemishes. Even his appearance was idealised, and said to be typical, into the bargain, "of the man bred of Southern blood and under the Southern civilisation". His figure was described as "tall" and "graceful", his profile "Roman", his whole carriage "calm, august, and imposing", while his dress was said to reflect the "simple dignity" of "a good knight, a true gentleman". As for his behaviour: "Such was the grandeur and urbaneness of his manner", one writer declared,

> the dignity and majesty of his carriage, that his only peer in social life could be found in courts and among those educated amid the refinement of courts and thrones.[15]

Even Lee's favourite horse was not exempted from the mythmaking. As an extension of the cavalier aspects of his persona, it was considered nothing less than a "noble animal" – "which attained", as one writer put it, "almost as much celebrity as the gallant form" it carried.

But it was when Lee's biographers came to his moral qualities that this attempt to turn a man into a legend was most obvious; nothing that could be accommodated within the patriarchal model was denied to him. In public life, he was said to have shown "dignity and moderation" and in private "humility, simplicity, and gentleness". Combining "moral strength with moral beauty", he was described as "polite" to subordinates, "courteous" towards equals, and "affectionate" and faithful with relatives. As a soldier, he was (we are told) intrepid, as a father and husband tender and caring, and as the head of the house gracious, hospitable, and kindly. He was, in short, the "compleat gentleman" once celebrated by Peacham and Brathwaite, "plain", "honourable", and "honest", showing "all of the virtues and few of the faults of a class selected to rule because fittest to rule". And being a compleat gentleman he revealed, by implication, the mixed heritage of that compelling figure: something that was suggested by what one writer said of Lee. "In devotion to duty", he declared,

> and calm reliance on God lay the secret of his life . . . It was the teaching of the Southern home, which produced the type of character, the deep foundations of which were devotion to duty and reliance on God.[16]

Lee was pictured, in fact, both as a noble Roman and a devoted Christian, a stoic in whose life everything was "made to square with duty's inexorable demands" and one of the faithful who saw everything in terms of his own deeply-held beliefs. There was no necessary contradiction in this, of course; in this respect, the Christian and classical traditions are perfectly reconcilable. But it is noticeable how, here as elsewhere, Lee's biographers refused to acknowledge even the potential presence of a problem, the possibility of personal conflict. As one of them suggested, there was no need for Lee to establish priorities, to compare and relate values, make moral choices and connections, because:

> His was a practical, every-day religion, which supported him all through his life, enabled him to bear with equanimity every reverse of fortune, and to accept her gifts without undue elation.[17]

His Christianity, in short, supported his stoicism and his stoicism reinforced his Christianity; everything, in the model, fitted into place — perfectly, and without apparent effort. Perhaps the biographer might admit that he himelf sometimes found it difficult to achieve a balance between the different aspects of Lee's life, or to establish the right degree of emphasis for each aspect ("His biographer hesitates what to choose for highest praise", one of them breathily admitted, "lingering in turn over Lee the son, Lee the husband, Lee the father, Lee the friend . . . Lee the Christian").[18] But such difficulties were never, for one moment, admitted to be a part of Lee's own experience. In this one character, apparently, perfection had been reached: "a just mixture of qualities", as one historian put it,

> a perfect balance of character at once rare and admirable . . . the precise adjustment of the virtues, . . . all . . . powers and dispositions knit in harmony, presenting a single majestic picture of human nature.[19]

It was an imposing picture but also, for those interested in something other than the perfection of archetypes or the smooth surfaces of models, a rather depressing one.

The virtual apotheosis of Lee in the years after the war had as its main aim the perpetuation and the development of the patriarchal image of the South. Working from the assumption that Lee represented "the true type of the Southern gentleman", the patriarchal ideal in its quintessence, Southern historians and biographers presented their hero as a tangible reminder of the lost cause, all that the Confederacy had fought for – a function he was pre-eminently suited to perform, of course, because he had been one of the leaders in the fight. Significantly, slavery was rarely mentioned in connection with Lee; or, if it was, it was hardly ever dwelt upon. What Lee had fought for, it was argued, was the defence of the South, "inherited conviction and constitutional right";[20] and more specifically for his home state of Virginia. The comparison with the heroes of the American Revolution, and in particular with Washington, was frequently used to buttress this argument: Lee, the contention was, had followed in the footsteps of other eminent Virginians who had fought for their liberty against an oppressive colonial power. Nor was the fact that Lee had survived the war ever left waiting for rhetorical embellishment, since that survival enabled him to act, not just as a nostalgic emblem, but as a beacon, a projection of hope for the future. Lee had survived, and so by implication had the patriarchal model. Both were still there, after Appomatox, waiting for the South to pay them the appropriate tribute by way of reverence and imitation; despite defeat, the cause was not really lost.

There was another way of looking at Lee, though, that was occasionally adopted by Southerners: which was to see him, not as an embodiment of the aristocratic ideal, but as generals frequently are, in time of war – as a representative of all the men he commanded. This was put very succinctly by one writer, when he insisted:

> The fame of Lee and Jackson . . . is but condensed and personified admiration of the Confederate soldier, wrung from an unwilling world by his matchless courage, endurance, and devotion. Their fame is an everlasting monument to the mighty deeds of the nameless host who followed them through so much toil and blood to glorious victories.[21]

The problem with this point of view was that it was difficult to sustain beyond the kind of vague rhetorical gestures illustrated here. Lee and "the Confederate soldier" might very well have been alike in their "matchless courage, endurance, and devotion" – alike, that is, in the way that nearly all fighting men are alike when commemorated by those whom they have fought for. But, when it came to portraying and celebrating the ordinary soldier in detail, he emerged as a very different figure from his gentlemanly leader – as this passage, taken from a long description of the Confederate forces, clearly illustrates:

> The vast majority were uneducated, many could not read or write; but they were as a class far from being ignorant, for they were "good listeners" and close

observers of current events . . . Their . . . houses were of logs, some hewn, many of skinned poles, and some so primitive that the bark was left on . . . As might be inferred, their lives were simple, and in general they were obedient to law. They were, however, high-strung and quick to resent an affront, and their ready appeal to the rifle and the hunting-knife in the settlement of personal differences was the chief exception to their common acceptance of . . . authority . . . They dressed with extreme simplicity, usually in cotton or woollen stuffs, raised, spun, woven, and tailored at home . . . they raised everything they ate, except sugar and coffee . . . their wants were few and easily supplied . . . Their convention was that freemen had the inherent right to do as they pleased, and as freemen they would stay in the Union or secede . . .[22]

It hardly needs pointing out that we have moved here from the patriarchal model to its populist equivalent: the simple farmer – unlettered but wise, law-abiding but independent, self-reliant but capable of communal action. The figure who was once seen as the nerve of the English army is here portrayed as the backbone of the Confederacy, defending its right to self-determination.

Several further points could be made about this passage, and the portrait of the Confederate soldier it offers. In the first place, it should be mentioned that it comes from a rather different kind of book from the ones in which Lee, Jackson, and their kind are celebrated. The latter purport to be histories of the war, or some significant aspect of it, or biographies of one of the Confederate forces' "great men"; they take a distanced view, and by no means all of them were written by people who participated in the conflict. The fuller accounts of life among ordinary troops tend, by contrast, to occur in personal memoirs, recollections, and sketches; they were written, in other words, by men fighting in the ranks – men who, by definition, were more literate than most of their comrades-in-arms but who otherwise shared many of their habits, tastes and prejudices. This passage, for example, comes from a book entitled *With Sabre and Scalpel*, written by a man who served in a humble capacity as a trooper and medical aide. In the second place, it is worth underlining the fact that although most of those who celebrated the Confederate soldier did not force the point home – and were not, probably, even aware of any latent contradiction – there was a clear difference between their perception of the lost cause and that offered by, say, Lee's biographers. Again, the passage just quoted alerts us to that difference: with its emphasis on a life so plain that it verges on deprivation, and self-reliance carried, if necessary, to the point of violence. This is the world conjured up in the stories of the Southwestern humorists rather than the fiction of Simms or Caruthers, the homeplace of Sut Lovingood or Joseph Jones, rather than that of Colonel Porgy; and it needs, perhaps, to be repeated that, however much these two worlds may coincide at particular points, they do depend on two quite different vocabularies and sets of priorities, two conflicting notions of how the world is and how it should be arranged. Finally, it should be emphasised that what is said here *is* typical: typical, that is, of a large number of books written to present the Southern side of the Civil War to the "tribunal of History". Not all these books may offer quite such a detailed portrait of the life from which the Confederate trooper issued and for which he fought. Underpinning all of them, however, are the assumptions on which this portrait is based; they begin, all of them, with the same model and consequently use the same idiom.

Like the writer of *With Sabre and Scalpel*, most of the authors of these books tended to stress above all the independence and individualism of their subjects. Confederate troops, it was argued, had fought to repel invasion, to defend their land. "They loved their State", declared one writer:

> They loved their homes and their families. They were no politicians. Most of them knew little of the warring theories of constitutional interpretation. But one thing they knew – armed legions were marching upon their homes, and it was their duty to hold them back at any cost.[23]

In some ways, it was admitted, this love of freedom, this self-reliance was a disadvantage: it made them reluctant to obey orders, on the assumption that they were as good as the men who commanded them, and unwilling "to submit to the routine duty and discipline of the camp or march". But, like the yeomen of English tradition, they were regarded as born fighters. The paradox was summed up by the author of a book called *A Rebel's Recollections*, who said of his comrades:

> The men who volunteered . . . were wholly unaccustomed to acting on any other than their own notion. They were hardy lovers of field sports, accustomed to out-door life, and in all respects excellent material of which to make an army. But they were not used to control of any sort, and were not disposed to obey anybody except for good and sufficient reason given.[24]

Gone from this account of things was that sense of deference to Christian gentlemen and cavaliers that was so insisted upon by the biographers of Lee, Stuart, and Hampton.

Other details of the portrait fleshed out this image of the yeoman-soldier. He was depicted as naturally proud, simple, and honest. Of a rough and even sometimes crude humour, evident particularly before and during battle (when, of course, such humour could be excused as a manly device for exorcising nervousness) he was also said to be endowed with "the purest . . . and gentlest feelings"; for all his roughness, the suggestion was, the Confederate soldier was "a man of honour". Indeed, it was a constant and not very well justified boast of these writers that, while the troops of the Union had destroyed everything that came within their grasp, without mercy or even an elementary sense of decency, Confederate soldiers, on the occasions when they had crossed into the North, had treated the people whose land they invaded with courtesy, restraint, and a considerable degree of kindness. This was all part of a fairly detailed contrast between the two sides that depended on the traditional opposition between those who cultivate the earth and those who swarm in the cities. The Confederate army, it was claimed, consisted of "stalwart men of brawny arm", each man fighting "for himself, on his own account", while the Union army was a "machine" – and, in that sense, a replica of the society it was fighting to extend – an anonymous force in which each member became simply "an indefinite portion of a mass". Some writers went even further, and accused the Federal soldiers of cowardice, of "running like squirrels" from the field of battle if they had the opportunity. Most of them, however, restricted themselves to the familiar catalogue of Yankee vices – fanaticism, greed, cunning, vulgarity, hypocrisy – and to the argument that the South's opponents consisted, for the most part, of a "servile" host, seduced into the conflict by mercenary considerations of loot or pay. The following passage is in this respect fairly typical; it is taken from a book entitled *Detailed Minutiae of Soldier Life in the Army of Northern Virginia, 1861–1865*:

> The Confederate soldier fought bounties and monthly pay . . . and all the fury and fanaticism which skilled minds could create . . . He fought good wagons, fit horses, and tons of quartermaster's stores . . . He fought the commerce of the United States and all the facilities for war which Europe could supply. He fought the trained army officers and the regular troops of the United States army, assisted by . . . swarms of men, the refuse of the earth – Portuguese, Spanish, Italian, German, Irish, Scotch, English, French, Chinese, Japanese – white, black, olive, brown. He laid down his life with this hireling host, who died for pay, mourned by no one, missed by no one, loved by no one; who were better fed and clothed . . . in the army than ever they were at home . . . When one of these fell, two could be brought in to fill the gap . . .[25]

The reference to a *trained* army and *regular* troops in the passage just quoted is almost certainly loaded with bitter irony. For Southern observers of the war, the Union army was one marked by its professionalism – consisting, as they saw it, of soldiers by vocation and an urban proletariat that had learned only too easily how to function as a war machine. And they viewed that professionalism with a curious mixture of contempt and resentment: the Southerner was naturally "a better fighter . . ., a practical horseman, and skilled in the use of arms" but the Northerner, it had to be admitted, had soon learned to equalise differences through "instruction and discipline".[26] This was something, at least, that those who followed the patriarchal model and those who preferred the populist could easily agree upon: the Yankee was not by instinct a warrior, and could never join battle by and for himself – but he could learn and, working hard and single-mindedly, he had become part of a successful military force. Somewhere, just beneath the surface, the familiar oppositions were at work here: Southern bravery and gallantry versus Yankee servility, Southern impetuosity and indolence versus the North's laboriousness and industry. And the oppositions could be embellished and enlivened by two pseudo-historical parallels, both of them already deeply embedded in Southern thought. The first of these parallels was with the English Civil War, with the Confederates inevitably being equated with their legendary Cavalier forebears, those country people "who had followed the banners of Newcastle and Rupert" and the Yankee army suggesting a comparison with the Roundheads. In both civil conflicts, it was argued, "fiery and impetuous valour was at last overmatched by . . . disciplined purpose and . . . stubborn constancy":[27] which, as so often in the Southern version of things, made failure sound far more enticing and glamorous than success. The other parallel was a more straightforward morale-booster; and consisted, quite simply, of William Gilmore Simms's device of comparing the conflict between the sections with the American Revolution. The men who had fought for the South, driven by "the God-implanted instinct which impels a man to defend his own hearth-stone" were, it was averred, the direct spiritual descendants of those who had defied King George and the Tories. Armed only with "old flint and steel muskets, long-barrelled squirrel rifles, and double-barrelled shot-guns",[28] they had proved themselves worthy of their "heroic sires" – and worthy to be compared, too, with other great defenders of home and liberty, such as (and both these parallels were also popular) the ancient Greeks or those Englishmen who had risen against King John.

Not that the homes and liberties so defended were usually described in detail: the subject was the war itself and the patriarchal and populist models as they defined themselves in military action – which necessarily excluded much analysis, or imaginative rediscovery, of life on plantation and farm. That life only came in by implication and invocation, as it were: through the qualities, learned from their background, that gentlemen and yeomen were said to bring with them to battle, and through the occasional, stirring reference to the blessings they had left behind. There are, in these books, few equivalents of that detailed reinvention of life on the old plantation that one finds in, say, Simms's novels or Caruthers's; and few equivalents, either, of the vivid projection of the backwoods, its customs, habits, and rituals, that enlivens so many of the stories of Longstreet and William Tappan Thompson. Admittedly, some of the minor personae and emblems of either model appear in military disguise, on a war footing. The loyal slave of the plantation tradition, for example, reappears as the faithful valet following his "massa" to battle and, when necessary, carrying him from the field and tending his wounds; while the plantation lady and her daughter, the plantation belle, are transformed into "sustaining angels", working indefatigably behind the front lines to bring "comfort and cleanliness to the gallant soldier".[29] But for the most part it is upon the men themselves that attention is focussed in these books, and the degree to which, taken into new surroundings and put to the extremest of tests, they embody – which is to say, give flesh, blood, and bones to – the inherited dreams of the region.

That these dreams, even in their conflicts and inconsistencies, were not wholly without substance is suggested, among other things, by the actual condition and composition of the army on to which they were projected. Contradictions there might be in the Southern account of the war: most notably between those who insisted that the gentleman-officer, as natural leader, exercised unquestioned control and those who argued that, on the contrary, the ordinary soldier was an "independent, intelligent unit . . . not . . . to be manoeuvred by his officers".[30] But such contradictions of thought were in fact no more and no greater than the contradictions of practice to be found in the day-to-day life of the Confederate army. Officers in that army, for example, might be democratically elected but they were usually drawn from the privileged classes; their orders, too, might be disregarded or even flouted if the individual judgement went against them but they were still, more often than not, regarded as best suited to lead.[31] Which is all by way of saying that the codes to which Southerners gave their allegiance affected their behaviour during the Civil War quite as much as their memories of it afterwards; as in earlier periods – as in Virginia, for example, during the colonial and Revolutionary periods – the terms in which the region strove to present itself were as much a matter of action as of language and thought. "To me", wrote the Southern writer John Peale Bishop in 1931,

> it is always the most interesting thing about a man what he thinks of himself. That is to say, what is the form he has conceived through which to live . . .[32]

And that, as Bishop instinctively recognised, was because such a form acts as a medium of perception, a standard of judgement, and a catalyst for behaviour; it helps to shape every area of a person's life, linguistic, intellectual, political, and social. The rhetoric of many of these early Southern versions of the war may strike us now as absurdly mannered and their portraits of life on the battlefield as highly coloured and contrived, and that whether they are talking of Christian gentlemen or humble, "butternut"[33] soldiers. Just the same, it is worth recalling that they represent an attempt – and a significant attempt, at that – not merely to commemorate the lost cause but to perpetuate and promote regional identity. Feeling with that Georgia girl that "the world will not hear our story", they tried to tell that story to themselves, so that they would not figure in their own imaginations at least as their enemies chose to paint them – and in the hope that the world might one day be willing to listen to what they had to say.

LOOKING BEFORE AND AFTER: WRITERS IN THE NEW SOUTH

If there was one thing most travellers in the South were agreed on just after the Civil War, it was that the old economic and political system of the region had broken down irretrievably. One observer, for instance, claimed to have seen "enough woe and want and ruin and ravage", during a visit of fourteen weeks to Georgia and the Carolinas, "to satisfy the most insatiate heart"; "enough of sore humiliation and bitter overthrow", he added, "to appease the desire of the most vengeful spirit". Another has left us this vivid account of the Valley of Tennessee:

> It consists for the most part of plantations in a state of semi-ruin, and plantations of which the ruin is total and complete . . . The trail of war is visible throughout the valley in burnt-up gin houses, ruined bridges, mills and factories, of which latter the gable walls only are left standing, and in large traces of once cultivated land stripped of every vestige of fencing. The roads, long neglected, are in disorder . . . Borne down by losses, debts, and accumulating taxes, many who were once the richest among their fellows have disappeared from the scene, and few have yet risen to take their places.[34]

"A dead civilisation and a broken-down system" was how another traveller described the region after the war; and, melodramatic though the phrase may sound, it was not without a grain of truth. For the planters who had retained most of the wealth and power in the Old South found themselves in a hopeless position: economically ruined and very often excluded from participation in politics. Control shifted from them to new forces, openly committed to industrialisation, accomplished under Northern direction by Northern capital, reducing the South to a colonial status and fastening on it a colonial psychology. Even with the ending of Radical reconstruction in the late 1870s, the pattern did not significantly alter, since very few of the new "Bourbon" leaders were primarily interested in agriculture. As a group, they had very few connections with the plantation regime, and were committed to the building of a new order of things, not the recovery of the old.[35]

And yet despite all this – perhaps even because of it – the old order kept its grip on the Southern imagination; and, in particular, the patriarchal image still held sway, still defined the terms in which many Southerners preferred to see themselves. There were different motives for this, depending of course on what *kind* of Southerners they were: where their interests lay and what their condition and aims were after the war. For example, those who found themselves ruined, and, as they felt, victimised and humiliated, naturally turned back to the good old days before the conflict – which, suitably apotheosised by distance, came to represent all they had suffered for and lost. Those Southerners in turn, who benefited from the changed conditions – the shopkeepers who extended credit, the merchants and bankers who represented Northern interests – lost no time, once they had acquired wealth, in looking back to those days and trying to imitate them: acquiring land with the same indefatigable industry that William Fitzhugh once had, discovering ancestors among once-prominent slave-holding families, and in general reinventing their own past along with that of their region. Finally, those who swept to power in the "Bourbon" reaction did so through an adept use of the patriarchal image: their interests might have aligned them with the New South, and the gospel of Progress and Profits, but they and their message were given colour and glamour by being wrapped in the pseudo-aristocratic trappings of the old. Naturally, there was no reason why these different motives should not overlap: a successful merchant, having made his money and adopted the role of patriarch, made an ideal member of the new political order but so, too, did someone with a suitably imposing name, redolent of times past, who was ready to allow that name to be used to restore white supremacy and drive the Republicans back where they belonged. Motives were mixed, as they always are: the same Southerner could, at one and the same time, look back with nostalgia to the rural past and forward with hope to the industrial future, and cloak everything – past, present, and future – in the language and imagery of the patriarchal model. But one ingredient in the mixture remained simple, constant, and unchanging: which was the willingness, or rather the fierce compulsion, to identify the great days of the patriarchal order with the time before the war. Aspects of that order might be recovered, people felt, its essential spirit might not be dead, but in itself in its entirety it was gone for ever.[36]

This willingness to locate the feudal ideal firmly in the past had several consequences, some of them obvious and others perhaps less so. It meant, first of all, that those many writers who chose to celebrate that ideal – like John Esten Cooke and Thomas Nelson Page – were no longer hampered by any sense of contingency, any restricting concern for the ordinary details of day-to-day life. Nostalgia could run riot, distance could give a romantic blur to everything, while if any gap was perceived between ideal and reality, word and thing – and, not surprisingly, there sometimes was – it could be equated with the gap between past and present; once things were perfect, the argument went, and, if they do not seem so now, then the war is entirely to blame. On top of that, this placing of the centre of interest in times past helped to blur the moral and intellectual focus as well. Since writers such as Page were concerned with a world that was, as one commentator has put it, "so irrevocably and satisfyingly lost",[37] what they had to say had no direct or obvious implications for the present and future. Like the planters who had fallen victims to the war, never to recover, they might have been lamenting the disappearance of the old system as the one, truly human way in which to live, and so by implication have been castigating the new system of things. Or, like the Bourbon politicians and their accomplices, they might have seen no inconsistency between their hymns to the past and hopes for the future; since to memorialise something, in however fulsome a way, is not necessarily to offer it as a viable design for living. They might in short, as some critics have suggested, have been offering a pastoral rebuke to an increasingly urban present; or they might, as at least one critic has argued, have been indirectly promoting the industrial ethic by placing its rural alternative in a picturesque vacuum.[38] The point is, really, that we, the readers, cannot say for certain which of these two things they thought they were doing, because there are so few references of any significance to the emerging order of things. The patriarchal model is presented to us in a sealed container: that interest in applying it to the contemporary experiences and problems of the South which we find – in however crude or occasionally misdirected a form – in the novels of Simms, Paulding, Caruthers, and Tucker is for the most part missing from the plantation fiction written after the Civil War. So instead of historical romance we are left with romance, pure and simple.

Just how romantic that could be is suggested by these writers' frequent use of an ex-slave as memorialist, the commemorator of the lost pieties and sanctions. *Colonal Carter of Cartersville*, for example, by F. Hopkinson Smith, includes this elegy from the Colonel's faithful servant Chad:

> "Dem was high times. We ain't neber seed no time like dat since de war. Git up in de mawnin' an' look out ober de lawn, an' yer come fo'teen or fifteen couples ob de fustest quality folks, all un horseback ridin' in de gate. Den such scufflin' round. Old marsa and missis out on de po'ch an' de little pickaninnies runnin' from de quarters . . . An' den sich a breakfast an' sich dancin' an' cotin'; ladies all out on de lawn in der white dresses, an de gemmen in fair-top boots . . . Dat would go on a week or mo', an' den up day'll all git an away de'y go to der nex' plantation . . ."[39]

"Dem wuz laughin' times", declares another and more famous of these elegists, Joel Chandler Harris's Uncle Remus, "an' it looks like dey ain't never comin' back." This use of a narrator to recall the "good ole times" before the war even made nostalgia dramatically permissible, since it could be presented as an aspect of character as well as a quality of the text. It was not that these writers wished to dramatise the process of remembering as later Southerners like Tate, Ransom, and Faulkner were to do, to show how the mind perseveres to turn things recalled into legend; it was simply that this narrative frame helped them to distance themselves still further from their material. In the Preface to one of his novels, *Red Rock*, Thomas Nelson Page declared that his story was set "in the vague region partly in one of the old Southern states and partly in the yet vaguer land of Memory";[40] and it was clear from his tone that Page regarded this vagueness as a positive asset. Ideally, the assumption was, the "old courts and polished halls" of the ante-bellum South should be seen through a series of receding frames: of which one could be provided, when necessary, by a Negro so involved with the old times and so loyal to their memory that he refused to acknowledge his emancipation – or, if he did so, often felt himself lost and anchorless as a result (see Plate 7).

One of the more curious aspects of this blurring and softening of the plantation image was the way in which aspects of the patriarchal character that had once been construed as faults, or at the very least weaknesses, were now transmuted, by the distorting mirror of time and loss, into positive merits. Rashness, impetuosity, and foolhardiness were now marshalled unhesitatingly under the banner of "courage".[41] The lavishness and financial carelessness for which Simms's Colonel Porgy had been criticised was now praised, when it was noted in Cooke's gentlemanly characters, or Page's, as a symptom of generosity of spirit;[42] and that lack of practicality for which Colonel Dangerfield in *Westward Ho!* had been mocked was presented as the most endearing – which is to say, the most chivalrous, romantic, and archaic – feature of Colonel Carter of Cartersville. In order to register the change, one has only to compare the comments on Porgy's indolence or Dangerfield's, quoted earlier, with these words from *Gabriel Tolliver*, a book by Joel Chandler Harris:

> The serene repose of Shady Dale no doubt stood for dullness and lack of progress in that day and time. In all ages of the world, and in all places, there are men of restless but superficial minds, who mistake repose and serenity for stagnation . . . when you examine the matter, what is called progress is nothing more nor less than the multiplication of the resources of those who, by means of dicker and barter, are trying all the time to overreach the public and their fellows in one way and another.[43]

"The civilisation which existed . . . in the old days before the war has perished", declared Page in *On Newfound River*:

> The Landons [the heroes of the novel] and others of their kind ruled unquestioned in an untitled manorial system; their poorer neighbours stood in

a peculiar relation to them, part friend, part retainer, the line between independence and vassalage being impalpable; and peace and plenty reigned over a smiling land.[44]

In such a world, with its noble mansion, verdant lawns, and broad acres, there was no place for doubts or reservations – nor even for those drastically restricted kinds of social criticism and historical analysis that one finds in plantation stories from before the war.

So the patriarchal model was accepted by these writers in a more or less wholesale fashion: with only a slight variation provided by the challenge of war. Plantation mistresses were seen according to type as uniformly thoughtful, caring, and efficient, and in time of conflict offering the appropriate rebuke to those Yankees who dared to invade their homes.[45] Situated around them and their husbands were all the familiar *dramatis personae* of plantation fiction: the plantation belle whose physical perfection issued from her "old blood and gentle breeding", the young squire "playing in the court of love" but "a stout-hearted and stout-armed cavalier"[46] into the bargain, the faithful banjo-playing darkies, the wise old Uncle Toms, and the kindly black Mammies. Very often, the narratives, too, seemed to have a preordained structure to them: with set-scenes that evoked the life of the old plantation – the tournament, the ball, the hunt, the horse-race, the dinner, the duel – leading eventually to some conflict that threatened to bring this life to an end. Even if this structure was missing, the villains of the piece tended to fall into certain familiar types just as the heroes did. In detail, they might be coloured according to period – the Puritan extremist, the fanatical Abolitionist, the "lowly-born and lowly-bred" overseer who rises to power and influence after the Civil War: but, in general, they were associated with all the conventional vices of the Yankee – cunning and vulgarity, greed and hypocrisy, and an unparalleled appetite for cant.[47] Again, a comparison with the early plantation romance is worth making. For, whatever their deficiencies, writers like Caruthers and Simms were not unaware of the strengths of the Yankee case: Caruthers, after all, made one of his heroes a cross between the Puritan type and the Cavalier, while in *The Sword and the Distaff* Simms had provided Millhouse (who, although a Southerner, is given all the traditional "Yankee" ammunition) with his own vision, his own vocabulary, and his own indispensable part in the recovery of the plantation way of life. In later plantation fiction, however, the equivalents of Millhouse are people like one Hiram Still in *Red Rock* or Wash Jones in Joel Chandler Harris's story, "Ananias". Like Millhouse, both men are overseers; and, like Millhouse too, both men are thrifty, energetic and, when necessary, cunning. Unlike Millhouse, however, both are viewed with an absolute lack of sympathy, and use their talents, such as they are, not to help their masters but to rob them. "He did not hesitate to grind a man when he had him in his clutches", Harris declares of Wash Jones, ". . . he often, in a sly way flattered the colonel [the owner of the plantation] into making larger bills than he otherwise would have made."[48] Still demonstrates the same rapacity and ruthlessness in tricking and supplanting the man he is supposed to be working for and ends up, like Jones, living in the plantation mansion, at least for a while. "Here I am settin' up", Still observes at the moment of his triumph,

> "a gentleman here in this big house that I used to stand over yonder on the hill in the blazin' sun and just look at, and wonder if I ever would have one even as good as the one I was then in as my own."[49]

This is a far cry from the earthy poetry and utter self-confidence of Simms's character: even the lowly-born in Page's work and Harris's judge things, and in particular themselves, according to the patriarchal model – and struggling for the place and prerogatives of a gentleman show, in the process, just how hopeless that struggle is. Millhouse retains a healthy scepticism towards Porgy's aims even while he is helping him to achieve them; whereas Still and Jones evidently revere the very standards that, in practice, they assault. Consequently, while he strikes the reader as a kind of double agent, rebuilding the patriarchal framework yet all the time inviting us to question its adequacy, they come across as little more than two further propagandists for the cause: pleading the aristocratic case directly, in what they desire, and indirectly – that is, by negative example – in what they do.

Mention of the overseer character, and more specifically those stories in which he is seen rising to power on the back of his master, leads to another point worth emphasising: that by no means all these later plantation romances were set in the period before the war. One common way of commemorating the old order was to concentrate on its vestiges, the few reminders of the patriarchal regime that had survived the conflict. Although such stories might literally be set in the present, however, they were just as much imaginatively committed to the past as other, more obviously elegiac plantation fiction was. Their purpose was to invoke the patriarchal model by implication, as it were: by showing what remained of the old order and how anachronistic – how charmingly, comically, or tragically inappropriate – it was in the new context and system of things. The lighter side of this particular brand of nostalgia is illustrated by this passage from John Esten Cooke's *The Virginia Bohemians* describing one, fictional neighbourhood in the Old Dominion after the war:

> Once the families had lived in affluence . . . and carriages stood at the door at any and all hours of the day . . . There was a plenty of hospitality still, but few

servants were seen now, and the wolf was at the door much oftener than the coach . . . The good people in the old country homes accepted their reduced fortunes cheerfully . . . Certain persons, it is true, called them aristocratic and "exclusive" . . . they were a poor aristocracy now . . . A rich aristocracy ought, of course, to be saluted respectfully – certain advantages may be derived from conciliating it . . . a poor aristocracy . . . is an effective anomaly and has no right to exist . . . You can laugh at it, and despise it even – no inconvenience will result – since nothing is to be expected from nothing.[50]

What is particularly interesting about this passage is its gradual alteration of tone as it proceeds: from gentle humour, it moves through a sardonic reference to the criticism of "certain persons" to a bitter résumé of the total lack of esteem in which "a poor aristocracy" is held – and (a not unconnected issue) its utter powerlessness. The echo of *King Lear* at the end is surely neither unintentional nor inappropriate, since it invites the reader to make a connection between Lear in his decline and the Southern gentry in their poverty: the greatness of both being, by implication, measured by the size of their fall. The imaginative thrust of the entire piece is, in effect, backwards: back to the heights from which "the Virginia Bohemians" have toppled, back from a resigned, smiling acceptance of the shabby present to an angry – if partially suppressed – awareness of what has been lost, back to wealth, better days, and, even beyond that, to a far more ancient and revered example of patriarchal power. And in this it neatly summarises the movement and concerns of most plantation stories that permit the contemporary world to intrude on to their pages. In the last analysis, they are hardly interested in that world at all; it exists only as a palimpsest, as it were, through which, if we read carefully, the messages of earlier times appear.

But not every Southern writer after the war was willing to locate his version of the pastoral idyll in the past and in the dream of a feudal patriarchy. For some, at least, the collapse of the plantation system was a basis for hope. Destruction, in their opinion, could and should be followed by the recovery of the Jeffersonian ideal; the turmoil of the immediate post-war years might very well act as a prelude to the return of the yeoman farmer, and the revival of those simple pieties and steadfast principles with which that figure was traditionally associated. One writer who thought very firmly along these lines was the poet, Sidney Lanier. Lanier was born in the small but bustling city of Macon, in Middle Georgia, and did not have any personal stake in plantation society. This may have been one reason why he was so willing to embrace the populist image in so much of his writing, but it was by no means the only one. Just as important, really, was his considered belief, as strong as Jefferson's in its own way, that subsistence farming was the true basis of personal independence and republican ideals. Some of this comes out in an early dialect poem of Lanier's, entitled "Thar's More in the Man

Than Thar is in the Land".[51] The poem depends on the contrast between a man named Jones who "couldn't make nuthin' but yallerish cotton" from his land, and Brown, the man who buys Jones's property from him eventually. Convinced that it is the poverty of his land that is to blame, Jones travels west to Texas to farm cotton there. Meanwhile Brown, we are told,

> picked all the rocks from off'n the groun'
> And he rooted it up and he plowed it down,
> Then he sowed his corn and his wheat in the land.

Within five years, Brown, having abandoned the exclusive cultivation of cotton, has grown prosperous and "so fat that he couldn't weigh"; while Jones's venture into commercial farming has failed once again, and he returns to Georgia seeking work. Invited to share Brown's "vittles smokin' hot", he is also treated to some homely wisdom from his host. "Brown looked at him sharp", the narrator tells us,

> and riz and swore
> That "whether men's land was rich or poor
> Thar was more in the man than thar was in the land".

The reader is left to speculate about what else, if anything, Brown said to Jones, but there can be no doubt about the substance of his message or indeed the thrust of his example: in order to prosper or even survive on the land, the implication is, a man had better abandon dependence on commercial farming.

A similar lesson is taught, in slightly different ways, in several of Lanier's other poems. In "Jones's Private Argument",[52] for instance, we are reintroduced to the hapless commercial farmer, who seems to have learned little either from his own experiences or the wise words of Brown. Publicly, the narrator tells us, Jones now embraces the gospel of self-subsistence. "Farmers *must* stop gittin' loans", he declares, "And git along without 'em." "The only thing to do", Jones goes on,

> Is, eat no meat that's boughten:
> *But tear up every I, O, U,*
> *And plant all corn and swear for true*
> *To quit a-raisin' cotton!*

Privately, however, he continues to believe that he can make a success of producing cotton. In the very last stanza, in fact, the narrator overhears Jones reasoning that, if most farmers listen to the advice being given them to plant corn (which, it should perhaps be said, is a kind of shorthand in much of Lanier's work for subsistence farming in general), then cotton will be in short supply and the price will rise. "*Tharfore*", he concludes triumphantly, "*I'll* plant *all* cotton!" Old habits die hard, it seems: Jones's instinct for self-destruction has not been substantially

altered by the evidence – or indeed by the arguments that he has learned
to reproduce with such facility. And the reader must assume that, at the
very best, he will continue to sink further and further into debt: like a
farmer called Ellick Garry, who is the subject of another of Lanier's
dialect poems, with the intriguing title "Nine From Eight".[53] The title,
as it turns out, refers to the arithmetic of misery: Garry has learned that
his debts for the year of over nine hundred dollars outweigh his earnings
of roughly eight hundred dollars from his cotton crop. As he puts it,

> My crap-leen calls for nine hundred and more.
> My counts o' sales is eight hundred and four
>   Of cotton for Ellick Garry.

So, at the end of the year, he is left with the bitter wisdom that "nine from
eight / Leaves nuthin'", and with the fear that he may never escape the
clutches of his creditors and "Them crap-leens, oh, them crap-leens!"

The crop-lien or sharecropping system that Lanier has his character
refer to here was one of the things that anyone interested in the state of the
real South after the war had to deal with – if only, like Lanier, to attack
and dismiss it. It was a system that made it possible for planters to obtain
labour without paying wages and for landless farmers to obtain land
without buying it or paying cash rent; in other words, it was a system that
enabled commercial farming to function at a time when the usual
commercial institutions had virtually disappeared from the South.
Instead of exchanging money, owner and tenant agreed to share the
proceeds of the crop. And in order to meet the immediate demand of the
farmer for food and appliances, the crop-lien merchant appeared, who
provided credit against the prospective harvest. The merchant in turn
obtained advances from a wholesale dealer or jobber, and the chain of
credit ran back eventually to a Northern manufacturer or his banker –
with, of course, everyone making more than a little profit along the way.
Once enmeshed in this chain, the farmer – who was being charged high
rates of interest, obliged to obtain all his goods from the credit merchant,
and buying in the highest possible market – found it difficult, if not
impossible, to escape. If, as usually happened, he failed to cancel his debt
with the proceeds from his crop, the contract bound him to renew his lien
for the next year under the same merchant. The arrangement was bad
enough in itself, but it was made worse by other factors. Normally, the
farmer did not control the marketing of his own crop, and so while he
was buying in the highest market he was more than likely selling in the
lowest. As even Jones recognised, the laws of supply and demand were
not totally irrelevant, and since so many farmers in the region depended
on cotton for their livelihood, they tended to drive the price down;
pathetically, their usual response to this was to increase cultivation, and
so drive the price down even further. Quite apart from all this, the

victorious Federal government could now favour industry with impunity, through those policies of high tariffs and currency contraction that the farming interests had always feared and opposed. In nearly every respect, then, the sharecropping system encouraged what one contemporary observer described as "helpless peonage";[54] and it was a system to which, by 1880, more than one-third of all Southern farmers had fallen victim.

This rather brief summary of sometimes immensely complicated financial arrangements is necessary for at least two reasons. In the first place, it says something for the enduring strength of the populist model that it was able to survive all this: not only survive it, but find stimulus and challenge in it. Writers and politicians did not abandon the idea of the simple husbandman, tilling his few acres with not a care for the storms and changes of the market-place; on the contrary, they struggled all the more fiercely to retain that idea and its supporting vocabulary – as, for instance, the arguments and rhetoric of the Populist movement make only too evident.[55] And, in the second, it helps to explain something like the fierceness of Lanier's commitment to the notion of "corn" and, equally, the unbounded intensity of his hatred of "trade". "Trade, Trade, Trade", he wrote to a friend,

> pah, are we not all sick? A man cannot walk down a green valley of woods, in these days, without unawares getting his mouth and nose and eyes covered with some web or other that Trade has stretched across, to catch some gain or other.[56]

Writers such as Lanier celebrated the yeoman almost as an act of desperation: because of the fear, eloquently touched upon here, that the alternative was imprisonment within the spider's web of urban capitalism and the destruction, eventually, of everything that was humanly worthwhile – everything that, for a man of Lanier's learning and interests, could be accommodated under the heading of culture.

Just how much could be accommodated under that heading, and just how powerful were the opposing forces, is the subject of one of Lanier's finest and best-known poems, "Corn".[57] The poem begins with a richly atmospheric description of the poet walking through some woods on a summer morning. These are the opening lines:

> Today the woods are trembling through and through
> With shimmering forms, that flash before my view,
> Then melt in green as dawn-stars melt in blue.
>   The leaves that wave against my cheek caress
>   Like women's hands; the embracing boughs express
>   A subtlety of mighty tenderness;
>   The copse-depths into little noises start,
>   That sound anon like beatings of a heart,
>   Anon like talk 'twixt lips not far apart.

The clotted vocabulary, the luscious verbal music, the evocative allusions to the touch, texture, and smell of things, and not least the only partially veiled pattern of erotic references: all these things recover for us both the sensuous details of a particular scene and a more general sense of the riotous abundance of nature. In this vivid, synaesthetic, and on occasion slightly claustrophobic world, there is little concern, it seems, for order, arrangement, or proportion. Everything melts into and mingles with everything else; throbbing with life, "With stress and urgence bold of prisoned spring / And ecstasy of burgeoning", nature seems to attack the senses, almost, and invite us to participate in its "ambrosial passion".

Then, "with ranging looks that pass / Up from the matted miracles of grass", the poet moves slowly to the edge of the woods,

> to the zigzag-cornered fence
> Where sassafras, intrenched in brambles dense,
> Contests with stolid vehemence
> The march of culture . . .

He has come, in fact, to the edge of a cornfield. Looking at the green, growing corn, he notices one stalk towering above the rest: "one tall corn-captain", which he takes as an emblem of "the poet-soul sublime". Odd though the comparison may seem to the reader at first, Lanier proceeds to give it substance, to justify it. Like the "poet-soul", Lanier insists, the "tall corn-captain . . . leads the vanward of his timid time", he is a leader. Like, the poet-soul, too, he grows "By double increment, above, below": drawing sustenance from the earth, and strength and inspiration from the sky. There are further analogies. Both bring together the many elements of which life is composed and metamorphose them, make of them a new synthesis – or, as Lanier puts it, addressing the "corn-captain" but also thinking, clearly, of his own function as poet:

> So thou dost marry new and old
> Into a one of higher mold;
> So thou dost reconcile the hot and cold,
> The dark and bright,
> And many a heart-perplexing opposite.

Above all, perhaps, both in their different ways preach reverence for the simple life: the pieties of hearth and home, the value of independence, the importance of depending on oneself for one's needs. Again, the direct address is to the corn, but the implications embrace the poet:

> O steadfast dweller on the selfsame spot
> Where thou wast born, that still repinest not –
> Type of the home-fond heart, the happy lot! –
> Deeply thy mild content rebukes the land

> Where flimsy homes, built on the shifting sand
> Of trade, forever rise and fall . . .

"The march of culture": this is the phrase with which the second movement of "Corn" begins, and it is evident from the lengthy comparison of the "tall corn-captain" and the "poet-soul" that comprises most of this movement that Lanier wishes this phrase to be interpreted in the widest possible sense. "Culture" here clearly embraces cultivation of both the land and the spirit; indeed, Lanier seems to believe that the one kind of culture grows out of the other – that "chivalry", "courtesy", and the things of the heart depend for their support and sustenance on the proper care of the soil and the "substantial spirit of content" that care fosters. It is not a startlingly novel idea, of course, but Lanier gives it a special purchase on the imagination in this poem through the dramatic encounter of poet and landscape, and through a series of analogies that are very often as densely rendered as they are ingenious. And it is given additional point and focus by the frame in which the cornfield first appears to us: the woodland scene, with its rich confusion of sense-impressions, "setting limb and thorn / As pikes against the army of the corn". This, we are led to infer, is the raw material of both the farmer and the poet; both try to tame nature, not by denying its plenitude and vitality, but by channelling its energies – enabling it to acquire fresh life, purer blood, and clearer direction. The farmer erects his fence, the poet arranges his language, rhyme, and metre; and, in doing so, both become cultivators, leavening "Strength of earth with grace of heaven", the power of the soil with the purposes of the mind. For both, too, there is a harvest, a "wondrous yield": on the one hand, the "cool solacing green" of the fields and, on the other, the rich evocations of language and enlargement of spirit that, so Lanier hopes, this movement of his poem achieves.

It is in the light of this idea of culture – and, more specifically, of the links indissolubly binding the simple farmer to the poet – that the third and final movement of "Corn" has to be read. This last movement has often been criticised: William Dean Howells, in rejecting the poem for publication in *Atlantic Monthly*, was only the first of many to complain that in itself it seemed overly rhetorical and that its connection with the earlier movements was at best obscure, if not non-existent.[58] The criticism is misguided, however. The alteration of perspective is in fact made very carefully and effectively. From the closeness and intimacy of the woodland scene, the poet has moved to the field of corn laid out before him; now he looks across the cultivated valleys to a barren and deserted hill, where once upon a time, we are told, "Dwelt one . . . who played at toil / And gave to coquette Cotton soul and soil." This leads him, almost inevitably it seems, into an attack on those who turn "each field into a gambler's hell" by dependence on commercial farming – and, by extension, on "trade" in general. Certainly, as the poet's vision extends into the distance, there is a change of tone and vocabulary – the language is much more combative here, much thinner and much less richly metaphorical – but the change, as it turns out, is part of the point. Lanier's subject now is barrenness and desertion: a subject that hardly requires the evocative imagery and lyric impulse of the second movement, still less the sensuous abandon of the first. "Corn" has moved us steadily from nature through culture to the sterile abstractions of trade – metaphorically, at least, we could say that we have travelled from the wilderness past the homestead and the clearing to the streets of the city; and the verbal equivalent of this has been our journey from the densely figurative language of the first movement, through the imaginative poise of the second, to the thoroughly small and dry idiom of the third.

All of which is not to say that the final movement of "Corn" is flawless. Unfortunately, Lanier cannot leave us where we are at the end of our journey, with this vision of abandonment and decay. He feels compelled, for some reason, to append sixteen lines in which he expresses the hope, or rather the dream, that even the "old hill" will one day yield "golden treasures of corn", thanks to the efforts of someone, anyone, willing to use "antique sinew and . . . modern art" – that is, presumably, native strength and scientific methods of crop cultivation. In a way, this is characteristic of both Lanier and his time. As far as Lanier himself is concerned, he never lost his optimistic belief that the yeoman would become a dominant force in the South. Admittedly, his later verse is less immediately or insistently concerned with the need for subsistence farming: but poems like "The Symphony" continue the attack on Trade, while others such as "The Marshes of Glynn"[59] develop the contrast between the rural life and the "terror and shrinking and dreary unnamable pain" associated with other forms of existence. More to the point, his last essay of any consequence, "The New South",[60] expresses his firm belief that "the quiet rise of the small farmer in the Southern states" had been "the notable circumstance of the period, in comparison with which the noisier events signify nothing". Lanier claimed to base this belief on contemporary evidence, in the form of "a mass of clippings" from Georgia newspapers. Significantly, however, as his biographer has noted, his essay seems to depend less on any knowledge of contemporary conditions than on his reading of earlier, English celebrants of the yeoman. One-third of it, in fact, draws on the sort of material with which the Virginia pamphleteers were familiar, such as the sermons of Bishop Latimer, describing the plight and potential of the "backbone of England." And just as significantly, the essay concludes, not with a programme for action, but with a gently nostalgic portrait of

Middle Georgia, the land where he was born, "It is a land", Lanier declared,

> where there is never a day of summer nor of winter when a man cannot do a full day's work in the open field; all the products meet there, as at nature's own agricultural fair; . . . within the compass of many a hundred-acre farm a man may find wherewithal to build his house . . ., to furnish it in woods that would delight the most curious eye, and to supply his family with all the necessaries, most of the comforts, and many of the luxuries of the whole world. It is the country of homes.[61]

It is a moving portrait, but it is moving precisely because of its use of a rich mine of personal memory and traditional ideas. For an essay whose avowed subject is the present and future, "The New South" seems remarkably backward-looking – preoccupied, to the point of obsessiveness, with the past.

"The New South", Lanier insisted, "means small farming"; and "small farming", he added, "means *diversified farm-products*". He could hardly have been more wrong: both in his failure to recognise that the real thrust of the New South was towards the growth of towns and factories, and in his unwillingness to recognise that Southern farmers were just as fatally and irretrievably enamoured of "coquette Cotton" as ever. In this, however, he was hardly alone. While writers such as Thomas Nelson Page and John Esten Cooke continued the regional infatuation with the gentlemanly image and the vocabulary of paternalism, there were others besides Lanier who drew on the populist model. For some, that model, like its patriarchal equivalent, was expressly associated with the good old days before the war. Richard Malcolm Johnston, for example, set his tales, reminiscent of Southwestern humour, in what he termed "the Grim and Rude, but Hearty Old Times in Georgia"; "it is a grateful solace", he admitted,

> to recall persons whose simplicity has been much changed by subsequent conditions, chiefly the Confederate War. Growth of inland towns and multiplication of outside acquaintance have served to diminish, or at least greatly modify, striking rustic individualities; and labour, become more exacting in its demands, has made life more difficult, and therefore, more earnest.[62]

Others, however, seemed to believe along with Lanier that the populist model defined the present and future rather than the past: that the New South could in fact be described in terms of the old pieties. As late as 1911, for example, an undeniably gifted and intelligent writer like Ellen Glasgow could say this about what she termed "the rise of the working man in the South":

> The land which had belonged to the few became after the war within the reach of many. At first the lower classes had held back, paralyzed by the burden of

slavery. The soil, impoverished, wasted, untilled, rested under the shadow of the old names – the old customs. This mole-like blindness of the poorer whites persisted still for a quarter of a century; and the awakening was possible only after the new generation had come to its growth.[63]

For all her attempts to appear temperate by putting things back a generation, Glasgow clearly belonged – at least, in the earlier part of her career as a novelist – with those who believed in the resurrection of the yeoman: who were convinced, in fact, that the old and supposedly feudal order could be replaced, perhaps had been replaced, by the "plain man . . . building the structure of the future".[64] That she and they were mistaken in their belief goes without saying: the New South belonged to quite different forces. That they believed it nevertheless suggests how powerfully encoded the South had become by this stage in its history: which was a decidedly mixed blessing for those who wanted to write about the region, its past, its problems, and its possibilities.

A SOUTHERN AUTOBIOGRAPHY: MARK TWAIN

Of all the writers born and raised in the South during the nineteenth century, Mark Twain was the only one to achieve greatness; and it was not until he came to write *The Adventures of Huckleberry Finn* that this greatness was clear. For it was not until then that he came to successful creative terms with the most significant part of his own life – and, by extension, with that region that helped mould his personality as a child and youth and haunted his dreams when he became a man. "My books are simply autobiographies",[65] Twain insisted once. True of every American writer, perhaps, the remark seems especially true of him: partly because he relied so much and so frankly on personal experience (as early works like *Innocents Abroad* and *Roughing It* amply testify) and partly because even those works by Twain that were the results of strenuous imaginative effort can be read as attempts to resolve his inner divisions and create some sense of continuity between his present and his past. The inner divisions and the discontinuity were, in fact, inseparable. For virtually all of Twain's best fictional work has to do with what Henry Nash Smith christened "the matter of Hannibal":[66] that is, the author's experiences as a child in a small town in the slave-owning state of Missouri and (even if only by extension and implication) his years as a steamboat pilot on the Mississippi. This was not simply a matter of nostalgia for the good old days before the war, of the kind that one finds in, say, the stories of Thomas Nelson Page or Richard Malcolm Johnston. Nor was it simply another example of the Romantic idealisation of youth: although Twain did firmly believe that, youth being "the only thing worth giving to the race", to look back on one's childhood was to give oneself "a cloudy sense of having been a prince, once, in some enchanted far off land, & of being in exile now, & desolate".[67] It was rather, and more simply, that Twain recognised intuitively that his years in the South had formed him for good and ill – organised his perceptions, shaped his vocabulary, and defined what he most loved and hated. So to explore those years was to explore the often equivocal nature of his own vision; to understand them was to begin at least to understand himself.

Not that Twain ever began drawing on the matter of Hannibal in a deliberate or self-conscious way: he was not that kind of writer. He frequently claimed, in fact, that he was only interested in writing a book if it would write itself for him. Like Poe's claim that he composed "The Raven" from back to front this was, of course, something of a lie, but it did nevertheless point to a deeper truth: that he wrote best when he allowed his imagination free rein, in a relatively impulsive and unpremeditated manner. As if by way of illustrating this, Twain's first significant venture into his Southern past started as a series of articles for *Atlantic Monthly*, undertaken – at least, according to his own account of it – at the suggestion of a friend. "Twichell and I have had a long walk in the woods", Twain wrote to William Dean Howells, the editor of *Atlantic Monthly*,

> & I got to telling him about old Mississippi days of steamboating glory & grandeur as I saw them (during 5 years) *from the pilot house*. He said "What a virgin subject to hurl into a magazine!"[68]

So Twain hurled his virgin subject into Howells's magazine: "Old Times on the Mississippi", as the essays were called, appeared in 1875, describing in colourful detail Twain's experiences as a steamboat pilot. They were well received, and Twain was reasonably pleased with them. Nevertheless, he turned to writing other things, among them *The Adventures of Tom Sawyer* and part of *Huckleberry Finn*, before using them as the basis for a book. In adding to the essays when he did come to write the book, Twain used his favourite motif of a journey, in this case one taken by himself up the Mississippi River from New Orleans to St Paul, in order to see how things had altered since his childhood and steamboating days. Further padding was provided by passages taken from the manuscript of *Huckleberry Finn*, material left over from *A Tramp Abroad*, and long passages quoted from travel books by other writers. Twain's attitude towards this rather cavalier method of composition was disarmingly frank. "I went to work at nine o'clock yesterday morning", he wrote to Howells during this period,

> and went to bed an hour after midnight. Result of the day, (mainly stolen from books, tho' credit given) 9,500 words. So I reduced my burden by one third in one day.[69]

Cobbled together in this fashion, *Life on the Mississippi* finally saw the light of day in 1883.

Given the way *Life on the Mississippi* was written – which was haphazard even by Twain's own standards – it is not surprising that the chapters originally prepared for *Atlantic Monthly* – that is, chapters IV–XVII – are easily the most deeply felt and compelling. Their fascination stems, at least in part, from the fact that they represent Twain's first serious attempt to map the geography of his spiritual home. The map that emerges, however, is a far from clear one. The famous description of what, in Twain's own opinion, he gained and lost by becoming a steamboat pilot illustrates this. In becoming a pilot, Twain explains, he learned to read "the face of the water" as though it were "a wonderful book" – a book, he adds, "that was a dead language to the uneducated passenger, but which told its mind to me without reserve". Twain's attitude towards books and literature in general remained painfully ambivalent throughout his life (Huck Finn, for example, like Sut Lovingood, invariably associates books with "study" and "Sunday school"); so it is hardly surprising to find that this painfully acquired mastery of the alphabet of the Mississippi River is not regarded as an unmixed blessing. "I had made a valuable acquisition", Twain admits:

> But I had lost something too, I had lost something which could never be restored to me while I lived. All the grace, the beauty, the poetry had gone out of the majestic river . . . All the value any feature of it had for me now was the amount of usefulness it could furnish toward compassing the safe piloting of a steamboat.[70]

In effect, Twain argues, an attitude founded on a kind of innocence and illiteracy was replaced once he became a pilot by a more knowledgeable, and in a sense more useful, but sadly disillusioned one.

Several points need to be made about this distinction. In the first place, as a distinction of fact it is not strictly true. As one critic has pointed out,[71] Twain did not lose the ability to appreciate the "grace" and "beauty" of the Mississippi and its surroundings – *Life on the Mississippi* is, after all, full of rather florid passages describing that grace and beauty: all he did lose was the belief that the simply aesthetic stance, and the vocabulary the aesthete deploys, could do justice to the empirical realities of the river. In the second place, as an imaginative distinction, a way of defining possible attitudes or structures of feeling, it is painfully inadequate. Twain presents his education as a process whereby one form of myopia, one drastically limited code or set of preconceptions, simply replaces another. The vision of the romantic dreamer, who sees the river in terms of an embarrassingly conventional landscape painting, is displaced by that of the gruff, commonsensical realist, who thinks of it as no more than a tool, something to be used and exploited. And finally, as a small piece of mythmaking, what Twain says here provides him with a frame for the entire book and a way of relating his own history to the history of his region. For in distinguishing between the South of his childhood and steamboating days and the South of his adult years – the South, in particular, that he had seen in his trip from New Orleans to St Paul – Twain falls back on the tired, and ultimately unsatisfactory contrast he establishes here between (to put it crudely) the romance of the past and the realism of the present.

This may make Twain sound like some of the plantation novelists of the post-war years, and make the distinction on which both this passage and the book as a whole depend sound like Sidney Lanier's elaborate comparisons between "culture" and "trade." In a way, this is true. *Life on the Mississippi* uses roughly the same codes, starts with broadly the same vocabularies as, say, *The Virginia Bohemians* and "Corn". There is a difference, however, and it is not simply that Twain, unlike John Esten Cooke or Lanier, chooses to suggest a connection between his own personal story and the history of his region. It is that, in addition, in suggesting this connection and in describing the contrast between the Old South and the New, Twain is – as anyone who notices the contrast in the first place will confirm – uncertain, his sympathies fiercely divided. There are, certainly, frequent criticisms of the "romantic juvenilities" of the Old South, and of poor Sir Walter Scott in particular, who is blamed for encouraging Southerners to fall in love with the "grotesque 'chivalry' doings" and "windy humbuggeries" of the past. There are constant and approving references, too, to "the genuine and wholesome civilization of the nineteenth century" and the way Twain's homeplace seems to have become an integral part of that civilization since the Civil War – "evidencing", we are told, "progress, energy, and prosperity". Yet, time and again, there is also a profound nostalgia, a sense of loss noticeable in Twain's descriptions of the world that is gone or the few, lingering traces of it that remain. Describing the changes that have occurred in the riverside towns since his own steamboating days, for instance, Twain ruefully admits, "a glory that once was [has] dissolved and vanished away".[72] And his actual descriptions of the old steamboats themselves, and the period when they reigned supreme on the Mississippi, convey an irrepressible joy, involvement, and affection – feelings that are conspicuously lacking whenever Twain turns his attention to the "quiet, orderly" river traffic and men of "sedate business aspect" associated with the needs and demands of a more "wholesome and practical" age. No attempt is made to resolve this contradiction: the glamour of the past is dismissed at one moment and then recalled with elegiac regret the next, the pragmatism and progress of the present is welcomed sometimes and at others coolly regretted. Even if such an attempt were made, however, it is difficult to see how it could be successful. For at this stage of his career, at least, Twain lacked the language to accommodate and reconcile his different attitudes to the past. All he could do, evidently, was take over the familiar vocabularies of his region, with their patriarchal dreams of the past and their populist hopes for the future, and their confused mixture of progressivism and nostalgia, utopianism and elegy; apply these vocabularies with far more enthusiasm, frankness, and energy than any of his contemporaries; and, in doing all this, offer his readers what can only be described as a verbal equivalent of double vision.

Similar, if not precisely the same, confusions of language and perception are to be found in *The Adventures of Tom Sawyer*, which was published in 1876. According to contemporary accounts, Twain began the book "with certain of his boyish recollections in mind"[73] and gradually wove together three quite separate strands: the "love story" of Tom and Becky Thatcher (which, among other things, parodies the rituals of adult courtship), the story of Tom and his brother Sid (which inverts the many Sunday school stories popular at the time about the Bad Boy who ends up in trouble and the Good Boy whose maturity is crowned with success), and the melodramatic tale of Injun Joe (which illustrates Twain's love of popular literature, the "dime novel" and the "court-room drama"). From the beginning, however, Twain seems to have been doubtful about the exact nature and age of his audience. Would it appeal primarily to children or to adults? Quite simply, he was not sure, although he did try to assume an appearance of certainty when the book was completed. "It is *not* a boy's book at all", he insisted in a letter to Howells. "It will only be read by adults. It is only written for adults." Howells was not convinced. "Treat it explicitly *as* a boy's story", he insisted; Twain's wife, Livy, agreed; and so, in the Preface to *Tom Sawyer*, the author hedges his bets. The book, he declares, "is intended mainly for the entertainment of boys and girls". Nevertheless, he goes on:

> I hope it will not be shunned by men and women on that account, for part of
> my plan has been to try pleasantly to remind adults of what they once were
> . . .[74]

The uncertainty of purpose and perspective implicit in these opening remarks is uncomfortably obvious when we turn to the story. Certain elements of *Tom Sawyer* certainly do seem to identify it with the best kind of children's literature, in that they involve the dramatisation of common childhood fantasies or the cathartic exploration of childhood nightmares. Tom Sawyer himself, for example, discovers hidden treasure. He becomes "a glittering hero . . . – the pet of the old, the envy of the young", when he identifies Dr Robinson's murderer. And he enjoys the delicious pleasure of feeling wronged, apparently dying, and then returning in secret to hear penitent adults lament their treatment of him and admit that "he wasn't *bad*, so to say – only mischeevous".[75] Injun Joe really belongs to this area of the book, too, in that he is not so much a fictional character as a bogey-man, designed to give protagonist and reader alike an almost voyeuristic thrill of terror: it is noticeable, for instance, that he is nearly always seen from a hidden point of vantage, so that the threat he offers is framed and contained. But while all this serves to confirm the opening claim in the Preface, certain other aspects of the story seem to assume a more adult and sophisticated audience, looking back on the past – their own past, the author's past, and the past of the South – from a distanced, sometimes amused and sometimes regretful, standpoint. The parodic element in Tom and Becky's courtship, for example, presupposes an adult audience that can appreciate the nature of the parody. This is also true of the inversion of popular sentiment and genteel literary convention implicit in the contrast between Tom and Sid. Quite apart from that, there is the simple fact that Twain as a narrator tends to maintain a distance, a lot of the time, between himself and the reader, on the one hand, and, on the other, Tom Sawyer, Huck Finn, their friends and enemies, and the unsophisticated folk of St Petersburg.

This last point is the important one. At times, as when for instance Twain is describing Tom and Huck's adventures on Jackson's Island, the language has the kind of immediacy that one associates with, say, *Sut Lovingood's Yarns*: an immediacy that presupposes and implies that the world of St Petersburg is available to us – because we are children, perhaps, or because simplicity, although it may be lost, is not irrecoverable. But for the most part it manages to create a sense of distance between character and reader because the narrator is clearly a person of some sophistication, maturity, and refinement, who is trying to make us aware of this through his vocabulary. In *Tom Sawyer*, people do not spit, they "expectorate"; they do not wear clothes, but "accoutrements"; breezes are "zephyrs", and buildings are "edifices". There is a measure of self-directed irony contained in such genteel diction, of course, but the irony acts as no more than a qualification. Twain may be slightly embarrassed and uncomfortable about the contrast between simple characters and sophisticated narrator (and to this extent shows himself to be a far more sensitive writer than Longstreet, say, and some of the other Southwestern humorists); the contrast remains, however, and is even insisted upon. We are constantly being reminded, in fact, that he and we are no longer a part of the "kingdom" of the child or, for that matter, of a small, "simple-hearted" rural community. Along with explicit statements to that effect, this message comes to us via the narrator's constant tendency to step back from the action to elicit a moral of some sort, and his placing of all the characters on a stage, as it were, with a "curtain of charity" and footlights between them and us. It comes, also, but with rather different implications, via a passage like the following (which acts as an introductory sketch to the second chapter):

> Saturday morning was come, and all the summer world was bright and fresh, and brimming with life. There was a song in every heart; and if the heart was young, the music issued at the lips. There was cheer in every face, and a spring in every step . . . Cardiff Hill, beyond the village and above it, was green with vegetation, and it lay just far enough away to seem a Delectable Land, dreamy, resposeful, and inviting.[76]

"Just far enough away to seem a Delectable Land": the reader is reminded, perhaps (if he has read them) of Richard Malcolm Johnston's tributes to the simplicity of earlier times and Sidney Lanier's fond recollections of "the country of homes" – or, for that matter, of some of the stories of Thomas Nelson Page or Joel Chandler Harris, with their hushed invocations of "a smiling land" situated somewhere in the vague territories of memory. St Petersburg may on the whole be closer to the populist model than the patriarchal: "simplicity" may be its dominant feature rather than gentility. Just the same, the traces of elegiac affection that seep into Twain's accounts of it here belong exclusively neither to post-war reminiscences of the plain farmer in the Old South nor to their equivalents in the plantation romance. They were part of the idiom of the times, part of the South's structure of feeling at that moment in its history. And they are there unmistakably in Twain's second imaginative venture into his region and its past, tempering and often even directly contradicting his gestures of condescension and mockery.

All of which is by way of saying that, in *Tom Sawyer*, the confusions of *Life on the Mississippi* are even worse confounded. There is immediacy and there is distance; there is the stuff of childhood fantasies and the staple of adult discourse; there is the tendency to be ironic and patronising and there is the impulse towards elegy. There is also, as it happens, a desperate attempt on Twain's part to impose some kind of coherence on his material, to create concord out of all this discord: an attempt which perhaps owes more to his own personal history at the time of composition than it does to the actual exigencies of the narrative. For it may not be entirely irrelevant that Twain's earliest reminiscences about his boyhood, which provided the beginnings of *Tom Sawyer*, coincided with the first year of his marriage to Livy. Whatever else may be said about their relationship, it seems fairly clear now that he used his wife as a civilising agent, the embodiment of his conscience, the more respectable side of himself. "You will break up all my irregularities when we are married", he wrote to her shortly before the wedding, "and *civilize* me, and make of me a model husband and an adornment to society – won't you . . .?"[77] Quite apart from offering a parody of his own courtship, therefore, the story of Tom Sawyer and his friends seems to have acted as a kind of safety-valve, a way of releasing rebellious feelings and indulging in evidently unrealisable dreams of freedom before committing himself to orthodoxy, respectability, and success. The three narrative strands of the book tend to reflect this cathartic process: for the pattern Twain tries to give to each of them is the pattern of rebellion followed by conformity, abandonment and adventure leading eventually to a sober acceptance of duty. As far as the love story goes, Tom finally assumes the conventional male protective role with Becky, by accepting a punishment which should by rights have been hers. As far as the contrast between Tom and Sid is concerned, Tom, it gradually emerges, is the *really* good boy – any of his more dangerously subversive appetites having apparently been satisfied by the time out on Jackson's Island. And as for the tale of Injun Joe: Tom, it emerges, is not an outlaw at all but the very embodiment of social justice. Like his creator Tom ends up, in fact, by accepting the disciplines of the social norm. Injun Joe, who seemed for a moment to be a projection of Tom's darker self, is killed; the integrity and sanctity of the community is confirmed; and Tom is even ready, it seems, to offer brief lectures on the advantages of respectability. Here again, as in his account of his education as a steamboat pilot and the contrast between Old South and New, Twain tries, really, to solve problems by imposing on his material the notions of personal development and social betterment – in a word, the myth of progress. And here again he is unsuccessful: *Tom Sawyer*, in fact, like *Life on the Mississippi*, is interesting precisely because of its discontinuity – to the extent, that is, that it reveals its author's inner divisions and (something not totally unrelated) the contradictions inherent in the New South's image of itself.

Only one character stands outside this pattern of rebellion, release, and moral improvement; and that, of course, is Huckleberry Finn. When Huck first appears in the book, he is seen from the outside, and almost with disapproval. Gradually, however, he is given his own voice, allowed to speak for himself and his own, profoundly anti-social values: so that, by the end, he is even beginning to hold his own in debate with the newly respectable Tom. The ground is prepared, in effect, for *The Adventures of Huckleberry Finn* (1885), Twain's greatest work, in which he moved even more fully back into the past – not merely remembering steamboat days or even childhood now, but speaking in and from the person of a child. The full significance of this movement seems to have been lost on Twain at first; for when he began *Huckleberry Finn* in 1876 it is fairly clear that he saw it simply as a sequel to *Tom Sawyer*. Several narrative threads are carried over, and in the opening pages at least, although Huck is now permitted to be the narrator, much of the comedy is as uncomplicated as it was in the earlier book. It took nearly a year, in fact, for Twain to realise that things were heading in a direction other than the one he had originally intended – and that, in particular, Huck and Jim, under the pressure of their relationship and the problem of Jim's slavery, were growing into complicated and even difficult characters, requiring more than just a series of set comic routines. When he did realise it, his response was characteristic: he put the manuscript aside, leaving Huck and Jim on a suitably apocalyptic note with their raft smashed up by a riverboat, and turned to writing other things.

Critics are divided as to exactly how long it was before Twain returned to the Huck Finn manuscript.[78] One thing is certain, however: when he did, his entire attitude to the project had changed. As nearly everyone who now reads *Huckleberry Finn* is aware, he decided – instinctively, of course, rather than with all due deliberation – to embark on a more serious kind of comedy, which would explore the conflict between (to use his own later description) "a sound heart and a deformed conscience".[79] As not everyone seems to realise, however, Twain somehow understood that the best and, perhaps, the only way in which he could dramatise this conflict was by using his Southern background, the years on or near the Mississippi, and the rich treasury of idioms and perceptions that background had given him. In *Huckleberry Finn*, and especially in the chapters written after Twain had returned to the manuscript, we are confronted with two radically different ways of looking at the world, two utterly opposed structures of thought and feeling; and Twain seems to have recognised that he could project both those visions, give flesh and blood to the two structures, without straying very far from his own regional past.

As far as Twain's portrait of society, the particular system that has deformed Huck's conscience, is concerned, Twain seems to have been helped by his reading. In between writing the first and second parts of the manuscript, Twain had been involved in the preparation of a collection of comic tales and sketches: which had required him, among other things, to reread the work of the Southwestern humorists. As several commentators have pointed out, this almost certainly encouraged Twain in his formulation of a new plan for the Huck Finn story; it could be, he saw, a series of comic scenes from old Southern provincial life along the lines of *Georgia Scenes* and *Sut Lovingood's Yarns*.[80] Not that Twain had been unaware of writers like Longstreet and Harris before this, or indeed of the possibilities of comic portraiture: Pap Finn, for instance, who dominates some of the earlier episodes of the story, is in many ways like a figure out of Southwestern humour. In his rapacity and cunning he

recalls, perhaps, Simon Suggs, in his violence and earthiness Sut
Lovingood, while his sheer garrulousness, his verbal energy and love of
hyperbole, echo any number of tall tale-tellers, backwoods boasters, and
front-porch philosophers in the stories of Longstreet and his kind. "Call
this a govment!" declares Pap Finn during the course of one of his many
orations:

> "Oh, yes, this is a wonderful govment, wonderful. Why, looky here. There
> was a free nigger . . . from Ohio; a mulatter . . . He had the whitest shirt on
> you ever see . . ., and the shiniest hat; and there ain't a man in the town that's
> got as fine clothes, as what he had; and he had a gold watch and chain, and a
> silver-headed cane – the awfullest old grey-headed nabob in the State. And
> what do you think? they said he was a p'fessor in a college . . . and knowed
> everything. And that ain't the *wust*. They said he could *vote*, when he was at
> home. Well, that let me out. Thinks I, what is the country a-coming to? . . . I
> says I'll never vote agin . . ."[81]

And yet this brief passage already begins to indicate, perhaps, the
difference of achievement between Twain and his Southwestern
predecessors: because it is at once more sharply satirical and more
comically exuberant than anything we are likely to come across in earlier
humour, more savage and dispassionate and at the same time more
intimate. Pap Finn is a classic, comic portrait of the poor white, that is
clear enough: in his fear of the unknown, his habitual drunkenness
followed by equally habitual bouts of repentance, his inverted Calvinism, his violence, and his bigotry.[82] But for all the venom with which he
is drawn, there is no denying the delight his creator takes in him: for
instance, in his comically revealing juxtapositions of thought and speech
("he . . . knowed everything. And that ain't the *wust*"), his absurdly
exaggerated notion of his own importance ("I'll never vote agin"), as
well as the sheer, abandoned exhilaration, the helter-skelter quality of his
rhetoric. Pap Finn, in short, is a character created out of love as well as
hatred, or at least out of joyful fascination as well as disgust and despair. It
is from this that his colour and power derives, and it is upon this that his
credibility depends; for Twain, the reader feels, really *knows* this man, as
if he were a loved and loathed member of his own family.

Quite apart from this difference of quality as far as the creation and
analysis of particular characters are concerned, Twain also goes beyond
his humorist predecessors in two other respects: in the sheer range of his
vision and the coherence and clarity of his perspective. None of the old
Southwestern humorists had ever attempted a portrait of Southern life
anywhere near as rich and detailed as the one that gradually emerges in
Huckleberry Finn – or, for that matter, established a critical vocabulary, a
way of arranging and viewing his imagined world, that even begins to
approach Twain's in the clarity of its focus or the incisiveness of its

judgements. The inclusiveness of Twain's vision of the Old South is perhaps the first thing that strikes any reader. In the course of the book, we are offered an account of every level of ante-bellum society: from planters with aristocratic pretensions, like the Grangerfords, through plain farmers like the Phelps family who own a little land and, at the most, only two or three slaves, to the poor whites of Bricksville and, below even them, the blacks.[83] With each additional detail, too, we understand more about the system that seeks to control Huck's mind and Jim's body: that tries to contain reality by controlling every possible form of language, thought, and behaviour – in short, by imposing its own, patently inadequate version of things. In this sense, the "style" that Huck innocently admires when he observes it in, for example, the Grangerfords infects every aspect of life: it dictates the words people use, the clothes they wear, the opinions they form. It is the essence of Twain's criticism, in fact, that the patterns ordained by this – or, indeed, by any – culture are at once intricate, interconnected, and inclusive: the Granger-fords are controlled by the same inexorable laws whether they are making a fine speech, writing sentimental poems, killing their enemies in the name of "the feud", or enslaving their fellow human beings. Florid words, fine clothes, and the exploitation of others all issue, Twain insists, from the same false consciousness: a consciousness which manages to be at once sentimental and crudely opportunistic – justifying its economic base, and the major historical crime on which that base was built, in terms of an absurdly romantic myth of gentility.

The contrast between this portrait of the Old South and the possibilities offered by Huck Finn is commonly explained in terms of illusion versus reality.[84] This is a seductive explanation, not least because Twain almost certainly thought of it in these terms himself: but it is hardly a satisfactory one. Whatever else it may be, the portrait of Huck and Jim's Adamic life on the river can hardly be squared with even the most capacious definitions of realism; and to call Huck's response to life "realistic" is to ignore the very problems about the nature of the relationship between experience and perception, life and language, with which Twain himself was to become increasingly obsessed.[85] There is, of course, a conflict between Huck and Jim on the one hand and most of the other characters on the other: but it is a conflict not between illusion and reality, fiction and fact, or whatever – but, quite simply, between two different systems of language and thought. The false system, the system that Twain attacks, grows out of the darker side of both the patriarchal and the populist myths. It offers a world in which Colonel Grangerford and Pap Finn are equally at home: where, one might say, Colonel Carter of Cartersville and Simon Suggs could meet and shake hands. Its patterns of language range from the high-flown to the demotic but are all alike in their radical exclusions and inconsistencies, the degree to which the words people use do not even begin to relate to things. And its patterns of thought can accommodate both cavalier pretensions and what W. J. Cash called "the helluva fellow" complex, the false consciousness of the planter pretending to be a feudal overlord and the equally false consciousness of the poor white who plays the role of vigorous, self-reliant yeoman. In many ways, it is a system that recalls the false opposites on which a book like *Life on the Mississippi* is founded; since it involves a paradoxical mixture of the genteel and the utilitarian, romantic dreams and crudely opportunistic motives. And this in itself is a measure of Twain's achievement in his third major journey into his Southern past. For, in effect, he has resolved the contradictions of his earlier work by the simple expedient of making those contradictions his subject rather than his premise: by subjecting them to creative analysis, that is, instead of allowing them to dictate his perceptions or provide a conceptual framework for his book.

But Twain's use of the Southern myths is not simply negative: for the true system — the system that he sets against all this and which finds its embodiment and apotheosis in the book's hero — is quite as much indebted to his creative use of his regional inheritance. In nearly every respect, Huck Finn brings together and synthesises the warring opposites of Twain's earlier work. Huck is a focus for all his creator's nostalgia, all his yearnings for childhood, the lost days of his youth, the days before the Civil War and the Fall;[86] and he is also, quite clearly, a projection of Twain's more progressive feelings, the belief in human development and perfectibility – he suggests hope for the future as well as love of the past. Among other things, this is indicated by Huck's language, in that it is precisely Huck's "progressive" attention to the use and function of things that gives his observations such colour and immediacy. His words do not deny the beauty of things on the Mississippi River – beauty that Twain claimed had vanished for ever for him when he became a steamboat pilot – but neither do they deny that things are there for a purpose. On the contrary, they acknowledge that each particular in the river scene has a reason for being there and a message to communicate, and they derive their grace and force from that acknowledgement. In a passage like the following, for example, it is no more and no less than Huck's ability to read the face of the water that enables him to pay homage to its fluent shapes and lively configurations. He is at once an interpreter and a celebrant, someone for whom the signs at dawn on the Mississippi are there both to decipher and to appreciate:

> The first thing to see, looking away over the water, was a kind of dull line – that was the woods on t'other side – you couldn't make nothing else out; then a pale place in the sky; then more paleness, spreading around; then the river softened

> up, away off, and wasn't black any more, but grey; you could see little dark
> spots drifting along, ever so far away – trading scows and such things; and long
> black streaks – rafts . . . and by and by you could see a streak on the water
> which you know by the look of the streak that there's a snag there in a swift
> current which breaks on it and makes the streak look that way; and you see the
> mist curl up off the water, and the east reddens up . . .[87]

This is neither the language of the "realist" in *Life on the Mississippi* nor
that of the "romantic", but another form of speech entirely which
accommodates both of those languages and then raises them to a higher
power. In the process, it reconciles the demands of the pragmatist with
those of the dreamer, the progressive impulse with its nostalgic
equivalent – and manages to treat the alphabet of the river as a medium of
communication and as an object with its own peculiar beauty.

"Where the philosopher seeks certitude in the sign", wrote Burck-
hardt,

> – the p of the propositional calculus – and the mystic in the ineffable – the
> "OM" of the Hindoos – the poet takes upon himself the paradox of the human
> word, which is both and neither and which he creatively transforms in his
> "powerful rhyme".[88]

In this respect, Huck Finn truly is – as he has often been called – a poet of
the river; because for him the language of the Mississippi is clearly at once
referential and substantial, a means and an end, something with a precise,
paraphrasable meaning and something with its own intrinsic symmetry
and grace. And, not unrelated to this, Huck is at one and the same time a
figure of utter simplicity of the kind that Jefferson and, before him, the
Virginia pamphleteers often celebrated – and someone with all the innate
nobility of Simms's plantation heroes, say, or the popular Southern
image of Robert E. Lee. In short, he is a populist hero with all the best
patriarchal qualities. For he is easily the most honourable and, indeed, the
most chivalric character in his world simply because he sticks far closer
than anyone else to his own, independent version of things; he is self-
reliant, like all good yeomen, and this self-reliance enables him to behave
with what Chaucer would call "Trouthe and honour, fredom and
curteisie"[89] in all his dealings with others. A résumé of his character reads
in some ways like a denial of all those distinctions on which much of
Twain's earlier work rested, and much of the Southern argument as well.
He is courteous, it seems, without being unctuous, noble without
appearing priggish, chivalrous without ever becoming sentimental. He is
plain and he is gracious; he is straightforward and he is mannerly; he is at
once a frontier hero and a "parfit gentil knyght". In fact, if Pap Finn and
Colonel Grangerford between them suggest the dark side of the populist
and patriarchal models then Huck Finn enables us to see its bright
opposite. And if most of the characters in the book demonstrate Twain's

powerful capacity for analysis, for dissecting the Southern myths and exposing their faults and weaknesses, then its hero reveals something more heartening: which is to say, Twain's equally powerful capacity for celebration – the way he can unravel the best possibilities of those myths and out of them formulate a legend of his own, a coherent vocabulary and a positive vision of things.

Which is not, unfortunately, to say that even *The Adventures of Huckleberry Finn* is perfect: as many commentators have observed, the last few chapters of the book do represent a decline of some sort – or to use Hemingway's more dismissive phrase, "just cheating"[90] – in the sense that Huck is pushed to one side of the action, Tom Sawyer is permitted to play his familiar games, and the issue of Jim's slavery is reduced to the level of farce. For all Huck's occasional protests at Tom's behaviour, or his famous final cry of defiance, the comedy loses its edge, the moral problems are minimised, and the familiar divisions and contradictions in Twain's writing begin to reappear. There are many possible reasons for this, but one that should not be overlooked is that Twain was perhaps beginning to have doubts about the effectiveness and viability of his hero. "I have always preached", Twain declared once:

> If the humour came of its own accord and uninvited I have allowed it a place in my sermon, but I was not writing the sermon for the sake of the humour.[91]

This, while not strictly speaking true, does point to a powerful impulse in his writing, which led him quite often to search for remedies for the ills he diagnosed, to offer his readers guidance, or to find models of belief and behaviour which he felt were relevant to his times. And it might well have been this, among other things, that prompted him to turn away from the figure of Huck Finn towards a rather different kind of hero: Hank Morgan, the narrator and protagonist of *A Connecticut Yankee in King Arthur's Court*. Like Huck, Hank is a vernacular hero with a strong commitment to his own, independent version of things. Unlike him, however, he is a down-to-earth, self-made man; he is very much a part of the new urban-industrial world that Twain saw growing up all around him; and he has a programmatic, reforming side to his character. In devising Hank, in short, Twain seems to have been trying to meet a criticism of Huck that someone with a more didactic approach to literature might have offered – someone like himself at times, in fact – the criticism that, for all his virtues, Huck was too much of a loner and a mythic figure to provide an imitable model, and too much a part of a vanishing agrarian world to offer hope to those trapped in the New South.

The basic plot device in *Connecticut Yankee* is simple and well-known. Hank Morgan, "a Yankee of Yankees" and an accomplished engineer, finds himself carried back into the world of King Arthur, where his knowledge of technology enables him to gain power and import "the civilization of the nineteenth century".[92] The stage is set by this device for a contrast between sound sense, liberal principles, and progress on the one hand and on the other the nonsense, barbarism, and romanticism of a society corrupted by its false consciousness, its patently inadequate version of things. What seems to have been intended, in fact, was a revised, updated version of the contrast between Huck Finn and the Old South, with sixth-century England acting as the Old South's *doppelgänger* (the gentlemen are now knights, the poor whites peasants, the slaves serfs, and so on). As so often happened with Twain, however, intention and achievement turned out to be two quite different things. Arthurian England certainly emerges as a shadowy version of Twain's childhood homeplace, and Hank certainly assumes the mantle of progressive hero. The book in which they meet and conflict, however, is not so much a development of *Huckleberry Finn* as a revised version of *Life on the Mississippi*. For in attempting to make his hero more 'relevant', Twain divorced him completely from that world of the past, the world of potent regional myths, that held such sway over his imagination. The power of the character of Huck Finn, it is perhaps worth repeating, issues directly from the fact that Huck is at once a progressive and a regressive figure for his creator; both an expression of his belief in populism and perfectibility and a gathering-point for all his deepest feelings about childhood and about the conflicting legends of the place where he was born. And in the absence of this synthesising figure the familiar divisions reappear, the old 'either-or' distinctions: between past and future, romance and realism, the patriarchal and the populist.

This is as much as to say that Twain is as ambivalent about the Arthurian kingdom as he had been in his earlier books about the kingdom of Tom Sawyer or that Mississippi River on which the riverboat pilot had reigned once as "absolute monarch". The "lost land" to which Hank Morgan finds himself returned is – it is perhaps worth repeating – a thinly disguised version of Twain's own "lost land"[93] of childhood and regional memory, and as such it exercises a profound pull on the author's imagination and, eventually, on the narrator's and reader's as well. Certainly, there is plenty of criticism of the backwardness, cruelty, and romantic silliness of early medieval England, just as there had been in *Life on the Mississippi* of the Old South and its legacy; and occasionally the parallels as well as the criticism are made quite explicit – as when, for example, Hank compares the false consciousness of the peasants (who, it seems, are ready to turn "their . . . hands against their own class in the interest of the common oppressor") to that of the poor whites in the Civil War (who, we are told, fought "to prevent the destruction of that very institution that degraded them").[94] The name of poor Sir Walter Scott is even dragged in once again as a means of belabouring romanticism in general. But these deliberate criticisms and conscious parallels are more than countered by those moments in the book when author and narrator alike appear to be thoroughly seduced, their imaginations captured by a world where – to borrow a phrase quoted earlier – they have had the cloudy sense of being a prince. Even in the first chapter, as Hank moves "as one in a dream" into the world of Camelot, there is an unmistakable sense of moving back into the author's past: there is the same mixture of poverty and glamour as we find in the portraits of the riverboat towns in *Life on the Mississippi*, the same "soft, reposeful, summer landscape, as lovely as a dream and as lonesome as Sunday".[95] And later passages serve merely to strengthen this tendency, to underline this suggestion; the haunting passage at the beginning of the twelfth chapter, for instance, which describes Hank and his aide setting off on a journey, moving "like spirits", dreaming alone "through glades in a mist of green light",[96] finds its echo in Twain's descriptions of the countryside surrounding the Quarles plantation where, as a boy, he spent long, idyllic summers.

If Hank's kingdom is seen at once as barbaric and romantic, a closed society and a vanished virgin land, it is not surprising that uncertainty and ambivalence come to characterise Hank himself. This ambivalence takes two forms really. When, as in for example many of the earlier chapters, Twain is distanced from Hank and can see him objectively, as a spokesman for reform, a progressive hero, then Hank is sometimes celebrated, praised for his technological innovations and his liberal politics, and sometimes regarded with profound distrust – for he is, after all, introducing irreversible historical change, guaranteeing that the lost land will be for ever lost. But when, as in the closing chapters, Twain begins to identify with Hank and his experiences and use him as a mouthpiece, then, in such cases, Hank tends to become as full of pessimism, doubt and self-contradiction as his creator – pessimism as to the possibility of progress, doubt as regards the value of what he is doing, and self-contradiction when it comes to describing the lost world of Camelot. The book is so rife in its inconsistencies, in fact, and in particular so contradictory in its attitudes towards agrarianism and industrialism, feudalism and populism, past, present, and future, that it reads sometimes as if it were a work of collaboration – written jointly, perhaps, by John Esten Cooke, Henry W. Grady, and Sidney Lanier. By its end, Hank Morgan has been returned to the nineteenth century; he is in exile with, as he puts it, "an abyss of thirteen centuries between me and my home and my friends".[97] And as he lies dying, dreaming that he has returned to his lost land, trying to pretend that it is the strange new world of technology and progress that is the dream, he offers a poignant reflection of the author's own predicament – caught once again between present and past.

After *A Connecticut Yankee*, Twain made several more attempts to deal with his experience of the South,[98] but only one of these attempts ranks as a notable achievement. This is *The Tragedy of Pudd'nhead Wilson*, which explores the themes that obsessed Twain by means of a story of exchanged identities: a black slave woman substitutes her master's son for her own, while the two are still in the cradle. The woman herself, Roxana, has only a small amount of Negro blood, and is to all appearances white. She, and her son, are only black by convention, a socially accepted fiction, just as her fellow slaves are only slaves, and inferior, according to a fiction; and in effect, Twain suggests, she is merely replacing one fiction for another when she makes the exchange. Her own son, now known as Tom Driscoll, consequently grows up to become a member of the privileged class, wearing the clothes and playing the role of gentleman; while his secret "twin", the real Tom Driscoll, grows up to become a "nigger", with the language and characteristics which were thought by apologists for slavery – and perhaps still are thought by some racists – to be the prerogatives or rather the disabilities of a particular race. "Training is everything",[99] we are told at one point in the book; and this process whereby a 'black' man is turned into a 'white' man, and a 'white' man is turned into a 'black' man, would certainly seem to bear this assertion out. From a bare summary of the plot, it might also be inferred that in *Pudd'nhead Wilson* Twain recovered the moral pungency and imaginative confidence of *Huckleberry Finn*, with Roxana assuming the function that had been assumed in the earlier book by Huck. After all, it could be argued, she too challenges the style, the inadequate and debilitating codes of the society in which she finds herself; more specifically, she does this just as Huck does, by helping a particular person escape from the horror of slavery.

As so often in Twain's work, however, there is something of a gap between intention and accomplishment: between what seems to be the case – and what the author may well have been aiming for – and what, in fact, *is*, in terms of the readings made available by the text. The small town in which Roxana lives, for example, called Dawson's Landing, is perceived with quite as much ambivalence as King Arthur's Camelot. It is a slave-owning community, Twain admits; its inhabitants are, in many ways, unattractive, particularly when they act as a mob; and its leading citizens are, in their own way, as deluded, romantic, and theatrical as the Grangerfords. But there is no escaping the idyllic nature of the opening description of the town, with its "snug little collection" of houses manifesting, we are told, "contentment and peace", or the way in which Twain's criticisms are continually blunted by a sense of nostalgic yearning. One eminent critic of the book, F. R. Leavis, has gone so far as to claim that the author "unmistakably admires" the town's leading citizens and sees the town itself as an example of "an expanding and ripening civilization".[100] This seems to me to be a misreading: but it does help to indicate the muted nature of Twain's approach here – the extent to which, that is, the irony or satire can soften into affection and the moral perspective is consequently blurred.

Quite apart from this problem of Twain's approach to Dawson's Landing and its more privileged inhabitants, there are the further confusions created by his treatment of Roxana and her child and by his choice of narrative point of view. Unlike Huck, Roxana does not tell her own story: she is presented from the outside by a third-person narrator who seems to possess much of the gentility of the narrator of *Tom Sawyer* and some of the ironic pessimism of the character who gives the book its title. And the terms in which she is presented to us seem precisely calculated to appeal to the prejudices that Twain elsewhere attacks. "Only one sixteenth of her was black," we are informed,

> and that sixteenth did not show. She was majestic of form and stature, her attitudes were imposing and statuesque, and her gestures and movements distinguished by a noble and stately grace.[101]

More important, perhaps, Roxana herself seems to share many of those prejudices. When she exchanges the babies, for instance, she defends it to herself by claiming that it is not an act of rebellion but part of the Calvinist scheme of things; and when her son Tom turns out to be vicious and a coward she rebukes him by reminding him that one of his ancestors was "Ole Cap'n John Smith, de highest blood dat ole Virginny ever turned out" – and by insisting that "it's de nigger" in him that has made him that way. "Thirty-one parts o' you is white", she declares, "en only one part nigger, en dat po' little one part is you' *soul*."[102] In fact, if Roxana is like Huck Finn in some ways, in others she is more like those humble darkies in plantation romance who derive a somewhat pathetic pleasure from their tenuous connections with what they term "de bes' of quality, de ve'y top de pot". It would be pleasant to think that Twain's purpose was satirical here, but the sheer power with which Roxana expresses herself suggests otherwise; and, in any case, satire is something that is conspicuously lacking from the author's general presentation of her.

And then there is Tom Driscoll: in a sense, he exposes the inner divisions of the book more clearly than any other character. The "degenerate remnant of an honourable line" Pudd'nhead Wilson (the nearest thing we have to a spokesman for the author) calls him long before he knows about the exchange, and in a profoundly unnerving way this is true. All the other 'aristocrats' in Dawson's Landing are merely silly, whereas Tom is *evil*: he steals, he sells his mother down the river, and he kills his adoptive father. So, in a sinister way, the hidden message of the book seems to be, not 'white and black are alike', but 'never give someone ideas above his station'. Which is not to say that Twain ever intended this message – merely that he is caught, by this time, in the trap of his own inner divisions and determinism. "Training is everything", and if blacks have been trained as a race to be inferior then, according to Twain's own philosophy of the prison-house, they are to all intents and purposes just that. There is no escape; the fate assigned to Roxana's son at birth is finally his at the end of the narrative when he is sold as a slave down the river. The belief in a figure like Huck, who can weave past, present, and future together in one significant pattern is replaced by an inexorable series of opposites, a set of inner divisions as painful as they are inescapable – and, more simply and sadly, by the feeling expressed in the epigraph to the Conclusion: "It was wonderful to find America, but it would have been more wonderful to miss it."[103]

"The most desouthernized Southerner I ever knew":[104] that was how William Dean Howells described Mark Twain, and one can see why. Twain, after all, spent most of his adult life outside of the South; he rarely referred to himself as a Southerner in his later years: and he was inclined to be sceptical (to say the least) about such evidently acid tests of regional loyalty as the myth of the noble Lost Cause. But this was by no means the whole of Twain; nor even, as far as his work was concerned, the most important part. Whatever he may have claimed, however he may have appeared to friends like Howells, and whoever he may have believed himself to be, his fictions betray the essential truth: that his commitment to his childhood and youth – and to the material and moral landscapes in which they were spent – came very near to being total. He was obsessed with his past, the years in the South, and it was those years that supplied him with an imaginative vocabulary: which is to say, a compelling subject, an appropriate system of ideas, and a possible means of locating his own life and interpreting the world about him. Admittedly, Twain only mastered this vocabulary once: in *Huckleberry Finn*, where the different idioms available to him – the populist code and the patriarchal, with their often confused and conflicting versions of the past, present, and future – were translated into an adequate language, a coherent, convincing, and in the main consummately satisfying reinvention and reading of things. To do this even once, however, was an achievement close to the miraculous, given the sheer abundance, the diversity of words, moods, and modes he had to deal with. And, whatever else may be said about them, Twain's other books are almost as seductive in their inconsistencies as they are in their occasional moments of synthesis. For, as their narratives twist and turn, catapulting back upon themselves and multiplying contradictions, they offer the reader not only an insight into the multitudinous vision of their creator but a kind of dictionary of the regional argument – the most inclusive statement available of what it meant to be from the South in the later nineteenth century. "In my end is my beginning", wrote another Missourian, T. S. Eliot, who was almost as fascinated as Twain was by the "strong, brown god"[105] of the Mississippi. Twain proved Eliot's point by continually going back to his own beginnings and trying to rewrite them, rediscover their meaning; and he proved it, too, by showing how very much his mind had been shaped by the alphabet, the habits of language and perception, he had learned when he was young. Far from being a "desouthernized Southerner", Twain was in fact a writer possessed by his Southernness, locked into a relationship with a place he simultaneously loved and despised. His best work is engraved with the imagery of the region, coloured by its dream of princely splendour and exile, and fired into life by its potent mixture of utopianism and elegy, millennial hopes, nightmare fears, and pastoral reverie; he tells tales that are haunted by dreams of home, the Southern vision of things, and he tells them with a regional accent, an unmistakably Southern voice.

4

A climate of fear: the South between the wars and the Nashville Agrarians

"The older I get", wrote Allen Tate to John Peale Bishop in 1931,

> the more I realize that I set out about ten years ago to live a life of failure, to imitate, in my own life, the history of my people . . . We all have an instinct – if we are artists particularly – to live at the center of some way of life and to be borne up by its innermost significance. The significance of the Southern way of life, in my time, is failure: those Southerners who leave their culture – and it is abandoned most fully by those who stay at home – and succeed in some not too critical meaning of success, sacrifice some great part of their deepest heritage. What else is there for me but a complete acceptance of the idea of failure?[1]

This may sound a little like Romantic posturing, something to which Tate was not averse; after all, he was perceptive and honest enough to recognise his spiritual kinship with a figure like Poe, and with any number of other writers since the Romantic revolution who have felt themselves born out of their due time – at odds with what Tate, in another letter to Bishop, called "the middle-class capitalist hegemony". Tate's pursuit of failure could, in this sense, be interpreted as a necessary consequence of his embracing of the aristocratic, reactionary position: to be equated with, say, Byron's calculated flouting of bourgeois standards, Poe's perversity and self-destructiveness, and Baudelaire's adoption of the roles of dandy and conservative pariah. And his rejection of success could be construed as just another aspect of the Romantic agony: part of that complex of feeling which responds to a crassly inadequate world by reversing its moral vocabulary, actively seeking its condemnation, and wearing its emblems of shame as if they were badges of courage.

However, there is more to what Tate says here than that. In writing to Bishop in this way, Tate may very well have been indulging in a touch of self-dramatisation, playing the part of fugitive fleeing the brute materiality and mediocrity of his times: a part which, it should be added, he could have learned equally well from Byron, Poe, or Baudelaire, from some of the glamorous figures he had met in Nashville or from earlier self-confessed Southern reactionaries like, say, John Randolph of Roanoke. But he was also trying to respond to what he saw as a significant moment in the history of his region; to be more precise, he was trying to define how he and those like him should react to the simple but radical fact of change. In the first decades of the century, as Tate once put it in a famous phrase, the "South reentered the world":[2] on the level of culture and society, it became an inextricable part of the urban-industrial complex (see Plate 8), and on the level of consciousness, its traditional systems of thought and belief were eroded by the new philosophies of modernism. All that was vital and precious in the regional heritage, in fact, everything that made the South distinct, was being worn away and destroyed: that was Tate's belief. To use Tate's own word, it was failing, it was succumbing to new idioms and standards (idioms and standards that were summed up in the new meaning given to that word, "success"). And the appropriate response to this, Tate felt, was not to desert the sinking ship but to cling all the more fiercely to its rails, so as to affirm – even if in a way that more opportunistic minds might regard as foolish – the instincts, the dignities and disciplines that were being lost.

Several points need to be made about this attitude to the profound social and intellectual changes that were taking place in the early part of this century (and which have been catalogued in almost excessive detail by historians and other commentators).[3] In the first place, it was an attitude that was hardly peculiar to Tate nor even to his friends but one that was widespread and, given the circumstances, quite predictable. Considering the problem of cultural change, the anthropologist Ralph Linton has observed:

> Even in the most progressive and forward-looking community, changes in culture produce some individual discomforts. At least some of the members of the group will develop nostalgic attitudes towards a past which appears rosy in the light of present difficulties. The more intense and widespread the discomfort due to change, the more widespread the attitudes are likely to be.[4]

For good and ill, the South was never "the most progressive and forward-looking" of communities; the changes it was confronted with were fairly radical; and so Tate was by no means the only Southerner to give what he termed "a backward glance" to an earlier and apparently more coherent time. In the second place, it is worth emphasising that this nostalgic impulse, this deliberate – and, in Tate's case, at least, almost violent – decision to identify with a code and culture which, it is recognised, has passed or is passing creates a peculiar double focus. Here, the theory of "cultural lag" formulated by the sociologist William Ogburn provides a useful gloss. According to Ogburn's *Social Change* (which was published, incidentally, at about the time when the South was experiencing its changes), material culture (which is to say, towns, factories, and so on) always pushes ahead of non-material culture (beliefs, customs, and institutions). "When the material conditions change", Ogburn argues,

> changes are occasioned in the adaptive culture. But these changes in the adaptive culture do not synchronize exactly with the change in material culture. There is a lag which may last for varying lengths of time . . .[5]

The result is not only disharmony between the material and non-material culture, but discontinuity and division *within* the non-material culture itself: the familiar vocabularies, the old codes and customs are seen to be threatened, there is a perceptible and evidently unbridgeable gap between them and the material conditions of existence, but they are clung on to – tenaciously, with increasing difficulty, and with growing self-consciousness.

It need hardly be said that this situation – in which the codes and patterns dictated by a particular culture no longer suffice because that culture has itself substantially changed – is hardly a satisfactory one, as far as such simple but valuable things as peace of mind and a secure sense of identity are concerned. But peace of mind is not something devoutly to be wished in every circumstance; and a secure sense of identity can be constraining as well as comforting, since it may inhibit any significant exploration of experience, ourselves and our means of perception. Which leads to the third point worth making about the sort of response to social change that Tate illustrates. No matter how difficult it might have been at times, no matter what efforts of the will or the imagination were involved, most earlier Southerners had managed to perceive their region in terms of the codes, the pastoral mythologies that had been attached to it since the time of its colonisation. The populist and patriarchal models had been their way of knowing the South, their tools for structuring and encoding it, the means by which they perceived their world and turned it into words. The advantage of this was that they could construct a coherent portrait of their homeplace, one they could be comfortable with and which could inspire affection and allegiance; the disadvantage was that – with a few, conspicuous exceptions – their perspective was consequently limited, their vision distorted, and their criticisms subverted or at the very least blurred. Southerners like Tate, however, born into a time of radical social change, could no longer take those codes for granted: like a suit of clothes that has grown too small, a shade unfashionable, and just a little torn and tattered, they had either to discard them altogether (which, as Ogburn indicates, was a very difficult thing to do, even supposing they wanted to do it), or they had to examine them carefully, perhaps alter and renovate them in some way, and then use them with a certain amount of self-consciousness, deliberation, and defiance. Something that Lucien Goldmann says is worth quoting here. "All forms of consciousness", Goldmann argues,

> express a provisional and mobile balance between the individual and his social environment; when this balance can be fairly easily established and is relatively stable, . . . men tend not to think about the problems raised by their relationship to the external world. On the social as well as on the individual plane, it is the sick organ which creates awareness, and it is in periods of social and political crisis that men are most aware of the enigma of their presence in the world.[6]

People like Tate were living at just such a moment of crisis as Goldmann refers to here: when the terms of their relationship to things – which included, most crucially, their language – were brought up for examination and review. Whether they liked it or not, they had been made unavoidably aware of the mythologies that made up what Tate, in that letter to Bishop, described as their "deepest heritage"; and even while clinging on to those mythologies they had to reinvent them, reinterpret them according to their needs, and in the process think more critically, argue more provocatively, and write with more imaginative force and daring than most of their predecessors in the region.

SHOUTING ACROSS IMMENSE VOIDS: APPROACHES TO THE AGRARIAN ARGUMENT

Of all the Southern writers who responded to the challenge of the times (and who felt, as Tate once put it, that they were "both inside and outside the old tradition")[7] none did so with more calculation and aggression than the Nashville Agrarians. The conventional starting-point for historians of the Agrarian movement is the anti-evolution trial, when a young man named Scopes who had taught Darwinian theories of evolution in a high school in Dayton, Tennessee, was prosecuted for doing so. The trial took place in 1925, and with William Jennings Bryan acting for the prosecution and Clarence Darrow the principal lawyer for the defence, the event was guaranteed nationwide coverage. Journalists poured down to Dayton in their scores, to cover the proceedings, offer satirical portraits of local folkways, and pour scorn on Fundamentalism and the benighted South. And in response to this, most historians argue, a group of poets known as the Fugitives – who included, among their number, Allen Tate, John Crowe Ransom, and Donald Davidson – discovered (or, at least, some of them did) that they were not as hostile to the South as they had once thought. As Davidson later put it, somewhat melodramatically perhaps, the trial broke in on their literary concerns like "a midnight alarm"; and, he added, "we began to remember and haul up for consideration the assumptions that – as members of the Fugitive group – we had not bothered to examine". Tate, also remembering this period some years later, even claimed a kind of synchronicity for events: as if he and his friends were so close in their beliefs that they renewed their allegiances, responding to the crisis, at almost exactly the same time. In 1926 or so, Tate said, he wrote to Ransom from New York in a very different vein to that of previous years. "I told him", Tate recalled, "that we must do something about Southern history and the culture of the South. John had written, on the same day, the same message to me. The letters crossed in the mail."[8]

This conventional account of the inception of the Agrarian movement is by no means wrong, but it does perhaps involve a slight distortion of emphasis. The traces of melodrama in Davidson's recollections, and the slightly pat nature of the account given by Tate, should alert us to this; we are, after all, in the presence of two good storytellers who want to give the random odds and ends of historical fact some of the coherence and symmetry of fiction. The Scopes trial was undoubtedly the catalyst, the specific event that precipitated action on the part of Tate and his friends, but it was not by any means the cause. That lay deeper: in the slow process of simultaneous erosion and accretion that was altering the fabric of Southern society and the structure of the Southern mind, and which, sooner or later, would have demanded some sort of response, some kind of active definition of the self *vis-à-vis* the region, from writers of this intelligence and vision. In this respect, it is perhaps worth reminding ourselves that Ransom began treating the South explicitly as a theme a year before the "monkey trial" and that, as Louis D. Rubin has pointed out, poems written even earlier, like "Armageddon", anticipate the making of the Agrarian symposium.[9] And it is worth adding that Tate – partly under Ransom's influence, and partly under Eliot's – was formulating ideas about tradition, ritual, and the dissociation of sensibility characteristic of modern times well before Scopes and his ideas became news.

Be that as it may, Davidson, Ransom, and Tate began to communicate with each other, feverishly and enthusiastically, about their new allegiances and, more important, about the notion of expressing these allegiances in a symposium. Their plans were helped along by various informal talks between Davidson, Ransom, and, later, others such as the historian Frank Owsley and the writer Andrew Nelson Lytle – and by a steady correspondence with Tate who, in 1928, departed for a while to France. Other contributors to the symposium were considered (including, rather ironically, Stringfellow Barr, who became one of the Agrarians' most vocal opponents), and some of them at least were recruited. Stark Young was enlisted from New York chiefly because both Tate and Davidson felt he could contribute a good essay: provided, Tate added sardonically, "he can be prevented from including anecdotes about his grandmother".[10] Robert Penn Warren, another ex-Fugitive regarded as a "sheer genuis" by one or two of the others, was asked to join in and readily agreed to do so. And John Donald Wade, a friend in particular of Davidson's and the author of a very fine work on Longstreet, was evidently cajoled into submitting what turned out to be one of the best essays in the book. Other contributions were sought and received from Herman Nixon, a young political scientist who, it was hoped, would give some socio-economic ballast to the book; John Gould Fletcher, perhaps best known as an Imagist poet; Henry Blue Kline, a Vanderbilt student of a later generation than most of the others; and Lyle H. Lanier, a psychologist. Little by little, *I'll Take My Stand* (as it eventually came to be called) took shape: with Ransom drafting the preliminary statement, Donald Davidson doing much of the donkey work normally associated with the job of editor, and Tate firing salvoes from wherever he happened to be. Two firms were found that were willing, in fact eager, to publish; Tate was authorised to sign with Harper's; and finally, on November 12, 1930, the book appeared.

It can hardly be denied, really, that there was a strong sense of unity felt throughout all these proceedings, and not merely because several of the contributors knew each other so well – forming, as Davidson put it once, "a unit of mutual understanding". "Our cause", Ransom declared triumphantly, "is, we have all sensed this at the same moment, the Old South . . . Our fight is for survival: and it's got to be waged, not so much against the Yankees as against the exponents of the New South."[11] But to leave things like that is to do less than justice to the sheer strength of personality of the different Agrarians. More important, it is to ignore the fact that, behind the apparent unity, there were quite radical variations of commitment and belief. The arguments over the title of the symposium are fairly well known, and they illustrate these differences very clearly. Taken, of course, from the song, "Dixie", the phrase "I'll Take My Stand" was apparently suggested by John Donald Wade when he was talking to Davidson, and then taken up with enthusiasm by both Davidson and Ransom. Warren, however, hated it. "I think the title . . . is the god-damnest thing I ever heard of", he wrote to Tate in May 1930, "for the love of God block it if you can."[12] Tate, who also hated the title, did try to block it. For him, as for Warren and Andrew Nelson Lytle, a less specifically local title such as "Tracts Against Communism" seemed much more appropriate. "I'll Take my Stand", Tate declared, made his ears burn. It would offend the "foreign" (by which he meant, the non-Southern) reader. And, besides, he added:

> It is an emotional appeal to ill-defined beliefs; it is a special plea. The essays in the book justify themselves *rationally* by an appeal to principle. It thus falsifies the aims of the book.[13]

It is rather doubtful, to say the least, that the essays in *I'll Take My Stand* appeal rationally to a sense of principle: but that is not the point at issue here. What is, and is worth emphasising, is the deeper significance of this quarrel. In the short term (and despite a hostile response from Davidson and Ransom), Tate did get some of his way; since he was allowed to run a footnote to his essay, explaining, in however discreet a fashion, his dissatisfaction with the title and his wish to dissociate himself from it. And, in the longer term, by raising the issue in the first place, Tate and Warren let some skeletons out of the cupboard. That is to say, they unearthed, in a way that was difficult to ignore, some fairly basic differences within the group concerning the nature and purposes of the symposium; by extension, they revealed just how elastic the pastoral mythologies they were using had become – just how much of the Southern code was now open to argument and available to change, and just how wide was the scope for reinvention.

Many of the differences within the Agrarian group, and the varying interpretations of the regional code which these differences engendered, are conveniently illustrated by the relationship between Tate and Davidson. Tate and Davidson were very close in many ways; their letters to each other, written over a period of forty-one years, testify clearly enough to that. But theirs was a closeness, an intimacy founded to some extent upon difference: difference of background, difference of temperament, personality, and belief, all of which necessarily affected the nature of their commitment to the South. For instance, from the beginning Tate seems to have thought of agrarianism in terms of another, larger context: which was, as he put it, the context of science versus religion. This comes out in a letter he wrote to Davidson in March, 1926. "For over a month", Tate declared,

> I have been collecting notes for an essay. The essay, I fear, will contain a discussion of Fundamentalism: not what the Methodist Bishops think it is, but what it really is. My purpose is to define the rights of both parties, and I'm afraid I agree with Sanborn that science has very little to say for itself.[14]

Davidson, by contrast, was much more specifically local in his concerns, more interested in his region as an end rather than a means; and the point at which his path diverged from his friend's came out with especially painful force when the two of them exchanged poems. At some time in March, 1926, Davidson sent Tate a copy of a new poem, which was later to be published as "The Tall Men". This poem in its published form constitutes, as one critic has put it, "an act of personal identification" – with the regional past, that is, and with the whole idea of a local tradition; and, reading it, Tate was horrified. For him, evidently, it was little more than propaganda. "I do not believe it was your intention to write a poem", he told Davidson, "you wished to do something else." "It isn't that I disagree with your 'ideas'", he went on:

> I am personally inclined to believe that Southerners are better men than Yankees, that the fall of the South meant a State for the pig, and that some sort of love is the keynote of ethics. But if I *dis*believed these doctrines, I should feel as much interest in them, *as poetry*, as I do believing them.[15]

"For God's sake, Don", Tate ended, "don't publish the poem in its present state." Davidson meanwhile, had received a copy of Tate's "Ode to the Confederate Dead", and responded in kind. "The Confederate dead", he declared,

> become a peg on which you hang an argument whose lines, however sonorous and beautiful in a strict proud way, leave me wondering why you wrote a poem on the subject at all.

"The poem is beautifully executed", Davidson added, damning with faint praise,

> but its beauty is a cold beauty. And where, O Allen Tate, are the dead? You have buried them out of sight – with them, yourself, and me.[16]

Already, even before the Agrarian symposium was under way, one can see a gap appearing here between the two friends: a gap that sometimes made Tate feel (as he put it) as if they were "shouting to each other across immense voids".[17] On one side of that gap stood Davidson the regionalist: a man looking for practical solutions to problems that were, first and foremost, specifically local ones – although they might, by implication, be of more general interest too. And on the other side was Tate, trying to assume the mantle of traditionalist, searching for a coherent, intellectual and spiritual, framework. Practical problems might arise for him, the Southern dimension might inspire him certainly. But his vision was fixed, really, on ultimates: on issues which, as he himself sensed even this early on in his career, could be dealt with only in theological terms.

There is no need, however, to impose too heavy a freight of meaning on this simple, and rather acrimonious, exchange about poems. The differences between the men began to come out even more clearly as they discussed the possibility of "a Southern symposium of prose".[18] The phrase occurs in a letter from Tate dated March 17, 1927, and represents the first reference in their correspondence to the book that was later to become *I'll Take My Stand*. Even before this, however, they had exchanged confidences about their new, and apparently fully shared, allegiance to the local. "I've attacked the South for the last time", Tate declared proudly; and Davidson responded, within three or four days of hearing this, by declaring, "my America is here or nowhere".[19] All the March 17 letter did, apparently – and it was admittedly a great deal – was provide a focus for their new commitments, something concrete to which they could attach their new enthusiasms and so give them tangible shape and direction. After its first mention, in fact, their letters are full of the new project, or plans and proposals that could be loosely related to it. Sometimes, when they write to each other, they sound like the Southern boys that one of Faulkner's characters describes in *Intruder in the Dust* for whom remaking the past, refighting the Civil War and turning defeat into victory, remains a continual and tempting possibility. "I am already convinced", declared Tate in May, 1927,

> that had Jackson been in chief command from the beginning we should be a separate nation and much better off than we are now: and that if Jackson hadn't been killed in 1863 the Battle of Gettysburg would have been won.[20]

"I quite agree", replied Davidson,

> . . . it is interesting to speculate on what could have happened if Jackson, not Lee, had been the supreme head. Also, I agree that we might have been a damn sight better off if Stonewall had lived to realize his ideas.[21]

Sometimes, with an apparently equal amount of energy and shared principles, they engaged in a little Yankee-baiting: as when, on one occasion, they egged each other on to say uncomplimentary things about Livingston Lowes's book, *The Road to Xanadu* and New England "ideals of 'scholarship'" in general. Always, though, behind the mutual back-slapping, the apparent sharing of interests, the gap between them was there, waiting to be noticed. So when, for example, Tate admitted to Davidson, "I am more and more heading toward Catholicism. We have reached a condition of spirit where no further compromise is possible", Davidson felt compelled to offer his friend some sound advice. "Surely", he said,

> you must not, like Eliot, give up the ghost in favour of a combination of classic-Anglo-Catholic-Conservative, principally because that combination (good as it may be) isn't good enough for you, however much its elements may attract you, or even serve your purposes now and then.[22]

"I like better", Davidson added, "to be tied up with no church at all . . . As matters stand, I seem to be bothered less by religious matters than by anything else."

But Tate was not to be deterred that easily. Davidson's kindly-meant lecture was immediately followed by a detailed account of plans for the new book: which was, as he envisaged it, to consist of "a collection of views on the South, . . . a group of openly partisan documents . . . with a strong bias toward the self-determinative principle". The collection would all be written by Southerners, Davidson insisted, and would call for action as well as ideas: and that word "action" was underlined for emphasis. Tate's reply to these proposals was characteristically convoluted. He agreed with Davidson, he said, but he then offered his own proposals, a "tactical program" which was at once more ambitious and vaguer than Davidson's project and, besides, implied only a minimal interest in action. The programme, Tate suggested, should include the formation of "a society . . . of Southern positive reactionaries" – made up to begin with of what he termed "people of our own group" and endowed with "a philosophical constitution", the establishment of a newspaper "to argue . . . principles on the lower plane", a weekly journal "to press philosophy on the passing show", and a quarterly "devoted wholly to principles". "Philosophically", he declared (using that word again),

> we must go the whole hog of reaction, and base our movement less upon the actual old South than upon its prototype – the historical social and religious scheme of Europe. We must be the last Europeans – there being no Europeans in Europe at present.[23]

This was in many ways at odds with Davidson's plans. Quite apart from anything else, Davidson (along with some of the other Agrarians like Owsley) was profoundly suspicious of the European tradition and preferred to see the South – and, indeed, the nation as a whole – in specifically nativist, even isolationist, terms: "I insist", he was to write in 1937, "on the uniqueness of the American establishment and on its separateness from Europe." Tate must have sensed this; for he went on, in his letter, to make a further proposal which at once sums up one whole side of his character, suggests something of the fierceness of his devotion to the new cause – and, above all, seems to acknowledge that he and Davidson, and the Agrarian group in general, might not be in complete agreement. "For the great ends we have in view", he insisted,

> – the end may be only an assertion of principle but that in itself is great – for this end we must have a certain discipline; we must crush minor differences of doctrine under a single idea.[24]

Differences were not to be crushed quite so readily, however. Tate's schemes remained, for the most part, grandiose, Davidson's simpler and, within the Southern context at least, more obviously attainable. Tate talked about asserting principles, formulating philosophies, standing at the end of Western civilisation; while Davidson insisted, rather testily perhaps, that they must "get down to the practical plane", to "act as well as speculate & talk". One must not exaggerate all this, of course: Tate was not uninterested in immediate issues, such as the structure and contents of the projected symposium, and Davidson could express enthusiasm for Tate's larger schemes and broader aims – while all the time wondering, nevertheless, where the money for them might come from. But the differences were there, and were apparent enough for Tate not merely to acknowledge them but to dwell on them and try to explain them: both to himself and his friend. It was just a year before the publication of *I'll Take My Stand* that he did so, in fact, in a letter to Davidson written from Paris. What he said there bears the mark of having been brooded over for a long time. Besides, it relates so closely to this problem of the disagreements within the Agrarian group, and describes them so incisively, that it is worth quoting at some length. "There is one feature of our movement that calls for comment", Tate wrote:

> We are not divided, but we exhibit two sorts of minds. You and Andrew seem to contribute one sort – the belief in the eventual success, in a practical sense, of the movement. The other mind is that of Ransom, Warren, and myself. I gather that Ransom agrees with me that the issue on the plane of action is uncertain. At least I am wholly sceptical on that point; but the scepticism is one of hoping to be convinced, not by standing aside to watch the spectacle, but by exerting myself. In other words, I believe there is enough value to satisfy me in the affirmation, in all its consequences, including action, of value. If other goods proceed from that, all the better. My position is that since I see the value, I am morally obligated to affirm it. That sounds pretty grand, but I can think of no other phrase.[25]

Tate was, of course, to find this division confirmed only a few months later, in the arguments over the title: which were to leave him complaining that the Agrarians had never worked properly as a group. And Davidson must have had similar feelings when he received Robert Penn Warren's contribution to the volume, which discussed the problems of the black and his place in the Agrarian scheme of things. Davidson was horrified. "Behind the essay", he protested to Tate,

> . . . are implications which I am sure we don't accept – they are "progressive" implications, with a pretty strong smack of latter-day sociology. Furthermore, I think that there are some things that would irritate and dismay the very Southern people to whom we are appealing . . . I simply can't understand what Red is after here. It doesn't sound like Red at all – at least not the Red Warren I know. The very language, the catchwords, somehow don't fit. I am almost inclined to doubt whether RED ACTUALLY WROTE THIS ESSAY! . . .[26]

Davidson's criticisms in this letter were curiously misdirected and confused, which was perhaps one symptom of his panic. For contrary to what he claims here, the position Warren assumed in his essay was essentially a conservative one, involving a fairly unabashed defence of segregation: the black, Warren suggested, should become a farmer, but situated "beneath his own vine and fig tree". Davidson, however, chose to label the essay "progressive" because, whatever its conclusions, it did question Southern institutions and the region's past in the name of certain fundamental principles. In other words – like Tate's "Ode" to which, a few years earlier, Davidson had taken such exception – it did place the regional heritage, for good *and* ill, within a larger and essentially traditionalist context. As far as Davidson was concerned, that heritage was itself the context, the measure by which everything else was to be judged. To question that was, in his opinion, to question the book's major premise; on a more emotional plane it was also, Davidson felt, to act with cold disloyalty to the region and renege on one's very identity as a Southerner.

The conflict between traditionalism and regionalism that is registered so clearly in the correspondence between Tate and Davidson is not by any means the only point of debate in *I'll Take My Stand*. It is, however, the most crucial and noticeable one and creates the largest fissures. Besides, it generates other divisions and discontinuities; and it raises a number of fairly radical questions about the function of the symposium and the kind of discourse it offers. The nature of those questions is suggested by the disagreements the Agrarians have provoked not only between themselves but among their critics, the people who have tried to explain and locate them. Is *I'll Take My Stand* what, say, Louis D. Rubin, Thomas D. Young, and Robert Heilman claim it is: part of the American pastoral tradition, a protest against the dehumanising influence of urban society that can be compared most profitably with *Walden*?[27] Or should it be placed where R. Alan Lawson, Richard Pell, and Michael O'Brien all tend to put it: in the context of the regionalist movement of the 1930s, along with books like Howard Odum's *Southern Regions of the United States*?[28] Is it, as Lewis P. Simpson has argued most forcefully, a predominantly backward-looking work, involved in a heroic and inevitably doomed attempt to recover that "webbed order of myth and tradition"[29] for which (in their own fashion) Henry Adams and T. S. Eliot also longed? Or is it on the contrary, as some critics have suggested, an essentially prophetic book, anticipating the ecological movement and the problems of post-industrialism by several decades? Is it a literary work or polemic? Does it offer an invitation to thought or incitement to action? Could it best be described as a meditation upon principle, an elegy for many, departed, lovely things, or a provocative call for a change of economic policy? Questions of this kind are quite impossible to answer in the long run, because none of the Agrarian group ever begins to answer them, either in *I'll Take My Stand* or elsewhere.

Not only that: the Agrarians often end up disagreeing with themselves as much as with each other, allowing self-contradiction to seep into their own, individual arguments. Of course, people like Ransom and Lytle exploited the mythic potential of the Old South in their poems and novels and elsewhere: but they also contributed articles to the *American Review* on the possibilities for agricultural reform, and joined up with some Distributists in 1936 to produce another symposium entitled *Who Owns America?*[30] Of course, Ransom himself developed a contrast between the European philosophy of establishment, perpetuated in the South, and the dominant American spirit of pioneering, a contrast the power of which clearly depends in some part on its fictive origins and possibilities. But he also wrote a number of essays in the 1930s proposing such mundane things as a reduction of the land tax, the graduation of farm bounties to benefit small farmers, and free land for those willing to become self-subsistent.[31] And, of course, Tate claimed in his letter to Davidson that the affirmation of values was an end in itself. But even he could remark despondently, just after *I'll Take My Stand* had been published and these values had presumably been affirmed:

> The trouble with our agrarianism is . . . that we don't believe in it in the way that demands sacrifice . . . I get a little bitter about all this. I came back to live in the South, and I've been let down.[32]

It was little wonder, really, that so many of the Agrarians were intrigued by the idea of discontinuity, the divided mind, since discontinuity was something they knew from their own lives, felt upon their pulses. "Shouting across . . . immense voids", they appear often to be shouting to themselves, conducting an *inner* dialogue; taking their stand, they seem occasionally to illustrate Donald Davidson's notion of the Southern writer – whose "tragic contradiction", Davidson tells us, "results in painful self-consciousness, in split personalities, in dubious retreats".

There is another contradiction at the heart of *I'll Take My Stand* that is worth considering in some detail: which has to do, not with the viability or practicability of the good life the Agrarians describe, but with its actual texture, its character. Quite simply, different contributors make use at different times of both the populist and the patriarchal models; and, no matter which particular model they choose, tend to emphasise quite different aspects of that model and so, in the event, emerge with some sharply contrasting designs for living. Andrew Nelson Lytle, for instance, in his essay on the symposium, celebrates a life of simple self-sufficiency. The farming family he describes survives on two hundred acres of land, works from dawn to dusk, lives in a house referred to as "a dog-run with an ell running to the rear", and finds its entertainment mainly in square dances and country ballads. Stark Young, by contrast, offers a rather more glamorous picture, stocked with white columns, magnolias, and gentlemen of the old school. "The aristocratic", Young insists at one point in his essay, "implied the possession of no little leisure"; and, as he makes it clear, it is the aristocratic strain – or, as he puts it, "the Southerner of good class"[33] – that *he*, at least, has chosen to defend. Recently, it has been suggested that there is no real conflict here: that what the Agrarians envisaged was a felicitous balance between the different interests, co-operation between farm and plantation in the common struggle against the capitalist entrepreneur. This position is summed up neatly by Richard H. King, who concedes that "the dichotomy between yeoman and planter ideals is certainly there"; however, he adds, this is "ultimately reconcilable in the vision of a hierarchical society".[34]

This is a seductive argument, certainly, and one that the Agrarians might well have appreciated, since if accepted it would give a much greater cohesiveness, and even symmetry, to their views. But it is difficult to see how it can be defended, either in terms of general principle, or in the context of the Southern and agrarian arguments. As celebrants of the populist ideal from the Virginia pamphleteers through Jefferson to Sidney Lanier have realised, the planter who relies on a staple crop has interests that are very different from those of the self-subsistent farmer: he depends upon quite sophisticated market arrangements, a fairly well established system of credit and finance, and all the paraphernalia of merchants and brokers, warehouses and contracts. He may, as both Ransom and Young suggest, take life easy but he is still, in his own way, an entrepreneur, interested in buying and selling so as to support his relatively privileged way of life. He is, in fact, a member of an elite (whether a patriarchal elite or a capitalist one is not, for the moment, our concern); and the social and political systems he favours, and the cultural forms – the modes of belief and behaviour – he embraces, all in their own ways express this. Of course, in any particular historical circumstances, planter and farmer may live side by side (just as, for that matter, a millionaire and a pauper may, or a white landlord and a black tenant-farmer): but this is hardly to imply that they subscribe to the same opinions or ideals, or that the values by which they live – the structure of feeling revealed in their every gesture, the codes that help them to perceive and assess their experience – are somehow reconcilable or interchangeable. Several of the Agrarians admit as much, by specifically excluding either the patriarchal or the populist model from their discussion at the outset: Stark Young, for example, mentions "the so-called poor whites" (see Plate 9) and "the . . . respectable and sturdy . . . yeomanry" only to dismiss them by insisting that "it is not they who gave this civilization its peculiar stamp". And several of the others make the same admission in a rather different way, by following a peculiar, zigzag course between patently irreconcilable models: Frank Owsley, for instance, seems undecided whether to commit himself to the kind of figure "whose hands were rough with guiding the plow" or to the kind whose principal amusements were "fine balls and house parties",[35] and so ends up by celebrating both at different points in his essay.

In this connection, the arguments of one Agrarian in particular, Andrew Nelson Lytle, are perhaps worth noting. For, in a number of the things he wrote after *I'll Take My Stand*, Lytle makes it quite clear that in his opinion it was the aristocratic tendency that effectively *destroyed* the South. The Southern gentleman, he argued in an essay written for the *American Review*, "was the agent of those disrupting forces which had been at work since the sixteenth century",[36] and which eventually promoted the disintegration of Southern society. A capitalist entrepreneur rather than a farmer, a cotton snob intent on making the agrarian economy of the South dependent on an industrial economy, the gentleman, Lytle argued, was the main person responsible for reducing "a union composite of spiritual and temporal parts to the predominance of material ends". This version of Southern history was given extended treatment in Lytle's biography of Bedford Forrest, published in 1939. As Lytle describes him, Forrest emerges as an embodiment and apotheosis of the populist virtues: a man who "had risen from obscurity, like the majority of Southern leaders", but, unlike many of them, had "no cotton snobbery in his make-up". Forrest's background and early years are described in detail: partly because they give Lytle the opportunity to celebrate a world in which a man could live "by hunting and fishing and by working as little of the ground as possible", and partly because they enable him to develop his thesis about the destructive nature of the plantation economy. By the time the third generation of white settlers had grown up in the Mississippi Valley, Lytle tells us, the region

> had set itself to accumulate land, not that it might live freely, but that it might grow cotton and be wealthy . . . An agrarian economy was basing its cultivation on the pay of an industrial economy, which by nature is hostile to it. This is full of peril . . .[37]

The change of tense here is significant, indicating that Lytle, good Agrarian that he is, is using the past as an example and warning to the present; and this continues in his account of the Civil War, where Lytle appears to be suggesting that the main reason for the South's defeat was the betrayal of the "butternut soldiers" by the generals, "representatives in military of 'cotton snobs'", and by the tendency of more than one political leader of the Confederacy to behave like a "feudal overlord".

Forrest, of course, is seen as a noble exception among the Confederate leaders, a man "with the virtues and vices of the wilderness still a part of his character". Playing a game curiously similar to the one played by

Tate and Davidson in their letters, Lytle even argues that if Davis "had had the vision and courage to appoint. . . Forrest to the command" then the outcome of the War might have been very different. The words he puts in his hero's mouth, too, make him sound like a curious compendium of the rough heroes to be found in old Southwestern humour and the simple infantrymen celebrated in Confederate memoirs. "I ain't no graduate of West Point", Forrest declares at one moment in the book, "never rubbed my back agin any college, but . . . I'll use my six-shooters and agree to whup the fight with any cavalry . . ." Forrest's contempt for the niceties of the aristocratic code, and gentlemanly pretension, is seen as part and parcel of all this, further proof of his backwoods virtues. For instance, when a young officer challenges him to a duel, Forrest – who, we are told, had little time for such refinements – simply knocks his challenger down; and his response, when another young officer refuses to perform some menial but necessary task on the grounds that it is beneath him, is to hit him hard enough to persuade him to change his mind. There is no question about Lytle's admiration for this kind of rough-hewn behaviour. Nor is there any question about his feeling that the central weakness in the Confederate strategy was its failure to recognise the centrality of the yeoman. This passage, for instance, describing the opening moments of the Civil War, leaves the reader in little doubt as to where Lytle takes *his* stand:

> The last of the Yeomanry . . . went to war. He brought with him no fine candies, but a jug of molasses, a sack of corn, and his father's musket . . .
>
> These young men were without medieval visions . . . They were plain people, the freest people in the South, whom the cotton snobs referred to as the "pore white trash". And they were going . . . to defend their particular way of life, although they would not have spoken of it in such flat terms. These men made up the largest body of people in the South . . . the rich snobs were ashamed of their pioneer ancestry and they were not. Davis and his advisers made one great mistake of policy that overshadowed all the other errors of policy: they chose to rest the foundations of the Confederacy on cotton and not on the plain people.[38]

Lytle's is then a vision of rural society that is not merely different from, say, Stark Young's, but one that is openly and self-consciously *opposed* to it. What he praises in *I'll Take My Stand*, and celebrates in the character of Forrest, is not a hierarchical society at all but a community of plain folk: a world in which, ideally, everyone has a decent competence and nothing more. Of course, the impulse behind it is just as conservative as the impulse behind the aristocratic ideal. But this is a conservatism that seeks its fulfilment in an almost primitive culture: a culture, that is, that having achieved a certain, relatively unambitious level of achievement has quite simply stopped developing. This, in turn, makes Lytle's version of the populist scheme of things different from (for example) Herman Clarence Nixon's; since what Nixon chooses to embrace is the idea of a balanced economy, with "a reformed agriculture", an industrial system geared to that agriculture's needs, and "an orderly process of evolution".[39] Earlier Southerners, like Lanier and Twain, had shown that the house of the yeoman had many mansions – that, in other words, the populist model contained a number of quite different possibilities progressive and regressive, hopeful and nostalgic; and one of the further complicating factors in *I'll Take My Stand* is that different essayists choose to dwell in different mansions, and concentrate on certain possibilities often to the exclusion of others. This is also true of the variations the Agrarians play on the patriarchal model. From the beginning, that model had tended to accommodate such contrasting, if not actually conflicting, emblems of the good life as the feudal overlord, the romantic cavalier, and the Tory squire. And the different contributors to the symposium push this tendency further: emerging, in the event, with versions of the aristocratic life that enjoy an at best uneasy coexistence.

John Crowe Ransom, for instance, is clearly sympathetic to the patriarchal design for living: which would suggest that he should be aligned with Stark Young. Unlike Young, however, he is distinctly reluctant to call the Old South aristocratic: "the so-called aristocrats", he admits, "were mostly home-made and countrified. Aristocracy is not the word which defines this social organization so well as squirearchy."[40] So does this align him with, say, Tate, who also tries to evade Young's romanticism? Hardly, since Tate differs from his friend and mentor in at least three crucial ways. In the first place, as his letters to Davidson testify, he was committed to a far more specifically feudal ideal. His reason for taking his stand with the Old South is, in fact, summed up in this telling passage from his biography of Jefferson Davis (a passage that incidentally suggests why Tate was so attracted to Eliot):

> The South was the last stronghold of European civilisation in the western hemisphere . . . In a sense, all European history since the Reformation was concentrated in the war between the North and the South. For in the South the most conservative of the European orders had . . . come back to life, while in the North, opposing the Southern feudalism, had grown to be a powerful industrial state which epitomized in spirit all those middle-class, urban impulses directed against the agrarian aristocracies of Europe after the Reformation.[41]

This vision of the decline of Christendom looks decidedly fierce and apocalyptic when placed beside, say, Ransom's assertion that the Old South's chief claim to cultural fame was its possession of "the eighteenth-century social arts of dress, conversation, manners, the table, the hunt, politics, oratory, the pulpit". "The South took life easy", Ransom claims "which is itself a tolerably comprehensive art." If this were so, one feels tempted to add, then it might have proved a congenial place for Ransom himself but not for his slightly younger and far more openly combative friend.

On a slightly less exalted plane, there is further, if implicit, disagreement between Ransom and Tate on the matter of foreign ties and allegiances. Shortly after the publication of *I'll Take My Stand*, Tate observed dryly to Davidson that there was "too much Anglo-nostalgia" in the volume. "Looking back on our Symposium", he wrote, "I am increasingly convinced that it was sacrificed to the English tradition . . . My only excuse is that I foresaw it, and tried to talk the Anglophiles out of it." Tate did not go on to say who exactly he thought "the Anglophiles" were. But it seems fairly certain that they must have included Ransom, who opens the second section of his essay in this fashion:

> The nearest of the European cultures which we could examine is that of England; and this is of course the right one in the case . . . England was actually the model employed by the South, in so far as Southern culture was not quite indigenous. And there is in the South even today an Anglophile sentiment quite anomalous in the American scene.[42]

Tate was completely out of sympathy with this sort of thing: partly because he was drawn to France rather than England, and partly because he could, at times at least, agree with Davidson that "as early as 1770 we had something very different".

And then, finally, as far as the differences between Ransom and Tate are concerned, there are the more serious and central matters of the adequacy of the Old South as a fulfilment of the patriarchal vision, and the possibility of the contemporary South recovering its past. For all his reluctance to use the term "aristocratic", and his insistence that the Old South "was . . . not so fine as some of the traditionalists like to believe", Ransom does seem to have been convinced that it offered "a way of life that had been considered and authorized"; he does seem to have felt that Southerners before the Civil War did enjoy "fullness of life" – wholeness of character, that is – rather than being forced to scatter themselves piecemeal. Furthermore, he also appears to have been in little doubt that the South was still a traditional society and could remain so, despite industrialisation – and this by the simple expedient of accepting innovation with (as he put it) "a very bad grace". "The South must be industrialized", Ransom conceded, "– but to a certain extent only, in moderation": in this way, he argued, the region could survive economically, accept the inevitability of "contact . . . with the Union", while nevertheless retaining "a good deal of her traditional philosophy".[43] Here, again, the contrast with Tate is radical and striking. For

Tate left his readers in no doubt that the Old South failed to measure up to the feudal ideal. It was, as he put it succinctly, "a feudal society without a feudal religion": relying for its theological base on Protestantism ("a non-agrarian and trading religion; hardly a religion at all, but a result of secular ambition"), it lacked in his opinion precisely the kind of wholeness, coherence, and inclusiveness that Ransom wanted to claim for it. Tate went even further than this and argued that it was precisely this flaw, this lack of an adequate ideological foundation, that brought about the South's surrender to the modern world. "No nation is ever simply and unequivocally beaten in war", he insisted, "nor was the South";[44] what ruined it was the simple fact that "the world was too much with it" – that it failed to break with the ideological structures of the rest of the nation, its way of reading and evaluating experience. As a result, it could never manage to erect a satisfactory alternative to capitalism, something that could be defined in its own language and defended on its own terms.

It hardly needs pointing out that the implications of Tate's argument were extraordinarily subversive. For, in effect, he was not only entering into a disagreement with Ransom but questioning the initial premise of the entire symposium: the assumption, that is, that the Old South *was* a traditional society, offering a satisfactory illustration of either the patriarchal model, or the populist one, or (in some mysterious fashion) both. More than that, as he developed this argument it became clear that he was placing an equally large question mark over the aims of all the Agrarians, including himself. The nature of this overriding question is clear enough from Tate's concluding remarks. "How may the Southerner take hold of his Tradition?" Tate asks, and then answers "by violence". "The Southerner is faced with a paradox", he continues:

> He must use an instrument, which is political, and so unrealistic and pretentious that he cannot believe in it, to re-establish a private, self-contained, and essentially spiritual life.[45]

"Paradox" seems too mild a word in the circumstances, since what Tate is effectively describing here is an impossible situation: in which "the Southerner" (a compound figure who includes, of course, Tate himself) is asked to use reason to recover the irrational, to rely on his self-consciousness to recover a form of life the essence of which is its spontaneity, instinctiveness, and spirituality. On the level of general principle Tate was raising a problem that anyone must face, once they accept the idea that our perceptions are encoded, that our experience is mediated for us by our culture and the patterns it dictates: which is how to turn the mind against itself, how to disrupt our vocabulary, our way of reading the world, when that vocabulary is all we can use, the only tool we have available for the task. On a rather more specific and local level, he was unearthing what he evidently saw as the contradiction at the heart of *I'll Take My Stand*; since by formulating a defence of tradition, Tate felt, he and the other essayists were announcing their estrangement from it – the fact that they were part of a far more theoretical and discontinuous culture. No amount of violence, directed outwards or self-inflicted, could alter this. The Agrarians, as Tate perceived it, were alienated, separated by their rationality and self-awareness – their immersion in the currents of modern culture – from the very codes they sought to embrace: which, to go back to a point made earlier, may have been unfortunate for them as men, part of that compound character known as "the Southerner", but a blessing in disguise for them as writers.

So the disagreement and contradictions multiplied, both between essays and within individual contributions. At times, Ransom sounds like a spiritual descendant of Ruskin and Carlyle, both of whom he invokes during the course of his essay, and at times like a harbinger of the New Deal (he was, as his biographer indicates, to become a New Dealer eventually). Frank Owsley, in his essay, blames the Civil War and Reconstruction for the corruption of the South while Tate, as we have seen, locates the principal fault elsewhere. Some Agrarians dismiss industrialism altogether, whereas others plead for a mixed economy. Some of them appear to believe in the existence of "the South" as a distinctive and identifiable region; while others prefer to concentrate on a particular area, like the mountains or the Delta country, and still others, such as Wade, on a specific state. And all this, it should perhaps be added, was not merely a matter of intellectual or theoretical disagreement but of personal background and upbringing: each Agrarian had his own individual memories, his own particular stock of images and affections to call upon, invoke, and exploit. In this respect, an essay written by Lytle on the way in which he came to write one of his novels is perhaps worth referring to briefly. The novel, *The Velvet Horn*, is Lytle's finest piece of fiction and an unjustly neglected work, but that is not the point that concerns us here. What is relevant for our purposes is that it is set in Tennessee some time after the Civil War – in other words, in very roughly the period and in broadly the place of Lytle's own childhood and youth – and that Lytle talks in this essay, as he does in *I'll Take My Stand*, of a vanishing agrarian perfection. The life of that time and place, Lytle tells us,

> seemed to me to be what was left of the older and more civilised America, which as well retained the pattern of its European inheritance. The Civil War had destroyed that life; but memory and habit, manners and mores are slow to die . . . As a boy I had witnessed its ghostly presence, and yet the people which this presence inhabited were substantial enough. They were alive in their entire being . . . The last active expression of this society seemed to fall somewhere between 1880 and 1910.[46]

"Somewhere between 1880 and 1910": in other words, somewhere about the time Lytle and the other Agrarians were born and started growing up (the oldest Agrarian, Stark Young, was born in 1881 and the two youngest, Henry Kline and Robert Penn Warren, in 1905). Like Twain, in fact, the contributors to *I'll Take My Stand* were doing something else besides registering an undeniably important set of cultural changes and something more than simply formulating a series of vivid proposals. They were recalling a lost land: lost in part, certainly, because of history but also for the simple reason that they had grown up and shades of the prison-house had started to gather around them. They were trying to recover, in their imaginations, what Warren has a character in his most recent novel refer to as "a land more glowing than even America . . . the country of the young".[47] In some ways, this country was the same for all of them: rural, backward-looking perhaps, a place of farms and small towns. But in others it was a matter of very personal ties, painfully intimate loyalties and associations. Thankfully, the country of the young is different for each of us – affected by what Lytle, in his essay, calls "complex interrelationships of blood and kin" – and any work, like *I'll Take My Stand*, that involves a number of individual attempts to chart it is bound to be one of multiple suggestions, rich confusion. All of the Agrarians shared allegiance to one, particular piece of land, but that piece varied in shape and texture for every one of them. So, in the last analysis, the ground on which each of them took his stand belonged to him alone; it was his to protect, explore, and commemmorate as – to use Faulkner's famous phrase, describing his relationship to Yoknapatawpha County – sole owner and proprietor.

SPEECH AND SILENCE: *I'LL TAKE MY STAND* AND THE DEFENCE OF THE SOUTH

So what, in view of all this, stops *I'll Take My Stand* from disintegrating? What, if anything, prevents complete confusion setting in and gives some sort of cohesion to the book? There are several answers to this, really. In the first place, it is worth responding to these questions with a further question. Is discontinuity necessarily a bad thing? The idea that any work can be reduced to an all-embracing formula – a particular genre, an identifiable kind of discourse, and a connected argument or narrative – may, after all, be misleading and debilitating: it may, in fact, give a false impression of why we were interested in that work in the first place. Unity, coherence, and inclusiveness may be a part of the critical orthodoxy, eminently respectable literary virtues (and virtues which, it might be added, the Agrarians themselves helped to popularise in their New Critical phase): but we can value a book just as much for its intractability, its eccentricities and paradox, and the circuitous, endlessly labyrinthine routes on which it manages to lead us. "Why is the writerly our value?" asks Roland Barthes in *S/Z*, and then answers:

> Because the goal of literary work (of literature as work) is to make the reader no longer a consumer, but a producer of the text.[48]

It would be going too far, perhaps, to call *I'll Take My Stand* a "writerly" work according to this definition: but it does come very close to imposing on the reader the sort of task Barthes refers to here. For as we move through the twelve essays – comparing, say, Lytle's essay with Young's or Ransom's with Tate's – we become aware that we are being enmeshed in a system of conflict, a text that requires us much of the time to establish priorities and distribute emphases and so participate in the job of making or (to use Barthes's term) "producing" it.

But discontinuity is one thing, and disintegration another. It would be plainly wrong, as well as painfully facile, to argue that because the Agrarians disagree over so many issues there is therefore nothing that binds them together. For all their differences, they did believe they were enlisted in a common cause. More important, the book they helped to produce only hovers on the edge of confusion; we are likely to feel after reading it that, however much the individual essayists may be at odds at times, there is something holding them together, some force other than sheer blind conviction that draws them into the same orbit, the same field of discourse. Which brings us back, remorselessly, to the original question. What is this 'something'? What, exactly, supplies some bearings for each of the essayists as he navigates his own particular territory? One possible answer to this might be the introductory "Statement of Principles", written by Ransom, which provides a convenient starting-point for the reader and a nicely combative gloss on the title. However, the "Statement" was never quite the corporate effort it was originally intended to be (the initial idea was for Ransom, Lytle, and Davidson to produce something in consultation with one another); the individual essayists did not, as was hoped, have it to refer to while they were writing their contributions; and, in the event, it is predictably much closer to Ransom's own essay, in terms of assumptions, argument, and idiom, than to any of the others in the volume. Another potential answer is to be found in the sense of crisis common to all the Agrarians: the feeling that they were fighting what Ransom called, at one point,

> a foreign invasion of Southern soil, which is capable of doing more devastation than was wrought when Sherman marched to the sea.[49]

But, again, this seems unsatisfactory, even if slightly less so. The sense of crisis certainly helps to explain (among other things) the pervasive imagery of battle, the continued use of military terminology, and the essayists' almost obsessive references to the Civil War. It is hardly enough by itself, though, to act as a means of giving focus, shape, and some sort of direction to the book. At best, it alerts us to the fact that there is something there exerting a gravitational pull on each contributor to the volume; it is not that 'something', that magnetic force itself.

Perhaps a useful way of getting at what that something is would be to remind ourselves of one simple fact: although the Agrarians take their stand on the idea of the Old South, they hardly ever refer to the Old South's "peculiar institution" of slavery. In fact, with the conspicuous exception of Warren's essay, they hardly ever refer to blacks in any specific way – as a particular problem, that is, an identifiable force in Southern society, carrying its own special burden of oppression and want. There is the occasional reference to a faithful "Uncle Tom" figure like the black servant, Anthony, in Wade's essay; one or two remarks concerning the supposed weaknesses of the Negro race (Owsley goes so far as to refer to blacks after the Civil War as "half-savage" and "hardly three generations removed from cannibalism"); and apart from that only a general, fairly submerged tendency to see the black man as (to use Louis D. Rubin's phrase) "a kind of peasant, an element in southern society fitted to be the hewer of wood and drawer of water". One or two critics have tried to defend this absence by claiming that since the Agrarians were, by definition, interested only in agrarianism, the formulation of a pastoral ideal, consideration of slavery was irrelevant to their purposes. Thomas D. Young puts the point trenchantly when he declares:

> To dismiss the central intent of the Agrarians because they did not deal adequately with the plight of the black man in the South . . . is to denigrate Thoreau for his apparent lack of compassion regarding the immigrant Irish railroad builders – thence ignoring the central thrust of *Walden* . . .[50]

But, however well put, this is a little misleading. The way of life that Thoreau recommends to our attention is not nearly as deeply embedded in a specific culture as the one celebrated by each of the Agrarians. It happens to be located in nineteenth-century America, it is clearly affected by Thoreau's New England inheritance: but, as Leo Marx has pointed out, it represents "an experiment in transcendental pastoral-ism",[51] its geography is primarily moral and its landscapes symbolic. More to the point, perhaps, even if Thoreau's pastoral ideal were more implicated in a particular culture than it is, there would still be a difference: because the oppression of Irish labourers in the infant American republic, no matter how deplorable, was hardly as crucial an economic factor or as definitive a social and cultural force as Negro slavery was in the Old South. It was not, in sum, a "peculiar institution". In this respect, *Walden* and *I'll Take My Stand* undoubtedly *are* different;

and the absence of many references to the black race, and to slavery in particular, remains conspicuous and remarkable.

At this point, something that Pierre Macherey says, in *A Theory of Literary Production*, is worth considering. "The speech of the book", Macherey argues, "comes from a certain silence, a matter which it endows with form, a ground on which it traces a figure." "The book is not self-sufficient", he goes on,

> it is necessarily accompanied by a *certain absence*, without which it would not exist. A knowledge of the book must include a consideration of this absence.
>
> This is why it seems useful and legitimate to ask of every production what it tacitly implies, what it does not say. Either all around or in its wake the explicit requires the implicit: for in order to say anything, there are other things *which must not be said*. Freud relegated this *absence* of *certain words* to a new place which he was the first to explore, and which he paradoxically *named*: the subconscious.[52]

For Macherey, in effect, textual absence, or rather structural absence, is constitutive of the text; when "speech . . . has nothing more to tell us", as he puts it, then "we investigate the silence, for it is the silence that is doing the talking". And, clearly relating this notion of constitutive absence to the Freudian idea of repression, he suggests that what that silence speaks of is the buried land of the subconscious, personal or cultural or both. Developing this idea, we could surely argue that the absence of any significant reference to slavery in *I'll Take My Stand* is not only remarkable; it helps us to locate the vision of the world – or, to use Raymond Williams's phrase, the structure of feeling and experience – that underpins all the essays in the symposium. It helps us to establish the models of belief and behaviour, and habits of language, that enabled the Agrarians to pattern the real and perform various crucial acts of exclusion. Like any code, the one the Agrarians employed is as notable for what it does not say as for what it does, for the absences by which it is haunted; and *their* code seems intent on not bringing into speech, and therefore into the orbit of its attention, one figure in particular – the black, especially in his role as slave.

It will perhaps be obvious what all this suggests: that *I'll Take My Stand* is not just Southern as a matter of historical accident but distinctively and determinately so. It belongs first and last to a body of writing for which the constitutive absence, the invisible or at best marginal character, is and always has been the black. Something of this aspect of the Southern mind is beautifully caught by William Faulkner, in that moment in *Light in August* when Joanna Burden learns from her father about the "curse" visited by the black race on the white, and then tries to explain how this lesson changed her attitude towards black people. "I had seen and known negroes since I could remember", she says:

> I just looked at them as I did at rain, or furniture, or food or sleep. But after that I seemed to see them for the first time not as people, but as a thing, a shadow in which I lived, we lived, all white people, all other people.[53]

The irony of this passage stems from the fact that Joanna does not really see or know the black people around her at any moment in her life. Far from progressing from simple seeing to deeper vision – which, of course, is her notion of the change effected by her father's lesson – all she does is move from one form of blindness to another. Like so many of Faulkner's characters, in fact (like, for instance, the deputy in the story, "Pantaloon in Black"), she uses her eyes and her idiom to perform an act of exclusion. To be more precise, she begins by regarding Negroes as an unremarkable part of life's furniture, something not to be noticed or noted, and then subsequently turns them into an object of fear – a tactic that seems to dematerialise them in a way, and certainly serves to dehumanise them. Joanna may appear to be talking about blacks and so by implication acknowledging their existence, understanding them by bringing them within the confines of speech. What she is really doing, however, is relegating them to silence, to a shadowy area where they must remain anonymous and unknown.

Of course, this is a more sophisticated example of constitutive absence than the one that distinguishes *I'll Take My Stand*. Faulkner, unlike the Agrarians, has not merely absorbed this aspect of the Southern mind and allowed it to shape his work; he has (in a way that, as we shall see, is characteristic of him) attempted to dramatise it and analyse its implications. Furthermore, he has introduced a typical piece of ironic legerdemain, since what Joanna illustrates is a paradoxical situation, in which an apparent acknowledgement of presence is actually a revelation of absence. With all these qualifications, however, the basic point remains the same: that it is a traditionally Southern strategy to place the black on the margins of language, to deny him the dignity of an adequate definition. Either a screen of words provides a form of concealment, or the gap between the word and object, signifier and signified, is widened to the point at which it becomes an unbridgeable abyss; in either case, language acts to exclude and suppress.

But there is no need to go to Faulkner to show just how deeply embedded in the Southern argument *I'll Take My Stand* is, and just how much the figure of the black man functions as an absent presence. There is another point of reference that is perhaps more significant, and more directly relevant, and besides connects the Agrarians with some of the darker recesses of the region's history. About a hundred years before Ransom, Tate, and their friends published their symposium, another group of Southerners found themselves faced, as they saw it with a Yankee invasion: one led by William Lloyd Garrison and the Abolitionists. And they responded to this invasion, not by apologising for their peculiar institution of Negro slavery, but by asserting quite simply that it was a positive good, an integral part of the South's established, agrarian mode of life. These defenders of slavery – and, by extension, the social system of the Old South – included people like George Fitzhugh, Chancellor Harper, Thomas Dew (a professor of political philosophy), James Henry Hammond (a Senator), and William Gilmore Simms. Fitzhugh wrote a number of things concerned with slavery, and in particular two books entitled *Sociology for the South; or, The Failure of Free Society* and *Cannibals All!; or, Slaves Without Masters*, while the others, among other things, all contributed essays to a symposium published in Charleston, South Carolina in 1852, the short title of which was *The Pro-Slavery Argument*.[54] Some of the arguments they produced need not concern us here: such as those drawn from the Bible, purporting to find a theological warrant for slavery, or certain, supposedly scientific theories concerning the separate, inferior origins of the Negro race. What is of interest, however, is that in defending the peculiar institution they all felt compelled to develop a theory of society that represented at once a reworking of traditional Southern arguments, and a base for attacking the capitalism of their Northern neighbours. In addition to that, while attempting to bridge the gap between principle and practice – between their essentially utopian visions of an organic society and their repressed knowledge of the realities of Southern life – they all felt the need, evidently, to develop an idiom almost as old as the region itself, which had found one of its most significant expressions prior to that in the work of John Taylor of Caroline. Just how much, if at all, these apologists for slavery actually influenced the Agrarians it is difficult to say: although it may be worth pointing out that Owsley talks about them in his essay in *I'll Take My Stand* and that at one time Tate wanted to include an essay on Harper and Dew in the symposium.[55] The question of influence, however, is not really a crucial one in this context. What matters is that these two quite different groups of writers responded to a situation of crisis in curiously similar ways, by drawing on almost exactly the same reserves of language and thought. In the process, they revealed just how involved they were in the same regional tradition, and just how much they employed the same codes, with the same – or, at the very least, analogous – habits of silence and exclusion.

Both the defenders of slavery, for instance, and the Agrarians begin by emphasising the importance of experience, the past. "If you can tolerate one ancient maxim", says Hammond in *The Pro-Slavery Argument*, "let it be that the best criterion of the future is the past."[56] This could lead, rhetorically, to constant references to earlier civilisations, the testimony of Greece and Rome; or it could usher in a kind of disingenuous pragmatism. "Slavery", declares Ransom blithely (in one of the very few overt references to the problem in *I'll Take My Stand*) "was a feature monstrous enough in theory but human in practice."[57] Ransom's remark finds its anticipation in this stirring pronouncement made by one political representative of Virginia:

> For my part, sir, I am not an advocate of slavery in the abstract . . . but I am not yet convinced that slavery, as it exists in Virginia, is either criminal or immoral.[58]

Or, again, in this argument offered by Hammond:

> If you were to ask me whether I am an advocate of slavery in the abstract, I should probably answer, that I am not . . . I do not like to deal in abstractions. It seldom leads to useful ends. There are few universal truths . . . We have no assurance that it is given to our finite understanding to comprehend abstract moral truth . . . We ourselves, our relations with one another and with all matter, are real, not ideal.[59]

It also finds a curious foreshadowing in the contrast many of the apologists insisted on making between their supposed realism and the nominalism of their opponents. "The Senator from New York said yesterday that the whole world had abolished slavery", declared Hammond during a speech in the Senate. "Ay, the name", he added triumphantly,

> but not the *thing*; all the powers of the earth cannot abolish it . . . your whole hireling class of manual labourers and "operatives" as you call them, are essentially slaves.[60]

Whether applied to the problem of slavery, though, or to some other issue, the implications of this argument remain essentially the same: the test of a thing is the actual experience of it, how it works and has been perceived to work in the past, rather than its abstract moral status. Experience – what one Agrarian terms "historical consciousness" and another "traditional background" – remains the key, what really matters.

Among the things that experience teaches, evidently, is a sense of evil, human fallibility and limitations. Indeed, both the apologists and the Agrarians embrace the idea of sin with an enthusiasm that borders on the morbid. "To say that there is evil in any institution", argues Chancellor Harper in the opening essay in *The Pro-Slavery Argument*, "is only to say that it is human": a sentiment which finds its echo in a remark made by Tate – "evil", he declares, "is the common lot of the race".[61] Embracing evil, they also embrace an extremely sceptical attitude towards the notion of progress. People are imperfect, so the argument goes; the world is a dangerous and mysterious place; and there is a vast difference, as Robert Penn Warren puts it, between a "paper victory and a workable system". Change, consequently, if it occurs at all, should occur very slowly. "I am satisfied with the existing laws", says William Gilmore Simms in *The Pro-Slavery Argument*, "until the gradual and naturally formed convictions of the community, and the progress of experience, shall call for their improvement." Or, as John Gould Fletcher has it in his essay in *I'll Take My Stand*, "so long as a system is producing good results, it is useless to meddle or tinker further with it".[62]

All this emphasis on experience, and on what one Agrarian calls "the futility of trying to deal with social problems in an abstract fashion", leads, as well it might, to a notion of society that is characterised by the recurrence of certain key-words: "roots", "harmonious", "balanced", "stable", "secure".[63] "The old South", Ransom suggests in his essay, "practiced the . . . European philosophy of establishment as the foundation of the life of the spirit"; it imitated the model of English provincial life, which

> long ago came to terms with nature, fixed its roots somewhere in the spaces between the rocks and in the shade of the trees, founded its comfortable institutions, secured its modest prosperity – and then willed the whole in perpetuity to the generations which should come after.[64]

This portrait of modest ease and leisurely stability was one favoured by nearly all the apologists. The following passage, from *The Political Economy of Slavery* by Edmund Ruffin, is not untypical in this respect:

> A farmer or planter of the South, not rich, but in independent and comfortable circumstances, gives a portion of his time to social and mental occupation. Perhaps his whole object in seeking such relaxation is pure enjoyment. But the final result is not the less the improvement of his mind and manners. His sons and daughters grow up under these advantages and influences of communication. And if, in the end, because of such indulgences of a family, even though moderately enjoyed, there may be less money accumulated, there will be acquired other values much more than compensating for difference of pecuniary gains.[65]

Society is seen, in effect, as a natural extension of the human personality, a kind of biological unit; or, to quote George Fitzhugh on this subject, "Society is a work of nature, and grows."[66] Lurking behind all statements of this kind, of course, is an essentially Aristotelian conception of the community: one which defines the social group as an organism, complex and inegalitarian, a harmony of different interests and castes. "All harmonies", declared William Gilmore Simms in a ringing passage in *The Pro-Slavery Argument*,

> whether in the moral or physical world, arise wholly from the inequality of the tones and aspects; and all things, whether in art or nature, social and political systems, but for this inequality, would give forth monotony and discord.[67]

And, using precisely the same sort of assumptions, the Agrarians come to very similar conclusions: as when, for instance, they praise (as Davidson does) the idea of "diversity within unity", a "harmonious" society and a "balanced life" – or as when they roundly condemn (as Fletcher does) "the American craze for simplifying, standardizing, and equalizing" everything. As these quotations indicate, difference is equated with inequality by both groups, and inequality can therefore be seen as a virtue, a positive good. What is to be avoided at all costs apparently, is the smooth, symmetrical notion of the group constructed by the abstracting intellect: the assumption made by some "theorists", that is, that they can "control nature and bend her to their views".

From this basis – this premise that, as Chancellor Harper put it, "inequality . . . is deeply founded in nature" – the defenders of slavery launched an attack on the entire liberal tradition. Man, they contended (echoing Calhoun in this respect) was not born free but "in a state of the most helpless dependence on others . . . to subjection . . . to sin and ignorance". Neither was he born to equality: that "much lauded but nowhere accredited dogma of Mr. Jefferson" was dismissed as "new-fangled philosophy" and, on a more personal level, as "the effusion of [a] young and ardent mind which . . . riper years might have corrected".[68] Out with the Declaration of Independence, also, went the contractual notion of society: which George Fitzhugh, for example, dismissed with the utmost scorn. "Fathers", Fitzhugh insisted, "do not derive their authority as heads of families, from the consent of wife and children"; and, since the family was simply "the first and most natural development" of man's social nature, it followed that the leaders of society did not derive *their* authority from the consent of those *they* led. The "abstract propositions . . . of . . . a Locke, a Jefferson", people like Fitzhugh argued, were the products of an era when "the human mind became presumptuous and undertook to form governments upon exact philosophical principles, just as men make clocks, or watches, or mills"; they represented nothing more than an "ignis fatuus", the airy "speculations of closet philosophers".[69] In the nineteenth-century American context, at least, this wholesale dismissal of the Whig interpretation of history was quite remarkable; and one of the apologists, Fitzhugh, took things even further than that. For what Fitzhugh (who was, in many respects, the Allen Tate of the pro-slavery group) realised was that, if the argument was to be carried to its logical conclusion, then the idea of free competition, the *laissez-faire* economy, would have to be rejected as well. "Free competition", Fitzhugh insisted, "simply means each man's eagerly pursuing his own selfish welfare unfettered and unrestricted by legal regulation." As such, it clearly violated feudal principles. Enabling the rich and strong to exploit the poor and weak, it was "not only destructive to the morals, but to the happiness of society".[70] It would lead, eventually, to the destruction of a system founded on a paternalistic sense of responsibility, the patriarchal model (which was what, as Fitzhugh saw it, the South was in fact or at least potential), and its replacement by one that was purely competitive, acquisitive – a jungle of speculative capitalism inhabited by "cannibals all".

Not all of the Agrarians were willing to be quite so open in their attack on their fellow countrymen's absolutes of liberty and equality. It is worth remembering however, that one of the essays in *I'll Take My Stand* is actually called "A Critique of the Philosophy of Progress", and that the assault on Enlightenment principles developed there is carried on elsewhere by the other contributors. The Agrarians, in fact, showed no hesitation in rejecting liberal capitalism, and the impulse behind every one of their essays is in the same direction: towards what a hostile critic might call a closed society. Like Fitzhugh, for instance, they regarded the world created by free competition as (to quote one of them) a "jungle of speculation" and argued for strict regulation and control. Like Simms, they insisted that equalitarian theories lead only to disaster: for example, the educational system should, they felt, be aggressively inegalitarian, so as to cater for different needs and abilities. And like most of the defenders of slavery, they poured scorn on the moral and religious life of industrial society: a society in which, they suggested, what is good and what is useful are invariably equated and theology is reduced to problem-solving. In this respect, Lyle H. Lanier only makes explicit what most of the other contributors leave to implication, when he claims that "the doctrine of progress" encourages "the decline of family life" and incites relativism, atheism, and revolution. His argument is fairly simple. "The corporate age", he tells the reader, ". . . leaves little to the family beyond the details of finance and the primary sexual function"; it is thus "incompatible with the conditions necessary to the stability and integrity of family life". At the same time, those notions of earthly power, practicability, and unlimited advancement that characterise the modern temper – and which besides, Lanier informs us, are indissolubly linked to "the positivistic spirit of British and French thought in the eighteenth century"[71] – must by their very nature promote scepticism and unrest: the impulse to question inherited beliefs, and challenge established institutions and, whenever it seems necessary, to destroy them.

Against this vision of a world in which the centre cannot hold, both the Agrarians and the apologists set their version of the rural South: which acts as a yardstick by which to measure the specific deficiencies of the industrial system and as an emblem of all the traditional rural virtues. "The greatest, most luminous defence of any point of view", Stark

Young asserts in *I'll Take My Stand* "is its noble embodiment in persons"; and, responding to this, many of the contributors to both arguments seek to defend and celebrate the Old Southern order by describing typical farmers and planters and by presenting scenes from an apparently perfect country life. The total picture that emerges is a fairly predictable one, for anyone familiar with Southern writing. The ideal Southerner, enjoying what George Fitzhugh describes as "the only condition in which reciprocal affection [can] exist among human beings", is apparently at once independent and part of a community: able to develop his entire personality to the full while at the same time living in fruitful communion with others. "He is lofty and independent, in his sentiments", Fitzhugh declaims, "generous, affectionate, brave and eloquent; he is superior to the Northerner in everything but the arts of thrift." This, as it happens, could serve as a succinct pen-portrait of someone like, say, John Donald Wade's "Cousin Lucius" or the anonymous Southerners "of the old school" whom Young celebrates. Nor is it necessarily an inaccurate account of the humbler figures that inhabit Lytle's imagined world: at basis, the virtues – pride, self-reliance, open-handedness, warm-heartedness, courage, and a native gift for speech – remain the same, as does the mean-spirited, acquisitive system with which this pastoral ideal is compared. At this level of argument, in fact, where both groups of writers are invoking an idea that is generalised to the point of ghostliness, it is not so much the concrete details of the picture that count as the frame within which that picture is set: the structure of assumptions with which these celebrants of rural ways are working. In the country, the initial premise is, a person can labour in a fashion that does not just answer to his material needs, but provides an effective basis for moral action as well. His leisure is filled with traditional pursuits, which are as much a part of his essential life as his work-patterns are. His code is grounded in the traditions of a particular locality (is a matter of blood, one could say, rather than abstract legality), and so appeals to his emotions and imagination as well as his reason. And his religious life issues directly from his contact with the earth. For from that contact, the day-to-day struggle with unpredictable conditions, he acquires what one Agrarian calls a "humble sense of man's precarious position in the universe"; or, as an apologist for slavery puts it, he learns that "we must . . . take the world as we find it, not as we would have it".[72]

The problem with all of these arguments, of course, was that they did assume a neat equation between rural life as it should be and Southern rural life as it was. This was a large assumption, to put it mildly; and, in order to buttress it, both the apologists and the Agrarians felt compelled to develop a peculiarly local kind of rhetoric, an idiom that tended to blur the distinction between word and thing. The Agrarians also had other reasons, which were largely their own, for developing this idiom. For it enabled them to ignore, or at the very least to minimise, the radical differences between them: over, for instance, the exact nature of the model they were embracing and the precise aspects of that model they wanted to emphasise. Furthermore, it made it that much easier for them to identify with their regional tradition, at least for the moment: to go some way – although by no means all the way – towards repressing the painful awareness that they were part of the modern world, and implicated in the confusions of modernism, whether they liked it or not. In this sense, the Agrarians unlike the apologists were responding to what they instinctively saw as *their own* spiritual plight; and, far more than the apologists were, they were using rhetoric to induce a willing suspension of disbelief *in their own minds*, to seduce *themselves* into gestures of assent as well as their readers. What Allen Tate said of John Crowe Ransom is, in fact, true of all the contributors to the symposium: Ransom, Tate suggested, suffered an "intolerable burden of conflict that only occasionally, and even then indirectly, came to the surface".[73] To which one might add that it was one of the several functions of the vocabulary, the patterns of language and imagery in *I'll Take My Stand*, specifically to keep that conflict secret, to push it down below the level of conscious perception, so that each of the Agrarians could present his case with apparent confidence.

Whatever their differences of motive, however, the fact remains that the defenders of slavery and the Agrarians developed a rhetoric that was remarkably similar. Its nature is suggested by these two, fairly representative passages, the first by James Hammond in *The Pro-Slavery Argument* and the second from Ransom's essay in *I'll Take My Stand*:

> The primitive and patriarchal, which may also be called the sacred and natural system, in which the labourer is under the personal control of a fellow-being endowed with the sentiments and sympathies of humanity, exists among us. It has been almost everywhere else superseded by the modern, artificial money power system, in which man – his thews and sinews, his hopes and affections, his very being, are all subjected to the dominion of capital – a monster without a heart – cold, stern, arithmetical – sticking to the bond – taking ever "the pound of flesh" – working up human life with engines, and retailing it out by weight and measure.

> In most societies man has adapted himself to environment with plenty of intelligence to secure easily his material necessities from the graceful bounty of nature. And, then, ordinarily, he concludes a truce with nature, and he and nature seem to live on terms of mutual respect and amity . . . But the latter-day societies have been seized – none quite so violently as our American one – with the strange idea that the human destiny is not to secure an honourable peace

with nature, but to wage an unrelenting war on nature . . . Man is boastfully
declared to be a natural scientist, whose strength is capable of crushing and
making over to his own desires the brute materiality which is nature . . . His
engines transform the face of nature . . . but when they have been perfected, he
must invent new engines that will perform even more heroically . . . Our vast
industrial machine . . . is like a Prussianized state which is organized strictly for
war and can never consent to peace.[74]

Ransom's is, perhaps, the more sophisticated approach here and what he
says may appeal more immediately to our ecologically sensitive ears. At
bottom, however, the vocabulary used in these two passages is one and
the same, and besides illustrates in a fairly uninhibited way the rhetoric
shared by all the apologists and Agrarians. Rural, and more particularly
Southern, society is natural, it is suggested; urban society – which is to say
the society of the North and, in Ransom's case, the New South – is
artificial, mechanical. Southern life is peaceful, idyllic, having made
allowances for human nature and reached an accommodation with its
natural surroundings; whereas Northern life is warlike, with its people
interminably engaged in destructive and self-destructive activity.
Southern life is in harmony with things; it is sane, balanced, and healthy;
and it offers the possibility of human affection and contact. Northern life,
by contrast, is unbalanced, unhealthy, characterised by disharmony and
fanaticism, and denies all bonds and connections other than the
economic.

This series of contrasts between North and South – and, in the case of
the Agrarians, between Old South and New – could lead in a number of
different directions. It could lead, for instance, to the assumption that the
South was a living thing, an organism which like any other organism had
developed and grown: that was old, and good because it was old. The
North, by comparison, being a machine was incapable of growth. It
remained, in a sense, perpetually young and even infantile. "Seasoned"
and "mature" became as a result terms of approbation for both groups; in
addition, the apologists (as we have seen) dismissed modern notions of
society as the product of adolescent folly, while Ransom refers to a "very
large if indefinite fraction of the population of these United States" as
"men in a state of arrested adolescence" – "boys", really, rather than
men. In this connection, it is perhaps worth noting that both the
defenders of slavery and the Agrarians tended to reverse the normal
connotations (or, at least, the normal American connotations) of certain
words: so that, for example, "young", "new", and "modern" all became
terms of abuse. Thus, we find George Fitzhugh declaring quite airily that
"Liberty and equality are new things under the sun" and Lyle H. Lanier
being equally dismissive: "Progress", Lanier tells us towards the
beginning of his essay, "is a comparatively modern idea."[75] Certainly, it

is worth mentioning the fact that there was a potential paradox at work here: since rural society was evidently being celebrated for both its vitality and its sophistication, its spontaneity and its maturity, while its urban opposite somehow managed to be artificial and youthfully barbaric at one and the same time. The paradox was resolved, of course, in the notion of *controlled* growth and the related, if largely implicit idea of good husbandry: culture, both the apologists and the Agrarians believed, represented a fulfilment, a bringing to fruition of nature, whereas lack of proper cultivation, the necessary care and pruning, left the human personality to waste itself and wither away.

The horticultural metaphor seems appropriate here, since lurking somewhere behind all the descriptions of the Old South, in *I'll Take My Stand* and the pro-slavery argument, was the myth of the garden, that "idealized reaction to modernity" as Lewis P. Simpson terms it, which the early settlers of Virginia brought with them across the sea. Sometimes, the myth could seem crudely and obviously inappropriate, completely out of key with the historical facts it sought to explain. Here, for example, is a passage from a pro-slavery book entitled *A Treatise on Sociology*: it is set in the future because its author is anticipating the day when slavery, to which he gives the euphemism "warranteeism", will be accepted everywhere in the United States:

> . . . in the plump flush of full-feeding health, the happy warrantees shall banquet in PLANTATION-REFECTORIES; worship in PLANTATION-CHAPELS, learn in PLANTATION-SCHOOLS; or, in PLANTATION-SALOONS, at the cool of evening, or in the green and bloomy gloom of cold catalpas and magnolias, chant old songs, tell tales . . . and after slumber in PLANTATION-DORMITORIES over whose gates Health and Rest sit smiling at the feet of Wealth and Labour, rise . . . to begin again welcome days of jocund toil.[76]

Ludicrous as this may be, it is the product of precisely the same impulse as leads Frank Owsley, for example, in his essay in the Agrarian symposium, to talk of the Old South in the following terms:

> Thoughts, words, ideas, concepts, life itself, grew from the soil. The environment all pointed toward an endless enjoyment of the fruits of the soil . . . The planter . . . kept vigil with his sick horses and dogs, not as a capitalist who guards his investment, but as one who watches over his friends.[77]

For that matter, exactly the same impulse lies behind, say, Lytle's moving evocation of a day in the life of a poor farming family, Wade's equally moving account of the life and death of Cousin Lucius, a gentleman from Georgia – and this passage from Stark Young's contribution to *I'll Take My Stand*:

> . . . a sense of family followed our connection with the land, a gracious domain where the events of the day began with the sky and light, the bread you ate

> from the fields around you, your father's, your own; and life has been led;
> where you have known man's great desire, that generation of himself in the
> body of life, of which the earth is the eternal and natural symbol; and where
> there was, of all occupations, the form of labor in which the mystery and drama
> of life — the seed, the flower and harvest, the darkness, the renewal — is most
> represented in us.[78]

The images conjured up by these writers can seem vivid, evocative, even credible sometimes; or, alternatively, they can appear inflated and little short of absurd. But, whatever may be the case as far as impact or effect is concerned, the ingredients, the controlling ideas remain just about always the same. There is nearly always the same willingness – or, perhaps it would be more accurate to say, the same desperate desire – to identify the actual world of the Old South with the ceremonies and innocence of pastoral, the same evident need to interpret the regional experience according to an inherited code. And allied to this, there is nearly always the same readiness, however qualified or concealed it may be in some cases, to ignore or mitigate the central problem of slavery, by making the black disappear into the garden and the mists of the agrarian dream.

On the other side of the coin, whenever Northern or urban society is referred to in any detail, there is another crucial paradox at work: a paradox that goes back at least as far, in the history of Southern thought, as the Yankee stereotype itself. For both the apologists and the Agrarians condemn their opponents for what may seem, at first sight, to be two quite different things: their obsession with material profit, the accumulation of property, and their tendency towards doctrinaire notions, the preference for theory rather than fact. The paradox is caught in, for example, Ransom's use of a curiously mixed imagery to describe the modern industrial state: the attacks on machines and the mechanical, like the one quoted earlier, are punctuated by references to "Americans . . . still dreaming the . . . dreams of their youth", by assertions that "the South as a culture had more solidity than another [sic] section", and by passages like this:

> A man can contemplate and explore, respect and love, an object as substantial as
> a farm or a native province. But he cannot contemplate nor explore, respect
> nor love, a mere turnover, . . . a pile of money, a volume of produce . . . or a
> credit system. It is into precisely these intangibles that industrialism would
> translate the farmer's farm.[79]

Similarly, the apologists for slavery were ready to condemn Northern society both for its mechanism and its abstraction: as a system in which life was controlled by engines and, at the same time, as a place where people were seduced by labels, and thought in terms of "names" rather than "things". The point of all this, of course, was that in the eyes of both groups of writers the typical member of an urban society suffered from a split personality. His mind, as they saw it, had been deeply and ineradicably divided by a system that turned people into products, and did so in the name of certain insubstantial theories concerning nature, human nature, and power. Admittedly, there were differences of detail here, between the arguments of the apologists and those of the Agrarians. An Agrarian like Tate, for instance, preferred to use the currently fashionable notion of the dissociation of sensibility to support his beliefs; while people like Fitzhugh talked in terms of discord, disharmony, or simple madness. But what they were saying was essentially the same, they were pressing home a similar irony: which was that a society that prided itself on its practicality, its attachment to facts, was in their opinion based on a fiction. It imposed on its members a radical case of false consciousness, and so reduced their lives to turmoil and perpetual frustration. "Why have you Bloomer's and Women's Right's men", asked George Fitzhugh rhetorically,

> and strong-minded women, and Mormons, and anti-renters, and "vote myself a farm" men, Millerites, and Spiritual Rappers, and Shakers, and Widow Wakehamites, and Agrarians, and Grahamites, and a thousand other superstitions and infidel Isms at the North . . . Why all this, except that free society is a failure?[80]

And Fitzhugh's portrait of nervous dissatisfaction, of a world full of people unable to fathom or perform their natures, was nicely echoed by John Gould Fletcher's claim that the typical "public-school product of New York City or Chicago" was "a behaviorist, an experimental scientist in sex and firearms, a militant atheist, a reader of detective fiction, and a good salesman". Clearly, this was not just a matter of *lack* of culture, but of a culture, a system that divided, warped, and denied.

Which was, it need hardly be said, the culture the Agrarians saw growing up and flourishing around them, even in their own region and their own home states: in the end, the emphasis has to be placed here. The apologists and the Agrarians were of like mind in many respects. They used the same arguments, the same structures of feeling and experience; they even used the same combative imagery, the same references to Northern imperialism and the South's colonial status, and the same allusions to earlier, heroic struggles against the unjust demands of an oppressor (the apologists invoked "the spirit of '76"[81] while the Agrarians, of course, went back to the "irrepressible conflict" of the Civil War). Equally, they both developed those arguments in the first place because they felt themselves threatened by history: "forced, by external pressure", as one of the apologists put it, "to re-examine the ground" on which they stood. For all this likeness, however, one crucial difference remains, and its importance should never be underestimated.

The Agrarians were writing nearly a century after the apologists. The times had changed; the material culture, the social and economic conditions of the South, had changed (and were still changing); and the non-material culture, its vision of the world, was also in the process of change, however slow. The Southern codes were breaking up, under the twin pressures of modernisation and modernism; and the Agrarians were actually registering that break-up by the simple fact of digging into the past, trying to find something to halt the process, or at least slow it down – something, also, that would resolve their own inner divisions, caught as they were between an old, loved world and a new one labouring to be born. "With us Western civilization ends", declared John Peale Bishop to Tate rather grandiloquently, but knowing that Tate, who had made the same point many times himself, would not hesitate to agree; and it is this sense of being at the end of things (a sense that, as Bishop's letter indicates, the Agrarians were not alone in experiencing) that gives point, force, and tension to the Agrarians' essays. Far more than the apologists – far more, for that matter, than any previous spokesmen for their region – people like Ransom, Davidson, and Tate had to will themselves into being Southerners: as Lewis P. Simpson acutely remarks, "No American writers ever worked harder at inheriting their inheritance than the Agrarians."[82] They suffered from the sick organ that creates awareness (to use that phrase quoted from Goldmann earlier); they suffered from it, and they benefited from it too. For it is precisely this that makes *I'll Take My Stand*, for all its faults, an edgy, splendidly rebarbative, and even moving book: an argument for the South, certainly, but also an account, however veiled, of personal crisis.

Just how much the Agrarian symposium depended on a moment of crisis – personal and, by implication, historical and ideological – is suggested by the subsequent history of the movement. Ransom, Tate, and the others had come together for a time in apparent agreement, responding to what as they saw it the times demanded; and they had tried to resolve the divisions and discontinuities each of them experienced by assuming certain kinds of Southern identity, certain specific models or roles. It was only for a time, however. As the process of change accelerated, and the regional code continued to shatter and fragment, the same impulses that had led them to embrace Agrarianism in the first place prompted them to turn in quite different directions, seeking other ground on which to take their stand. Of course, the Agrarian movement did not immediately disappear with the publication of the symposium. It was followed by several public debates, one of which (between Ransom and Stringfellow Barr) attracted an audience of well over three thousand. And many of the Agrarians continued to write things that were related to the cause. But none of the grandiose ambitions of Tate were ever realised; neither, for that matter, were any of Davidson's rather more modest schemes. Gradually, the sense of a group effort, a heroic struggle to recover the past and reaffirm dying values, began to disappear: to the point where, as Tate put it, "the Agrarian Movement . . . degenerated into pleasant poker games on Saturday nights". "Of course", Tate conceded, "from the ashes the Phoenix rises in new strength"; however, he went on sardonically, the Phoenix seemed too honorific an emblem in the circumstances – "we had better name him a Buzzard".[83]

What was to arise from the ashes of Tate's own involvement in Agrarianism was, as his essay in *I'll Take My Stand* had anticipated, religious faith: commitment to the Roman Catholic Church and to the kind of feudal beliefs or "right mythology" which, he had argued in 1930, the Old South fatally lacked. Eventually, he was willing to be quite charitable towards his old convictions. He informed Davidson in 1942, for instance, that in his opinion Agrarianism had been a success because it represented "a reaffirmation of the humane tradition" – "and to reaffirm that", he added (summoning up a familiar argument), "is an end in itself". However, if he was being charitable it was only because, as he saw it, he could now afford to be: he had finally reached a position of security, and so could feel reasonably comfortable about giving the old cause a few generous pats on the back. Looking down from the high altar, in fact, Tate tended to treat his earlier Agrarian self like a precocious child, someone who instinctively knew the right questions but had only a very few of the correct answers. Writing to Davidson in 1953, for example, about what he called "our old views of the late twenties when we were rebelling against modernism", he declared rather dismissively, "We were trying to find a religion in the secular, historical experience as such, particularly in the Old South. I would now . . . say that we were idolaters." "As far as our old religion went", he added, "I still believe in it":[84] but, as Tate indicated, as far as it went was not nearly far enough and, besides, it was quite clear that he was using the word "religion" with cauterising irony.

John Crowe Ransom, meanwhile, moved in a direction quite different to that of Tate, but one that seemed equally to imply the impossibility of sustaining a regional faith. He chose to take *his* stand, in fact, on art: "salvation", he wrote in 1945, had to be found in

> individual works of art, or religious exercises which are works of art institutionalised and rehearsed in ritual. All these are compensatory concretions – they return us to primitive experience, but only formally; by no means do they propose to abandon the formal economy.[85]

This passage comes from an essay called "Art and the Human Economy" which represented, as Davidson angrily put it, "John's first open & public recantation of his agrarian principles". Unlike Tate, and most of the other former Agrarians, Ransom felt that he had to make his new position clear by measuring the distance he had travelled since the days of *I'll Take My Stand*. Certainly, he was willing to give his old beliefs their due: "the agrarian nostalgia", he declared in his essay, "was very valuable to the participants, a mode of repentance not itself to be repented" – among other things, "it matured their understanding of the forward-and-backward rhythm of the human economy". But that did not prevent him from putting those beliefs very firmly in their place. "The Southern agrarians", he pointed out, borrowing a criticism made very frequently of the group in earlier days,

> did not go back to the farm, with exceptions which I think were not thoroughgoing. And presently it seemed to them that they could not invite other moderns . . . to do what they were not doing themselves. Nor could they even try to bring it about that practising agrarians . . . should be insulated from the division of labour and confined securely in their garden of innocence.[86]

In short, they could not reassert models of belief and behaviour that quite patently did not fit. Nor, Ransom insisted, was this entirely to be regretted. A more difficult society had arrived, and with it "the habit of specialized labour", but this carried certain compensations in its wake. For as he put it,

> without consenting to division of labour, and hence modern society, we should have not only no effective science, invention, and scholarship, but nothing to speak of in art, e.g. *reviews* and contributions *to reviews*, fine poems and their exegesis.

"The arts are expiations", he added,

> but they are beautiful. Together they comprise the detail of human history. They seem worth the vile welter through which homeless spirits must wade between times, with sensibilities subject to ravage as they are. On these terms the generic human economy can operate, and they are the only terms practicable now.[87]

Ransom's recantation was a curious one, as he must have realised, since at one point he seemed to be embracing modern society with a measure of enthusiasm, for what he saw as its active promotion of the arts, while at others he seemed to see it in a considerably less flattering light, as a "vile welter" from which the arts themselves provided a temporary refuge. But any uncertainty over the nature of modern times did not carry over into Ransom's attitude towards historical change: such change, he now clearly felt, was inevitable and irreversible. "We have fallen", as he put it in the essay; the "garden of innocence" was no longer available; and, whether one liked it or not, "we cannot actually go back".

Most of the other former Agrarians tended to agree with Ransom on this score, although they did not necessarily put it quite so brutally. Robert Penn Warren, for instance, gravitated towards existentialism and an increasingly liberal position, not least on racial matters: his eventual attitude to his Agrarian stance is perhaps best summed up by a remark he made during a discussion of the movement in 1980. "I think", he said,

> we were very weak on the side of suggestions, on the positive side, what to do about things: I think we were dead center on the negative side, as it was focussed on the implicit dangers, the growing dangers of the kind of society we were creating.[88]

In other words, like Tate and Ransom, Warren never reneged on the impulse that made him try to interpret historical experience according to the Southern code: but only on the belief, embraced with a fierce obstinacy at the time, that that code supplied a satisfactory interpretation. Herman Nixon, in turn, worked actively for the New Deal ("I am", he said, "for the constructive acceptance of the inevitable"); Henry Blue Kline, like Nixon, was employed by several government agencies, promoting the economic development of the South; while Stark Young, taking a very different path, seems to have found his last love, as well as his first, in the theatre. "Art's function is to extend life into dream", Young declared in an autobiography covering his first twenty years, ". . . for the actuality of real things has no solidity as compared to the reality of our illusions."[89] It was as a drama critic that Young made his living and fame, and as a critic devoted to the ideas of "style" and "glamour". Literal realism was never popular with him ("Art is not art", he wrote once, "until it ceases to be life"); and, in a sense, his interest in the Old South and the patriarchal myth seems to have been merely a by-product of all this – just one way, among others, in which he could satisfy and express his overriding preoccupation with artifice.

And then there were those who stayed at home, or tried to go home again: people like John Gould Fletcher who returned to his homeplace, after nearly a quarter of a century in England, to spend his final years in a remote house surrounded by pine trees – or like Andrew Nelson Lytle, who has spent much of his life working a farm, while rarely regarding himself as a "proper farmer". The case of John Donald Wade is interesting in this respect. Resigning his post at Vanderbilt University, Wade returned to his home in Marshallville, Georgia, where he assumed the role of benevolent patriarch: organising a boy's club, financing a much-needed bridge, and providing his town with new amenities including a library. It was a role, however, that was assumed very deliberately and in the full awareness that it represented a retreat from the challenges and the confusion of the modern world. "I can't make up my mind . . . about 'intellectualizing'", he wrote in 1938:

> I hardly know *how* in the present state of life. I remember how Chesterton
> grumbled for some *limits* to do his thinking in. There seem to be so few limits in
> our time; and thought is always so likely to turn purely volatile! And the
> Bridge and the boys club have been comfortingly tangible.[90]

Tempting as it may be to interpret Wade's return home as an attempt to
put Agrarian principles into practice, a remark like this surely puts things
in their proper perspective. Wade was not trying to reinvent the
Southern code, still less was he trying to provide a model for others to
imitate; he was simply seeking a way of keeping his mind quiet, at least
for a while, a comfortable routine that would help him to forget larger
questions.

Of all the former Agrarians, perhaps, the only one who never really
moved very far from his position in the early 1930s, and never really
strayed for long from Nashville either, was Donald Davidson. Times
continued to change, but he did not; gradually, his opinions hardened
into prejudices, and he became a vigorous supporter of Senator Joe
McCarthy and a vociferous opponent of school desegregation. Staying
on at Vanderbilt, and trying desperately to cling on to the Agrarian
cause, Davidson suffered more acutely than anyone else from the gradual
loss of rapport, the disappearance of a sense of group purpose. A letter
that he wrote to Tate in 1940 brings this out in a quite moving way. It is
worth quoting at length, not only because it is so affecting, but because it
registers just how far apart the Agrarians had moved. Some, like Tate
and Ransom, had gone off in pursuit of other gods; some had made their
accommodation with the modern world; and some had retreated from it
altogether into the landscapes of childhood and the simple routines of
age. Only he, Davidson felt, was left in the fortress, apparently deserted
by his friends and suffering acutely from a sense of absence, betrayal, and
loss. "You have used the word *isolation*", Davidson wrote:

> Well I certainly am isolated. No doubt of that. I do not grieve, however, over
> the kind of isolation that may occur from the disregard . . . of the Communist
> reviewers of New York. I do not respect them; they can all go to hell. But I am
> decidedly grieved by being isolated from my friends. I don't mean physical
> isolation, deplorable though that is. I mean I find myself suddenly at a
> disagreeable intellectual distance, for reasons that I do not in the least
> understand . . . It is this intellectual isolation, this lack of communion, which I
> feel the most. And it began before any of you left these parts. Why, is a mystery
> I can't solve. What fault was I guilty of? Did I just fail to keep up with your
> patterns of thinking, and, though once worthy, thus become unworthy? . . .
> But since I can't solve the mystery, I am going to stop thinking about it, and
> don't propose to return to the subject.[91]

The one counter to this centrifugal movement, this general flight from
the Southern codes and a sense of group purpose, was provided by the

New Criticism: in which some of the former Agrarians – and notably Tate, Ransom, and Warren – participated. The New Criticism was not by definition aligned with the values on which the Agrarians had chosen to take their stand. Some of the Northern New Critics were liberal, not to say left-wing, in their inclinations and far from unhappy about the technological age. But the Southern New Critics, at least, did carry over into their New Critical phase many of the principles that had guided them as Agrarians; and the impulses that made them cherish certain kinds of poetic structures were precisely the same as the ones that had prompted them to celebrate the social structure of the Old South. To put it another way, what people like Ransom and Tate seemed to be seeking for in works of literature was what they had once sought for in historical institutions: a harmonious system, an organism in which there was a place for everything and everything was in its place – and which, ideally, was part of an identifiable tradition, referring back to systems of a similar kind. This put them at odds with the tradition of American poetry typified by Walt Whitman in the nineteenth century, and in the twentieth by William Carlos Williams; since their idea of poetic form was that it should be closed rather than open, and orthodox and inherited rather than imitative and experimental. Of course, they allowed for, and even insisted upon, personal manoeuvre within the prescribed structures: but this, in fact, only made their ideal poet sound even more like the ideal farmer or planter of Agrarian myth.[92] "There is always a variation to this ritual" of farming, Lytle had insisted in *I'll Take My Stand*. Precisely so: there was always a variation to the poetic rituals too, the Southern New Critics argued, room for the free play of the imagination, the setting off of texture against structure. Like Wade's Cousin Lucius or Ransom's anonymous squirearchy the poet was described as *actively benefiting* from the forms he inherited; they allowed him to give palpable shape and tangible expression to an otherwise amorphous inner world. And the reader, as it turned out, benefited from those rituals as well. For, as Ransom indicated in "Art and the Human Economy", the effect of an aesthetic order on those who perceived it was to produce a momentary feeling of balance and wholeness, and so offer some sort of redress for what Ransom – together with Tate and Warren – now regarded as an *irredeemably* unbalanced and incomplete world.

Even the New Criticism was not simply a movement against the grain, however. It may have involved an attempt to drift back to familiar principles: but that attempt was made on the assumption that the old, active faith had been shattered irretrievably and that, even if parts of it could be reclaimed, this could only be done in a masked way, by indirection and stealth. Agrarianism, as most of the Agrarians realised, had become a lost cause: something to be remembered, occasionally with regret, but more often with affection and approval, on the grounds that the impulses which had fired it into life were not entirely misguided. The Agrarians had begun with a profound sense of historical displacement, the suspicion that an accelerating process of change was threatening to destroy not merely the contours of their physical world but their modes of being and perception, the solidity of their social and moral selves and the terms in which they interpreted things. They had found in Agrarianism a kind of nucleus, and a catalyst: something around which they could gather their feelings of unease and which, in addition, could help transform those feelings into a coherent aim. Quite simply, the Agrarian idea seemed to offer balm to their divided minds, to allay some of their anxiety about the immediate moment by discovering possible redemption in yesterday and tomorrow; the present might be confused, their belief was, but with the help of the regional codes a bridge over it might be built, uniting a past apotheosised by memory to a future transfigured by hope. But the bridge was never completed; they felt themselves compelled to accept historical displacement as inevitable; and they then went on to seek some other form of deliverance, some more strictly personal mode of salvation, that would enable them to confront inevitability without succumbing to despair. "Is not civilization", asks the narrator in Allen Tate's novel, *The Fathers*, "the agreement, slowly arrived at, to let the abyss alone?"[93] Tate, Ransom, and their friends were inspired by the idea of civilisation, certainly, but they could never quite forget about that abyss. It yawned beneath them, even while they tried to balance themselves on what remained of the Southern mythologies; and it gave to everything they said in *I'll Take My Stand* a sense of peril, incipient failure, and fear.

5

Out of the South: the fiction of William Faulkner

Nearly everyone agrees that William Faulkner's work as a whole is greater than the sum of its parts. Malcolm Cowley, for example, in one of the first important discussions of Faulkner's writing, declared that all the books in the Yoknapatawpha series belonged to "the same living pattern". They could be compared, he argued, to "wooden planks . . . cut, not from a log, but from a still living tree": something that was effectively there before they came into being and somehow remained apart from them, susceptible to change and capable of further growth. A similar point has been made by more recent commentators. John T. Irwin, for instance, in his speculative reading of Faulkner, proposes the existence of what he terms an "imaginative space that the novels create in *between* themselves by their interaction"; while Estella Schoenberg and Joanne Creighton prefer to talk in terms of a "multi-novel" or a "meta-novel that exists above and beyond the individual stories which inform it". Some critics pursuing this idea have made use of the contemporary notion of a literary career: "a self-reflexive system" (as one of them puts it) "which is rather more than either the sum of . . . the works produced . . . . or the writer who produced them".[1] Others, in turn, have fallen back on the more traditional idea of the Saga – the suggestion here being that Faulkner, while actually inventing his narratives, manages to create the impression that he has recovered them from an inherited body of anecdote and wisdom; consequently (so this argument goes), his work achieves that quality of resonance so characteristic of ballad and epic, the sense of a thousand other, anonymous stories hovering just behind the one being remembered and retold. The explanations vary wildly, and will presumably continue to do so, but the initial assumption remains the same. The tale of Yoknapatawpha County, the premise is, can somehow be separated from the books in which it is told, and indeed from its teller;

it stands apart from them, even though it is they who give it tangible shape and expression, enjoying its own independent authority and status.

One reason why this belief in the independent status of the Yoknapatawpha story is so strong among Faulkner's readers is because Faulkner himself evidently shared it. As his biographer has shown, Faulkner had the greatest admiration for a writer like Balzac, who could create not just individual novels but "an intact world of his own". "I like the fact", declared Faulkner in an interview,

> that in Balzac . . . people don't just move from page one to page 320 of one book. There is continuity between them all like a blood-stream which flows from page one through to page 20,000 . . . The same blood, muscle, tissue binds the characters together.[2]

This sense of inter-relatedness, of overlapping stories and interwoven character and incident, was clearly something that Faulkner was after himself – and, in his more optimistic moments at least, actually believed he had come near to achieving. "It sometimes seems to me", he told Malcolm Cowley in an unusually self-congratulatory mood, "that all the people of the imaginary county, black and white, townsmen, farmers, and housewives, have played their part in one connected story." Continuity, however, was not quite the right word to describe it. For, as Faulkner recognised most of the time, such connections as he achieved took place within a framework of ultimate *dis*connection. Ends might be tied up but other ends would have to be left hanging loose; the stories that were told, the patterns that were traced, rested upon certain initial acts of selection and exclusion.

Faulkner's recognition of this, the discontinuity of his work, was registered in several ways, varying considerably in obviousness and importance. In the first place, and most obviously, there were his frequent references to the apocryphal status of his fictions: for example, his famous account of his discovery of his "own little postage stamp of native soil" talks of the creative process in terms of "sublimating the actual into the apocryphal".[3] To anyone brought up in the Christian tradition, as Faulkner himself was, such references invariably rang with suggestions of the partially disclosed and secretive, a text that was at best only deviously connected to the truth, a series of words that enjoyed no more than the loosest of associations with the Word. In the second place, there was something rather more fundamental in that it was related to a belief underpinning all Faulkner's work: the belief, that is, that no story could be told finally and for ever. *Maybe nothing ever happens once and is finished*, thinks Quentin Compson in *Absalom, Absalom!*; and that *maybe* became certainty for Quentin's creator, a man who invariably left room for imaginative manoeuvre in his novels, reinvention and reinterpretation, and who liked to insist on the dialectical nature of the relationship between past, present, and future, the tale and the particular context in which it was being told. As far as Faulkner's own relationship to his imagined world was concerned, this belief in what one critic has termed "the 'always deferredness' of meaning" issued in a distinct reluctance to iron out the creases, to resolve the differences between the various versions of an event or person that he offered to his readers over the years. Aware, for instance, that there was something of a discrepancy between his account of the Compson family in *The Sound and the Fury* and the one offered in an appendix to that novel, written many years later, he said simply this:

> Would rather let the appendix stand with the inconsistencies, perhaps, make a statement (quotable) at the end of the introduction, viz.: The inconsistencies in the appendix prove that to me the book is still alive after fifteen years, and being alive is still growing, changing; the appendix was done at the same heat as the book . . . and so it is the book itself which is inconsistent: not the appendix. That is, at the age of thirty I did not know these people as at forty-five I now do: that I was even wrong now and then in the very conclusions I drew from watching them, and the information in which I once believed.[4]

The assumption that lay behind a passage like this – or, for that matter, Faulkner's brief preface to *The Mansion* – was that Yoknapatawpha County and its inhabitants existed somewhere 'out there', in a space of their own quite separate from the one the author occupied. Understanding of them would have as a result to remain partial and even distorted; it might be developed, added to or improved, but, like any body of knowledge that referred to something possessed of its own identity, with its own self-authenticating existence, it could never be assumed to be complete.

A third, and perhaps even more intriguing way in which the otherness of Yoknapatawpha was registered by Faulkner has to do with his attitude, not to stories and storytelling, but to something quite different although equally close to his heart: the land. That attitude is summed up very neatly in a brief passage in *The Unvanquished*, describing two members of the McCaslin family, "Uncle Buck" and "Uncle Buddy". The two men, the narrator informs us,

> believed that land did not belong to people but that people belonged to land and that the earth would permit them to live on and out of it and use it only so long as they behaved and that if they did not behave right, it would shake them off just like a dog getting rid of fleas.[5]

Nobody owns the land, to think so is a snare and a delusion. That is the point made here, and insistently throughout Faulkner's work: in, for instance, the story of the 'education' of Ike McCaslin in *Go Down, Moses*, or in the poignant account of people like Mink Snopes in *The Mansion* who, we learn, never had owned even temporarily the land which they believed they had rented between one New Year's and the next one. It was the land which owned them, and not just from a planting to its harvest but in perpetuity; not . . . the landlord . . . but the land . . .[6]

The ironies implicit in all this are explored in, say, the story of Thomas Sutpen in *Absalom, Absalom!*, a man who is destroyed by his assumption of power over nature; and they reverberate through the account, in *Requiem for a Nun*, of the several generations from Ikkemotubbe to the present who believe that they have set an indelible stamp on their surroundings. More to the point, they put in doubt Faulkner's own proud claim to be the "Sole Owner & Proprietor" of his county. Faulkner might have cherished his postage stamp of native soil, he might have tilled it in his imagination and reaped the appropriate rewards: but, as he evidently realised in the end, he could never exercise complete dominion over it. In this respect, his relationship to Yoknapatawpha was analogous to that of his characters: claiming to possess it he was in fact possessed by it, wishing to appropriate it he could do no more than inhabit it temporarily. Perhaps this is why the illusion of ownership is described so powerfully in his novels: because it was an illusion that he himself shared at times, or at least felt sorely tempted to embrace. Certainly, it was another reason why he saw the very best art, including his own, as a "gallant . . . magnificent failure"; and why, more specifically, he came to believe that there was more to Yoknapatawpha County than even he was ever likely to know.

A further reason why Yoknapatawpha assumed this peculiar substance and authority for Faulkner, and perhaps the major one, was that for him it *became* the South: not just an emblem for the South but his way of understanding it and using it to encode experience. Like the Nashville Agrarians, Faulkner found himself living at a peculiarly difficult time: when, as he put it in one of his class conferences, his region was experiencing the "change from the land to the town and city". "It's not particularly unique to the South", he added. "It's only that the South is a little behind the rest of the country." But, again like the Agrarians, he was well aware of the fact that the difficulties were commensurate with the possibilities. "It was not my intention to write a pageant of my county", he declared once:

I simply was using the quickest tools to hand. I was using what I knew best, which was the locale where I was born and had lived most of my life. That was just like the carpenter building the fence – he uses the nearest hammer.[7]

In a way, this was true: Faulkner could no more avoid using his locality as a "tool", a means of shaping experience, than anyone born in any culture can. However, as he must have realised, he did have the advantage of being born at a moment when *his* culture, his particular locality, offered two peculiar advantages to the writer: a complex code, an elaborate blueprint or vocabulary, and a sense of displacement, sufficient critical distance from that code to allow any person willing to do so to locate and explore it – to know it, one could say, even while employing it as a means of knowledge. This was at least one reason why Yoknapatawpha County came to seem larger than the books in which its story was told: that in becoming the South for its creator it acted as a focus of suggestion, generating far more in the way of potential discourse than he could reasonably encompass. Its relationship to the region and its codes was like that of the tip of the iceberg to the larger mass supporting it beneath the water; and it was not the least of Faulkner's achievements that he evidently recognised this.

Certain, and possibly more useful, ways of defining the connection between Yoknapatawpha and the South are offered to us by contemporary linguistic theory and structural anthropology. Ferdinand de Saussure, for instance, in his *Cours de linguistique générale*, begins his consideration of language by identifying what he sees as its two fundamental dimensions: that of *langue* and that of *parole*. *Langue* is what in English might simply be called 'language', which is to say the abstract language-system pertaining to a particular culture. *Parole*, on the other hand, might be roughly translated as 'speech', the individual utterances made by the various members of that culture. The illustration Saussure himself uses, to explain the distinction he is trying to make, is the game of chess: *langue*, he argues, corresponds to the abstract rules and laws known as 'chess', and *parole* to the actual games of chess played by people in the ordinary world. The rules can be said to exist quite apart from any individual game, or indeed from the sum of all games played or conceivably to be played: but they can only ever assume concrete existence in such games, and in the relationships that develop between them. In the same way, *langue*, the basic structure of language, can be said to exist above and beyond *parole*, the individual examples of speech the nature of which it in fact determines: but it has no concrete life of its own, it receives its only concrete manifestation in the piecemeal form that speech supplies. The traditional theological distinction between the Word of God and the word of man is perhaps as useful an analogy as the game of chess to which Saussure refers. Like the divine Word, *langue* achieves its only tangible realisation in *parole*, the verbal transactions of the visible world; and it is from a synchronic, associative examination of *parole* that we can infer the presence of *langue* and begin to abstract some understanding of its nature. However, the Word is never contained by the word, even though it may be invoked by it: a peculiarly absent presence, *langue* is never fully there in any particular discourse, any specific instance of *parole*, nor for that matter in the sum total of all discourses.[8]

Saussure's distinction between *langue* and *parole* has proved fruitful not only for other linguists but also for anthropologists: and not least for Claude Lévi-Strauss, in his discussion of myth. "Whether the myth is recreated by the individual", argues Lévi-Strauss in his *Structural Anthropology*,

> or borrowed from tradition, it derives from its sources – individual or collective . . . – only the stock of representations with which it operates. But the structure remains the same, and through it the symbolic function is fulfilled.[9]

That is to say, the relationship between the myth and any particular telling of it is precisely the same as the relationship between *langue* and *parole*: Sophocles' *Oedipus Rex*, for example, derives as *parole* from the *langue* of the total Oedipus myth. Above and beyond any particular use of a myth, any individual narrative located in time, lies the myth itself. Behind the several versions of the story of Oedipus scattered through history is the code, the structure that generated and determined them: a structure that is never completely encompassed or circumscribed by those versions, taken separately or in the aggregate. Which is not to suggest, of course, that the structuring myth cannot be apprehended. Just as with *langue*, it can be abstracted from the particular case, the specific text or discourse by reading it synchronically: by effectively perceiving it, not as a series of sequential, linearly progressive relations, but in terms of its associative, coexistent, "vertical" ones – the way it opens a door on the entire storehouse on which it draws.

Turning back to Faulkner, it is probably not difficult to see how all this applies to his "discovery" of his imaginary county. Yoknapatawpha stands in the same relation to the South and its codes as, to use Saussure's terms, *parole* does to *langue* and as, to borrow from Lévi-Strauss's discussion of myth, any particular telling of that myth does to the myth itself. All the Yoknapatawpha stories can, or rather must, be read diachronically, which is to say sequentially, line by line: but they also demand to be read synchronically – as a concrete manifestation of something, some means of interpreting the world and establishing significant connections, that they invoke but by no means contain. "An orchestra score", Lévi-Strauss argues,

> to be meaningful, must be read diachronically along one axis – that is, page after page, and from left to right – and synchronically along the other axis, all the notes written vertically making up one gross constituent unit, that is, one bundle of relations.[10]

In the same way, he suggests, any version of a myth works simultaneously on two axes and must be read along both. And in the same way, one could add, Faulkner's Yoknapatawpha fiction must be perceived with a kind of double vision. We must read it "page after page, and from left to right" as a narrative performance in time. And we must read it, too, in terms of its resonances: the codes that are operative within it, the full pattern of systematised relationships that it presupposes and, to some extent, explores.

This, of course, begs the question of just what those codes are and how, exactly, they operate in the world of Yoknapatawpha – how Faulkner utilises them, how he examines them, and how he places his work in relation to them. As good a way as any, perhaps, of beginning to answer these questions is to recall some of Faulkner's own remarks concerning his region. Such remarks as a whole tended to be characterised by one thing: an ambiguity, bordering on self-contradiction, of which Faulkner himself was well aware even when, as on occasion, he pretended not to be. Asked about the South when he was in Japan, for instance, he declared:

> I love it and hate it. Some of the things I don't like at all, but I was born there, and that's my home, and I will still defend it even if I hate it.[11]

This was a refrain repeated throughout his life: in interviews, in an autobiographical essay like "Mississippi", and not least in his fiction: one thinks, for example, of the anguished note on which *Absalom, Absalom!* ends (*I don't hate it! I don't hate it!*) or the tortured, ambivalent relationship of Bayard Sartoris III, Horace Benbow, Ike McCaslin, and even Gavin Stevens to their heritage. As one of his biographers has said, "Oxford was what Faulkner knew . . . Yet it never became completely his home", "drawn to it he could half enter it; offended by it, he became uneasy and pulled back". Faulkner admitted as much himself when, writing to Malcolm Cowley, he said that after the war he had come back to find that "he was at home again in Oxford, Mississippi, yet at the same time . . . not at home". Such an equivocal stance to his "native land" (as he termed it in "Mississippi") naturally encouraged a dual focus and peculiar self-consciousness in his fiction. The map of the South that the Yoknapatawpha stories present us with seems, in fact, to have been drawn by a double agent, someone who knows what it is both to be an insider and an outsider; it discloses plans, and explores dreams, that possess both observed and observer.

Just as crucial a factor in promoting this duality and self-consciousness was something that has been mentioned in passing already: Faulkner's sense of living at a moment of crisis. There is a curious, if perfectly understandable, inconsistency about the opinions he expressed on this matter. At times, he could talk as if there were no doubt in his mind that the South survived as a recognisable entity, with its own peculiar and ultimately definable codes. "In the South", he declared once in an interview, "there is still a common acceptance of the world, a common view of life, a common morality": a declaration that had been anticipated by Gavin Stevens in *Intruder in the Dust* – who declaims (on behalf of Southerners faced with the possibility of enforced desegregation):

> We are defending not actually our politics or beliefs or even our way of life, but simply our homogeneity . . . only from homogeneity comes anything of a people or for a people of durable and lasting value.[12]

However, such claims ring decidedly hollow when placed beside a passage like the following. It is taken from an Introduction to *The Sound and the Fury*, written by Faulkner in 1933 but only published fairly recently:

> . . . the South (I speak in the sense of the indigenous dream of any given collection of men having something in common, be it only geography or climate, which shape [sic] their economic and spiritual aspirations into cities, into a pattern of houses or behaviour) is old since dead . . . There is a thing known whimsically as the New South to be sure, but it is not the south. It is a land of Immigrants who are rebuilding the towns and cities into replicas of towns and cities in Kansas and Iowa and Illinois, with skyscrapers and striped canvas awnings instead of balconies, and teaching the young men who sell the gasoline and the waitresses in the restaurants to say O yeah? and to speak with hard r's, and hanging over the intersections of quiet and shaded streets where no one save Northern tourists in Cadillacs and Lincolns ever pass at a gait faster than a horse trots, changing red-and-green lights and savage and peremptory bells.[13]

The explanation seems to have been that Faulkner found himself at the cutting edge of history: a corner from which he could see the road that lay behind and the road lying ahead. On occasion, especially in his discursive prose when his imagination was not thoroughly captivated by his fictive county, he would set his eyes in one direction, towards past or future. But more often than not he could and would face both ways, and so was able to use the "indigenous dream" of the South in a simultaneously distanced and engaged way, with a sharp sense of the historical ironies involved and a nicely graduated measure of self-awareness.

Just how this expressed itself in the texts themselves is perhaps best seen in the variations Faulkner played on the Southern code, as it fed into the substance of each narrative. And exemplary in this respect was his use of *place*: that feeling of belonging to one dear, particular spot that characterises so much Southern writing. "More than any other people of the world", declared one Southern novelist, "the Southerners have that where-do-you-come-from-sense";[14] and, with very little hesitation, one would have to agree. The point is illustrated by a fairly minor novel,

Fire in the Morning by Elizabeth Spencer, which draws its strength from its typicality. The action of the book turns on a contrast between families: on the one hand, the Armstrongs and McKies, and on the other the Gerrards. The Armstrongs and the McKies, as a result of "living in one pleasant place" all their lives have become identified with that place, feel that they belong to it and cherish it. The Gerrards, by contrast, appear to have no vital connection with the land whatsoever; interlopers, they are like the Yankees of a previous era, bringing "fire in the morning", waste and destruction, in their wake. What they lack is briefly summed up by one of the Armstrongs. He listens to a friend reciting from Thomas Hardy's poem "Neutral Tones" the lines, "Since then, keen lessons that love deceives, / . . . have shaped to me / Your face, and the God-curst sun, and a tree / And a pond edged with grayish leaves", and then comments in this fashion:

> "You see . . . something very rare in this poem; namely the correct order of things . . . Objects do not go about teaching us little lessons. No, but when a man remembers those times which he cannot forget, he will forever find, too, implicit in his memory and not to be torn away from it, the physical object of the scene . . . present simply as they are, self-assertive and undescribed, 'shaped to me' . . ."[15]

"*Feelings* are bound up in place . . ." insisted Eudora Welty in one of her essays, "It is by knowing where you started that you grow able to judge where you are":[16] a sentiment that finds its echo in a remark made by another Southern writer – "to know the certain things to which a man belongs", he insisted, "with which his deepest self is identified, is to know the man". Variously expressed, this belief in the power of environment, this feeling of attachment to landscape, remains the same and inescapable, one of the structuring principles of Southern myth. As such, it inevitably became operative in Faulkner's work as soon as he began to write: not just after he made his famous return journey to Oxford, but as soon as he had found his vocation.

It is important to emphasise this: that the sense of place was there in embryo in Faulkner's early work, even if it took his discovery of Yoknapatawpha to bring it into full, breathing life. In *Soldier's Pay*, for example, the plight of characters like Donald Mahon, Margaret Powers, and Joe Gilligan stems ultimately from their placelessness. The men, in particular, return to their homes only to find – or, at least, sense – that, like the characters in *Pylon*, they have "no place . . . to go back to . . . even if it's just only to hate the damn place good and comfortable". In the simplest possible sense, they are homeless; and the portrait Faulkner offers us of Charlestown, the setting for most of the narrative, serves as an ironic counterpoint, a reminder of the cosy securities that are no longer available to them:

Charlestown, like numberless other towns throughout the South, had been
built around a circle of tethered horses and mules. In the middle of the square
was the courthouse – a simple utilitarian edifice of brick and sixteen beautiful
Ionic columns stained with generations of casual tobacco. Elms surrounded the
courthouse and beneath these trees, on scarred and carved wood benches and
chairs the city fathers, progenitors of solid laws and solid citizens who believed
in Tom Watson and feared only God and drouth, in . . . the faded brushed grey
and bronze meaningless medals of the Confederate States of America . . . slept
or whittled away the long drowsy days while their juniors of all ages . . .
played checkers or chewed tobacco and talked.[17]

The anticipations of Jefferson here are perhaps too obvious to be
· remarked upon: one almost expects to see Benjy Compson appear in a
carriage rattling from left to right. What is perhaps worthy of remark,
though, is the way that Faulkner, while drawing on a tradition of
portraits of sleepy Southern towns that goes back at least as far as *Life on
the Mississippi*, manages to give it an additional dimension, an extra edge.
This he does simply by setting his portrait within a context of loss: a
narrative framework that is defined chiefly by characters who do not
belong to their surroundings, who are at best only loosely attached to the
imagined places in which they are set. In this respect, the protagonists of
Soldier's Pay stand at the beginning of a long and distinguished line. One
thinks, for example, of Bayard Sartoris III in *Flags in the Dust*, watching
"the noon throng" and noting a painful contrast between their easy
"murmuring and laughing" – their ability, as Walker Percy might have
put it, to be one hundred per cent themselves – and his own nervous
agitation and restlessness. Or one thinks, perhaps, of Horace Benbow in
Sanctuary, whose agony and sense of displacement are quietly mocked by
the people he sees around him on the courthouse square: "slow as sheep",
possessed of the "mild inscrutability of cattle", revealing the same
patience, impassiveness, and even mystery as the "imponderable land"
they inhabit. Nor should the autobiographical reference be forgotten
here, the connection between Faulkner's deployment of people like
Mahon, Bayard Sartoris III, and Benbow, and his own sense of being "at
home . . . yet at the same time . . . not at home". It was not just that,
through the use of this context of loss, Faulkner found a way of
expressing those feelings of crisis and exile he shared with other major
Southern writers of his time: writers as otherwise different as, say,
Thomas Wolfe and Allen Tate. It was also that, in this fashion, he
managed to inject a special, and discomfitingly personal, tension into his
work, since in their relationship to place Faulkner's protagonists
frequently act as masks, a means of fictionalising their creator's peculiar
status in Oxford, his role of double agent.

Of course, it would be wrong to suggest that Faulkner's use of place as a tool was never simple or straightforward, in line with the mainstream of the regional tradition. It could be just that: as Charles Mallison, one of the narrators of *The Town*, indicates when he declares right at the beginning of the novel, "when I say 'we' and 'we thought', what I mean is Jefferson and what Jefferson thought".[18] The sense of identification with a place that is thoroughly known and cherished is unmistakable here: just as it tends to be in some of the short stories, like "The Tall Men" and "Shall Not Perish". As a general rule, however, there is nearly always this edginess and self-consciousness, and not merely because of Faulkner's use of a framework of loss, or preference for characters who are at least partially displaced. Just as important, in this respect, is his willingness to suggest that landscape, place possesses a degree of anonymity that is ultimately inescapable and indelible: that our efforts to identify and know it are, in the last analysis, doomed. This is far more than the perception offered by a lesser Southern writer like Spencer that one attaches one's feelings and memories to something that is, objectively speaking, neutral, that the sense of belonging to a spot is largely a matter of projection. It is a matter of seeing place as a product of human creativity. We make the spaces we inhabit, Faulkner's message is, because we structure them, we call them into being by naming them; to put it with brutal simplicity, the nature to which we seek to fasten ourselves is a cultural artifact that will last only as long as we and our vocabulary do. It goes without saying, perhaps, that this reading of place would have been unavailable to Faulkner had he lived in stabler, more culturally contained times. But it is worth adding that the reading did not come easily or inevitably: only Faulkner and a very few other Southern writers were able to reinvent a segment of the regional code in this way – by using it, and at the same time subjecting it to radical reappraisal.

Perhaps the nature of this reinvention of the sense of place could be made clearer by means of a comparison. In traditional Southern writing, in the novels of William Gilmore Simms, for instance, and the poems and prose of Sidney Lanier, the place, wherever it may be, seems already located and identified, a prepared landscape structured by innumerable previous activities and perceptions. It is there, the impression is, for the writer to record and for the characters to enter into and be defined by. But in Faulkner's work, and that of a few other Southern writers of the period, there is a far more conscious, more open and deliberate sense of the landscape being organised: tamed by the particular eye that confronts it, given shape and substance by the particular imagination that comes to grapple with it in the text. In John Crowe Ransom's poem, "Antique Harvesters", for instance, a sense of place seems to be created by the seeing eye of the narrator as he observes the land on the banks of the Mississippi and gradually attaches to it the notions of ceremony and chivalry, the belief in a usable past and an inheritable pattern of living. What seemed at first little more than "a meager hill of kernels, a runnel of juice" is transformed during the course of the poem into a spiritual resource, a setting that evidently furnishes roots and identity; and that process of transformation, whereby an anonymous and apparently unpromising environment becomes an heroic land (whereby, one could say, the earth becomes "our Lady")[19] is as much a matter for the reader's attention as the purported subject is. "The process of definition is the intent of the poem", wrote Robert Creeley; and, altering the phrase a little, one could add that the process of *creation*, the act of making a landscape, is at least part of the intent of this particular poem – and constitutes a vital part of the *content* too.

Which is also true for Faulkner: on the simplest level this takes the form of several major characters attempting to transmogrify their surroundings, and so fill "a kind of vacuum" – which is how Shreve describes the South, at one point, in *Absalom, Absalom!* – with solidity and moral presence. So, in *Absalom, Absalom!*, the landscape of Sutpen's Hundred is made by the protagonist and the narrators, man acting and man thinking (Faulkner hardly bothers to make a distinction since, for him, the creative process is at work in both); each of them fashions a place that gives their inner lives geographical location, a local habitation and a name. And so the people Faulkner describes in the inter-chapters of *Requiem for a Nun* seem to will Jefferson into being: in order, like the girl who scratches her name on a window-pane in the town jail, to leave some "fragile and indelible" evidence of themselves on the surface of the earth – something that says, *Listen, stranger: this was myself, this was I.* This is only the simplest level, however. In a deeper way, the making of a landscape in Faulkner's work involves the open and active participation, not only of the characters and narrators, but of the author himself, just as it does in "Antique Harvesters". Repeatedly, the reader is presented with moments when the sense of place seems to be created by the seeing eye of the writer, as he observes some particular portion of Yoknapatawpha and gradually reinterprets it in terms of certain ideas, a specific vocabulary and values. The scene at the beginning of *Light in August* is a case in point, describing Lena Grove travelling across the Mississippi countryside towards Jefferson and encountering Henry Armstid in his wagon. She has been travelling for almost four weeks, we are told,

> a long monotonous succession of peaceful and undeviating changes from day to dark and dark to day again, through which she advanced in identical and anonymous and deliberate wagons as though through a succession of creak-wheeled and limpeared avatars, like something moving forever and without progress across an urn.
>
> The wagon mounts the hill toward her . . .

> . . . Though the mules plod in a steady and unflagging hypnosis, the vehicle does not seem to progress. It seems to hang suspended in the middle distance forever and forever, so infinitesimal is its progress, like a shabby bead upon the mild red string of road. So much is this so that in the watching of it the eye loses it as sight and sense drowsily merge and blend, like the road itself, with all the peaceful and monotonous changes between darkness and day, like already measured thread being rewound onto a spool. So that at last, as though out of some trivial and unimportant region beyond even distance, the sound of it seems to come slow and terrific and without meaning, as though it were a ghost travelling a half mile ahead of its own shape.[20]

Some of the effects of this passage are fairly obvious, if nonetheless impressive: its onomatopoeic force, for example ("the sharp brittle crack and clatter"), the evocative movement ("Though the mules plod"), or the repetitions of word and phrase that at once focus the reader's attention on the right particulars and capture something of Lena's "identical and anonymous" days as well. Others, though, are much subtler, more elusive: the reader is much less likely to notice them even though his reading of the scene has been shaped by them. The use of imagery and descriptive detail offers a useful illustration here, because on close inspection it seems to rest on an implicit paradox: not just contradiction, but a dialectically stimulating and fruitful paradox. Many of the images Faulkner uses are bright and vivid and their vivacity and clarity serve to draw us into the scene, so that we are involved in the experience described. But the emphasis he places on the smallness of certain objects (the road, the wagon, the people) has a very different impact: it tends to set us above and apart from things, so that we also receive an impression of the experience's shape and wholeness. As so often in Faulkner's work, in fact, the reader senses that he is at once inside events and outside them, a participant and an observer. The imaginative place the author is describing captures his attention, and consequently ours, but it is not by any means permitted to monopolise it; we are made aware of the existence of a larger framework, other possibilities of perspective and language, and so end by sharing in Faulkner's equivocal status.

Another way of putting this, the effect achieved by Faulkner's use of a dual perspective, would be to say that in his rendering of scene he places primary emphasis on the act of seeing: the way in which the disposition of author, narrator, and reader, the stance from which they perceive some small corner of the earth, serves to shape it in a particular fashion. This is something that is underlined in the passage in several ways. Most obviously, Faulkner actually draws our attention to the process of active perception and, in effect, reinvention: watching the wagon, the reader is told, "the eye loses it as sight and sense drowsily merge and blend" with results that are then catalogued in some detail. The eye reshapes and restructures things, remakes them according to its own habits and laws; and so, the implication is, does language. For this is the eventual message carried to us by the language Faulkner uses: a language that never ceases calling attention to its artificiality. His prose is insistently figurative, intricately playful, as if he were trying to remind us all the time that what he is presenting us with is, finally, a verbal construct: within the space of a few sentences, for instance, we are invited to consider Lena Grove in terms of the figures on Keats's Grecian Urn, to compare motion to stasis (the wagon) and sound to silence (its creaking wheels), and to think of the country wagons that carry Lena towards Jefferson as "a succession of creak-wheeled and limpeared avatars". This is not just verbal bravado, nor is Faulkner merely intent on violently yoking the most heterogeneous particulars together. The calculated, 'high profile' vocabulary used in a scene like this, the elaborate conceits and patent fictiveness, are simply another way of making the point that this scene, this place like all others, is a product of human creativity: fashioned out of words, tropes, grammar or, it may be, codes, conventions, and rituals.

At this point, it may be objected that anyone describing a place is to that extent 'making' it, and that there is consequently no difference between, on the one hand, writers like Faulkner and Ransom, and, on the other, earlier or minor writers from the region. In a way, this is true; anyone is creating a landscape when they write about it, turning a world into speech. There is a difference, however – and a crucial difference at that – and it is a matter of consciousness and impression. With writers like Simms or Lanier, or for that matter Elizabeth Spencer, the language refers us to something that is supposed to be objectively there, more or less in its entirety, its fundamental patterns established and requiring only a frame. Place, "the physical objects of the scene", the assumption and implication is, may be coloured by the writer but it is in no sense restructured by him; its essence precedes the existence he has given it. With someone like Faulkner, though, or Ransom, language becomes much more creative, insists more on its status as an invented object, and the writer is very much more his own explorer and topographer. In turn, place becomes far more amorphous and fluid because, like the settings in many of Wallace Stevens's poems, it is clearly and indeed sometimes ostentatiously (thanks to the obtrusive, oratorical idiom) the product of an interchange between code and environment, the mind and its surroundings; constantly created and then recreated out of a feeling of need, it seems to depend for its essential character – which is to say, the qualities for which it is known – upon its existence within the writer's fragile web of words.

The feeling that existence precedes essence also characterises Faulkner's treatment of another crucial aspect of the Southern code: that sense of the past which led one minor writer from the region to claim that "everything flows into everything and carries with it all the lives of . . . other life". Southern literature, as Allen Tate put it once in a famous phrase, is "a literature conscious of the past in the present"; and Southern books are full of characters who are destroyed because they forget "the simple fact of the continuity of life" (as one such book puts it),

> the single thread that is never cut but which goes on generation unto generation to the end of time. The simple truth that the future and the past are a part of the same passage.[21]

This is the theme of, for example, *A Buried Land* by Madison Jones, one of the best minor Southern writers of recent years, the power and limitations of whose work derive precisely from his deliberate, willed and more or less complete, commitment to the traditional codes of his region. At the centre of the novel is Percy Youngblood, a character who attempts to deny the past in two ways, political and personal, which eventually coalesce. On the public level, he gives his full, uncritical support to the forces of progress and, more specifically, to the Tennessee Valley Authority, which wishes to bury some of the old world quite literally in the name of a new order, yet to be born. And on the private, he rejects his father, who opposes the Tennessee Valley scheme; and he attempts to evade responsibility for the death of his lover, killed in the course of a botched abortion, by concealing her body in the land about to be flooded. "It's a kind of sickness, isn't it, that dwelling on the past", claims a friend and mentor of Youngblood's, "people leave ruin behind them, it's the nature of things." It is the entire purpose of Jones's novel, however, to disprove this claim, and to lead Youngblood towards some recognition of its falsity: a recognition that takes a form characteristic of so much Southern writing – a return to the family home or, in this case, to the place where the home had once been, and where it still seems to exist, "only submerged . . . a ghostly shadow".[22] "We Southerners are accused of living in the past", complains another minor writer from the region and rough contemporary of Jones's. "What else can we do?" he asks defiantly:

> The past lives in us. And not just that single episode which those who accuse us have in mind: the Civil War – but all of the past. If the Civil War is more alive to the Southerner than to the Northerner it is because all the past is, and this is so because the Southerner has a sense of having been present there himself in the person of one or more of his ancestors.[23]

Such a claim might stand as a useful epigraph not only to a novel like *A Buried Land* but to the entire body of work written from within the Southern tradition.

"The past is never dead. It's not even past": this famous remark from *Requiem for a Nun* will serve to remind us, if reminder is necessary, that Faulkner's obsession with the past is quite as marked as that of any of his Southern predecessors or contemporaries; time and again, he and his characters play on what is called at one point in *Absalom, Absalom!*, "the resonant strings of remembering". Very often, too, this obsession takes a fairly commonplace form (commonplace for the region, that is) of presenting us with someone who is so haunted by ghosts, whether he likes it or not, that he is like "an empty hall echoing with sonorous defeated names". Old "Colonel" Bayard Sartoris, for example, is portrayed in this way in *Flags in the Dust*, as a man so overshadowed by things past that he seems less of a substantial presence than they are; while several of the characters in *Sanctuary* and *Light in August* behave like – and, indeed, are compared to – sleepwalkers for the simple reason that their immersion in memories has deprived them of the ability to function properly in the present. For such people, who often seem reminiscent of Poe's febrile and distracted protagonists, the phrase associated with Joe Christmas in *Light in August* might serve as an appropriate epitaph: "Memory believes before knowing remembers." More to the point, to their stories as a whole the title of Madison Jones's book could easily be attached: as this passage, taken from *The Town*, tends to illustrate. It is Gavin Stevens, one of Faulkner's favourite characters, who is speaking and the perception he offers here – one that shapes his life and vision – clearly links the past, in both a literal and a metaphorical sense, with the notion of "a buried land".

> There is a ridge; you drive on beyond Seminary Hill and in time you come upon it . . . And . . . looking back and down, you see all Yoknapatawpha in the dying last of day beneath you . . .
>
> They are all here, supine beneath you, stratified and superposed, osseous and durable with the frail dust and phantoms – the rich alluvial river-bottom land of old Issetibbeha, the wild Chickasaw king, with his Negro slaves and his sister's son called Doom . . .; the same fat black rich plantation earth still synonymous of the proud fading white plantation names whether we – I mean of course they – ever actually owned a plantation or not: Sutpen and Sartoris and Compson and Edmonds and McCaslin and Beauchamp and Grenier and Habersham and Holston and Stevens and De Spain . . . Then the roadless, almost pathless perpendicular hill-country of McCallum and Gowrie and Frazier and Muir . . . everywhere you look about the dark panorama you still see them, faint as whispers . . . And you . . . standing there while there rises to you, about you, suffocating you, the spring dark peopled and myriad . . .[24]

But Faulkner's rendering of the past does not simply take this form of describing for us the idea of a buried land and presenting people who are so affected by their surroundings that they feel (to borrow a phrase from *Absalom, Absalom!*) "older at twenty than a lot of people who have died". Far more interesting and central to his work are his attempts to show the past not as a ghost, however substantial, but as a living presence capable of growth. Again, this is something that Faulkner shares with those few of his contemporaries in the South whose relationship to the traditional codes was founded on a recognition of crisis: who did not simply acknowledge the facts of change and displacement (most modern Southern writers have done that, at one time or another), but who tried to express that acknowledgement in their response to the region's structuring myths. One thinks, for example, of Robert Penn Warren and Allen Tate, both of whom have portrayed the relationship between past and present as a dialectical one, involving alteration on both sides. A poem like Tate's "Ode to the Confederate Dead" illustrates this. The narrator, a man who is unmistakably a victim of the contemporary crisis, stands by a Confederate graveyard; and, as he tries to imagine what the lives of those buried there might have been like, it is clear that what he is doing is reconstructing an *idea* of "the Confederate dead", something by which to measure his own sense of failure. He is haunted by ghosts, certainly, but they are ghosts that he has helped to invent, using the hints and guesses that are available to him. Tradition, the sense of a usable past, is by no means assumed in the poem – a *donné*, to use Henry James's handy term – for the simple reason that the making of a tradition constitutes its leading subject. What we are asked to consider, in fact, is the way in which the present actively shapes the past, not merely remembers but reinvents it.[25]

It is, however, Faulkner himself who has given the most succinct, memorable expression to this idea of deliberately recreating the past, in a famous passage in *Intruder in the Dust*. Again, it is Gavin Stevens who is speaking: "yesterday wont be over until tomorrow", declares Stevens,

> and tomorrow began ten thousand years ago. For every Southern boy fourteen years old, not once but whenever he wants it, there is the instant when it's still not yet two o'clock on that July afternoon in 1863, the brigades are in position, the guns are laid and ready in the woods and the furled flags are already loosened to break out . . . and it's all in the balance, it hasn't happened yet, it hasn't even begun yet.[26] (See Plate 10)

It is a measure of just how deeply embedded in Faulkner's work this idea of reimagining yesterday is that it is adumbrated in his very first novel. At the centre of *Soldier's Pay* is Donald Mahon, a living corpse badly wounded in the First World War, who has been cut off from the past by the loss of memory. A dangling man, he appears to be waiting for something, as another character comments: "Something he has begun, but not completed, something he has carried over from his former life that he does not remember consciously." The nature of that "something" eventually becomes apparent: towards the end of the novel he remembers the day on which he was wounded and, having done so, he then dies. His past has been reimagined, the clear implication is; and because it has he can have a present; the story has been recovered, retold, and can now be given the sense of an ending.

A comparable but infinitely more complicated process occurs in Faulkner's later novels, where character after character appears to be reinventing the past so as to create a sense of identity. Faulkner used various analogies to try to define this process. In the original version of *Sanctuary*, for example, he compares Horace Benbow to an archaeologist "who, from a meagre sifting of vertebrae, reconstructs a shape out of the nightmares of his own childhood". More frequently, he referred to the figure of the detective: not just literally in the sense that Gavin Stevens acts as an amateur sleuth in *Knight's Gambit*, solving a number of local mysteries, but in the metaphorical sense that people like Quentin Compson and Shreve in *Absalom, Absalom!* – or, for that matter, Benbow in *Sanctuary* and Stevens himself in *Requiem for a Nun* – try to construct a coherent and plausible version of past events. "The hero of a detective novel", argues R. G. Collingwood in *The Idea of History*,

> is thinking exactly like an historian when, from indications of the most varied kinds, he constructs an imaginary picture of how a crime was committed and by whom.[27]

Which suggests a further analogy: the narrators and protagonists of many of Faulkner's stories could also be compared to Collingwood's ideal historian, who weaves together "a web of imaginative construction stretched between certain fixed points provided by the statements of his authorities". History, Collingwood insists, is a re-enactment of past experience; "The history of thought, and therefore all history, is the re-enactment of past thought in the historian's mind." This does not involve "a passive surrender to the spell of another's mind", he goes on, but rather

> a labour of active and therefore critical thinking. The historian not only re-enacts past thought, he re-enacts it in the context of his own knowledge and therefore, in re-enacting it, criticizes it, forms his own judgement of its value, corrects whatever errors he can discern in it. This criticism of the thought whose history he traces is not something secondary to tracing the history of it. It is an indispensable condition of the historical knowledge itself.[28]

It is not difficult to see the parallel here. The activity Collingwood describes is not that far removed, after all, from (to take just one example)

Quentin and Shreve's attempts to reinterpret the Sutpen story by relating it to their own experience and the broader historical experience of the South: to recover the past by resurrecting its inhabitants and attempting to 'become' them – trying to imagine how they thought and what they believed.

The parallel is not perfect, however, and for one seminal reason. In constructing his imaginative web, Collingwood suggests, the historian tries to use "nothing that is not necessitated by the evidence", but nevertheless to supply sufficient "points" (in the form of documents, artifacts, and other data) for only one "thread" or hypothesis to fill the space between. And,

> if these points are frequent enough and the threads spun from each to the next are constructed with due care . . . the whole picture . . . runs little risk of losing touch with the reality which it represents.[29]

The essence of something like the Sutpen story, though, is that the "points" are *not* frequent enough: that, as one critic has put it, "there are too many holes in it and no possible access to factual filler for the holes. At best, it is a series of dramatically potent pictures." A narrative that links those pictures, and binds yesterday to today, is something that Quentin and Shreve clearly yearn for, as they work together with, as their raw material, "the rag-tag and bob-ends of old tales and talking". But all they can weave out of this is something that is disconcertingly artificial, self-evidently fictive: a world inhabited by

> people who perhaps had never existed at all anywhere, who, shadows, were shadows not of flesh and blood which had lived and died but of shadows in turn of what were . . . shades too, quiet as the visible murmur of their vaporizing breaths . . .[30]

The past in Faulkner's work, like place, seems to be a kind of vacuum which the observer must populate with his own imagined inhabitants. Or, if not that exactly, it is at any rate an uncharted territory containing a few clues, one or two points of reference, to tease even the least curious or speculative of minds.

The net result of this attitude towards the past and its interpretation is to make Faulkner's readers feel quite frequently as if they had been caught in a Chinese box of fictions, in which everything comments on its own origins, making, and development. *Absalom Absalom!* is again the classic instance here, if only because it is the work of Faulkner's that is most insistently preoccupied with the problem of understanding past events and placing them in some kind of significant conjunction with the present. Most of the story comes to us mediated by not one but several narrators, and is punctuated by such remarks as "I was not there", "All I ever heard", "I have this from something your grandfather let drop", "the tale came through the negroes", "That was how he told it". The account of Sutpen's experiences in Haiti, for example, is offered by Quentin to Shreve; Quentin, in turn, learned it from his father, who learned it from *his* father General Compson, who learned it from Sutpen. The reader is presented with a series of receding pictures – Quentin and Shreve at Harvard, Quentin and his father in Oxford, Quentin's father listening to General Compson, General Compson listening by the campfire to Sutpen – all of which revolve around the act of storytelling, constructing a version of things. Nor do these pictures end with the version Sutpen supplies, since he seems to be quite as distanced from the story he tells as anyone else. "It was not absolutely clear" to him, we are informed,

> – the how and the why he was there and what he was – since he was not talking about himself. He was telling a story . . . he was just telling a story about something a man named Thomas Sutpen had experienced . . .[31]

In this context, something that Mary McCarthy said once about Vladimir Nabokov's *Pale Fire* seems relevant. When we read *Pale Fire*, she explained,

> a novel on several levels is revealed, and those "levels" are not the customary "levels of meaning" of modernist criticism but planes in fictive space . . . Each plane or level in its shadow box proves to be a false bottom; there is an infinite regression, for the book is a book of mirrors.[32]

"The book is a book of mirrors": it is not just that the several narrators of *Absalom, Absalom!* offer versions of the past that tell us as much about their creators as they do about their apparent subject, or that in doing so they dramatise Faulkner's notion of the historical process as a recreation of the past by the present. It is that (as several commentators have pointed out) each reader, every time he reads the book, is compelled into this act of recreation too: compelled, that is, to compare versions, fill in gaps, and discover inconsistencies. *Absalom, Absalom!* is 'about' the making of history and enforces just such a making on its audience, every member of which therefore becomes a part of the "infinite regression". Nor does the regression end there, with this one novel. "I am telling the same story over and over", Faulkner admitted once, "which is myself and the world."[33] The entire Yoknapatawpha series – with its recurring characters, its repetition and revision of familiar stories, and its slow accumulation of character and incident – ends up by offering us a microcosm of history in which "nothing ever happens once and is finished" either for the author or for the reader.

Of course, one common result of emphasising and exploring past experience – instead, that is, of future possibilities – is that one ends up with a profound sense of evil. Viewed in terms of what they have done (or at least what they are believed to have done) rather than what they might do, people seem no longer innocent and perfectible but, on the contrary, deeply flawed, weighed down by the burden of inherited failure. This, evidently, is what has happened within the traditional Southern scheme of things: a preoccupation with the past (combined, as C. Vann Woodward has pointed out, with the fact that the region has had to suffer failure and defeat on a scale unparalleled elsewhere in the United States)[34] has encouraged Southerners to believe that, to quote one of them, "without the knowledge of evil . . . there is no life". As far as Southern writing is concerned, this sense that (as another minor Southern author puts it) "there is evil in the world and it is strong" has found expression in several ways. There is, for example, a recurrent tendency to subject Adamic protagonists, idealists and innocents, to withering criticism and even humiliation, quite simply because of their inability to perceive the dark side of human nature, their blindness to the power of blackness and what one writer from the region has called "the power of the swamp". One thinks, in this context, of characters like Virginia Cranston in John Peale Bishop's novel *Act of Darkness*, Henry Brent in Andrew Nelson Lytle's book *A Name for Evil* and, more recently Jonathan Cannon in *Forest of the Night* by Madison Jones. And just as pervasive is the use of the trappings of Gothic fantasy, landscapes of nightmare and characters who seem designed to prove the claim that (to borrow a remark made by one character in *Forest of the Night*) "human beings is a heap like animals . . . You ain't a–going to get that out of them".[35]

The books of the Tennessee novelist Cormac McCarthy are particularly interesting in this respect, since they manage to combine an apocalyptic vision with a lean, meticulous prose and to locate incidents of perversion and violence in settings of unnerving peace, disturbing quietude. In *Child of God*, for instance, McCarthy's third published novel, we are introduced to a poor white Southerner called Lester Ballard: who is described as "small, unclean, unshaven . . . with a constrained truculence. Saxon and Celtic blood. A child of God much like yourself perhaps." That last phrase reverberates with irony, since in the course of the novel Ballard becomes a voyeur, a murderer, and a necrophiliac. Moving to levels of existence that are ever more primitive, ever more elemental and subhuman, he retreats eventually into a cave with a cathedral-like ceiling where he places the bodies of his victims "on stone ledges in attitudes of repose". There is a peculiarly suggestive mixture of animalistic and theological references in these later pages. "Here" in the cave, we are told,

> the walls with their softlooking convolutions . . . had an organic look to them, like the innards of some great beast. Here in the bowels of the mountain . . . on ledges or pallets of stone . . . dead people lay like saints.[36]

The mixture is in some ways reminiscent of Flannery O'Connor: as, indeed, is the last act in this macabre drama. Ballard dies suddenly, and then is subjected to the final stage in this process of dehumanisation, as piece by piece his body is dissected by medical students:

> His head was sawed open and the brains removed. His muscles were stripped from his bones. His heart was taken out. His entrails were hauled forth . . . At the end of three months when the class was closed Ballard was scraped from the table into a plastic bag and taken with others of his kind to a cemetery outside the city and there interred. A minister from the school read a simple service.[37]

A passage like this illustrates the power of the book, and of so much Southern writing. That power, such as it is, depends on a single-minded, almost obsessive dissection of the human animal's claims to authority and status, a stripping-away of his pretensions and, to some extent, even his dignity. And it also relies on the reader's feeling that this unnerving process is performed, not for sensationalism's sake, but in the service of a vision that approaches the religious – which is to say, in the name of three things: a sense of moral displacement, a fear of pride and abstraction, and a belief in something – force, fate, environment, or whatever – that lies beyond the human capacity to know and control.

"There is a logical pattern to evil", thinks Horace Benbow in *Sanctuary*; and in Faulkner's work, more than in that of any other Southern writer, that pattern is intricate and interconnected. Something of this has been suggested already, in the discussion in chapter 4 of Joanna Burden's attitude to the "curse" visited upon the white race by the black. Like many writers from the region, Faulkner tended to associate the idea of evil with the black man or black woman's potent if shadowy figure; since the black, whether as a slave or more simply the member of an oppressed race, brings with him a disconcerting reminder of inherited guilt. To white Southerners, including white Southern writers, he becomes a potent emblem of Original Sin, simply by being there, standing on the periphery of things: a reminder of a crime committed not so very long ago by some mythic, communal ancestor. Unlike most of his contemporaries, however, Faulkner went further than this. Certainly, the guilt is there, ingrained in the texture of his books; more specifically, the association of blacks and evil is part of their mythological framework, their structure of thought and feeling. But as that passage quoted earlier from *Light in August* indicates, it is also the object of creative analysis: Joanna Burden's speech proves, if proof is necessary, that Faulkner's sense of evil, like his sense of place and the past, was self-aware, self-dramatising, and above all self-critical. From the legion of other possible illustrations of this one need only cite that moment in *Go Down, Moses* when Roth Edmonds feels that he can no longer sleep beside Henry Beauchamp, the black boy who up until then has been his closest friend and constant companion. There is no particular reason why Roth feels this way, Faulkner tells us. It is just that "one day the old curse of his fathers, the old haughty ancestral pride . . . descended to him".[38] Roth simply inherits the racial prejudice, and the guilt, of his ancestors and re-enacts their Original Sin: a Sin that is compounded by the fact that, since he and Henry share the same great-great-great-grandfather, he is denying his brother in a double sense. The power of this moment is extraordinary; and it stems directly from the fact that it encapsulates a feeling provoked by the entire narrative. For all the stories that go to make up the book present the black as a kind of Nemesis: a bringer of doom and a provoker of shame and fear. We are, in effect, invited to observe and examine evil, how it originates and expresses itself, and we are also made to feel it, to share in the sense of its presence. And this dual process is made possible because the writer is describing one of his own obsessions as a Southerner, not just a facet of observed behaviour; it is something that, having inherited, he cannot ignore or suppress, and that he is now inviting us to explore.

"Then he was . . . enclosed . . . in that unmistakable odour of Negroes", Faulkner writes of Charles Mallison in *Intruder in the Dust*,

> – that smell which if it were not for something that was going to happen to him . . . he would have gone to his grave never once pondering . . . He had smelled it for ever, he would smell it always; it was a part of his inescapable past, it was a rich part of his heritage as a Southerner . . .[39]

Remarks of this kind run through Faulkner's work: there are references, for instance, to "the frank odour of. . . Negroes" in *Soldier's Pay*, to their "animal odour" in *Flags in the Dust*, and to the "smell" of the hordes of ex-slaves hurrying North in *The Unvanquished*. Ugly as such remarks may seem at first sight, they do have a positive function: which is to express, in peculiarly persuasive because sensory terms, the elusiveness and omnipresence of blacks. Odour, says Jean-Paul Sartre, is "a disembodied body, vaporised, remaining complete in itself, and yet transformed into a volatile essence". As such, it provides an extraordinarily apt way of registering the nature and position of blacks in Faulkner's world, who always seem to be around even when the white characters refuse to see them, creating subtle feelings of discomfort and unease. Faulkner's black characters, one could say, are there in the sense that their white neighbours have appropriated them, use them and rely on their labour, but not there to the extent that whites never grant them full reality, true identity – never acknowledge their existence as human beings. They are an absent presence: just as, as Sartre indicates, smell is because it is all around, quite literally part of the air one breathes, but something that must remain tantalisingly diffuse, undefined and intangible.

There is only one other aspect of experience, one other corner of his imagined world, that Faulkner describes quite so remorselessly in terms of the olfactory sense: and that is human sexuality, and more specifically the discovery of the fact or possibility of sexuality in women. Quentin Compson in *The Sound and the Fury*, Horace Benbow in *Sanctuary* (especially the original version), Joe Christmas in *Light in August*: all these characters feel suffocated by the odour of burgeoning honeysuckle that they associate with the sexuality, the physicality of the women they know. And not only honeysuckle: the moment when Benbow decides that he can no longer bear living with his wife Belle is worth remembering at this point, since for him the experience of married love appears to be summed up by his weekly expeditions to collect a package of shrimps. Belle adores shrimps, Benbow explains, and every Friday he goes to collect a pack of them from the train and then carry them home; "I have done it for ten years" he says, "since we were married." "I still don't like to smell shrimp", he goes on:

> "But I wouldn't mind the carrying it home so much, I could stand that. It's because the package drips. All the way home it drips and drips, until after a while I follow myself . . . and stand aside and watch Horace Benbow . . . thinking, Here lies Horace Benbow in a fading series of small stinking spots on a Mississippi sidewalk."[40]

It does not require a particularly subtle or intensive reading of this passage to see that it involves a covert reference to female sexuality, or to be more precise to the fact of menstruation. "Delicate equilibrium of periodical filth between two moons balanced", Mr Compson calls it in *The Sound and the Fury*, while Joe Christmas thinks in terms of "something liquid, deathcoloured, and foul". The terms may vary (although, in fact, Joe also uses the phrase, "periodical filth"): but the response to the menstrual cycle remains the same, and points to a set of perceptions and associations shared by many of Faulkner's white male characters. *Women . . . have an affinity for evil*, the assumption is, they are "older in sin than man", "not interested in morals", and "are born already bored with what a boy approaches only at fourteen and fifteen with blundering and aghast trembling". Mud, filth, blood are the elements that suggest this; anything "womansmelling" supplies the appropriate, evocative imagery; and the entire complex of feeling is summed up by certain trigger words ("knowledge", "nature", "earth") that derive ultimately perhaps from the mythic figure of Eve.

One reason why women are so often associated with the idea of evil in Faulkner's work has to do with something that will be discussed later: which is, quite simply, their 'otherness', the fact that for Faulkner's white male protagonists (and, of course, Faulkner himself) they constitute and embody the world outside the Self. Even more, perhaps, than the black characters (who can be dehumanised or ignored, if necessary), they represent the alien and unknown; as a result, they call into question established codes, habitual methods of mediating, organising, and explaining experience.[41] Another reason is worth noting, however, if only because it reminds us once again of Faulkner's regionalism, the extent to which he was involved with the South's structuring myths. And *it* has to do with that cult of Southern Womanhood which – as W.J. Cash explains in *The Mind of the South* – made it possible to associate certain white women with "the very notion" of the region. The cult, Cash says, rested on a clear division of roles. Black women, and some white women, were assigned the sexual function; which is to say, not that they were the only ones ever engaged in sexual relations, but that they were those with whom the sexual dimension of experience was habitually and mythically associated. This made it possible to transform the bulk of white women into creatures of angelic perfection, stainless expressions of the ideal, whose sexuality was minimised even if it was ever acknowledged. The white woman, Cash suggests, became

> the South's Palladium . . . – the shield-bearing Athena gleaming whitely in the clouds, the standard for its rallying, the mystic symbol of its nationality in face of the foe. She was the lily-pure maid of Astolat . . . And – she was the pitiful Mother of God . . . There was hardly a sermon that did not begin and end with tributes in her honor . . .[42]

Despite the rather flamboyant way in which this is expressed, Cash is surely locating a significant pattern here, and one that profoundly affected Southern thought and life. By means of it, it was possible, not only to establish a convenient standard around which defenders of the region could rally, but to contain sexuality by compartmentalising it, acknowledging it only on a suppressed, subterranean level.

The degree to which Faulkner's characters are capable of compartmentalising females and sexuality in this way is suggested by what we are told of Henry Sutpen in *Absalom, Absalom!* Henry, we are informed, had "a simple and . . . untroubled code in which females were ladies or whores or slaves"; for him, the other sex was

> separated into three sharp divisions, separated (two of them) by a chasm which could be crossed but one time and in but one direction . . . – the virgins whom gentlemen someday married, the courtesans to whom they went while on sabbaticals to the cities, the slave girls and women upon whom that first caste rested and to whom in certain cases it doubtless owed the very fact of its virginity . . .[43]

As always in Faulkner's work, it is as well to remind ourselves who is telling the tale, since this has a lot to do with what is told. In this case, it is Mr Compson speaking to Quentin; and it does not take a great deal of effort to see that he is describing a complex that has profoundly affected both of them, although in rather more convoluted ways than these remarks might suggest. Henry, in Mr Compson's eyes, is (at this stage in his development, at least) a kind of innocent; and he is regarded as such largely because he reminds Mr Compson of himself when he was young. As several commentators have pointed out, Mr Compson is a disillusioned idealist, and one of the things he has clearly become disillusioned with is women – or rather, Woman. Having subscribed once to the cult of Southern womanhood, according to which some women at least are regarded as "virgins", he has now come to see them all as contaminated by sexuality and "periodical filth": as all "whores" with a *natural affinity for evil*. "No woman is to be trusted", he tells Quentin. What he means is that he "trusted" Woman once, in other words idealised her; and that, when she turned out to be real rather than ideal, he felt humiliated and betrayed.

Some of this is hypothetical, of course; we know relatively little of Mr Compson's early life and have to draw inferences from what, in later years, he says and does. However, there is no need to fall back upon hypotheses in Quentin's case – or, for that matter, the cases of Horace Benbow and Joe Christmas. Quentin, Benbow, and Christmas all struggle gamely to protect their notion of Woman as a figure of stainless perfection: dressed in white, it may be, a temple or sanctuary for ideals, as free from the contaminations of time as Keats's Grecian Urn. But all of them find this notion challenged by events, and in particular by their own unwilling acknowledgement of the menstrual cycle, or female sexuality, or both: the dress seems muddied as a result, the sanctuary collapses, the urn is irreparably cracked. Quentin is so shaken by this that he simply tries to escape, to evade this disabling knowledge by committing suicide. Even he, though, is tempted towards the conclusion that Benbow and Christmas reach once they feel that their goddess is a false one: that Woman, if she is not the expression of a sort of bodiless good must be the all too fleshly embodiment of evil. *They're all bitches,*[44] Caddy's lover Dalton Ames tells Quentin; and Quentin, to his intense discomfort and despair, feels himself seriously tempted to agree. If Caddy is not a virgin, then she must be a whore: that is the devastating logic that is beginning to go to work in his mind before he puts a stop to it, terminates it in the most effective possible way.

The matter does not stop there, however, as a problem of Quentin's or Benbow's or Christmas's: as something to do simply with Faulkner's characters. Here again it is worth emphasising that what Faulkner is doing is dramatising and exploring a complex of feeling he shares, a code that was his as a (white, male) Southerner. Several attempts have been made to label Faulkner a misogynist – which is surely wrong. His attitude towards women is far too intricate to be described in such terms. Furthermore, one of his purposes in presenting us with people like Mr Compson or Joe Christmas is to help us to place them: to understand, certainly, the motives behind the equation 'woman = evil' but also to criticise it, to see it as a symptom rather than an explanation. One does not have to subscribe to the wound and the bow theory, however, to realise that one reason why Faulkner describes this particular obsession so powerfully is that it was his, part of his own experience and psychological make-up. *Sanctuary* is the classic instance here. It is a disturbing book, and not simply because it dwells on various incidents of violence and perversion. It is also because the author appears to be implicated himself, involved however circuitously in those incidents. The manner in which Faulkner observes Temple Drake, for instance, is disconcertingly close to the voyeuristic ("long-legged, thin-armed, with high small buttocks . . . she moved swiftly, . . . writhing into her scant, narrow dress"); while he even seems to participate, to be involved in her rape in a distanced, vicarious way (like Popeye, he cannot perform the act himself, and so recruits someone else to do it for him while he watches). Moreover, he is often painfully close, embarrassingly sympathetic to Horace Benbow, sharing in his protagonist's sense of betrayal – and in his related suspicion that woman is evil, "older in sin than he would ever be". Admittedly, the eventual published version of *Sanctuary* is much less introspective and narcissistic than the original, less preoccupied with Benbow, his Prufrockian postures, and what his wife mockingly terms his "complex". But even here the opulent and crushing inwardness of the prose, its febrile intensity and scarcely suppressed hysteria, provide the best possible proof that Faulkner understands that "complex" because he was the man, he suffered, he was there:

> . . . he . . . plunged forward and struck the lavatory and leaned upon his braced arms while the shucks set up a terrific uproar beneath her thighs. Lying with her head lifted slightly, her chin depressed like a figure lifted down from a crucifix, she watched something black and furious go roaring out of her pale body. She was bound naked on her back on a flat car moving at speed through a black tunnel, the blackness streaming in rigid threads overhead, a roar of iron wheels in her ears. The car shot bodily from the tunnel . . . towards a crescendo like a held breath, an interval in which she would swing faintly and lazily in nothingness filled with pale, myriad points of light. Far beneath her she could hear the faint, furious uproar of the shucks.[45]

With the loss of his sanctuary, Benbow, like many a disillusioned idealist, becomes prey to the belief that the world is broken, pointless. And it is precisely this sense of a broken world that comes through the narrative, with its apparently wilful refusal to explain things, to link character and motive to event (What makes Popeye tick? Why does Temple testify against Goodwin?), or to connect one event, one moment in time, to another. *Sanctuary* has often been called Faulkner's "vision of evil". It would surely be more accurate to describe it as the book of his that most clearly illustrates his relationship to his region's cult of Woman: a relationship that was characteristically balanced between love – or, at least, identification – and hate. More generally, it provides yet another example of how, in drawing us a map of the regional code, he was also charting his consciousness of himself, his own spiritual geography.

Self-consciousness: it may be an inadequate term, but it provides the most convenient, short-hand way of referring to a particular quality that Faulkner demonstrates in his work, along with a few other Southern writers of the period. The deliberate making of a landscape, a sense of place; the urgent, dramatised reinvention of the past; and an obsessively personal, self-critical investigation of certain inherited names for evil. These are all characteristics that Faulkner shares with people like John Crowe Ransom, Allen Tate, and Robert Penn Warren, and that can all be included under the heading of self-consciousness – as long, that is, as the term is interpreted in a fairly generous fashion.[46] It is perhaps significant too that Southern history and literature constantly present us with people who are self-conscious in a more primitive, straightforward sense, and whose self-consciousness leads them into a concern with manners, ceremony, and self-dramatisation. Needless to say, there is none of Faulkner's self-reflexiveness, none of his tendency towards internally directed criticism, contained in *this* kind of self-consciousness: what it has to do with is a desire to elevate life by ritualising it, turning it into a game or a kind of art. But apart from 'self-conscious' there is no adequate, understandable term to describe this aspect of the regional character – except perhaps two slightly more limiting phrases, a sense of theatre or feeling for the heroic.

Anyway, whatever term is used to describe this element of the Southern code and character, the ways in which it expresses itself are perfectly clear. One thinks, for example, of the theatricality of so many local heroes (in fairly recent times, people like Cotton Ed Smith, Pitchfork Ben Tillman, or Huey Long) or, to take an instance from Faulkner's own family history, of the Old Colonel, William Clark Falkner – a man who seems to have lived most of his life on the histrionic plane, with the instinctive aim of turning himself into a legend. Alternatively, staying strictly within the field of literature, one could cite perhaps the relative flamboyance of Southern writing, its dash, stylishness, and *bravura*, and its more or less wholehearted commitment to the notion of artifice. Something that one of the Virginia writer James Branch Cabell's characters says is worth quoting here. Of man he observes, "The things of which romance assures him are far from being true." "Yet", he goes on,

> it is solely by believing himself a creature but little lower than the cherubim that man has . . . become, upon the whole, distinctly superior to the chimpanzee.[47]

It would probably be superfluous to point out that this was something Cabell believed himself, firmly underwritten as it is in so much of his work; and equally superfluous, perhaps, to add that he shared this notion with many other Southern writers – this belief in, if nothing else, then in the possibility of belief, the therapeutic value or redemptive power of illusion. "They are merely trying to live up to an image they have created of themselves", one character says of others in a book by Hamilton Basso (a Southern novelist roughly contemporary with Faulkner). With very little alteration that could stand as an epigraph to numerous other books from the region. For time and again in Southern writing people are presented as "actors in a spectacle", to be judged solely by the brilliance of their role and the excellence of their performance; and the heroic impulse is portrayed as a potential agent of redemption – or, if not that exactly, then at least as a way of making life tolerable.

Of the different veins of Southern writing tapped out of this heroic mode, two are especially notable. One is illustrated by *A Woman of Means*, a novel by Peter Taylor, who is probably better known for his short stories. Despite what the title seems to imply, the most interesting character in the book is in fact the narrator's father. He is a sad, slightly pathetic figure, the butt of the storyteller's humour and family jokes because he is always trying to play a heroic role – that of "Kentucky colonel", as his son puts it – in what are felt to be the most unfavourable of surroundings. Born on a plantation, but now removed to St Louis, where he is required to play the more mundane part of "go-getter", he is a man so torn between desire for a role no longer available to him and dislike of the role his circumstances impose that his behaviour frequently verges on the schizophrenic. "My stepmother", recalls the narrator,

> said . . . he baffled her German servants, treating them sometimes as equals and sometimes as black body servants, who might at any time be sent to the fields if they didn't toe the line . . .
>
> My father never lied, I had heard Grandmother say, but he never told but one set of truths at a time.[48]

The tone is comic, certainly, but it is comedy used to a purpose: to suggest that the gap between the individual and the part to be played may be so wide that it can only be reconnoitred by the most extraordinary of efforts, and quite probably not even then. Taylor never labours the point, but it is clear enough, and so too is his sense of the reasons why this is so. In "the new order of things", as he calls it in one of his short stories, there is simply no room for anyone to play the hero with any degree of credibility; unlike the old order, which at least aspired towards heroism even if it did not necessarily attain it, there is nothing there – nothing, that is, except ruthless pragmatism and the meanest, most impoverished of parts. So the choices are sadly simple: to surrender to that pragmatism, or to retreat into some anachronistic private drama reflecting the old pieties and pretensions, or to do as the father does in *A Woman of Means* – fluctuate nervously between the two, never wholly committing oneself to either.

That old order which is conspicuous only by its absence from *A Woman of Means* is the principal subject of *Tournament*, the first novel of Shelby Foote, a Southern writer who, like Peter Taylor, is a generation younger than Faulkner. *Tournament* has a fairly simple narrative core, involving the rise of a character named Hugh Bart to prosperity and eminence just after the Civil War. A legendary glow is cast over the narrative, however, by presenting Bart's story as the product of hearsay, tales told by those who hardly knew him but wished they did. Not only that, this glow is deepened and enriched by the reasons Foote gives for his protagonist's success, which have to do with Bart's mythologising tendencies and those of the people around him. Bart fought for his wealth, we learn, because he saw it as a means of transmuting himself, a way of becoming "the proud tall figure . . ., immense and knightly" of his secret "hero-worship". And the fight was successful partly because his neighbours were willing, indeed eager, to cast him "in the heroic mould": eager because they wished to cast themselves in that mould too, to live according to a dream "projected to include not only what was, not only what was to be, but even what was wished to be". Not surprisingly, references to the theatre run through the entire novel. Of Bart himself, for instance, we learn that, having become a wealthy planter, "he dressed the part" and laboured to assume the appropriate "habits and gestures". "He watched, and as he watched he began to acquire: from this man he took one thing, from that another." And the whole point is that Bart is *typical*. Stories of men like him punctuate the narrative: men whose chosen roles may be different from Bart's but behind whom, too, the heroic "pattern" looms "like a firm-bodied ghost". The "new, tight, practical twentieth century", to which Foote turns rather uneasily towards the end of the novel, looks poor by comparison, a place where "men build their dreams on expected promotions".[49] It seems to be lacking entirely in that fictive sense, that mythmaking impulse which Foote, like so many Southern writers, clearly finds so attractive and which, obeying quite consciously his *own* mythmaking impulse, he chooses to associate with the past of his region. Life is in fact turned into art in a double sense – by the author as well as by his characters; and so the book becomes, in a way not untypical of Southern writing, a product, an example of the heroic strain – albeit a fairly sophisticated, knowing one – as well as a celebration of it.

To an extent, Faulkner's participation in all this is obvious. Of the great modern American writers he is easily the most epic and heroic, and the one most interested in the theatrics of living. "Jesus, the South is fine, isn't it", Shreve says sardonically at one point in *Absalom, Absalom!* "It's better than the theatre, isn't it. It's better than Ben Hur, isn't it." And the histrionic tendency the young Canadian notes here seems to possess every other character in the book. Thomas Sutpen, for example, is sometimes seen as a "fiend blackguard and devil", a Gothic villain "from abysmal and chaotic dark to eternal and abysmal dark completing his descending . . . ellipsis", and sometimes as a person rather like Hugh Bart, someone who has to will himself into the part of gentleman: Sutpen, Mr Compson suggests,

> was like John L. Sullivan having taught himself painfully and tediously to do the schottische, having drilled himself and drilled himself in secret until he now believed it no longer necessary to count the music's beat.[50]

In the one case, in Rosa Coldfield's version of him as a "light-blinded, bat-like" being, the theatricality of Sutpen's life is something that he himself is supposed not to be aware of: a quality that clings to him instinctively, like the "faint sulphur-reak" that he carries with him "still in clothes and beard". In the other, as Mr Compson describes him, he is much more calculated and knowing. All the world's a stage, Mr Compson implies, with "Fate, destiny, retribution, irony – the stage manager" deciding the dénouement even while we are "still playing the scene to the audience"; and Sutpen acknowledges this by attempting (just as the woman who becomes his second wife does) to rise "to actual stardom in the role" that he feels most appropriate to his desires. But in either case, whatever the differences of interpretation, it is the heroic strain that determines the approach, the terms in which the protagonist is seen. Sutpen is presented as a larger-than-life creature, heroically evil or heroically "gallant . . . proud . . . brave" and resolute; and the extra dimension of reality he possesses then spills over into the people around him, all of whom are required to take their places on the stage.

This extra dimension is there, for instance, not only in Sutpen's family as Mr Compson and Rosa Coldfield describe them, but in the versions of them that are fashioned by Quentin and Shreve. "Maybe", says Miss Coldfield as she begins to give Quentin her account of Sutpen, you will enter the literary profession as so many Southern gentlemen and gentlewomen are doing now and maybe some day you will remember this and write about it . . . and submit it to the magazines.[51]

As "the town's and the county's poetess laureate", Rosa has a natural interest in nurturing literary ambition, encouraging young people to carry the artistic torch after her: but beyond that her remarks register, with a nice touch of irony, the several levels of theatricality and role-playing that operate in the book – and that eventually incorporate Quentin's own version of events. Sutpen writes his own play, he is the keystone of his own self-appointed drama. So, too, do each of the narrators, each of the people trying to rewrite that drama (this of course, includes the reader as well as Shreve and Quentin), since each of them is attempting to dispose the *dramatis personae* around his or her individual consciousness; and so, in turn, do each of the characters, each of the players placed around Sutpen. Henry Sutpen is a good example. As Quentin's "dark twin", a projection of all his repressed feelings about his sister Caddy, Henry is seen in Quentin's version of things both as a hero and a villain. He is a hero in so far as he can be regarded as the protector of his sister, just as Quentin (or, for that matter, Horace Benbow) devoutly wishes to be: an "academic Hamlet waked from trancement" who kills in the name of "honour"; whereas he is a villain to the extent that he can be seen as the seducer: someone seeking to give expression to his incestuous desires. "Perhaps", speculates Mr Compson,

> this is the pure and perfect incest: the brother realizing that the sister's virginity must be destroyed in order to have existed at all, taking that virginity in the person of the brother-in-law, the man whom he would if he could become, metamorphose into, the lover, the husband; by whom he would be despoiled, choose for despoiler, if he could become, metamorphose into the sister, the mistress, the bride.[52]

Perhaps so; and, if so, Henry becomes a person capable of claiming with some justification that he has committed incest, just as Quentin does, even if it is not literally true. If so, too, then Henry as Quentin sees him ceases to be a noble creature, a man of honour, and becomes someone as doomed and damned as Poe's Roderick Usher – or as, in some moods, Quentin perceives himself to be. Whether as protector or seducer, though, knight in shining armour or figure of doom, Henry remains larger-than-life, like a character out of a dream play: which he must do simply because he is the principal object of Quentin's desire – a rabid need he shares with almost all the other people in the book – to enlarge life and render it significant by turning it into drama.

But what if the drama is not of one's own choosing? What if the role is a difficult one, or even unpleasant and impossible? This other typically Southern theme, of a gap opening up between the player and the part he plays, is one on which Faulkner offers his own personal variations. Not surprisingly, those variations are complicated, subtle, and imply a characteristically self-conscious stance towards the region and its structuring myths. There are, of course, many examples in Faulkner's work of characters like the father in *A Woman of Means*, who seem comic or pathetic or both because they try to play a part that is beyond them or anachronistic. These include Simon, Old Bayard Sartoris's black servant in *Flags in the Dust*, who "with his race's fine feeling for potential theatrics", is always trying on different roles like that of regal coachman or local philanthropist and looking triumphantly absurd as a result. But such characters are less interesting, because further from the core of Faulkner's concerns, than those whose uneasy, equivocal relationship with their roles can be assigned, not to the passing of time or a comic lack of self-knowledge, but to the formulaic nature of the role itself, the fact that it can imprison, deaden and distort. In this respect, Addie Bundren's attack on words in *As I Lay Dying* is worth remembering. "Words are no good", she insists, while of course using words to express this intuition, ". . . words don't ever fit what they are trying to say at." Expanding the notion of language, as semioticians do, we can see how this belief relates to role-playing, the masks and disguises we use to mediate experience. Roles are perhaps necessary, just as words are necessary for Addie: because without them human transactions cannot occur, people are unable to function in society. But if those roles are confused with reality, the signifier with the signified, then the only possible result will be waste, blindness, and confusion. The world will become a world of puppets like the one Darl Bundren sees from within the prison-house of his language, in which human behaviour is reduced to the purely automatic and functional: what Darl refers to as the "dead gestures of dolls".[53]

Significantly, the characters of Faulkner's who suffer most from the potentially imprisoning nature of roles are those who have had very little, if anything, to do with the actual writing of the play: blacks (or at least those assigned the part of black within the Southern scheme of things) and women. As far as blacks are concerned, the two most hypnotising illustrations of this predicament of being trapped within an alien vocabulary are Lucas Beauchamp and Joe Christmas. In both *Go Down, Moses* and *Intruder in the Dust*, Beauchamp is presented as a man whose entire life has been spent fighting against his role: insisting on his rights both as a direct descendant, by the male line, of Lucius Quintius Carothers McCaslin, and as a man, an individual. In the earlier book, this takes the open, active form of actually confronting Zack Edmonds, his landlord (and relative), and attempting to kill him because Zack has taken Beauchamp's wife into his house. Beauchamp is not, it seems, content to accept the role of "nigger" by allowing Edmunds to do with him and his family as he wishes; and he is even willing to use violence to make the point. In *Intruder in the Dust*, despite the melodramatic violence of the story, Beauchamp's resistance to the part imposed on him is quieter and perhaps more deeply subversive, expressed in innumerable little habits and gestures. He studiously avoids addressing whites by name, so as not to have to call them "Mister", or, if he does use "sir" or "Mister", he says it in such a way that it is somehow obvious he does not mean it. He will not accept the presents of Charles Mallison, offered in a patronising, squirearchical spirit, without responding in kind. And, having been rescued from the charge of murdering a white man, he even refuses to respond with the sort of abject humility and gratitude expected of "Sambo": carefully paying his rescuers ("I authorized you", he tells Gavin Stevens. "How much do I owe you?") and then, in the last breath of the book, demanding a receipt. There is clearly the implication that one reason why Beauchamp is accused of murder in the first place is that this is the only way that white people can "make a nigger out of him for once in his life". Nor is the animosity towards him confined to whites; his behaviour seems to irritate some black people as well: "It's the ones like Lucas", declares Aleck Sander (Mallison's black companion) "makes trouble for everybody."[54] Evidently, not all those imprisoned in their roles object to it, since one man's prison may be another's safety and security. For some, like Beauchamp, the part of "nigger" may be a source of anger and despair: but for others, for whom Sander appears to speak at this moment, it is just a way of avoiding trouble.

In some ways, Lucas Beauchamp continues the idea of the "tragic mulatto" that goes back in Southern writing at least as far as the books of George Washington Cable, and Charles W. Chesnutt, and of course Twain's *Pudd'nhead Wilson*. Far more than slavery, Faulkner focussed on miscegenation as the repressed myth of the Southern past. Furthermore, he focussed on it in ways that indicated he was not just interested in what Chesnutt termed "the problems of people of mixed blood"[55] in and for themselves, but for the chance they offered him to explore the linked questions of role, identity, and knowledge. This comes out with particular force in the story of Joe Christmas, whose dilemma stems not from the fact but from the *idea* of mixed blood. Neither Joe nor the reader ever knows whether he is white or part-black; Joe, however, has been convinced by his culture that he needs to know this in order to know who he is. Unable to see the issue of race as one that is incidental to the definition of self, and unable to accept wholeheartedly the role of black or that of white, he seems to be at once imprisoned and empty: imprisoned by the false notions of identity that constitute the only ones he has been taught, and empty because, lacking the ability to create his own notions, his own vocabulary of selfhood, he ceases really to exist as anything more than a cipher. It seems appropriate that his name should be no more than an arbitrary label attached to him by people who neither know who he is nor care: for, even more obviously than Beauchamp's, his problem is one of names rather than things. "Joe Christmas" is little more than a linguistic convention, a shape to fill a lack. It is not an authentic name because Joe's is not an authentic language – which is to say, a language that relates directly to his own experience and expresses his personal needs; and without an authentic name or language, Joe is without the tools necessary for any understanding of himself. "The nature of our society is such", wrote the black novelist Ralph Ellison, "that we are prevented from knowing who we are."[56] Faulkner would clearly have agreed with this, and with the larger implications of Ellison's remark: that the question of role is vitally related to the larger issue of how we relate to reality – including the reality of ourselves – and begin, at least, to understand it.

This same attitude towards role, as a mode of knowing rather than being, is evident in Faulkner's treatment of a number of women characters: whose confusions of perception and identity clearly stem from their unwillingness to accept the part offered them by their culture and their inability to find a viable alternative. Drusilla Hawk in *The Unvanquished* provides a remarkable illustration of this. Drusilla loses her sweetheart in the Civil War; and therefore finds herself reserved for what her mother, at least, regards as "the highest destiny of a Southern woman – to be the bride-widow of a lost cause". However, she rejects the part and tries instead to adopt a male role, leaving her home in Alabama to spend the last years of the war fighting in Colonel John Sartoris's troop. In pursuit of her ambition, she even has her hair cut short and assumes the garments (as her mother puts it, with a palpable shudder) *not alone of a man but of a common private soldier*. Even when she comes back to Jefferson with Sartoris after the war, she continues to work and dress like a man: until her mother arrives from Alabama, forces her daughter into a dress, and insists that in order to regularise things – that is, place the relationship on a conventional footing – Drusilla and the Colonel should get married. There is more than a touch of comedy in Faulkner's presentation of these events; and not least in his account of the horror with which most other Southern ladies regard their aberrant sister. "It is not myself I am thinking of", declares Mrs Hawk a trifle disingenuously:

> . . . I think of my husband who laid down his life to protect a heritage of courageous men and spotless women looking down from heaven upon a daughter who . . . deliberately cast away that for which he died, and . . . I think of my half-orphan son who will one day ask of me why his martyred father's sacrifice was not enough to protect his sister's good name . . .[57]

Like Lucas Beauchamp, in fact, Drusilla is regarded with evident dissatisfaction by her fellow prisoners, those who have managed to accept the role she rejects; and, like Joe Christmas, the eventual result of her dilemma – the fact that she is uncomfortable in the part prescribed for her and unable to formulate any other – is that she seems deprived of a credible identity.

This second point comes out in the last story in *The Unvanquished*, "An Odour of Verbena". The story, told as all the stories in the book are by Bayard Sartoris II, describes how he defies the traditional Southern ethic by refusing to kill the man who has killed Colonel John, his father; and its principal interest here stems from the fact that it is Drusilla who speaks for that ethic and, after the death of the Colonel, struggles to persuade Bayard to seek revenge. Continuing her pursuit of the male role, in fact, Drusilla tries to assume the mantle of Duty. She attempts to turn herself into a spokesman for the code of honour, an embodiment of those stern martial virtues that once drew her into the Civil War, requiring a life to be taken for a life. "There are worse things than killing men, Bayard", she proudly declares a few weeks before her husband dies:

> "There are worse things than being killed. Sometimes I think the finest thing that can happen to a man is to love something . . . hard hard hard, then to die young because he believed what he could not help but believe . . ."[58]

Her position is embarrassingly compromised, however, by her demand, following shortly upon this declaration, that Bayard should kiss her. In other words, she tries to use her sexual attractiveness to support her case: she speaks 'as a man' and then acts 'as a woman'. A similar discontinuity is even more noticeable in the scene where Drusilla tries to prepare Bayard for vengeance by handing him two duelling pistols:

> "Take them, Bayard", she said, in the same tone in which she had said "kiss me" . . ., already pressing them into my hands . . . speaking in a voice fainting and passionate with promise: "Take them. I have kept them for you . . . Do you feel them? the long true barrels true as justice, the triggers . . . quick as retribution, the two of them slender and invincible and fatal as the physical shape of love?"[59]

The sexual dimension is even more obvious here, as is the "passionate and voracious" nature of Drusilla's approach; again, she seems to be fluctuating between two quite disparate roles. At one moment assuming the male, martial role and at another that of seductress, her behaviour is equivocal to the point of incoherence: something that is nicely caught in her description of the pistols, instruments of death that are temporarily transfigured in her eyes into instruments of love. Drusilla's dissatisfaction with the Southern versions of womanhood has been enough to distance her from the conventional, even though she now dresses as a woman.

However, it has not enabled her to repress her sexuality, that force which makes her imitation of a man less than convincing, or to follow a more appropriate path.

People, particularly women, and roles — the parts written for them to play, the names attributed to them, and the words given them to speak: at this point, the discussion is shading into what is perhaps the most fundamental level in Faulkner's relationship with the structuring myths he inherited as a Southerner. Something of that level has been suggested in passing already: it is, to put it briefly, Faulkner's preoccupation with the relationship between reality and language, our given world and the models we employ to facilitate understanding of it. "Man is free and he is responsible, terribly responsible", said Faulkner in an interview:

> His tragedy is the impossibility — or at least the tremendous difficulty — of communication. But man keeps on trying endlessly to express himself and to make contact with other human beings.[60]

"Maybe", he added on a more personal note,

> I will end up in some kind of self-communion — a silence — faced with the certainty I can no longer be understood . . . Sometimes I think of doing what Rimbaud did — yet I will certainly keep on writing as long as I live.[61]

Speech or silence, the impostures and artifice visited on us by the acts of perception and communication or the blankness and impenetrability of a world where the effort to understand and make contact has stopped, somehow been laid in abeyance. Remarks like this indicate just how fascinated Faulkner was by language, and exactly how conscious he was too of the dangers latent in the fictive act, the process of structuring and encoding: dangers that included the possibility that words might act as a screen, disguising the subject rather than exposing it. To some extent, Faulkner was attracted to such considerations by the simple fact that he was a writer, bound like any craftsman to be aware of his tools and occasionally check them. But it went further than that, because his interest in language and all that it implied was also something actively encouraged by his region (see Plate 11). On this level, indeed, what the South offered Faulkner was precisely that awareness of words which intensified, raised to a higher power, enabled him to examine with care the very words his Southern inheritance had given him: to turn awareness into self-reflexiveness by exploring the tools of communication at the same time as they were being used. Speaking of the Southerner's interest in role-playing and his related fondness for rhetoric, W. J. Cash remarks:

> . . . rhetoric flourished here far beyond even its American average; it early became a passion — and not only a passion but a primary standard of judgment,

the *sine qua non* of leadership. The greatest man would be the man who could best wield it.[62]

Just so; and it was this apparently inexhaustible fascination with language that Faulkner absorbed and then used in his own peculiarly displaced, critical way. He was a rhetorician, of course, and could be as passionate in his love of speech as Cash's notional Southerner: capable of sonorous word melodies, long, labyrinthine or elaborately balanced, sentences, and metaphors that startle the reader with their bravado. Coming from a culture of the spoken word, he also tended to admire anyone with a marked oral gift, natural orators like the Reverend Shegog, Gavin Stevens, or V. K. Ratliff. For all that, though, he was also acutely, uncomfortably conscious of the sheer slipperiness of language, the possibility that, to quote that remark of Addie Bundren's again, "Words are no good"; and while his region did not actually teach him this distrust it was something that he owed ultimately to its tutelage, because it was the South that had taught him the subject, prompted him to attend to language, in the first place.

"Talk, talk, talk", thinks the sculptor Gordon in *Mosquitoes* while listening to a conversation:

> the utter and heartbreaking stupidity of words. It seemed endless, as though it might go on forever. Ideas, thoughts, became mere sounds to be bandied about until they were dead.[63]

Of course, one can think of reasons for dismissing this comment, or at least minimising its importance: Gordon is, after all, a fairly laconic person hardly likely to give words their due, and his criticism does not seem entirely misplaced in a book where the characters never seem to stop chattering. But it is not so easy to dismiss it when we remember that other characters in the book, despite their garrulousness, echo Gordon's sentiments. The writer Dawson Fairchild, for instance, argues at one point that there is "a kind of sterility" in words. "You begin to substitute words for things and deeds", he suggests,

> "like the withered cuckold husband that took the Decameron to bed with him every night, and pretty soon the thing or the deed becomes just a kind of shadow of a certain sound you make by shaping your mouth in a certain way."[64]

Still more to the point, this association of words with blockage, sterility and frustration runs through all Faulkner's work: one sees it, for instance, in his account of his sad young men, whose impotence seems to derive in part from the fact that, as Horace Benbow says of himself, they "have always been ordered by words". Even the actual metaphor, of taking art to bed rather than a body, reappears in only slightly altered form in one of Faulkner's favourite points of reference: to "the old pagan who kept his Byzantine goblet at his bedside and slowly wore away the rim by kissing it". In this respect, the Introduction that Faulkner wrote in 1933 for *The Sound and the Fury* is well worth quoting. "There is a story somewhere", Faulkner concludes after giving an account of how he came to write the book,

> about an old Roman who kept at his bedside a Tyrrhenian vase which he loved and the rim of which he wore slowly away with kissing it. I had made myself a vase, but I suppose I knew all the time that I could not live forever inside of it, that perhaps to have it so that I could lie in bed and look at it would be better . . .[65]

Two things need to be said about this remark of Faulkner's. In the first place, it illustrates just how paradoxical his attitude towards language could be. The image of the "old Roman" carries reverberations of impotence, certainly, but it also manages to suggest consummation, a denial of life but something of an apotheosis as well; there may not be a body there with the old man, but what he does have brings its own compensations and is a not entirely unwelcome substitute. Another way of putting this is the way Dawson Fairchild puts it. Having dismissed the sterility of words in the part of his speech just quoted, he then backtracks more than a little by claiming that, while words do not "have life in themselves", nevertheless, "brought into happy conjunction", they can "produce something that lives, just as soil and climate and an acorn in proper conjunction will produce a tree". It would be an act of supererogation to point out that, while Faulkner could deride those who depended on the "false authority" of language or confused a "fragile web of ink and paper"[66] with experience, he continued to commit ink to paper and tried to use language to interpret things. But it is worth reminding ourselves that, although an uneasiness about words thickens the texture of his books – providing them with a further dimension of self-consciousness – it does not really undermine their structure. The scope and success of his own verbal constructs may be continually brought into question, but he rarely if ever challenges the need for such constructs, the importance of at least trying to encode reality.

The second thing that needs to be said about Faulkner's reference to the "old Roman" has to do with the terms in which he thinks of the act of substitution: the process whereby, in writing his book about the Compsons, experience was turned into language, the "thing or the deed" into art. A woman and an urn: these are the terms of the act. "I, who never had a sister", Faulkner says in another version of the Introduction, "and was fated to lose my daughter in infancy, set out to make myself a beautiful and tragic little girl": that is, he set out to turn a female who was simultaneously there (to the extent that she was sensed and desired) and not there (because she was never reached or embraced) into a palpable presence, a tangible shape – to capture her essence in a fragile web of ink and paper. In this context, it is perhaps worth noting that Faulkner very often attributes his own distrust of artifice in general and the artificial structures of language in particular to a woman. "Women", we are told in his first novel, "know more about words than men ever will. And they know how little they can ever possibly mean." This is a sentiment echoed in *Mosquitoes* ("They don't care anything about words except as little things to pass the time with"), and either illustrated or expressed by such otherwise diverse figures as Laverne Schumann in *Pylon*, Charlotte Rittenmeyer in *The Wild Palms*, Eula Varner and her daughter Linda (Linda, because she is deaf, is actually said to live "immured, inviolate in silence", "outside human sound . . . outside human time too . . .").[67] There is more to this than just a fairly commonplace belief in 'feminine intuition'; although Faulkner was not averse to the idea that a woman's intelligence was different from a man's, more concrete, less interested in abstraction. For behind it lay something mentioned earlier: Faulkner's impulse, his fundamental inclination, to associate women with otherness, the world outside the ego – what Wallace Stevens once referred to as "the inconceivable idea of the sun".[68] Small wonder, then, that his women tended to distrust words, since what they distrusted was, as he saw it, the machinery devised to capture and contain them. Small wonder, either, that they despised words, or were indifferent to their claims, for what they were despising or dismissing were the pale shadows of them, the reflections that pretended to be them, the substitutive object that dared to challenge comparison with the subject.

Of course, in conceiving of women in these terms Faulkner was not being particularly original: for obvious reasons, the male imagination has perennially used woman as an archetypal image of the Other. But he was unusual, if not original, in the persistence, or rather the obsessiveness, with which he pursued this image and explored its different manifestations: in the way in which he kept coming back and then coming back again to what he referred to, in a story written early in 1925, as "that imminent . . . that troubling Presence". The story, "Nympholepsy", was itself derived from two earlier works, "L'Apres-Midi d'un Faune" published in 1919 and "The Hill" published in 1922; and it shows just how early and deeply embedded in Faulkner's mind the image of the seductive, elusive, ineffable female was. Briefly, it describes how a young man returning from work just before sunset suddenly sees "a golden light among dark pines". The light turns out to be a girl, a nymph-like figure who seems to partake of the sun's brilliance and who makes the boy feel hopelessly "swinish" by comparison. He pursues this "ghostly" vision, "not knowing whether it was copulation or companionship that he wanted"; and, for a moment, as he sinks into a woodland stream,

where "the water murmured in a dark and sinister dream", he seems to
reach out and touch her, to make contact with "something more than
water". "Beneath his hand", we are told,

> a startled thigh slid like a snake, among dark bubbles he felt a swift leg; and,
> sinking, the point of a breast scraped his back. Amid a slow commotion of
> disturbed water he saw death like a woman shining and drowned and waiting,
> saw a flashing body tortured by water . . .[69]

But then he loses her. "Like a match flame", she appears for a moment
against the darkness of the trees and then disappears, leaving her pursuer
with the rather cold comfort that maybe he did achieve some strange sort
of consummation – that perhaps, for a moment, "I touched her!"
"Nympholepsy" is saturated in the kind of *fin-de-siècle* romanticism that
Faulkner was later to control and criticise (although he was never to
reject it – as Brooks points out, he remained "a romantic . . . to the end,
though a reformed or foiled or chastened romantic"). Nevertheless, it is
of vital interest because it is packed with so many anticipations of its
author's later work, prophetic guides to the country of his imagination.
A woman like a spirit or a twilight dream, a woman offering the
otherness of love or death, a woman associated with the primal element
of water – a woman, too, to whom the man who pursues her reaches out
like the lover on Keats's Urn and who may, or may not be, touched for a
moment: no reader of Faulkner needs to be reminded just how much of
the fabric of his novels is woven out of these ideas, with their deployment
of the male as the poet, lover, maker of words and the female as his
beloved, tantalisingly ungovernable object. Nor, probably, does he need
to be told what the animating conception, the primary belief is behind all
such ideas: that, like Eula Varner as she is described in *The Town*, woman/
reality is "too much" for any man, that there never will be "enough of
any one male to match and hold and deserve her".[70]

Mention of Eula Varner is a useful reminder that by no means all the
women in Faulkner's work possess the teasing bodilessness of the girl in
"Nympholepsy". Quite the contrary, for every nymph, every woman
whose epicene figure, shimmering clothes, and rapid movements express
her elusive, uncontrollable otherness, there is someone like Eula or Lena
Grove who is other in a quite different sense: because she is of the earth,
earthy, clinging to its curves and rounds – while man seeks to climb up,
further and further away from the concrete surfaces of things. The two
versions of woman, which appear so different and yet issue from the
same equation, are both sketched out in Faulkner's first novel. Here, the
part of nymph is taken by the boyish, irritatingly unpredictable Cecily
Saunders, whose body is compared by her lover to "a narrow pool,
flowing away like two silver streams from a single source".[71] In turn, a
warmer, maternal, and yet still elusive presence is supplied by Margaret

Powers. Married twice, to men who never even begin to know her, pursued by others whose passion is matched only by their sense of impotence, her unreachability is summed up in the last moment when we see her: as she departs on a train one of her admirers runs wildly and desperately after her vanishing image, like the "bold lover" who can never quite catch his beloved in "Ode on a Grecian Urn". A similarly double image of the female is projected in *Mosquitoes*; and here – not surprisingly, given the more discursive nature of Faulkner's second novel – it is more openly explored, even explained. Pat Robyn suggests that aspect of "the feminine nature" which, we are told, makes it "impalpable as moonlight": a slim, boyish figure with a "clean, young odour . . ., like that of trees", she is so light and bodiless that she seems to make no sound as she walks. Like the girl in "Nympholepsy" (or, for that matter, Temple Drake or Laverne Shuman), she is all activity: possessed of a "childish delight in strenuous physical motion" that comes out especially in the descriptions of her swimming by night, moving fluently and "naked and silver as a ghost". Likewise, her admirers are reminiscent of the young man in that early – and, for a long time, unpublished – short story: pursuing her "with . . . unutterable longing", or simply gazing at her, and objects associated with her, with "passive abjectness", "an utter longing, like that of a dog". Paired with Pat is her friend of a day, Jenny Steinbauer. Her appeal is equally powerful but quite different: stemming, as one of the other characters observes, from "an utterly mindless rifeness of young pink flesh, a supine potential fecundity lovely to look upon". One of Jenny's many admirers, Dawson Fairchild, seems to have her in mind – or, rather, the particular image of woman she suggests – when he declares, "Women can do . . . without art – old biology takes care of that . . . Creation, reproduction from within . . . [is] the dominating impulse in the world feminine."[72] Woman is, man does, it seems; woman is a creator, a part or function of reality, while all man can do is attempt to *re*-create.

Just what man re-creates is implied by that image of the vase or urn; "I had made myself a vase", said Faulkner of *The Sound and the Fury*, and as he said it he must have realised the multiple ironies packed into that phrase. After all, it could hardly have been mere coincidence that the woman/urn comparison (or contrast) occurred to him so often, or that he felt compelled to allude time and again to "Ode on a Grecian Urn". Lena Grove, we remember, is compared to something moving interminably across an urn, while when Joe Christmas learns about menstruation he has a vision of urns cracked and bleeding. Later, in *Go Down, Moses*, Ike McCaslin reads the Keats poem and then, to the suggestion that the lines "She cannot fade, though thou hast not thy bliss, / For ever wilt thou love and she be fair" refer to a girl, retorts that the poet was also "talking about truth": an observation that suggests not only the permanence of "truth" but just how teasingly elusive it can be. Linda Snopes is described in *The Mansion* as "the bride of quietude and silence"; and in a much earlier book, *Flags in the Dust*, we are twice told that Horace Benbow addresses his sister as "Thou still unravished bride of quietude". The first time we are told this is well worth quoting – and not least because it bears such a striking resemblance to those two passages, quoted earlier, from *Mosquitoes* and the Introduction to *The Sound and the Fury*. Horace, we learn, took to blowing glass as a hobby,

> and produced one almost perfect vase of clear amber . . . chastely serene and which he kept always on his night table and called by his sister's name in the intervals of apostrophising both of them impartially in his moments of rhapsody over the realization of the meaning of peace and the unblemished attainment of it, as Thou still unravished bride of quietude.[73]

Again, the suggestiveness and serviceability of this image is striking. The act of creation as an act of substitution; the ambiguous relationship between art and narcissism; the notion that any attempt to translate things into other terms can be seen as both a consummation and a gesture of impotence; the belief that the world's body remains immune to the raids made on it by the plundering mind. All these ideas and possibilities are contained within a passage that perceives making and encoding in a paradoxical way, as both a triumph and a failure: a marriage that apparently keeps the bride "unravished", and an escape from the self into language that seems to leave otherness unrevealed, intact, and quiet. Another way of putting all this would be in terms of the obvious. The vase is not Horace's sister; nor, for that matter, could *The Sound and The Fury* ever begin to compensate for the absence of a sister in Faulkner's own life, or his loss of an infant daughter. Nevertheless, both artifacts, the urn and the book, were cherished, both had their substitutive use and expressive value: as Horace's behaviour here and Faulkner's habitual, loving references to the story of the Compson family – and Caddy Compson in particular – clearly indicate.

The notions of triumph, failure, and Caddy Compson are, of course, intimately related; since *The Sound and the Fury*, as Faulkner saw it and never tired of saying, was "the one that failed the most tragically and the most splendidly". "I like the one which caused me the most trouble", he declared in an interview. "That is *The Sound and the Fury*." And elsewhere, in his class conferences at Virginia, he continued this line of thought: *The Sound and the Fury*, he insisted,

> was the best failure. It was the one that I anguished the most over, that I worked the hardest at, that even when I knew I couldn't bring it off, I still worked at it . . . The others that have been easier to write . . . I don't have the feeling toward any of them that I do toward that one . . .[74]

One reason why the book held such a special place in Faulkner's affection was that it was the one most intimately related to his own personal experience. "I am Quentin in *The Sound and the Fury*",[75] he once admitted; and recent commentators have shown how the book grew out of a moment of exceptional crisis, and just how much of its detail can be traced to biography – the author's own life seen, as it were, through a glass darkly. But another, not unconnected reason was surely Faulkner's devotion to Caddy Compson. Explaining why a short story called "Twilight" gradually turned into a novel called *The Sound and the Fury*, he spoke with an open, autobiographical candour that was unusual for him – that is, *except* when he was talking about Caddy. "I loved her so much", Faulkner said,

> I couldn't decide to give her life just for the duration of a short story. She deserved more than that. So my novel was created, almost in spite of myself.[76]

To an extent that was unmatched in any of his other work, Faulkner made a woman the abiding, guiding presence of this, his fourth novel; and, in doing so, he raised the whole problem of otherness with a fierceness and intensity unparalleled elsewhere. The question of just how, if at all, the shimmering light of reality is related to the artifacts we make, the words we use, the myths we devise: that question hovers behind every section of the book, as well as its author's subsequent accounts of its genesis, making, and achievement. If for no other reason, then, a brief look at *The Sound and the Fury* seems an appropriate point on which to end this discussion of Faulkner and his work.

Faulkner's account of the beginnings of *The Sound and the Fury* is well known and suggests just how seminal Caddy was, just how much she acted as the book's source and inspiration. "It began with a mental picture", Faulkner said:

> I didn't realize at the time it was symbolical. The picture was of the muddy seat of a little girl's drawers in a pear tree where she could see through a window where her grandmother's funeral was taking place and report what was happening to her brothers on the ground below.[77]

Not only its source, she was also the book's subject. "To me she was the beautiful one", Faulkner admitted,

> she was my heart's darling. That's what I wrote the book about and I used the tools which seemed to me the proper tools to try to tell, try to draw the picture of Caddy.[78]

And not only *that*, she could also be seen as its ideal audience: that is, if we accept the proposition put forward by a character in *Mosquitoes* that "every word a writing man writes is put down with the intention of

Plate 1. "The First Day at Jamestown" (painting by an unknown artist)
Plate 2. "Westover", the Virginia home of William Byrd II

Plate 3. Thomas Jefferson (engraving by J. C. Buttre after a painting by Gilbert Stuart)

Plate 4. "Scene on a Southern Plantation" (painting by an unknown artist)

Plate 5. Peachtree Street, Atlanta (photographed by George Barnard in September 1864, shortly after Union troops under Sherman had occupied the city and evacuated the civilian population)

Plate 6. Robert E. Lee

Plate 7. Old slave cabin near Macedonia, Christian County, Kentucky (photographed in 1938)

Plate 8. A farm on the edge of an industrial development in Ensley, Alabama (photographed in 1937 by Arthur Rothstein for the Farm Security Administration)

Plate 9. Bud Fields, a poor white farmer, and members of his family (photographed in 1935 by Walker Evans for the Farm Security Administration)

Plate 10. Pickett's Charge, July 3, 1863 (painting by an unknown artist)

Plate 11. A gathering in front of a barbershop in Vicksburg, Mississippi (photographed in 1935 by Walker Evans for the Farm Security Administration)

Plate 12. Peachtree Center, Atlanta (photographed by Bob Glander)

impressing some woman". This is a contentious suggestion, perhaps. But two further points can hardly be denied: that it was from Caddy's story that Faulkner tried to "extract some ultimate distillation" by telling it four or five times, and that it was while trying to extract this distillation, to capture this essence, that he seems to have experienced certain quite extraordinary feelings. As he put it later, what was absent in the preparation of *As I Lay Dying* was precisely what made the writing of *The Sound and the Fury* such a painful pleasure:

> . . . that emotion definite and physical and yet nebulous to describe; that ecstasy, that eager and joyous faith and anticipation of surprise which the yet unmarred sheet beneath my hand held inviolate and unfailing, waiting for release.[79]

At the very least, such feelings matched in intensity the ones he attributed to the Compson brothers, Quentin and Benjy: in their intensity, that is, their ephemerality, and also in their sexual connotations.

So Caddy Compson was and is the novel's beginning, middle, and end, its *raison d'être* just as Narcissa Benbow was the reason why Horace's "chastely serene" vase was brought into existence. Both book and vase, we could say, represent an attempt to imitate the shape of the beloved object, the curves of her being, and a possible way of commemorating, containing her. Imitation and containment are not so easy, however. Faulkner may "try to tell, try to draw the picture of Caddy" in words, but she seems somehow to resist his efforts; she seems to exist apart from or beyond the narrative frame, and so escape the clutches of Faulkner and all the other storytellers. To some extent, this is because she is the absent presence familiar from many of Faulkner's other novels: a figure like Donald Mahon, say, or Thomas Sutpen, who obsesses the other characters but very rarely speaks with his or her own voice. Far more important, though, are two simple facts. Caddy is a woman – and so by definition a reminder for Faulkner of what lies outside the parameters of language – and she is a peculiarly haunting woman even by her creator's own standards. She is Eve and Lilith, virgin and whore, mother, sister, daughter, and lover, and she is these with an unmatched passion, a ferocious intensity. She is also a nymph and a maternal figure, combining many of the teasing qualities of Cecily Saunders with the soft receptiveness and warm protectiveness of Margaret Powers: a slim, boyish, active figure like Pat Robyn who yet also, to her brother's despair, has some of the "mindless rifeness", the "supine potential fecundity" of Jenny Steinbauer. In short, Caddy is compounded of paradox to a degree that is rare even among Faulkner's female characters.[80] So it is hardly surprising to find that, while she is there in the sense that she is the focal point, the eventual object of each narrator's meditations, she is not there to the extent that she remains elusive, intangible – as transparent as the water, and as invisible and disconcerting as the odours of trees and honeysuckle, with which she is constantly associated. More than any of Faulkner's women – more, even, than Eula Varner – she is "too much" for her men, too various and unpredictable for them to handle. As each of them, including the author, tries to focus her in his camera lens she seems to slip away, leaving little more than the memory of her name and image.[81]

Not that Faulkner ever stops trying to bring her into focus – for himself, his narrators, and of course for us. Each section of the book, in fact, represents a different strategy, another attempt to know her. Essentially, the difference in each section is a matter of code and rhetoric: in the sense that each time the tale is told another language, an alternative model is devised and a different series of relationships between author, narrator, subject, and reader. The opening section, for instance, is marked by an attempt to melt language and experience down into a series of separate, all equally egocentric, units, and to obliterate the distance between narrator, subject and reader. Benjy wants to ignore the otherness of his sister; and for him, unlike his older brother Quentin, this leads to very few immediate problems since, according to his own radically limited perception of things, otherness simply does not exist. There is nothing 'out there', as he sees it, everything is merely an extension, an adjunct of his own being. The whole purpose of Benjy's monologue is, in fact, to deny the irreducible reality and particularity of the objective world and to absorb every experience, each person or thing that confronts him, into a strictly closed and subjective system. There are other denials, too. The reader, for instance, is simply ignored; there is no attempt made to address him or explain things to him, because his otherness is never acknowledged any more than Caddy's is. Even the gap between thing and word, Caddy as she is and Caddy as she is perceived and named, is extinguished in Benjy's consciousness; for him, the signified and the signifier are one and the same. This emerges on the very first page of the book, when the punning cry of the golfers, "caddie", is enough to make Caddy present for her idiot brother: she is there for him, it seems, because her name is there. "I was trying to say", says Benjy at one point, when he recalls the time he chased some schoolgirls, confusing them with his lost sister,

> and I caught her, trying to say, and she screamed and I was trying to say and trying and the bright shapes began to stop and I tried to get out. I tried to get off of my face, but the bright shapes were going again. They were going up the hill to where it fell away . . . and I tried to keep from falling off the hill and I fell off the hill into the bright whirling shapes.[82]

This passage is fairly typical of Benjy's habits of language and perception, and it shows how rigidly constricted they are. Vocabulary is kept to a minimum; the sentences are simple, declarative, and repetitive; and the distinction between predicate (once again, a girl) and subject (Benjy, who does not even see her, realise who she is) is almost completely flattened out. Benjy's "trying to say" involves little more than an attempt to simplify by identifying knowing with being – an effort, not to understand and communicate, but to reduce everything to a private code; and, in response to it, the reader is likely to fluctuate between feelings of strangeness and "defamiliarisation" and a more radical, less pleasurable sense of alienation.

Undoubtedly, there is something of Faulkner in Benjy: not least because Faulkner occasionally seemed to share Benjy's assumption that words had a talismanic power, and could summon into being the things they described. But as he himself admitted ("I am Quentin in *The Sound and the Fury*") there was far more of him in Caddy's oldest brother. Faulkner tends to identify with Quentin to the point where the second section can become almost impenetrably private. Quentin, for his part, tries to abolish the distance between Caddy and himself – although, of course, not being insane he is less successful at this than Benjy; and he tends sometimes to address the reader or, at least, try to address him and sometimes, like his idiot brother, to forget him. Whether addressing the reader or not, however, his language remains intensely claustrophobic: based not on a logic of the senses as Benjy's is, nor on the appearance of rational logic as is his other brother Jason's, but on a tortuous and convoluted series of personal associations. The style is intense and disjointed, ranging between attempts at orderly narration and uncontrolled stream-of-consciousness: Quentin, it is clear, is continually attempting to place things within conventional linguistic structures only to find those structures slide away or dissolve.

> The three-quarters began. The first note sounded, measured and tranquil, serenely peremptory, emptying the unhurried silence for the next one and that's if people could only change one another for ever that way merge like a flame swirling up for an instant then blown cleanly out along the cool eternal dark instead of lying there trying not to think of the swing until all cedars came to have that vivid dead smell of perfume that Benjy hated so. Just by imagining the clump it seemed to me that I could hear whispers secret surges smell the beating of hot blood under wild unsecret flesh watching against red eyelids the swine untethered in pairs rushing coupled into the sea . . .[83]

The disintegration of syntax in passages like this one finds its analogue, in the second section as a whole, in Quentin's failure to tell his story in an orderly manner. Quentin cannot quite subdue the object to the word; equally, he cannot quite construct a coherent narrative for himself because, in losing Caddy, he has lost what Henry James would call its "germ" – the person, that is, who made sense of all the disparate elements of his life by supplying them with an emotional centre.

It is perhaps worth noting, however briefly, the particular model, the series of assumptions that Quentin uses to mediate between himself and the world. Unlike his brother Benjy, Quentin has a very self-conscious sense of how life should be, which derives most of its force from notions of gentility and *noblesse oblige* traditionally attached, in the South, to the plantation aristocracy. Much of the comedy of this section, in fact, derives from Quentin's absurdly misplaced idea of himself as "a half-baked Galahad" (to quote Caddy's husband, Herbert Head), "a champion of dames" (to cite Quentin's friend at Harvard, Spoade): in short, a gentleman of the old school. For example, at one point he tries rather disingenuously to dissuade Caddy from marriage by telling her that her prospective husband "was dropped from his club for cheating at cards": a remark that draws the gloriously sardonic reply, *I'm not going to play cards with* [him]. The comedy always has a serious thrust, though: as Quentin's relationship with blacks memorably illustrates. Not surprisingly, given that he sees himself as a young Southern gentleman, Quentin tries to adopt a paternalist role with black people: throwing quarters to grateful darkies ("Thanky, young master. Thanky"), and making arrangements for Deacon, his black factotum at Harvard, to inherit one of his suits of clothes after he commits suicide. Black people, in turn, play the role of Uncle Tom with him: for convenience's sake, it may be, in order to survive – and in Deacon's case for the purpose of exploiting the "young master", making him "completely subjugated" and dependent. "A nigger", reflects Quentin, "is not so much a person as a form of behaviour, a sort of obverse reflection of the white people he lives among"; and while, as this remark indicates, Quentin knows he is being exploited by his black "guide mentor and friend"[84] he can never do anything about it. The reason is simple. The role Deacon plays fits perfectly into the idealised version of things that Quentin has constructed: a version that has himself as gentleman at its centre, and the purity of white womanhood (and of one white woman in particular) as its emblem and apotheosis. In this respect, the whole of the second section could be seen as a sly comment on the patriarchal model, with its assumptions about paternalist responsibility, its allegiance to fixed standards of refinement, and its careful deployment of male and female roles, and white and black. All models, all systems of language, thought, and behaviour are held up for criticism in this book, however implicitly: but the plantation model comes in for especially fierce dissection here. For it is, Faulkner suggests, absurdly innocent and anachronistic, at least in the wholesale, literal terms applied by Quentin.[85]

If the second section draws some of its power and interest from Faulkner's anatomising of the patriarchal model, then the third section involves among other things an even more ruthlessly critical look at its populist equivalent. Jason Compson has been compared by several critics to Simon Suggs and Sut Lovingood, because of his racy colloquial speech, his brutal wit, and brutally sensible – not to say, selfish and opportunistic – approach to things.[86] A more appropriate comparison, however, would be with Pap Finn, and for two reasons. Like Pap Finn, Jason Compson is a classic, comic portrait of white populist bigotry, a man whose verbal energy is matched only by his detestation of blacks, women, Jews, intellectuals, Yankees, or anyone else who appears to threaten his self-esteem. Moreover, like Mark Twain, Faulkner combines a fiercely satirical dissection of his character's greed, hypocrisy, and egotism with evident delight in him: not, that is, in his opinions and prejudices but in him as an imaginative creation – provoking both humour and horror, and condemning himself out of his own, forever open mouth. Which is to say that Faulkner is evidently fascinated by this figure he has brought into existence, even while he is also disgusted by him, not that he feels in any way close or affectionate; on the contrary, the Jason section is marked by a much greater sense of distance than the others – a much larger gap, not only between author and narrator, but between narrator, subject, and reader. Faulkner is clearly out of sympathy with this Compson brother, even if he is amused by him: he once said, in fact, that Jason was the character of his that he disliked most.[87] Jason, in turn, while obviously obsessed with his sister and her daughter, never claims any intimacy with either of them. And the reader is kept at some remove by the specifically public mode of speech Jason uses, full of swagger, exaggeration, and desperate attempts to bolster his image of himself:

> Once a bitch always a bitch, what I say . . .

> I never promise a woman anything nor let her know what I'm going to give her. That's the only way to manage them. Always keep them guessing. If you can't think of any other way to surprise them, give them a bust in the jaw.[88]

A vividly self-contradictory character, Jason conceals his irrationality behind vociferous appeals to commonsense and reason, invokes principles he never practices, and tries to conceal his precarious sense of his own identity by adopting the role of a straight-talking, hard-working hell-of-a-fellow. Quite as much as his two brothers, he uses an idiom that hardly begins to bridge the gap between himself and the world; and in his case otherness is not only evaded, it is blamed.

And what of Dilsey, and the last section of the novel? Here, of course, the reader is addressed directly and with consideration, in an attempt to communicate that scrupulously avoids the self-conscious swaggering of Jason's monologue. Caddy, in turn, is recalled with understanding and warmth – but with the acknowledgement that she is a separate person whose separateness needs to be remembered and respected. And

Faulkner himself – or, to use Wayne Booth's term, the "implied author" – appears for the first time as a distinct voice and a distinctive presence, ready to embrace Dilsey and her point of view while describing them strictly from the outside. In effect, all the relationships here between author, narrator, subject, and reader are characterised by a combination of intimacy and detachment; while the language carries us into a world where significant contact between quite separate individuals does at least appear to be possible.

> She [Dilsey] had been a big woman once but now her skeleton rose, draped loosely in unpadded skin . . . as though muscle and tissue had been courage or fortitude which the days or the years had consumed until only the indomitable skeleton was left rising like a ruin or a landmark above the somnolent and impervious guts, and above that a collapsed face that gave the impression of the bones themselves being outside the flesh, lifted into the driving day with an expression at once fatalistic and of a child's astonished disappointment . . .[89]

For once the closed circle of the interior monologue is broken, the sense of the concrete world is firm, the visible outlines of things finely and even harshly etched, the rhythms exact, evocative, and sure. And yet, and yet . . . Here, as in that opening scene from *Light in August* discussed much earlier on in this chapter, the language is emphatically figurative, almost obsessively artificial; and the stress throughout is on appearance and impression, on what *seems* to be the case rather than what is. We are still not being told the whole truth, the implication is, there remain limits to what we can know; despite every effort, in fact, even this last section of the novel does not entirely succeed in naming Caddy. So it is not wholly surprising that, like the three Compson brothers, Dilsey is eventually tempted to discard language altogether. In this respect, Benjy's howling, Quentin's suicide, and Jason's moments of impotent, speechless fury find their equivalent in the mindless chant that the Compson's black housekeeper and cook shares with the congregation at the Easter Day service: in ways that are, certainly, very different all four characters place a question mark over their attempts to turn experience into speech by turning aside from words, seeking deliverance and redress in a non-verbal world.

Not that Dilsey's voice is the only one to be heard in this section: it is frequently and conveniently forgotten that almost as much space is devoted here to Jason and Benjy – in other words, almost as many pages are given over to a counterpointing movement, something that casts a further shadow over things.[90] This movement is at its simplest and most obvious in the account of Jason's frantic pursuit of Miss Quentin. For his feverish haste offers an unmistakable contrast to the deliberate rituals of Dilsey and her fellow worshippers; his pride, rage, and isolation clearly set themselves against their humility, love, and sense of collective movement; above all, his experience of blockage and frustration, of not getting what he wants in any respect, provides a brutal response to their evident feelings of spiritual consummation, their belief that they have indeed "seed de first en de last . . . seed de beginnin, en . . . de endin". With Benjy, who takes over the very last pages of the novel, matters are slightly more complicated because the sense of an ending appears to be at once underlined and denied by his actions; things seem at once complete and incomplete. To an extent, the very reintroduction of the youngest Compson brother carries us back to the beginning of the book, as if the author were making a gallant attempt to make the wheel come full circle. And the feeling of circularity – or, to use a more familiar critical phrase, 'rounding things off' – is reinforced by the reappearance of certain familiar motifs, including the fence, the golfers, and Benjy's habit of whimpering and moaning. Even the famous closing lines of the novel seem at first sight intended to round things off, and put everything in its appropriate place. The objects of this world have now been arranged, the initial impression is, the artifact has been completed and can stand there in its own right, entire and "chastely serene".

> The broken flower drooped over Ben's fist and his eyes were empty and blue and serene again as cornice and facade flowed smoothly once more from left to right; post and tree, window and doorway, and signboard, each in its ordered place.[91]

The problem is, of course, that this is the order of an idiot, dependent on certain radical acts of exclusion. It is as if Faulkner were reminding us that the ending of *The Sound and the Fury* is no ending at all: that it represents, at most, a continuation of the process of encoding – the process, that is, of trying to put things "each in its ordered place" — and an invitation to us, the readers, to continue that process too. Benjy's "empty" eyes are poignant reminders that no system is ever complete or completely adequate. Something is always missed out, it seems, some aspect of reality must invariably remain unseen; and, since this is so, no book, not even one like this that uses a multiplicity of systems, can ever truly be said to be finished. Language may be a necessary tool for understanding and dealing with the world, the only way we can hope to know Caddy; yet perversely, Faulkner suggests, it is as much a function of ignorance, idiocy, as of knowledge. It implies absence, loss, as well as fulfilment.

It is often said that, being a modernist, Faulkner belongs primarily to the American and European literary tradition: that he is closer, say, to James Joyce, T. S. Eliot, and Ezra Pound than to other writers from below the Mason–Dixon line.[92] This is not without its grain of truth. His is, after all, a literature of the edge, marked by a sense of discovery and experiment, unafraid to explore the fundamentals of expression: as such, it does have much in common with the writings of Joyce, Eliot, and Pound, or in other arts with the work of Stravinsky or the Post-

Impressionists. However, it would be wrong to assume that, because of his modernism, Faulkner cannot be regarded as a literary regionalist. And it would be quite as wrong to suggest that – being a Southerner born and raised at a time when the Southern myths, although challenged, still possessed the imagination – he expressed his modernist tendencies in an unlocalised way, in anything other than Southern terms. Faulkner may, for example, have been encouraged by reading Eliot to consider the problem of tradition, the possibility of a usable inheritance. All the same, that problem was there to be perceived in his own corner of the earth: in the South's habitual preoccupation with the past, its long romance with memory, and the evident rift, the growing discontinuity it was experiencing between its notions of the past and the present. Equally, James Joyce may have helped Faulkner to become aware of the fictive impulse, the difficulties of naming and telling. But that awareness was in any case implicit in the regional preoccupation with artifice – and, in particular, with legend, rhetoric, and ritual. All it needed really was a sense of cultural disorientation (something that was readily supplied by the times) and personal displacement (something painfully provided by Faulkner's own life) to add an extra edge of self-consciousness: awareness of myth could then develop into a creative absorption in the mythmaking process, while a concern for rhetoric and an interest in ritual could be translated into, in turn, an imaginative analysis of speech, its limits and possibilities, and a dramatic inquiry into the nature of codes. All of this is not to say that Faulkner was ultimately uninterested in writers like Eliot or Joyce, or was uninfluenced by them. Of course he was interested in them – although he was sometimes misleading about the degree of his interest – and was affected by them – although perhaps less than is commonly imagined. But it is to say that, for the most part, what Faulkner responded to in those writers were forms of knowledge and discourse that he could also find in the regional experience; and that what he absorbed from the crisis of his times was used principally to question, comment upon, or develop that dream (to use his own word), those models of language, thought, and behaviour that were the special gift of the South. "You know", Faulkner said once in an interview,

> sometimes I think there must be a sort of pollen of ideas floating in the air, which fertilizes similarly minds here and there which have not had direct contact.[93]

For Faulkner, that "pollen of ideas" was primarily Southern in origin, of a very particular place and time; with its help he managed to produce fiction that was regional in the best sense – something that could speak from Oxford, Mississippi and the land he loved and hated to anyone anywhere willing to listen.

6

The Southerner as amphibian: the region since the war

A HOUSE DIVIDED AGAINST ITSELF: AN APPROACH TO RECENT SOUTHERN CULTURE AND WRITING

In 1970, a review entitled "The Last Good One?" appeared in the *New Republic*. The review was of Eudora Welty's novel, *Losing Battles*, and in it the reviewer, Jonathan Yardley, found himself wondering if "the Southern tradition in literature" was not falling into decline, or rather a state of terminal decay. *Losing Battles*, he argued, was "a work motivated in large measure by nostalgia", and "nostalgia not merely for a lost South but for a lost Southern literature". "Undoubtedly", he went on,

> someone will come along to prove me wrong, but I suspect that *Losing Battles* is the last "Southern novel" – or should I say the last good one. There is nothing self-consciously or affectedly Southern about it, yet in mood, setting and central concerns it is very much in the tradition that began when Faulkner sat down to write *Sartoris*. That tradition is now four decades old, and dying an early death.[1]

As Yardley saw it, the reasons for this early death were very simple: Southerners, and more particularly "young Southerners", no longer had "anything *unique* to teach", no sense of the past or place or anything else that made them different from other Americans. Eudora Welty's generation, he suggested, was "the last to know intimately the Southern land before the highways and the quick-food joints took over"; they were the last "to know the Southern myth before it grew stale, to know the Southern family before it disintegrated". If Welty wrote "naturally and easily" about "yesterday's South" it was because this was "her South", the country of her imagination; and there were very few if any younger writers of whom this could truthfully be said.

Yardley's review raises any number of minor issues. For instance, his

217

claim that *Losing Battles* is a work motivated by nostalgia seems unnecessarily reductive; while it would surely be more accurate to say that it was the Southern *renaissance* that began in the 1920s, not "the Southern tradition in literature". These, however, are not what concerns us here. What matters, in this context, is the question Yardley posed in his title and then tried to answer. Is Southern literature dead or dying? Is there still a body of writing that is recognisably *of* the South, identifiable with a specifically regional structure of feeling? Yardley was not, of course, the first person to ask this question, nor by any means the last; on the contrary, it has become one of the most popular debating points in Southern literary studies. And for every commentator who has agreed with him, arrived at similar conclusions, there is at least one other who has argued for survival – who has insisted that (as one of them put it, borrowing his words from Tennyson) "though much is taken, much abides". On the one side, lined up with Yardley, are people like Walter Sullivan, Floyd Watkins, and Thomas Daniel Young, all of whom insist that "that literature produced in the South has lost its unique regional flavor". There may be disagreements about precisely when this loss occurred (Sullivan, for example, sees *All the King's Men*, published in 1946, as "the philosophical swansong", marking "the literal end of the Southern renascence",[2] while Young seems to put things a little later): but, they agree, it certainly has occurred, the regional tradition has been exhausted. On the other side are a number of critics, including Louis D. Rubin, Paschal Reeves, and Lewis Simpson, who suggest that all we are witnessing now is "a new stage in the southern literary imagination, different from anything that has gone before". Simpson's argument – from which that last quotation is taken – is particularly interesting in this respect. The Southern renaissance, he suggests, has had "two major stages". The first lasted "from the early 1920s to about 1950" and was one in which Southern writing recorded "an attempted reconstruction of the past by the literary mind", a conscious effort to restore the idea of civilisation. The second, dating from roughly "the period of the Second World War and the beginning of the Cold War" registers something quite different: "the breakdown of the endeavour in reconstruction" and an accompanying sense "that the process of the destruction of memory and history . . . cannot be halted". In this second stage, which of course is still continuing, the writer no longer attempts to resurrect civilisation but simply to preserve his own personal integrity. He abandons the search for "a new literary covenant with the past" in the certain understanding that "the only meaningful covenant" for him now "is one with the self on terms generally defined as existential".[3]

There may be a peculiar and persuasive rigour in the tone of Simpson's argument, but its thrust, the assumptions on which it builds, and the direction in which it is developed are fairly typical – more or less characteristic of critics who insist on Southern literature's survival. Southern writing has changed, the suggestion is, and yet it is still Southern, attached to an identifiably regional code; or, as Paschal Reeves puts it, "the South is changing . . . but there's still enough of the South remaining so that it is able to produce a Walker Percy". The problem here, however, is one of assumptions – premises that, for want of any other word, can only be called philosophical. Simpson demonstrates very effectively just how depleted the Southern reserves of memory and imagination have become – by pointing out, for instance, how remembrances of "the War, the Surrender, and Reconstruction" are mediated for the contemporary writer by several generations, so that "a close contact" with the past is no longer possible for him. He even admits that many recent Southern books and stories "seem logically to indicate the eventual frustration of the writer as Southerner".[4] But having done all that he still insists on seeing the emergent forces in writing from the South as being definitively *of* the South, belonging to a new stage in the development of the regional argument. The reasons for this seem to be two: a quantitative sense that enough distinctively Southern characteristics have survived to justify retention of the term "Southern literature"; and something more fundamental and ineffable – a belief in some mysterious form or essence, some shaping spirit or Idea of Southernness, that is presumed to be there, to exist still, but is never satisfactorily defined. This has to be largely a matter of inference, though; for the most part, what Simpson refers to are those changes of mind and temperament that have made Southern writers less noticeably regional, more like those from elsewhere. Reduced to a simple formula, in fact, Simpson's argument could be presented thus: "A" (that is, Southern writing) has become "B" (that is, existentialist writing, or postmodernist writing, or whatever) in its manifest shape, and yet it still somehow remains "A" in its hidden form, in some way to do with its Platonic essence. And to this could be added a subsidiary formula: "A" is becoming "B", and yet it still retains enough of its "A" qualities, whatever they may be, to be called by its old name rather than its new. What seems to be missing from all this is the realisation that anything, including a literary tradition, can change so much that it assumes a new identity and must be described in fresh terms; or, alternatively, the acknowledgement that anything undergoing a process of change deserves to be seen in terms of its emergent shape, its developing identity, as well as the one it is discarding – to be given a name that expresses its ambivalent nature. To call a body of writing Southern, as Simpson does, and then to call it existentialist is really to beg the question. It is either Southern or it is existentialist or it is a richly confused and confusing mixture of the two: but it is not and cannot be described as if it were a coherent, unequivocal example of both.

The whole question of the survival of Southern writing is, of course, inextricably connected to the larger question of the survival of the South: that is, as a homogeneous culture with its own peculiar systems of thought and behaviour. And here the evidence is, to say the least, mixed. Admittedly, as far as the material culture is concerned, there can be little doubt that the changes over the past few decades have been radical. They are summed up in this way in a recent book on the subject, *Media–Made Dixie* by Jack Temple Kirby:

> By the late 1970s the easy geographical, economic, political, and demographic characteristics that had traditionally defined *southern* were long gone. The "national" urban-industrial mode so despised by the Agrarians of 1930 was firmly entrenched. The air above Chattanooga . . . was among the nation's most polluted in the sixties. Poverty was no longer a dominating characteristic.[5]

Sweeping as this may sound, it is nevertheless accurate: the Southern economic, political, and social structure *has* altered drastically, and in the ways that Tate, Davidson, and their friends feared it would. The Southern economy, in particular, has been transformed by what C. Vann Woodward, in a characteristically evocative phrase, christened "the Bulldozer Revolution". A seminal article written in the early 1970s is worth citing here, because it brings together the vast quantity of statistical detail on which people like Kirby and Vann Woodward depend for their evidence. Entitled "The Changing South: National Incorporation of a Region", it was written by two social scientists, John C. McKinney and Linda B. Bourque and it begins with this forthright statement:

> The South has been changing *more rapidly* than the rest of the nation during the last forty years . . . Such development and all it entails have enabled the South to become more like the rest of the American society in terms of its primary dimensions of living.[6] (See Plate 12)

The evidence McKinney and Bourque present in support of their claims seems incontrovertible. For instance, they reveal that, whereas in 1940 only 35 per cent of the Southern population lived in metropolitan areas, by 1960 that figure had risen to 52 per cent. In just twenty years, in effect, the South changed from "a predominantly rural region here and there scattered with cities" to a substantially urban area with a rural–urban balance much closer to that of the rest of the nation.

Accompanying this change, McKinney and Bourque point out, there have been others just as dramatic. Not surprisingly, given the drift to the towns, the proportion of the regional population engaged in agriculture has steadily decreased, from 33.4 per cent in 1940 to 10.2 per cent in 1960: and, moving things on a few years, "there is a much greater similarity in the industrial distribution between the South and non-South in 1968 than there was in 1940". Certainly, there are still differences between the *kinds* of industry characteristic of Southern and non-Southern areas. The South, McKinney and Bourque indicate, still generally favours "primary industries" – textiles, food processing, wood and furniture production, and so on – all of which represent a first-stage use of raw materials and are labour-intensive, employing a high percentage of unskilled or semi-skilled workers at a relatively low wage. By contrast, the general tendency in the non-South has been away from such primary industries into "secondary" or "tertiary" ones: which are dependent on, respectively, supplies from primary industries rather than raw materials and on research and development. Less labour-intensive than primary industries, they are also considerably more lucrative as far as the individual worker is concerned; and, as a result, there is still something of a gap between *per capita* income in the South and in the rest of the country. As McKinney and Bourque put it, "the 12 Southern states regularly fall among the lowest 15 to 17 nationally". But this gap should not be exaggerated, any more than differences in the type of industry characteristic of the two areas should. Personal income in the South has increased dramatically, they emphasise (by 300 per cent between 1940 and 1950, alone); the dependence of the region on primary industry is gradually decreasing; and it seems reasonable to assume that the Southern states are simply going through a stage of industrial development already experienced by most of the others and will eventually catch up. Besides, McKinney and Bourque argue, the growth of education in the South seems destined to alter the picture even if nothing else were to. Educational opportunities have improved to the point where the region is not far behind the rest of the nation: the percentage of the population in education at the age of eighteen, for instance, has grown from 24 per cent in 1940 to 40.2 per cent in 1960, which is just 2.8 per cent less than the non-Southern norm. And as a larger proportion of the Southern population attend school for longer periods of time, so a more skilled workforce will become available: a workforce that is, as McKinney and Bourque quietly suggest, "sharing in a national (in many respects international) culture".[7]

Since the publication of this influential essay on economic change in the South, many of the predictions made by its authors have been fulfilled. The metropolitan population has continued to grow (to 68.8 per cent of the total, in fact, by 1984), the secondary and tertiary industries have undergone a rapid expansion, and both educational opportunities and income have substantially improved (the median household income in 1983, for instance, was $19,386, as compared to $21,818 in the North-east and $21,086 in the Middle West). As a very recent commentator puts it, "the South has not only caught up with the rest of the nation in economic productivity, but has even surpassed some regions in economic growth".[8] Other changes, no less significant, have also helped to alter the tone and texture of regional life – some of which are suggested by this colourful remark made by the Southern political scientist, William C. Havard:

> cotton has moved west, cattle have moved east, the farmer has moved to town, the city resident has moved to the suburbs, the Negro has moved north, and the Yankee has moved South.[9]

As late as 1940, approximately 69 per cent of the black population of the United States lived in the eleven states of the former Confederacy, and about two-thirds of Southern blacks were located in rural areas. By 1960, the same eleven states had only 48.6 per cent of the total black population – for the first time in its history, in fact, the South had lost its majority of the Afro-American population – and ten years later, by 1970, about half of the Southern black populace was living in urban areas. Meanwhile, the 1970 population figures showed another "first": for the first time in a century the South had experienced a net gain, despite the loss of many blacks, because of immigration from other parts of the United States. In effect, the character of the Southern population has altered quite considerably. It is still altering and will, presumably, continue to alter, creating still further problems for those who want to hold on to the old, self-interpretative myths.

Mention of the Southern blacks perhaps helps bring into focus another way in which the region has altered over the last twenty or thirty years: politically, that is, thanks to what has come to be known as "the Second Reconstruction". For the civil rights movement, and the changes in law that accompanied or issued out of it, have served to abolish the four inherited institutions of political sectionalism in the South: dis-franchisement, malapportionment, the one-party system, and *de jure* racial segregation. The South is no longer "solid". On the one hand, the percentage of black voters has increased enormously: from 29.1 per cent to 66.3 per cent of the black voting-age population between 1960 and 1970 alone. On the other, the Republican party has steadily grown in power and influence. As one Southern political scientist put it, in 1975:

> One hundred years after Reconstruction the South is far along the road back to the mainstream of biracial, two-party American national politics . . .

> Three of the formerly solid Democratic southern states – Virginia, Tennessee, and perhaps Florida – have viable two-party systems. North Carolina, Texas,

> Arkansas, and Georgia are nearing the end of one-party dominance while
> Alabama, Louisiana, and South Carolina . . . have unstable political situations
> that could rapidly move the state Republican parties to positions of
> competitiveness.[10]

This movement back towards two-party politics was accelerated by the
results of the November, 1984 election. Republicans doubled the
number of their House and Senate seats in North Carolina and increased
their representation in Texas, South Carolina, Florida, and Arkansas.
They lost one seat in the United States Senate to the Democrats but still
remained not far behind them in terms of overall Southern representation (they now have thirteen seats while the Democrats have nineteen).
As for the Presidential race, there was, as one Texan commentator put it,
"a literal white flight from the Democratic party all across the South":[11]
Southern whites voted for Ronald Reagan by 71 per cent to 29 per cent.
The majority of white Southerners have not, in fact, supported a
Democratic Presidential candidate for over thirty years, not even Jimmy
Carter! Of course, it might be argued that the expression "solid South"
was in any case a misnomer – or, to adopt the spicier expression of one
Southerner, "hardly worth a proverbial damn" – since there was always
considerable factionalism within state Democratic parties. But as
William Havard points out, "competitiveness within the framework of a
one-party system hardly provides a substitute for the sort of organized
political opposition that is possible under a two-party system". And
although the South may not have a fully-fledged two-party system as yet
– what it has now, Havard suggests, could be more usefully described as a
"no-party" system – it is well on the way to acquiring one. A few
observers go even further than this, suggesting that the Republicans may
end up with something rather more than parity. "My impression", said
Curtis Gans, director of the Committee for the Study of the American
Electorate, shortly after the re-election of Reagan, "is that the Republicans are going to be a competitive party in the South, and maybe the
dominant party, in the next six years." "It has been building for quite
some time", he added, "and this was a real breakthrough year for them as
far as the South was concerned."[12]

   This last point is a purely speculative one, of course. What is not
speculation but a matter of fact, however, is that the economic and
political fabric of the region is being woven into a new design – and that,
at the same time, the social landscape of the South is experiencing a
metamorphosis, assuming more characteristically American arrangements. Again, Jack Temple Kirby had something to say about this, the
transformation of most Southerners' daily environment. "Since World
War II", Kirby observes,

> the region became urbanized, standardized, neonized. Visually, there is little
> difference between the superhighways and streetscapes of Ohio and Alabama.

The cars, gasoline stations, subdivision architecture, glass-faced office towers, and gaudy fast-food stands are the same.[13]

Most Southerners would be able to confirm this simply by looking out of the windows of their cars. "One drives", the Georgia writer Marshall Frady sadly reflects, "through a Santa Barbara gallery of pizza cottages and fish 'n' chip parlors, with a 'Tara Shopping Center' abruptly glaring out of the fields of broom sedge and jack pine." Taking things further, many seem to feel as, clearly, Frady does here – and, to some extent, even Kirby – that panoramas of this kind can be interpreted symbolically; to be more specific, they appear to think that changes in the Southern environment can be read as symptomatic — signs of a more fundamental alteration in its codes, its structure of feeling and perception. "There is every good reason to believe", wrote McKinney and Bourque in the conclusion to their survey of the regional economy,

> that to the extent that the daily occupational and educational environment of the Southerner becomes similar to that of the non-Southerner, the attitudes and values of the two will also become indistinguishable.[14]

Working from this assumption, many Southern observers argue that the alteration of consciousness anticipated by McKinney and Bourque has actually occurred: in other words, that along with its landscape the spiritual geography of the region has been "urbanized, standardized, neonized".

Of course, the implications of this assumed displacement of traditional codes are interpreted differently by different Southerners. The distinguished commentator on Southern affairs Robert Coles, for example, tends to see it as something to be regretted. The South, he claims, has been contaminated by

> The world of sex manuals, of Masters and Johnson, of *Playboy* and *Penthouse* and *Viva*; the world of talk, talk, talk, about me, me, me; the world of military hardware, of hydrogen missiles, dozens and dozens, stored all over . . .[15]

And as an inevitable accompaniment of this, he says, it has acquired "the soft psychological and moral belly of secular, agnostic liberalism". Others read things in more hopeful terms: arguing that (as one of them puts it) "the New South . . ., transforming its bigoted past . . . seems like a new frontier where those of talent and capability can meet their success". According to these, more optimistic interpreters of the Southern landscape, one event is of particular significance, the elevation of Jimmy Carter to the Presidency in 1976. For here was the first person from the Deep South to enter the White House since Zachary Taylor 128 years earlier. Not only that, here was a Southerner who hardly fitted into the traditional vocabularies or subscribed to the familiar pieties: a racial liberal, a progressive farmer, sympathetic to feminist causes – a

conservationist certainly, and to that extent not totally untouched by
agrarian feeling, but at bottom someone who was favourably disposed
towards the ideas of urban investment and industrial advance. The
arrival of Carter on the American stage, so this version of the regional
story goes, was more than just a personal success or a victory for the
Georgia political machine. It marked "the emergence of the
postsegregation South, economically confident and eager for national
recognition"; it was "the symbol of a South risen again"[16] – born again,
not as Carter had been to a form of Christianity, but to a whole new and
better series of commitments.

Seductive this interpretation of recent Southern history may be, not
least because of its symmetry: on this point, at least, many traditionalists
and progressives feel they can come together – that the outward and
visible signs of alteration in the South have been accompanied,
underwritten, and in a sense rendered coherent by an inward and
ideological change. Unfortunately, when the evidence is examined in
detail things become less symmetrical. As far as the reading of the 1976
election is concerned, there is the simple fact mentioned earlier that the
majority of white Southerners did not vote for Carter: so, if the election
did mark a transition in Southern thinking, then one is tempted to
suggest that white people in the South – those who, for good or ill, still
largely dictate the terms of Southern culture – were among the very last
to hear about it. And on a more general level all the signs are that the non-
material culture of the region, although not unaffected by changes in the
material culture, has so far been less substantially altered than one might
expect – less, too, than many Southerners have assumed. It may very well
be that McKinney and Bourque are right as far as the long-term future is
concerned. The fact remains, though, that for the moment there is what
one Southern commentator has referred to, somewhat paradoxically, as
"deep-rooted continuity behind the symptoms of basic change" – and
another has described, using a rather more direct and memorable phrase,
as "subcultural persistence in mass society".[17] "Belief systems", one
Southern progressive recently (and ruefully) observed, "although subject
to conditions of material change, do have a life of their own": which is a
point expanded upon by the North Carolinian journalist, Edwin M.
Yoder. Looking back at Cash's *The Mind of the South* some twenty-five
years after its first publication Yoder asked, "has the essential behavior of
the South as Cash described it changed radically . . .?" and then
responded to his own question in this way:

> On the whole the answer seems to me No – . . . In truth "the mind of the
> South" seems today to defy the impersonal forces. When you put aside the
> spread of television sets, the advent of jet air travel, the larger cash incomes (all
> consistent with national developments), you are left with a mental pattern
> familiar to Cash . . .[18]

This answer may suffer from its own kind of simplification; since it ignores the point that the old, self-reflexive codes of the region have been under exceptionally heavy assault for the past few decades and can hardly have remained unbruised. But it has its grain of truth. The South has not yet been "happily homogenized" (to use C. Vann Woodward's caustic phrase) – at least, not entirely; some of what another Southern journalist, Ralph McGill, has called "the clan virtues"[19] survive – even if in faltering or diminished forms; the picture, in short, is still far from clear.

Some notion of the ways in which systems of perception have survived material change can be gathered from an extensive survey of opinion polls conducted in the late 1960s: *The Enduring South* by John Shelton Reed. Southerners, it emerges from the polls Reed examined, still tend to think in identifiably local or regional terms. They are more likely than other Americans to choose kin and local people as those they most admire; more likely to be Christian and, being Christian, more likely to be fundamentalist. They are more likely, too, to rely on themselves and their own notions of honour, right and wrong – to fight, for example, rather than call the police or go to law; and more likely to oppose any challenge to, or possible infringement of, their right to bear arms. Inclined to think in regional terms generally, they tend to think of *themselves* in the same way, Reed discovered. This he established by asking a cross-section of Southern people to list the words or phrases that, as they saw it, most accurately described Northerners, themselves, and the American people as a whole. The four terms used most frequently to describe white Southerners were conservative, tradition-loving, courteous, and loyal to family ties; while white Northerners were usually depicted as industrious, materialistic, intelligent, progressive, and sophisticated. In turn, the adjectives most often favoured for the American people generally were materialistic, industrious, pleasure-loving, and progressive.[20] The Southerners interviewed in effect associated the national system of values with one quite alien to their own. They tended to see themselves as a distinctive minority, not nearly as "American" – nowhere near as much a part of the cultural mainstream – as most observers of the South's material development would like to believe.

Other studies of regional attitudes have tended to confirm Reed's findings and reinforce the notion of subcultural persistence. Two very recent surveys, for example, have unravelled a peculiar anomaly in the position of Southern women. On the one hand, there has been a rapid growth in the number of women in professional and executive jobs. *The Atlanta Constitution* referred to it, in fact, as "a staggering statistical leap"[21] – a claim that does not seem too much of a journalistic hyperbole in the circumstances. For while women's portion of the total Southern workforce only grew from 38.7 per cent to 42.9 per cent between 1970 and 1980, their share of executive and managerial positions jumped during the same period from 19.5 per cent to 31.4 per cent; in fact, the South now has a greater percentage of female accountants, administrators, and managers than any other part of the country. A dramatic change of this kind might be expected to put a dent in the traditional image of the white Southern lady, "beautiful, fragile, good, and ultimately irrelevant to reality": that notion of womanhood that a recent commentator, echoing Cash, described as being "at the core of the region's self-definition". But, it seems, things have not turned out this way. On the contrary Colette Dowling, reporting in 1982 on a visit she had recently made to Atlanta, revealed that the women she met, all from the middle class, seemed to have a hidden fear of independence. As one of these women observed to Dowling, "The point of pride, for a lot of women in Atlanta, is still how much money your husband makes and how well he takes care of you."[22] More recently, a series of interviews with successful professional women in the South (and the husbands of some of them) has revealed just how stubbornly the old codes survive. Successful the women may be, and economically independent. But they still tend to equate male success with a non-working wife; they still think of home as the female domain and everything outside it as male territory; and they are still inclined to play the part of gentle female in male company. "I do agree", admitted one of the interviewees,

> that southern women do still have somewhat a tendency to present themselves as sweet and genteel and cottony-soft and must not get out in the sun because you'll freckle and that sort of thing. But that's not the way it is at all.[23]

Which reveals the paradox sharply. The economic position of many Southern women has changed, certainly. Nevertheless, men of their acquaintance continue for the most part to treat them as "ladies": that is, to adopt protective rituals that are in effect forms of domination. In turn, the women, who may well be aware that "that's not the way it is at all", frequently choose to accept the roles assigned them. This, it may be, is for the same reason that many people accept an assigned role – because it is the easiest way out, the simplest and least troublesome thing to do. Alternatively (and most recent studies tend to support this), they may do so because they are not completely without false consciousness: in other words, not entirely untouched by the myth that the image of the white lady helps to sustain.

A similar, but rather more tragic, survival of traditional structures of feeling is noticeable in the attitudes of white Southerners towards blacks. On the basis of the available evidence, it seems clear that the industrialisation of the South has changed the character of race relations (although not necessarily for the better: for example, recent housing development appears actually to have promoted segregation). Whatever the changes in overt relations, though, inherited biases stubbornly remain. All that has altered is the terms in which those biases are expressed: as the author of one recent survey Margaret Andersen puts it, "the rhetoric of race prejudice has been replaced with a new vocabulary of class opportunity" – a vocabulary that ignores the differences of opportunity available in a black, urban ghetto and in a white, middle-class suburb. Nor have the terms necessarily changed that much, as some of the remarks quoted in the survey indicate. "I feel that colored people in the South get along far better than colored people in the North", observed one woman who, ironically, considered herself to be "in the vanguard of social change in the contemporary South"; "I think that colored people here know their place." "My husband's feeling is that southern blacks are much nicer than northern blacks", declared another; "Northern blacks are more defensive, more aggressive."[24] Of course, this is not to imply that the racial prejudice such remarks betray is, or ever has been, peculiar to the South: that is patently unfair and absurd. Nor is it to deny that there have been significant improvements below the Mason–Dixon line in race relations and racial attitudes. But, it does seem to be the case that the modernisation of a region's economic structure does not necessarily or immediately lead to the development of more liberal belief systems. Here as elsewhere there remains a gap between what many observers believed would happen to Southern thinking as a result of material change and what, so far at least, has occurred.

But perhaps the most startling and controversial example of subcultural persistence was offered by the social scientist, Raymond Gastil, in a paper entitled "Homicide and a Regional Culture of Violence". In his paper, Gastil argued from the available evidence that the region still manifested a distinctive attitude towards violence: that, to be precise, there is a "subculture of violence"[25] in the South probably attributable to the survival of military and hunting traditions, frontier habits, and obsession with the code of honour. Both Gastil's methods and his thesis have been vigorously contested. His critics have not, however, been able to provide any viable alternative explanation for observed differences between the regions as far as gun ownership, violence, and murder are concerned; and subsequent evidence has tended to confirm his findings. For example, the most exhaustive study of gun owners in the United States, conducted by the National Commission on the Causes and Prevention of Violence, discovered that owners tended to be concentrated in rural areas and the South; while a recent examination of urban pistol ownership concludes quite simply, "the best single predictor of pistol ownership is southernness".[26] If such findings are to be believed (and there is no reason not to believe them), then it would seem that the spirit of Captain Porgy and Sut Lovingood, Colonel John Sartoris and Johnny Reb — all of them men ready to defend their dignity with violence when they felt it to be threatened – is still very much alive and well.

A distinctive, even ritualistic attitude towards the otherness of women and blacks, a preoccupation with violence and the idea of honour: such qualities characterise both the populist hell-of-a-fellow and his partriarchal opposite – although it should be clear by now that they assume quite different implications according to the code, the system of argument and metaphor, with which they happen to be associated. And while these dark, Faulknerian themes evidently survive in certain forms, so too do some of the more comforting pieties: most notably, perhaps, an attachment to locality and the sanctions of memory. The journalist Willie Morris, for instance, concludes a short memoir of his Mississippi boyhood by claiming that what his upbringing taught him above all was "an allegiance and a love for one small place".[27] While Eudora Welty's account of her childhood ends in an analogous way, by declaring "memory . . . is the treasure most dearly regarded by me"; and this for a simple reason – "all that is remembered joins and lives", she says: "the old and the young, the past and the present, the living and the dead".[28] A similar note can be heard in the work of writers from a younger generation. The central character in *The Annunciation*, for example, a first novel by the young Southerner, Ellen Gilchrist, has memories that, we are told "she must carry with her always. Her cargo." More remarkably, the main figure in *Meridian*, a novel by the black writer from Georgia, Alice Walker, seems like a not-too-distant relative of Quentin Compson. "But what none of them seemed to understand", Walker says of her protagonist,

> was that she felt herself to be, not holding on to something from the past, but
> *held* by something in the past: by the memory of old black men in the South
> who, caught by surprise in the eye of a camera, never shifted their position but
> looked directly back; by the sight of young girls singing in a country choir,
> their hair shining with brushings and grease, their voices the voices of angels.[29]

Which is not to claim that Walker is in any definitive sense a Southern writer: merely that the regional voice can find many curious echoes, in even the most unexpected of places, and speak sometimes in hardly noticeable terms.

One final point needs making on this question of the South's relationship to the rest of the nation since the Second World War. A minority group is the product not only of self-definition but of definition by others; and here again, as far as the attitudes of other Americans towards Southerners are concerned, there is a perceptible fissure. Despite the steady erosion of social, political, and economic differences, in other words, there is still a tendency on the part of the rest of the nation to think of people from the former Confederacy as different. As the geographers Peter Gould and Rodney White have established, many non-Southerners retain distinctive "mental maps", a consistent pattern of regional evaluation that has as its centre a sharply negative image of the South.[30] This emerges with particular force from a survey of Northern attitudes towards Jimmy Carter that set out to discover if (as many observers claimed) Carter's election really did signal a change in outsiders' perceptions of the region. The survey revealed that, whatever impressions Northern people had of Carter – and, for the most part, they were favourable – they did not perceive him as Southern at all. More to the point, their notions of the South and Southernness fitted into the familiar stereotypes without much difficulty: Southerners were, it was felt, inherently provincial and traditional and usually at odds with the rest of the nation. Of those questioned 77 per cent even declared that, given a choice, the Southern region was the one from which they would least prefer their President to originate.[31] "What makes the mind of the South different is that it thinks it is",[32] observed a reviewer of Cash's book when it first appeared. If that has an element of truth to it, then so has a closely related point: that what may also make the mind of the South different is that Northerners persist in thinking it is as well. In fact, according to one recent survey Northerners still think there are greater differences between Southerners and themselves than between rural and urban residents, immigrants and residents of the United States, or males and females!

So, it seems, the essential paradoxes remain. The material culture has changed substantially since the Second World War, far more even than in the period when the Agrarians and their friends were taking their stand. But the non-material culture, although altered, still enables Southerners to think and talk of themselves in terms of their regional identity, the inherited codes, and, to some extent, still permits Northerners to do the same. "Psychological adherence is still strong in the South", observed one political commentator, "and the vast majority of southern whites retain their emotional identification as Democrats even though some of them have not supported a Democratic presidential candidate for . . . decades."[33] Exactly so; and it is only necessary to expand the terms a little to see how this applies to regional life in general. Southerners may live in a predominantly urban and surburban society and depend on an industrial economy; and the foundations of their lives may gradually be shifting under the impact of mass culture. They may watch television, eat at Macdonald's, and listen to popular music. But old habits die hard; alterations in the material fabric of society are not necessarily or immediately accompanied by alterations in the consciousness of its members. So the cultural lag persists, even if in weakened form;

and the war between the old codes and the new continues, with the new slowly but steadily gaining ground. The Southerner, in effect, still belongs in two worlds, two moral territories, even if he is turning back ever less easily or frequently to one of these; in terms of his mind or imagination at least, he remains an amphibious creature.[34]

Which is surely the right way of looking, not only at the Southerner and Southern culture, but at contemporary Southern writing: it is amphibious, attached partly to the old structures of perceptions and partly to the new. As a body of work, it is no longer distinctively regional in the way that the writing of previous generations was; there is no longer the sense of working from within a culture – inside a vocabulary, using models of belief that are shared and more or less self-contained. But the regional code is still operative in individual books. Some writers are still implicated – in different ways, of course, and to differing degrees – in the inherited arguments; while others find themselves worrying about the possibility that they are involved, whether they like it or not, in "a worn-out tradition" (to borrow a phrase from William Styron's most recent novel), an "ancient and noble literary heritage" that has "petered out, rumbled to a feeble halt".[35] Another way of putting all this is to say, quite simply, that Southern writing now is a very mixed bag: neither definitively Southern nor belonging to contemporary, postmodernist culture in any unequivocal sense. There are, certainly, writers like those mentioned in the previous chapter: people like Elizabeth Spencer, Madison Jones, Shelby Foote, and Cormac McCarthy, who have continued to write within the regional tradition, offering personal reworkings of familiar preoccupations and themes. But there are others whose relationship to that tradition is far more tenuous and uncertain: among them, Lee Smith, Sylvia Wilkinson, Reynolds Price, and William Styron. Still more to the point, perhaps, there are others – including some of the most intriguing of recent writers from the South – who seem actively to resist, consciously to defy, regional identification: such as John Barth, Barry Hannah, and Walker Percy.

"Signs of the times", thinks one of Lee Smith's characters as she looks at a large Pepsi sign throwing its light on the Confederate statue in the town square. "Everywhere you looked, you saw them."[36] To register change is not, of course, a conspicuously un-Southern thing to do. Writers from the region have always done it; and indeed it could be said that the best Southern writing has issued from precisely that sense of crisis that accelerated, or at least unexpected, change brings about. What is new, though, remarkably different from the traditional Southern manner of doing things, is the way such changes are duly registered in the fabric of a good deal of recent writing from the region: in its structure or texture, the models it uses for perceiving, encoding, and presenting experience. In a less radical sense, this is illustrated by Sylvia Wilkinson's use, in a novel like *Bone of My Bones*, of the forms and procedures of feminist fiction: which include, among other things, the idea that the book is about a woman preparing to liberate herself by writing a book. "Any girl can have a baby Mama", Wilkinson's protagonist Ella Ruth Higgins writes in her journal:

> I have all the things inside me to make one and they probably would work if I used them. . . . But I have to make my life into something it wasn't going to be naturally.[37]

That "something" turns out to be authorship. By the end of the novel, Ella Ruth has chosen her vocation, and given the reasons for her choice. "That's the way things come to me", she declares:

> They go into words so I can deal with them. And then I feel better. But I know it's more than that. I know it's something I want to share.[38]

Rejecting the conventional female role, Ella Ruth takes a path familiar to readers of contemporary feminist fiction, towards the freedom offered by the written word. Unlike Faulkner's Drusilla Hawk, in fact, and like her own creator, she resists identification in traditional Southern terms and forges a new identity for herself, devises a model of reality using a language that is at least partly of her own invention.

But perhaps a better example of this less radical, more equivocal stance towards the old structures of feeling is William Styron's novel, *Sophie's Choice*. Quite as self-reflexive as *Bone of My Bones*, *Sophie's Choice* – whatever else it may be about – is about its own making: a making that involves a painful but deliberate and necessary disengagement from the South and all that it entails. "You're at the end of a tradition", the protagonist Stingo (a plainly autobiographical character) is told by his Jewish friend Nathan, ". . . Southern writing as a force is going to be over in a few years." The time, significantly, is 1947, just after the Second World War. Stingo has travelled North to New York to become a writer, and there, as a kind of preparation for his new life, he gradually takes on a new identity. Many things contribute to his metamorphosis, but of these easily the most important is his relationship with a Polish girl Sophie, a survivor of Auschwitz. For what he learns through her, about the concentration camps, suffering, and human nature, transforms him, alters his vision and vocabulary. As a Southerner, Stingo believes in guilt, Original Sin; indeed, he could hardly do otherwise since, like Ike McCaslin, he is descended from slave-owners and has profited at whatever distance from the sale of human flesh. In the course of his conversations with Sophie, however, and as a result of his love for her and a sense of shared, vicarious experience, this belief is changed beyond recognition: into an inherently, desperately modern obsession with the banality of evil. Real evil, Stingo learns, is not "aggressive, romantic, melodramatic, thrilling, orgasmic"; it is not Gothic, nor has it any Biblical resonance. It is "gloomy, monotonous, barren, boring", a void or blankness that provides little or nothing on which the human imagination can acquire a purchase. The lesson is learned slowly and reluctantly, but Stingo does eventually learn it; and in doing so he moves from being a Southerner, an honourable, stoical, and liberal gentleman like his father, to being a part of what he himself bitterly terms at one point "the fucked-up twentieth century".[39]

Of course, it would be wrong to suggest that Stingo's metamorphosis is total or that his break with his Southern past is complete: he remains, for instance, deeply attached to his father, although he sees him as a touchingly anarchronistic figure, and for a while he even cherishes the notion of setting up home in Virginia with Sophie. Equally, it would be paying less than due tribute to Stingo's regional inheritance if it were not pointed out that that heritage actually helps him to learn his lesson: by mediating, providing him with a preliminary model or structure to facilitate understanding of his new experiences. He begins to understand Auschwitz, for example, "a vast enclave dedicated to the practice . . . of a new form of slavery", by seeing it through the prism of the South's peculiar institution; while knowledge of Poland, Sophie's "beautiful, heart-wrenching, soul-split" mother country, is assisted by his belief that it "conjures up images of the American South" and that there is "a sinister zone of likeness" between it and his own place of birth. The model, however, is only used for a while; like a bridge built for just one journey, it is then left behind. Stingo can no more retain the traditional Southern structures of feeling, after his migration to New York and his meeting with Sophie, than he can return to the South or do as his father wants him to do by sliding "into that great Southern tradition of writer-farmers". The traditional vocabularies and vision sit uneasily with more contemporary ones, even if they can never be totally forgotten or discarded. The point is nicely underlined at one moment about half-way through the novel: when Stingo remembers one morning he lay in a Manhattan hotel room, dreaming about his home in Virginia and its history. He was awoken from his day-dream, he tells us, by "a dim demonic warble", "the ululation of a police siren on the street below". "I listened to it", he says,

> with the faint anxiety which that shrill alarm always provoked; the sound faded away, . . . at last disappeared up into the warrens of Hell's Kitchen. My God, my God, I thought, how could it be possible that the South and that urban shriek co-existed in this century? It was beyond comprehension.[40]

Stingo seems to speak for Styron, his creator, here as well as himself. The idiom of the South is one thing, both tell us, the "urban shriek" another. They are separate languages, predicating quite different notions of reality; and both the author and his protagonist find themselves moving, during the course of this novel, from the old language to the new one.

With all that said, though, a case still could be made for the existence of some sort of positive relationship between writers like Wilkinson and Styron on the one hand and the traditional structures of feeling on the other – some kind of connection, however tenuous or tangential. Both writers could be seen as developing, albeit in strictly contemporary ways, certain familiar regional narrative types and structures. There is more than a trace in *Sophie's Choice*, for instance, of the traditional Southern *Bildungsroman*: with Stingo continuing the story of Quentin Compson and Eugene Gant, only taking their sense of displacement, their feeling that they can't go home again, rather further. Similarly Ella Ruth Higgins affronts her destiny and challenges convention in a fashion that is reminiscent of some of Ellen Glasgow's heroines, or for that matter those of Katherine Anne Porter. There is a vexed question here of the point at which a quantitative change becomes so great that it deserves to be seen as a qualitative one. Or to put it in more concrete terms, there is the problem of deciding just when a character has become so separated from his region, and a writer looks upon his regional inheritance with such a distanced, alien eye, that regional definitions no longer seem to apply. There is a moment when old systems of reference, old categories become less important than new, and perhaps with people like Styron and Wilkinson that moment has been reached. This is all by way of saying, of course, what was said earlier: that Styron, Wilkinson, and other writers like them are profoundly equivocal about the Southern model, but do seem to be moving away from it rather than towards it. They are uneasy, uncertain, finding the old voices drowned out by the "urban shriek"; and in this respect they are probably no different from many other Southerners.

Many other Southerners, but not all: quite apart from writers like Madison Jones and Cormac McCarthy who still appear to be capable of working from within the Southern model, there are others who have rejected it altogether. Along with Walker Percy and John Barth, the most interesting of *this* group is probably Barry Hannah, who declared in a recent interview that what he was after was not to "tell some cranked up southern story again" but through "skipping, illogical skipping" to devise "a new logic", something akin to John Berryman's *Dream Songs*. Of course, Hannah's work uses Southern backgrounds and is not devoid of traditional Southern references: Jeb Stuart, for example, appears in several of his short stories. But his imaginative landscape is not so much regional as drastically contemporary: the pages jostle with references to Jimi Hendrix, the Rolling Stones, the Vietnam War, joggers, *Penthouse*, and all the *dreck* of modern culture. More to the point, all his best work is loose, disjointed, fragmented, registering in sometimes quite violent ways his own evident belief that life is fluid to the point of chaos. In his best book, *Ray*, for example, the narrator, who gives his name to the title, moves backwards and forwards in time ("I live in so many centuries", he says at one point. "Everybody is still alive"), delights in the random and arbitrary ("If I could happen", he suggests, "anything could"), and lives a life of eccentricity and violence. There is no plot to speak of: "I just don't care about plot that much", Hannah has admitted. The characters have the bizarre, exaggerated features of a cartoon. And the narrative is divided into small lumps, segments, some of which are only a few sentences long: thus one segment reads simply, "To live and delight in healing, flying, fucking. Here are the men and women." Time and again, the author via the narrator pokes fun at conventional narrative patterns. After one scene of particular violence, for instance, Ray cheekily declares:

> Now I guess I should give you swaying trees and the rare geometry of cows in the meadow or the like – to break it up. But, sorry, me and this one are over.[41]

The only constant, in fact, is the rhythm of the narrative voice: a rhythm that Hannah says he learned from jazz and rock music and which clearly responds to the rapid, disjunctive movements of modern life. Evidently aware of the objections that might be made to the bewildering instability of his book, Hannah has Ray come out and defend it at one moment. "And yet", Ray insists,

> without a healthy sense of confusion, Ray might grow smug. It's true, isn't it? I might join the gruesome tribe of the smug. I think it's better with me all messed up.[42]

In this book, it seems, it is not only the traditional Southern structures that are rejected but structures of any kind and the actual *idea* of structure – and not just rejected, but openly challenged.

Which is all by way of saying that Hannah is not so much a Southern writer as a postmodernist one: someone whose very idiosyncrasies serve to identify him with a world of discontinuity, anxiety, and experiment and with a culture hostile to both regionalism and traditionalism. "Fragments are the only forms I trust", wrote Donald Barthelme in one of his short stories; and this phrase by itself suggests where Hannah's allegiances lie – with writers like Barthelme, John Barth, and Richard Brautigan, some of them from the South and some not, for whom the book is a sort of playing-field, a place for sport, random collage, and radical fantasy. Something that Richard Gilman said is worth quoting here, when he was reviewing a novel by Barthelme. Gilman saw Barthelme's novel as an example of a new kind of art, implying an altered sense of reality. This art, Gilman explained, was

> open-ended, provisional, characterized by suspended judgements, by disbelief
> in hierarchies, by mistrust of solutions, denouements and completions, by self-
> consciousness issuing in tremendous earnestness but also in far-ranging
> mockery.[43]

Gilman did not use the term 'postmodernism', that was to come later,
but it was clearly the postmodernist belief in a random, unstructured
world and an equally random, unstructured art that he had in mind. And
it takes no great effort to see that writers from the South such as Hannah
participate in this postmodernist consciousness; in doing so, they have
shrugged off their Southern identity – that "pollen of ideas" which,
Faulkner believed, fertilised his mind and the minds of his contemporaries
– and are obviously not very sorry about what they have done. Perhaps
one, brief vignette will help to measure the distance between someone
like Hannah and the founding fathers of the Southern renaissance.
Hannah was interviewed while he was staying in Oxford, Mississippi, in
a small frame house through whose fence Faulkner had Benjy Compson
look out at the world. During the course of the conversation, the
interviewer remembered a time when he was taken by his parents to the
battlefields at Shiloh and was so moved by the memories and pressures of
the past that he broke down and cried. Hannah's reply to this was laconic
and coolly iconoclastic: "I've never been there", he said, "but I
understand it will make you cry if you're into it." Evidently, that sly put-
down was not enough, though. For a few minutes later, when the
discussion turned to the rock guitarist Jimi Hendrix, Hannah added a
further, quietly subversive touch. "I saw Hendrix's grave when I was in
Seattle", he observed. "It was very moving, like one of these Civil War
things you were talking about."[44]

"Well", remarked Walker Percy once, "the so-called Southern thing
is over and done with I think."[45] Percy's remark certainly holds good for
writers like Hannah; and the course of William Styron's career indicates
that the "Southern thing", while not necessarily "over and done with",
is rapidly becoming peripheral for many others who once accepted it as a
means of mediating experience. For all that, though, there are still quite a
few Southerners, writers or otherwise, who give the lie to Percy's claim,
by managing somehow to cling on to aspects of the Southern code and to
perceive reality in terms that are as old as the region itself. A radical
alteration of consciousness has been going on in the South for more than
half a century, it has reached a terminal stage, but it is not quite
completed. The emergent culture, with its accompanying habits of
belief, has gained the upper hand; the high tension between old customs
and new – the tension, that is, that helped to precipitate the Southern
renaissance – has slackened as the old customs have lost their grip on the
regional imagination; nevertheless, the 'subculture' persists, not all

Southerners have ceased to be 'Southern', and experience is still organised for many by the regional myths. There are many possible ways of illustrating the present, mixed state of things: by appealing as John Shelton Reed does to surveys of public opinion, or by examining as Jack Temple Kirby does the development of popular culture, or by showing as others have done how the South's changing image of itself has affected its political life. But perhaps as good a way as any of portraying and exploring things – this richly confused situation in which one code, one system of perceptions and relationships has been slowly, almost imperceptibly shading into another – is on the level of individual sensibility, in the imaginative details of particular works. Here, the choice almost makes itself. Writers like Styron or Hannah may make their own contributions to the present "mind of the South" its richly ambivalent – not to say, contradictory – notions of reality. Their contributions are not nearly as significant, however, nor as central as those of two other writers who have been mentioned several times already and who, although of different generations, have produced what is arguably the best fiction from the region over the past two decades: Eudora Welty, the author of that "last good one", and Walker Percy, for whom (to quote that remark just one more time) "the so-called Southern thing" is evidently "over and done with".

ON THE NECESSITY OF LOSING BATTLES: EUDORA WELTY

In one of her short stories, called simply "A Still Moment", Eudora Welty describes a chance meeting on the Old Natchez Trace between Lorenzo Dow, an itinerant preacher, James Murrell, the outlaw, and Audubon, the artist and naturalist. Suddenly, in that quiet moment when they meet, a "solitary snowy heron" dips down out of the sky to feed beside the marsh water near them. Seeing the heron, all three men seem captivated by their vision: but, as it turns out, for different reasons. To Lorenzo Dow, the man of God, the heron is simply a divine messenger, an animate emblem of his special relationship with heaven; while for Murrell the outlaw – who is planning, in fact, to rob and murder the preacher – it is a messenger of quite a different kind, a reflection of his own moral brigandage and dedication to the wilderness. Only Audubon sees what is actually there, or at least tries to: the heron, in its beauty, separateness, and utter self-containment. And in response to what he sees, recognising that he cannot paint his vision from memory, he then shoots the heron and carries it with him into the forest. Even before he has begun to paint the bird, Welty tells us, he knows the best he can make will be "a dead thing and not a live thing, never the essence, only a sum of parts".[46] For the paradox of art – Audubon's art, any art, and indeed any attempt to structure and reinvent the world – is that it must kill in order to create. Registering the irresistible otherness of things, the artist must take them out of their living context and place them within another, and essentially still, frame; in doing so, Welty suggests, he can be seen as both a liberator – since he is freeing his subject from time – and a murderer – since he is reducing the bewildering variety of experience to a system, or series of signs.

"Ours is the century of unreason", writes Welty in an essay on Jane Austen,

> the stamp of our behavior is violence or isolation: non-meaning is looked upon with some solemnity; and for the purpose of writing novels, most human behavior is looked at through the frame, or the knot-hole, of alienation.[47]

Seeing things through the knot-hole of alienation is not Welty's way, however, even though she may be aware of the reasons for doing so: reasons that include those feelings of displacement, the belief that life is arbitrary, contrary, and unmanageable, that probably characterise our age more than any other. What *she* is after, clearly, is that habit of mind she attributes to Austen, "of seeing both sides of . . . [a] subject – of seeing it indeed in the round": an ability to recognise the importance of codes, custom and ceremony, while all the time acknowledging that the volatile essence of life will be squeezed out or escape from any of the structures we may choose to devise for it. The habit, Welty admits, "is a little unusual . . . to writers and readers of our day", but it is absolutely necessary if sense is to be made of things and experience is to be rendered tolerable. A celebration of order leavened with irony, of the sort one finds in Austen's best work – and, for that matter, in all the best traditionalist writing: that for Welty is the only alternative to numb surrender to the "century of unreason". As far as Welty's fiction is concerned, this deliberate, if necessarily qualified, commitment to the notion of structure issues in a distinct reluctance either to condemn that impulse to arrange, interpret, or commemorate that Audubon illustrates or to celebrate it in any full-throated way. Those of her characters who try to organise experience, to turn it into a comprehensible language, are invariably criticised, their limitations exposed. They are not necessarily artists, of course; they may simply want to inject some feeling of system into their lives with the help of little rituals or carefully assigned roles. Whatever, they are gently ridiculed, their activities seen as destructive or, at the very least, reductive. But the criticism is never carried too far, the criticism is hedged about with reservations, because the alternative to such activities is – as Lorenzo Dow and James Murrell make only too clear – solipsism and moral anarchy. The consciousness is either building and rebuilding systems all the time, no matter how constricting each one of them may turn out to be, or it is consigned to absolute separateness and oblivion:

that, eventually, is the message that comes to us via the apocalyptic dreams of violence dreamed by the robber and the narcissistic visions of his intended victim.

Not that the alternatives "A Still Moment" describes are necessarily parcelled out between individuals: often, especially in the longer fiction, each character is turned into a battlefield, drawn simultaneously to systems and the denial of them. He or she becomes, as a result, like some creature out of Ovid's *Metamorphoses*, capable of what seems like infinite secretiveness and change. This is particularly true of *Delta Wedding*, the book in which Welty examines most closely the patriarchal model of the South. It is set on a Mississippi plantation in 1923, a year Welty chose from an almanac as being one in which there were no wars or natural disasters to disrupt the normal patterns of domestic life. The un-eventfulness of that time allowed her, she said later, "to concentrate on the people without any undue outside influences . . . to write a story that showed . . . life that went on on a small scale in a world of its own".[48] Uneventful the novel certainly is, at least in the conventional sense; indeed, as one recent critic has observed, it was the very absence of a strong linear plot that led to a good deal of criticism being levelled at it when it first appeared. A young girl arrives to visit the plantation; she participates in the rituals of family life; and towards the end of the novel, one of the daughters is married. The one major event that causes a ripple on the smooth surfaces of domestic routine has occurred before the novel begins: George Fairchild, a member of the family that owns the plantation, has saved his niece from being crushed by a train – an act the foolhardiness of which has so offended his wife, apparently, that it has prompted her to leave him. But before long she returns, the family circle is completed, and the wedding affirming tribal solidarity can go ahead without any embarrassment.

At first glance, then, the book seems to do no more than celebrate the traditional, patriarchal way of life, and to lace this with an Austenian relish for domestic detail. Beneath the surface of events, however, a very different story is being told, of people living alone, leading lives of extraordinary solitude and even mystery. The plantation house suggests something of this. It has, we learn, an "undeterminate number of rooms" which make it seem "like a nameless forest, wherein many little lives lived privately". But of far greater importance is the actual narrative structure of the book. Welty weaves her way continually between different viewpoints and narrators: each character is seen, consequently, as a participant in the prescribed rituals and as a separate being responding in his or her own way to those rituals – each appears to be a part of and yet also apart from things, both in the dance and yet somehow out of it. Along with the ceremonies that punctuate the narrative, one character in particular, George Fairchild, acts as a touchstone here. Most of the Fairchilds are born storytellers, and George's story is told and retold by them in such a way as to affirm both community and separateness. For all the family, George has certain fundamental qualities: courage, for instance, and a concern for other members of the group that he demonstrates most memorably when he risks his life to rescue his niece. As each person recalls or describes him, however, it becomes clear that he has assumed a different, deeper significance for every one of them. What they cherish about him, it turns out, are chiefly personal memories and associations – potent reminders of the fact that in many ways they are, as Welty puts it at one point, "more different and further apart than the stars".[49] Not only that, their very fascination with George (for it is *his* story that obsesses them, far more than anyone else's) has a special edge to it, since the qualities they admire in him above all are his independence and generosity: he can stand alone, they sense, in utter self-assurance, "wholly singular", and yet also give of himself with unrivalled warmth. In trying to tell his story, then (an act which in some respects recalls Audubon trying to commemorate the still moment of the heron), they are implicitly testing their own capacity to see things, neither through the knot-hole of alienation nor simply from within the closed circle of the family, but, like their creator, from both sides, in the round.

"Ambiguity is a fact of life",[50] Welty declares in one of her essays, an observation that, phrased in different ways, she has repeated many times; and this alone should alert us to the subversive nature of *Delta Wedding*. She celebrates the plantation order, certainly, but that celebration is hedged around with criticism, mockery, and irony, with quiet reminders of all that has been excluded. There are sly references, for instance, to the other culture outside the plantation – a culture that belongs to quite another world, without traditions or regional or familial loyalties. The Fairchild family tell old tales but some of the younger ones also want to read *The Beautiful and the Damned*; folksongs and traditional ballads vie for their attention with "The Sheik of Araby" and "I Wish I Could Shimmy Like My Sister Kate"; they make their own music, enjoy their own time-honoured pastimes, but they also have a Victrola and go to the movies. Too much should not be made of this: Welty is not intent on being a social historian, nor clearly does she see the old order as hovering on the brink of a precipice. But this context of cultural change, sketched out in a characteristically elusive fashion, helps to remind the reader that, quite simply, time is passing, customs are altering, and elsewhere the world is different. For the moment, the world of *Delta Wedding* does not seem actively threatened by the change but it does seem, as a result, all the more private, all the more special and exclusive – and perhaps, even if only by implication, all the more cut off from the abrupt, syncopated rhythms of history.

And then, quite apart from these covert references to cultural change, there is the violence that plays just below the surface of things. Significantly, much of this violence is associated with blacks: in other words, with those who have at most a peripheral role to play in the dramatic rituals of plantation life. Early in the novel, for example, one of the characters remembers "a day in childhood" when she witnessed a knife-fight in which "two . . . little Negroes had flown at each other with extraordinary intensity",[51] only to be stopped from virtually killing each other by George Fairchild. And towards the end, Troy Flavin, the plantation overseer and prospective bridegroom in the "Delta wedding", narrowly escapes serious injury when he has to disarm a field hand who, having wounded two other blacks, is threatening him with an ice pick. The violence of such episodes is exacerbated by the contrast they offer with the quiet, spry tone and the relative uneventfulness of the rest of the story: as in so much traditional Southern writing, in fact, what the black characters do is remind us of a secret, subterranean, and slightly frightening dimension of experience that the patriarchal order tends to minimise, ignore, or strenuously exclude. With some writers, such as Faulkner, the effect of using black figures in this way is radical, to make that order seem fatally myopic or intolerably oppressive. However, this is not the case with Welty. The violence in *Delta Wedding*, while not contained, is never so great as to disrupt either the narrative structure or the structures of feeling, the patterns of existence she describes; the blacks are there to measure the limits of plantation life, but not to call it into serious question. Welty's criticisms, in sum – her sense that the plantation system, like any system, is constricting, arbitrary, and provisional – is balanced by sympathy and affection, her understanding of the human need to create systems and her attachment to, indeed her love of, this one in particular. Believing that "all things are double", what she tries to do is give her readers, along with her characters, a kind of dual focus or double vision: "the power", to quote her own words, while observing the patriarchal model, "to look both ways and to see a thing from all sides".[52]

That last phrase comes from *The Robber Bridegroom*, a novel published four years before *Delta Wedding*, which is set in the Natchez Trace region of Mississippi in the late eighteenth century. Based loosely on a Brothers Grimm folk-tale it is not, Welty has insisted, "a *historical* historical novel": its action is determined by some often bizarre cases of mistaken identity and the *dramatis personae* include a talking raven and a talking head. Nevertheless, it *is* concerned with history if only because it explores the ways in which we try to understand the past and accommodate it to the present. Essentially, Welty's strategy in the story is to mingle the actual and extraordinary to the point where the line between the two becomes virtually indistinguishable; so, inhabiting the same space as the talking head and the paraphernalia of fairy-tales, we have the Natchez Indians, New Orleans merchants, and slaves. Several of the minor characters, like Mike Fink and the Harpe brothers, seem to respond equally to the pressure of actuality and the power of myth, while the major characters are all at once recognisable frontier types and figures replete with legendary associations: Jamie Lockhart, for instance, the hero, is both a rather ordinary, polite young man and the "robber bridegroom", a romantic thief of the wilderness, and Rosamund Musgrove, the girl he comes courting, is both a beautiful captive heiress and "Clement Musgrove's silly daughter". Some also have a *doppelgänger*: twice another woman is mistaken for Rosamund and set upon by bandits, and, at least at one point in the narrative, Clement Musgrove considers the possibility that his first wife and his second have been "the one person all the time".[53] And nearly everyone can move, without apparent effort, from the colloquial to the mannered, from the language of getting and spending, and survival in the wilderness to the exotic or elevated idioms of legend.

The end result of all this might have seemed merely whimsical: but it does not, mainly because Welty distils out of this mixture of the everyday and the mysterious the essence of the place she is writing about. "Location pertains to feeling", she says in one of her essays, "feeling profoundly pertains to place"; and *The Robber Bridegroom* captures that feeling, the spirit of her own small postage stamp of native soil – which, she hints, is partly a product of human invention. Like a few other Southern writers, in fact, including most obviously Faulkner, Welty starts from the belief that place, as we attach ourselves to it, is in some measure an artifact, something that we, using our imaginations, help to create. Where she differs from most of them, however, is in the terms in which she expresses this belief. This passage, taken from the account of one of Clement Musgrove's several journeys, will serve as an illustration:

> He rode south on the Old Natchez Trace and then took another trail branching off to the deepest woods, a part he had never searched before. The wind shook the long beards of the moss. The lone owls hooted one by one and flew by his head as big as barrels. Near-by in the cane the wildcats frolicked and played, and on he rode through the five-mile smell of bear, and on till he came all at once to the bluff where deep down, under the stars, the dark brown wave of the Mississippi was rolling by.[54]

The basic details of this scene are accurate and credible enough, but there is a touch of the bizarre, the thoroughly rich and strange, about everything, as if we were looking at a primitive painting, or something by *le douanier* Rousseau. There is a playful opulence in the landscape and vegetation, a magical quality to the behaviour of the animals; the lines are emphatic, the colours simple and bright, the sensory details almost dizzyingly vivid. For the equivalent of this passage in prose one would have to turn to, say, fairy-tale or Chateaubriand's description of the wilderness around the Mississippi at the beginning of *Atala*; and even then the parallel is far from exact. For Welty knows her subject better than Chateaubriand does, and is far more knowing than the average teller of fairy-tales: which is to say that she is not indulging in fancifulness for its own sake, nor trying to promote some alternative world of legends but reminding us of how our minds work in *this* world. In some ways, the implication is, this is what place is; it may not always be quite as obviously artificial, so self-evidently 'made', as the landscape in *The Robber Bridegroom* but it springs from exactly the same sources as those landscapes do, the same interchange between the objective and the subjective. Strictly speaking, it is a *fiction*, spun out of certain given geographical facts; and in being so – simultaneously 'out there' and 'in here', a matter of actuality and a thing of fantasy – it shares the divided, dual nature of its creators.

Quite apart from this tendency to show landscape as simultaneously a matter of fact and of myth, Welty manages to persuade us that history involves a similarly dialectical process. The past, she suggests, may be something that we do not merely remember but reinvent: not quite as extraordinary as the tale of the robber bridegroom, perhaps, but responding just as clearly both to the visible contours of things and the power, the shaping presence, of the mind. The repetitive narrative structure is relevant here – many things happen not once but several times: Rosamund is twice set upon by the robber bridegroom, twice captured by Indians, twice hides behind a barrel to eavesdrop on a conversation, while her father twice loses his wife to the Indians while he himself is spared. In addition, certain tales are told and then compulsively retold (an incident in which Rosamund is robbed of her clothes, for instance, is recounted by Welty, Rosamund herself, and another, minor character); while individual characters tell stories to do with themselves over and over again (thus, Rosamund tells one story to her father and stepmother seven times!). All of this, compounded by the fact that each time a story is told there is further embroidery, different details are omitted or emphasised, adds to the feeling that what has gone before is continually being reimagined. New plots are forever being devised, it seems, fresh patterns spun from what is called at one point "the dream of time passing". Significantly, the only character who tries to exclude herself from this process, insisting that truth is single and there is a clear distinction between facts and "lies", is Rosamund's stepmother, the chief villain of the piece. And her insistence on a simple, fixed notion of things seems absurdly inappropriate in this world: where, as the following passage suggests, everything is constant only in its inconstancy –

changing shape, requiring a succession of fresh names and narratives. The speaker here, incidentally, is Clement Musgrove:

> "Men are following men down the Mississippi, hoarse and arrogant by day, wakeful and dreamless by night at the unknown landings. A trail leads like a tunnel under the roof of this wilderness . . .
>
> ". . . And even the appearance of a hero is no longer a single and majestic event like that of a star in the heavens, but a wandering fire soon lost . . . . Like will-o'-wisps the little blazes burn on the rafts all night, unsteady beside the shore. Where are they even so soon as tomorrow? . . .
>
> "Yet no one can laugh or cry so savagely in this wilderness as to be heard by the nearest traveler or remembered the next year. A fiddle played in a finished hut in a clearing is as vagrant as the swamp breeze. What will the seasons be, when we are lost and dead? The dreadful heat and cold – no more than the shooting star."[55]

Eventually, even the reader is caught up in the task of repetition and revision, just as in Faulkner's stories. For the elusive idiom, the ambiguous narrative detail, and not least a hauntingly inconclusive denouement: all, in the end, combine to make us feel that we too must become our own storytellers and, in the process, construct our own individual versions of the past.

Maybe nothing ever happens once and is finished:[56] that is the feeling generated by *The Robber Bridegroom*. It is basic, too, to the book that Jonathan Yardley termed the last good Southern novel: *Losing Battles*. In some respects, *Losing Battles* also recalls *Delta Wedding*. A family meets for a special occasion (in this case, the ninetieth birthday of the oldest member, "Granny" Elvira Jordan Vaughn). One of the male members (Jack Renfro here) is waited for and welcomed with particular enthusiasm by the others. Several things threaten to disrupt the family unity, but in the end that unity appears to be maintained. The differences, however, are at least as important as the parallels. "I wanted", Welty has said, "to get a year in which I could show people at the rock bottom of their lives." So, instead of a wealthy Delta family in good economic times, we are presented with some poor farmers from the hill country during the Depression; and instead of the ceremonies of the plantation we have the customs of a plainer, more specifically folk culture. Stylistically, too, there are differences. "I wanted", Welty has also explained,

> to see if I could do something that was new for me: translating every thought and feeling into speech . . . I felt that I'd been writing too much by way of description, of introspection on the part of my characters.[57]

A novel like *Delta Wedding* has a gently elegiac tone to it and is deeply involved in the secret, inner lives of its characters; in many ways, it is a drama of sensibility. *Losing Battles*, however, is a comedy. With sympathy and humour, it describes people waging a disgracefully unequal struggle with circumstances who remain hopeful despite everything – and who, above all, use old tales and talking as a stay against confusion.

"Can't conversation ever cease?" asks one character, an outsider, towards the end of the novel, and one can see what he means; for the Beechams and Renfros who make up the bulk of this family reunion never seem to stop talking. There are tall tales, family legends, personal memories, folk humour, religious myth, stories of magic and mystery; and everyone seems to possess his or her own storytelling technique. People comment on one another's tale-telling abilities: for instance, when Uncle Percy Beecham begins to imitate the characters he is describing, his sister-in-law Birdie Beecham comments appreciatively, "He gets 'em all down pat . . . I wish I was married to him . . . He'd keep me entertained." The dead, too, along with the living, are praised for their verbal gifts. Grandpa Vaughn, for example, is chiefly remembered for his eloquence as a preacher, which his replacement as the local Baptist leader, the unfortunate Brother Bethune, can never match: "the prayer he made alone was the fullest you ever heard", recalls one of his grandsons, Uncle Noah, "The advice he handed down *by itself* was a mile long!" Sometimes, advice is offered to a novice speaker while he or she is speaking: "What's Normal?" asks Lexie Renfro when Jack Renfro's wife Gloria refers to her time at Normal School, "Don't skip it! Tell it!" And always, accompanying the main text, the talk requiring the reunion's attention, there is a subtext of comment, criticism, and anecdote, like that background of anonymous voices, inherited folk-speech and wisdom, that gives resonance to traditional ballads and epic. There is the constant sense, in fact, that each tale and conversation, however trivial, belongs to a larger body of speech, a continuum of storytelling: stories knit into one another, one anecdote recalls another in the series, and tales are told which we learn have been told many times before ("I wish I'd had a penny for every time I've listened to this one", murmurs Ralph Renfro as his wife Beulah begins to recall the story of her parents' mysterious drowning). Even the reunion that provides the setting for most of the novel is given substance and weight, a sense of authenticity, by the feeling that the things that have happened this day will become a part of the story by being woven into the fabric of speech. "Gloria", Uncle tells his young niece,

> "this has been a story on us all that never will be allowed to be forgotten. Long after you're an old lady without much further stretch to go, sitting back in the same rocking-chair Granny's got her little self in now, you'll be hearing it told to Lady May [Gloria's baby daughter] and all her hovering brood . . . I call this a reunion to remember . . .!"[58]

Part of the "story" Uncle Noah refers to here is the suspicion, entertained at least for a while, that Gloria may in fact be a Beecham, entitled by blood rather than by marriage to be a part of the reunion. And clearly, the possibility of incest that this raises is of little interest to the family: what excites them is the bright hope that they can press this apparent outsider into the group ("Say Beecham!" the women chant at her, "Can't you say Beecham? What's wrong with being Beecham?"), and so close the magic circle around themselves even tighter. Just like the Fairchilds in *Delta Wedding*, in fact, the Beechams and the Renfros constitute a world apart, a charmed society with its own customs and totems. Unlike the Fairchilds, however, the world of the Beechams and Renfros is a populist rather than a patriarchal one; more to the point, it depends for its defence upon language in its most fundamental sense, on a barrier spun out of a fragile thread of speech.

"A reunion", Welty has said in an interview,

> is everybody remembering together – remembering and relating when their people were born and what happened in their lives, what that made happen to their children, and how it was that they died. There's someone to remember a man's whole life, every bit of the way along. I think that's a marvelous thing.[59]

This suggests very clearly just why the Beechams and Renfros talk. It enables them to escape from their loneliness; it gives them a feeling of identification with a particular place and past (need one say again, however, that that place and that past are things their talk helps to create?); and – to borrow a term from Walker Percy – it seems to "certify" experience for them, to make it manageable and real. In sum, their language gives them a sense of being and a feeling of belonging; or, to put it more crudely, they feel they are there because they say they are and other people say so too. Yet all the while they are saying so, there are (as always in Welty's fiction) warnings about the other side of things: the mystery of personality, the secret phases of experience, the accidental moments in life – the things that no code, no model of reality can ever quite accommodate. As far as those present at the reunion are concerned, these warnings or reminders come chiefly through two characters: Gloria Renfro and Judge Oscar Moody. Despite all the pressure that is put upon her, which approaches a frightening level at times, Gloria insists that she is different – not a Beecham or a Renfro but an orphan, alone and apart. "I'm here to be nobody but myself", she declares at one point, and elsewhere, "I'm one to myself, and nobody's kin, and my own boss, and nobody knows the one I am or where I came from." Sometimes she comes close to feeling defeated: "Oh, if we just had a little house to ourselves . . . And nobody could ever find us", she exclaims to her husband, and then adds hopelessly, "But everybody finds us. Living or dead."[60] At the end of the book, however, she has not given up. She is still insisting on her separateness, her and other people's essential privacy ("people", she declares, "don't want to be read like books") – still standing out against the family and what she, at least, sees as the imprisoning web of its stories.

Judge Oscar Moody is a rather different matter: a comic ghost at the feast, brought there by chance, cut off by education and position from the easygoing manners of his hosts, and slightly embarrassed by the recollection that it was he who put Jack Renfro in jail. The event that brings him and his wife to the reunion is a car accident: swerving to avoid Gloria and her baby, the Judge drives his Buick off the road and it ends up balanced uncertainly on the edge of a precipice called Banner Top. There, it provides a grotesque reminder of the way things happen to spoil even our best-laid plans: the accident, in short, calls our attention to the accidental. It seems elephantine, or at least less than responsive to Welty's light touch, to add that it also offers a comic emblem of the precarious nature of things, the abyss that hovers beneath us and our arrangements. Nevertheless, the emblem is there, however delicately or allusively it may be sketched in; and it is pointed by such nice touches as the fact that the hickory sign on which the Buick rests, as it sticks out over Banner Top, asks the question, "Where Will you Spend Eternity?" The question is never answered, of course, just as the plaintive demands made by the Judge's wife to be returned immediately to "civilization" never meet with a satisfactory response: but the reader is reminded by such things, or rather warned, that there are other dimensions of experience and different cultures standing on the edge of this closed world, and in the process helping to mark out its boundaries.

As far as warnings of this nature are concerned, however, one character stands head and shoulders above the rest: the woman who used to be the local schoolteacher, Miss Julia Mortimer. During the course of the reunion, the news is brought that Julia Mortimer has died. Many of those present were taught by her and they remember her, not necessarily with affection, as a magisterial presence. Now they rehearse her story, try to recollect what sort of impression she made on them: and this impression is summed up, really, by their response to a letter that Judge Moody, another of her ex-pupils, reads out to them. The letter, written by Julia Mortimer not long before her death, is a sort of apologia, an explanation or defence of the aims that sustained her throughout her career: "All my life", she confesses defiantly, "I've fought a hard war with ignorance. Except in those cases that you can count off on your fingers, I lost every battle." And the reaction of the Beechams and Renfros, as they listen, is notable for three things above all: uneasiness, incomprehension, and amusement. "Don't read it to us!" several of them cry before the Judge begins; then, when he has begun, "I can't understand it when he reads it to us. Can't he just tell it?" "I don't know what those long words are talking about", complains one hearer, Aunt Birdie Beecham; while another one, Beulah Renfro, appears to speak for most of the Judge's audience when she concludes, "Now I know she's crazy. We're getting it right out of her own mouth, by listening long enough."[61] Julia Mortimer, it is clear, spoke in another idiom, a language foreign to most of those assembled at the reunion. She believed in enlightenment, progress, making something of oneself: "She had designs on everybody", Uncle Percy Beecham recollects; "she wanted a doctor and a lawyer and all else we might have to holler for some day." She also believed in travelling beyond the horizons of one's local community and culture; for instance, she told one Beecham, Uncle Nathan, to see the world – "He took her exactly at her word", comments Beulah Renfro, Nathan's sister. "He's seen the world. And I'm not so sure it was good for him."[62] All her life, in fact, she was committed to a vision and vocabulary that demoted the Beechams, the Renfros, and all that their reunion represents to the level of the provincial, the backward, and the ignorant ("you need to give a little mind to the *family* you're getting tangled up with", she apparently told Gloria just before her marriage). The Beechams and Renfros, in turn, hardly began to understand her when she was alive, nor even want to now that she is dead; as they see it, she was domineering, eccentric or, more simply, crazy. Welty's point is not, of course, that either side is right; although, by setting her book well back from the present, she may just possibly be working from the assumption that the forces of progress, represented by Miss Julia, have been losing less of this particular battle recently than those embodied in the family reunion. What she is doing, rather, is giving a further edge to her portrait of farm life – throwing her version of the populist model into sharper relief by reminding us emphatically of the forms of intelligence that, for good *and* ill, it chooses to exclude.

And then there is the simple, brute fact of Julia Mortimer's dying. Lexie Renfro was Miss Julia's nurse, and the news of her death prompts Lexie to recall what she was like during the final stages of her life. "All her callers fell off, little at a time, then thick and fast", Lexie remembers, put off by her abrasive manner, her unwillingness to suffer fools gladly; and Miss Julia was left waiting, sitting in the front yard, for people who never came. "I used to say", Lexie declares, " 'Miss Julia, you come on back inside the house. Hear? People . . . aren't coming visiting. Nobody's coming.' " But evidently Miss Julia took no notice. So for her own good, Lexie insists, with that bland authoritarianism characteristic of so many nurses, she tied her charge to the bed: "I didn't want to, but anybody you'd ask would tell you the same: you may have to." Miss Julia was reduced to writing letters, incessantly and feverishly: with her tongue hanging out, Lexie recalls with amazement, "Like words, just words, was getting to be something good enough to eat." Lexie mailed them, she admits, because she "couldn't think . . . what else to do with 'em"; and it is, of course, one of these letters that Judge Moody reads out to the bewilderment of the family. Eventually, though, even this resource was taken away from her, Miss Julia's pencil was snatched from her hands by her ever-solicitous keeper ("I could pull harder then she could", says Lexie triumphantly), and she was reduced to the mere gesture of writing – shaping words with her finger on the bedsheet or her palm. Then Lexie left her – "I had the reunion to come to, didn't I?"[63] she asks her audience plaintively – and it was while she was by herself that Julia Mortimer died: virtually imprisoned, it seems, denied books and writing material, without close friends, visitors, or even sympathy. The final picture she presents is a pathetic one, certainly, but pathos is not Welty's primary aim: far more important to her are two other things, two ways in which Lexie's account of Miss Julia serves to develop and complicate the conceptual framework of the book. In the first place, this account reveals that the former schoolteacher shared the other characters' preoccupation with language, the need to turn the world into words. In her case, the language was more a written than a spoken one, but it served essentially the same purpose: to substantiate and communicate, to create a sense of identity and community – a feeling of being someone somewhere rather than just anyone anywhere. And in the second place, the sheer isolation of Julia Mortimer's last days, as Lexie describes them, acts as a *memento mori*, a haunting reminder of the vacuum over which any bridge of words is built. They offer a chilling emblem of the fact that, whatever companionship or contact we may enjoy during our lives – and, in particular, on occasions like a reunion – we must all eventually die alone.

Julia Mortimer is undoubtedly an important character, an absent presence curiously reminiscent in some ways of several of Faulkner's major figures. Quite as important as any person or event, however, as a way of focussing the paradoxes on which *Losing Battles* turns is the staple idiom of its descriptive and narrative passages – a vocabulary that seems intent on showing just how far words can go. In some respects, this is a long way, as these few sentences from the book's memorable opening pages illustrate:

> When the rooster crowed, the moon had still not left the world but was going down on flushed cheek, one day short of full. A long, thin cloud crossed it slowly, drawing itself out like a name being called. The air changed, as if a mile or so away a wooden door had swung open, and a smell, more of warmth than wet, from a river at low stage, moved upward into the clay hills that stood in darkness.
>
> Then a house appeared on its ridge, like an old man's silver watch pulled once more out of its pocket . . .[64]

A description such as this is a triumph of specificity and containment: Welty presents us here with a shifting, evanescent, metamorphic world which nevertheless seems to have been grasped for a while and composed. Something of the Mississippi hill country at a particular moment on a particular summer morning has been caught, snatched from the dream of time passing, and framed; and in catching it, Welty matches up to her own description of the ideal photographer or story-writer who knows, she says, just "when to click the shutter", the precise instant at which people or things "reveal themselves". Yet for all that something, it is intimated, has been squeezed out and remains elusive: some quality of the moment remains uncaught, seems to slip through the artist's fingers, eluding every one of her traps and snares. The way in which this is intimated to the reader is subtle but nevertheless inescapable. The prose never stops emphasising its own fragility and artfulness. It is compulsively metaphorical, insistently sportive, as though the author were trying to point out that this is, after all, an artifact, a pattern made out of words. Within the space of three sentences, for instance, a cloud is compared to a name; the air is said to change "as if . . . a wooden door had swung open"; and a house suddenly appears in the dawn light like a watch pulled out of a pocket (and not just *any* watch or *any* pocket: here as elsewhere, the figurative reference assumes a dramatic status of its own). The very insistence of all this, as well as the constant use of "like" or "as if", serves to remind us that the writer's language, like every other means used to alleviate our separateness, is an imprecise and not entirely trustworthy medium. Even when fought with this weapon, it seems, all battles must be losing battles, although they are never irretrievably lost.

Of course, the idea of art as a losing battle is not peculiar to this novel, it is implicit in all Welty's writing; and not merely art – the paintings of Audubon, the ceremonies of the Fairchild family, the legend of the robber bridegroom, the customs and storytelling of the Beechams and Renfros are all of them seen as examples of a primitive human impulse to render life comprehensible, orderly. Her work is an attempt to see and know by establishing a possible frame, and it describes other attempts, sometimes noble, sometimes comic or pathetic, and sometimes a cunning mixture of all three.[65] Nearly always, these attempts – Welty's, that is, and those of her characters – are characterised by extensive use of the regional codes: either the patriarchal code, as in *Delta Wedding*, or the populist, as in *Losing Battles* or, as in *The Robber Bridegroom*, elements that are common to both. And *always*, glimmering just below the surface of the text, there is the suggestion that something must remain apart from our stories and ceremonies, because even as we try to frame the object it will be gone. Just as we click the shutter, Welty implies, it will disappear leaving "never the essence, only a sum of parts". One of the more haunting reminders of this, the sheer elusiveness of things, occurs in Welty's most recently published novel, *The Optimist's Daughter*. It is when the daughter of the title, Laurel McKelva Hand, gazes at the dead body of her father Judge McKelva, a man whom she believes she has known intimately. The Judge, we are told,

> appeared . . . as . . . one listening. His upper lip had lifted, short and soft as a child's, showing ghostly-pale teeth, which no one ever saw when he spoke or laughed. It gave him the smile of a child who is hiding in the dark while others hunt him, waiting to be found.[66]

NOTES FOR A NOVEL ABOUT THE END OF THE SOUTH: WALKER PERCY

"There is a disintegration of the fabric of the modern world which is so far advanced that the conventional novel no longer makes sense." This remark of Walker Percy's, made in 1963, offers as useful a means as any of beginning to understand his work. Percy starts from the simple premise that, as he put it once in an interview, "now, the world is much more fragmented, people don't understand themselves as well or what they are doing as well". "The theories of man of the former age no longer work", he insists (in one of the essays in *The Message in the Bottle*), "and the theories of the new age are not yet known"; so in the mean time people either live "as the organisms and consumer units their scientists understand them to be" or feel "anxious without knowing why". In their different ways and moods, they are

> like the cartoon cat that runs off a cliff and for a while is suspended, still running, in mid-air but sooner or later looks down and sees there is nothing under them.[67]

And, Percy argues, they require new imaginative strategies, different forms of perception and expression; they need, in fact, to be seen in "postmodern" terms. "The subject of the postmodern novel", he says (this, in an essay with the apocalyptic title, "Notes For A Novel About The End of the World"),

> is a man who has very nearly come to the end of the line . . . The American novel of past years has treated such themes as persons whose lives are blighted by social evils . . . or perhaps the dislocation of expatriate Americans, or of Southerners living in a region haunted by memories. But the hero of the postmodern novel is a man who has forgotten his bad memories and conquered his present ills and who finds himself in the victorious secular city. His only problem now is to keep from blowing his brains out.[68]

There are some personal reasons, certainly, why Percy has been attracted towards experiment, innovation and postmodernist forms of discourse. He has, as he admits, been more heavily influenced by Russian writers like Dostoevsky and French writers like Sartre, Camus, and Marcel than by their American or English counterparts, and therefore more inclined to use fiction as a quasi-prophetic, quasi-philosophical medium, a vehicle for exploring such problems as "the quality of consciousness" and the nature of reality. His position as a Christian existentialist, too, has encouraged him to disrupt conventional narrative structures and accepted idioms: partly because, as he has put it, "The old words of grace are worn smooth as poker chips and a certain devaluation has occurred, like a poker chip after it is cashed in." Specifically personal motives like this, however, pale into insignificance beside Percy's initial contention that the fabric of our world has altered radically and that the tools we use to understand it are either obsolete or ludicrously inadequate. Regardless of who we are, Percy contends, or where we come from (provided, that is, we come from the industrialised West), it is up to us to build new structures of perception. Southernness, in this context, ceases to be a problem because it more or less ceases to exist. Or, as Percy puts it,

> nowadays . . . a writer, unless he goes out of his way, or goes back and deals with rural themes . . . or long recollections, that sort of thing, he's pretty much looking at the same sort of reality in New Orleans or Birmingham or Atlanta as his counterpart in Cincinnati or Los Angeles. The similarities are much greater than the differences.[69]

Of course, Faulkner said something very similar to this once or twice: but in his case that statement was qualified by his tendency to say something different or precisely the opposite on other occasions. Percy, by contrast, has remained consistent. For him, he insists, "the Southern scenery, the Southern backdrop" is used "just as that, as a place where a young man can react"; it is a geographical accident, a neutral medium. The distance between the two writers can perhaps be measured by the contrast between their equally distinctive narrative voices. Faulkner, it was noted in the previous chapter, tends to adopt the stance and voice of the person who is "at home . . . yet at the same time . . . not at home". Percy's narrators, however, are utterly displaced persons or – to use his own analogy – terrestrial Martians. "Since I am . . . a novelist", Percy has said,

> a somewhat estranged and detached person whose business it is to see things and people as if he had never seen them before, it is possible for me not only to observe people as data but to observe scientists observing people as data – in short to take a Martian view.[70]

A double agent or "a visitor from Mars". The man who is ambivalent about the land where he lives but acknowledges that, if he has a home, it is here – and the man who feels continually homeless, "homesick" because he knows that any home he may have is not here but some place else, in some world elsewhere. The distance between these two narrative *personae* accounts for the difference between Faulkner's furious, ghost-ridden narrative voice and the cool, sardonic tones of Percy's fiction. More important, it measures the gap between a body of writers who still think of themselves in regional terms, still see themselves as marked by the Southern brand, and those for whom the brand has been scorched out, obliterated – and in whose name new terms, fresh vocabularies have to be invented.

"Man is alienated by the nature of his being here", Percy has said. "He is here as a stranger and as a pilgrim, which is the way alienation is conceived in my books." All of Percy's novels ask the question asked at the very beginning of *The Message in the Bottle*: "Why does man feel so sad in the twentieth century?" And all of them begin with a particular man – a particular "sovereign wayfarer" as Percy would call him – coming into some dim awareness of the fact that he is like a castaway living on a desert island, "who despite a lifetime of striving to be at home on the island is as homeless now as he was the first day he found himself cast up on the beach".[71] So, in *The Moviegoer*, Binx Bolling becomes aware of "the possibility of a search": which, Binx explains, "is what anyone would undertake if he were not sunk in the everydayness of his own life".[72] While Will Barrett in *The Last Gentleman* and Thomas More in *Love in the Ruins* discover that man is not (to quote *The Message in the Bottle* again) "of a piece, . . . a whole creature" but split, sundered in two, into mind and body, "carnal knowledge" and "angelic knowledge", "bestialism" and "angelism".[73] In turn, Lancelot Andrewes Lamar in *Lancelot* sets out to search for sin on the assumption that "If there is such a thing as sin, evil, a living malignant force, there must be a God!"[74] And Will Barrett in Percy's most recent novel, *The Second Coming*, tries "to settle the question of God once and for all" in his own idiosyncratic way, by challenging God to save him from dying. "For some time he had been feeling depressed without knowing why":[75] this sentence, which appears on the opening page of *The Second Coming*, sums up the initial state of all Percy's protagonists. Living inauthentic lives, deprived of adequate models, they become aware of their own inauthenticity and search for a solution, a way of becoming "a hundred percent themselves". As Percy himself has pointed out, and numerous critics have noted, the conceptual framework of this fiction is existentialist: the opening phase of each of the novels can be described in terms borrowed from Heidegger or Sartre, while most if not quite all of Percy's protagonists are supposed to travel, during the course of the narrative, from Kierkegaard's aesthetic mode through the ethical to the religious. Existentialist, then, and Christian too: but not Southern, except in the minimal sense that the South – or perhaps it would be more accurate to say, "the Sunbelt" – is the place where people like Binx Bolling and Will Barrett happen to live and where they try to complete their pilgrimage. It is no more than that: a particular spot on the desert island where they chance to have been cast away, there to wait and seek "for news from across the seas".[76]

Just how far Percy demotes his region and its models of belief is fairly obvious from his use of landscape. The South where most of the action of most of his novels occurs is blank and anonymous, a world of urban decay and sterile suburban affluence indistinguishable from the rest of the United States. Avoiding "the old-world atmosphere of the French Quarter or the genteel charm of the Garden District", for example, Binx Bolling lives in the Gentilly district of New Orleans, in an apartment "as impersonal as a motel room". And although his consumption is more conspicuous and he lives in North Carolina, Will Barrett's homeplace in *The Second Coming* is in no way essentially different. Surrounded by all the comforts that advanced technology can furnish, the rhythms of Will's existence are dictated by

> socking little balls around the mountains, rattling ice in Tanqueray, riding $35,000 German cars, watching Billy Graham and the Steelers and M★A★S★H on 45-inch Jap TV.[77]

This is the landscape of most of Percy's novels: the landscape of middle America where the mass media, muzak and the credit card hold sway. And close to it is that other expression of what is sometimes called post-industrialism, the decaying urban centre where the only people who remain are those who cannot afford to go anywhere else. Percy rarely focusses on this other landscape for long, but something of its horror is captured in his third book, *Love in the Ruins*. A futuristic novel, set in "those dread latter days of the old violent beloved U.S.A and of the Christ-forgetting Christ-haunted death-dealing Western world", it presents a terrain over which are scattered cars abandoned by their owners, shops, motels, and gas stations burnt out and abandoned after riots, and other urban *detritus*. "In recent months", the narrator Thomas More tells us,

> the vines have begun to sprout in earnest. Possum grape festoons Rexall Drugs yonder in the plaza. Scuppernung all but conceals the A&P supermarket. Poison ivy has captured the speaker posts in the drive-in movie, making a perfect geometrical forest of short cylindrical trees.[78]

This is not Southern Gothic, of course, although it possesses some of the sinister resonance of, say, Faulkner's description of the Old Frenchman

Place in *Sanctuary*. It shares more with the imaginative spaces of contemporary fantasists like Barth and Pynchon than it does with the places described in traditional Southern writing; and what it communicates, above all, is a feeling of entropy.

Percy does not leave his treatment of place there, however. Very often, he offers the reader ironic or parodic versions of the traditional Southern idea of the patriarchal homeplace: the Vaught castle in *The Last Gentleman*, for instance, Tara in *Love in the Ruins*, and Belle Isle in *Lancelot*. Two of these houses are reproductions, imitations. The Vaught castle, we are told, with its "fat Norman tower and casement windows with panes of bottle glass" was built in the 1920s for a family of "cheerful, prosperous go-getters"; while Tara, "a preposterous fake house on a fake hill", was built for a gangster using "the drawings of David O. Selznick's set designer" for *Gone With the Wind*. The third, by contrast, is an old house belonging to Lancelot's family, which his second wife enthusiastically restores. In its restored state, however, it seems just as much of a fake as the others. "Did you know", Lancelot asks wryly, "that the South and for all I know the entire U.S.A. is full of demonic women who . . . are desperately restoring and preserving *places*, buildings?" For him (and clearly for his creator), his wife's restoration of his ancestral home is on a · par with her attempts to recreate *him*: according, he says,

> to some . . . image of the River Road gentry, a kind of gentleman planter without plantation, a composite . . . of Ashley Wilkes . . ., Leslie Howard . . ., plus Jeff Davis home from the wars . . ., plus Gregory Peck, gentle Southern lawyer, plus a bit of Clark Gable as Rhett.[79]

It bears no more relation to historical reality than "the Confederate Chevrolet agency" that Mr Vaught sets up in *The Last Gentleman*, staffed by "salesmen in Reb-colonel hats and red walking canes". Like the movies Lancelot alludes to here, it represents at best a tranquillising device, a way of avoiding what Binx Bolling habitually calls "the malaise".

It is worth considering for a moment the function of irony and parody in Percy's novels, particularly as this pertains to his treatment of such things as place. Gilles Deleuze, in *Logique du sens*, quotes a passage from Kierkegaard that illuminates the logic of irony, showing how the ironic mode depends on a strategy of displacement:

> The soul that practises irony is like the soul that travels throughout the world according to the doctrine of Pythagoras. It is constantly moving . . . Like children in a game, the ironist counts on his fingers: rich man, poor man, beggar man, etc. All those incarnations represent no more than pure potentialities for him, with the result that he can run their gamut as fast as children at play . . . If reality thus loses its value in the ironist's eyes, it is not

because it has been outgrown and must make room for a more authentic
reality, but because the ironist embodies the "essential I" to which there is no
corresponding reality.[80]

According to this formulation, irony liberates the subject, the perceiver,
by depriving the object of its claim to reality. It is a destabilising device,
and as such has become a crucial weapon in the armoury of the
postmodernist novel, which delights in avoiding resolutions and
suspending meaning. So, too, is parody: which acts as a liberating agent
by relegating other people's words, codes, conventions – that is, the
things parodied – to the level of the fictive and illusory. And in using such
devices, whenever the patriarchal homeplace is his object, Percy
announces both his distrust of it as a particular, talismanic image and his
separation from the patriarchal model in general. This is not the tortured
reluctance of a Faulkner to allow the aristocratic code all that it claims for
itself; still less does it bear any resemblance to Welty's spry reminders that
the plantation community, whatever its merits, leaves some aspects of
the inner life untouched. What Percy is doing, effectively, is rejecting
both code and community as worthy objects of contemplation. They,
and the structure of feeling that shaped them, he suggests, are not to be
taken seriously because the real, if it exists, does not exist there.

Of course, other aspects of the Southern code come into play at this
point: it is not just Percy's treatment of landscape that reveals his irony
and sense of displacement. His uses of time and history are just as
revelatory, and in particular his manipulation of what one of his
protagonists refers to as "the banality of the past". The person who coins
this phrase, Lancelot Lamar, also praises New Orleans (where, like Binx
Bolling, he lives) because, he claims, in "three hundred years of history
. . . it has never produced a single significant historical event". An
arguable point, perhaps: Percy may be inclined to use his protagonists to
express his own ideas, but he certainly does not intend us to take
everything they say on trust. Still, it *is* true that history is simply not there
in many of Percy's imaginative settings; and even when it is there it is
usually coolly dismissed. This, for example, is how Binx Bolling reacts to
a fort left over from the Civil War which he visits one day in the
company of a girl-friend:

> It is the soul of dreariness, this "historic site" washed by the thin brackish water
> of Mississippi Sound. The debris of summers past piles up like archaeological
> strata. Last summer I picked up a yellow scrap of newspaper and read of a
> Biloxi election in 1948, and in it I caught the smell of history far more
> pungently than from the metal marker telling of the French and Spanish two
> hundred years ago and the Yankees one hundred years ago. 1948. What a far-
> off time.[81]

As Binx's comments suggest, his field of vision has narrowed to the point that it can only incorporate things that happened a few years ago; "the smell of history" is, in fact, hardly distinguishable from the odour of personal memory. The only yesterdays that really matter for him are his own, recovered by what he calls "repetition": moments of *déjà vu* in which "the events of the intervening . . . years" between the past event and its recurrence are "neutralized", wiped out by the simple fact of recurrence, and "There remain[s] only time itself, like a yard of smooth peanut brittle." There is no imaginative reenactment of the distant past here of the kind one finds in, say, *Absalom, Absalom!*; Binx is not seeking to involve himself in the processes of history. On the contrary, he is trying to detach himself from those processes, to extricate himself from history's "dreariness" and absurdity: something that Percy, both as a postmodernist writer and a Christian existentialist, can only applaud.

"He remembered everything", one section of *The Second Coming* concludes, describing Will Barrett's predicament. "She remembered nothing", begins the next section, which returns us to Alison, the girl whom Will is eventually to fall in love with. These two brief remarks describe the extremes between which most of Percy's major characters gravitate. One extreme is "repetition": those rediscoveries of the past moment in which "nothing is . . . forgotten" and the experiences intervening between that moment and the present seem somehow to be obliterated. And at the other extreme is that condition to which people like Binx aspire for most of the time: a total immersion in the present that squeezes out all afterthought or forethought, all notions of yesterday or tomorrow. This condition is just as unresponsive to the idea of time as process as the moments of repetition are, just as indifferent to any sense of temporal or historical continuity. And it gives a peculiar angle or quality to the vision, as this passage from *The Moviegoer* illustrates:

> Yes! Look at him. As he talks, he slaps a folded newspaper against his pants leg and his eye watches me and at the same time sweeps the terrain behind me, taking note of the slightest movement. A green truck turns down Bourbon Street; the eye sizes it up, flags it down, demands credentials, waves it on. A businessman turns in at the Maison Blanche building; the eye knows him, even knows what he is up to. And all the while he talks very well.[82]

Binx Bolling is describing his friend Eddie Lovell here, whom he has met by chance on the street. And what is extraordinary about his description is its quality of detachment, distance; far from giving a sense of 'you are there' immediacy, the use of the present tense actually adds to the sense that we are examining this specimen under glass. The main reason for this is that it is part of Binx's immersion in the present moment to resist any resort to the past as a source of explanation. He refuses to place Eddie in a context that would make him understandable; there is no guide to personal motive, no reference to biographical or historical background – no use of 'was' to render the 'is' intelligible. As a result, Eddie seems trapped in the instant just as Binx is, turned into a series of odd or at the very least remarkable gestures. He is defamiliarised, as if– to use Percy's own analogy – he were being observed by a visitor from Mars.

This sense of being insulated from the processes of time is just as strong when Percy's protagonists turn away from the present moment to a form of remembering. Binx Bolling recalling "the time the kitten found Orson Welles in the doorway in *The Third Man*", Will Barrett remembering the night his father died, or lapsing into the past to such an extent that "Everything he saw became a sign of something else" from his youth: on such occasions, the characters involved seem to be cut off from their immediate environment. Just like the "little objects closeted away" under glass that Percy refers to in both *The Moviegoer* and *Lancelot* (relics from the Civil War, books published in 1850, or whatever), they appear to be "not merely locked in but sealed in forever": so trapped in the air of another time that they are unable to gauge the temperature of the world about them. Pushing even further than this, Percy sometimes applies his techniques of irony to these moments of turning away, particularly on those few occasions when the turn is to the historical rather than the personal past. Once or twice, for example, Will Barrett falls into reveries about what might have been if the South had won the Civil War:

> . . . he imagined how Richmond might be today if the war had ended differently. Perhaps Main Street would be the Wall Street of the South . . . Here in the White Oak Swamp might be located the great Lee–Randolph complex, bigger than GM and making better cars (the Lee surpassing both Lincoln and Cadillac, the L'il Reb outselling even Volkswagens). Richmond would have five million souls by now, William and Mary be as good as Harvard and less subverted. In Chattanooga and Mobile there would be talk of the "tough cynical Richmonders", the Berliners of the hemisphere.[83]

The difference between this and the famous passage in *Intruder in the Dust*, explaining how every Southern boy tries to rewrite the story of the War, is the difference between parody and the thing parodied. Faulkner is serious about the impulse he – or, rather, Gavin Stevens – describes: because, however futile in a practical sense he perceives that impulse to be, he clearly regards it as an expression of something fundamental and true – which is to say, the dialectical nature of history. Percy, however, dismisses the notion of the historical past as something to be reinvented (as Faulkner believes) or something to be remembered and imitated (which is the more Southern conventional way). The comical nature of

Barrett's day-dreams places them as just that: day-dreams. They, and the sense of the past as either a burden or a resource that they point to, are not taken seriously. The past may be a joke, perhaps, or a nightmare, or something too foreign and remote to be of much use to anyone now: these possibilities are still open to debate. But to think in any other way, Percy suggests – to think, in fact, as Barrett does here – is to do nothing less than surrender to absurdity.

If the sense of the past is observed in Percy's work only to be dismissed or parodied, then that feeling for evil which has characterised so much Southern thought is equally conspicuous by its absence. "There is very little sin in the depths of the malaise", says Binx Bolling:

> Christians talk about the horror of sin, but they have overlooked something. They keep talking as if everyone were a great sinner, when the truth is that nowadays one is hardly up to it . . . The highest moment of a malaisian's life can be that moment when he manages to sin like a proper human.[84]

Sin is not present as a *donné* in Percy's work for the simple reason that it is not present in the world as he sees it: there is only amorality, a studious avoidance of responsibility – or, to quote Lancelot Lamar, nothing but "curiosity and interest and boredom". As these remarks of Binx's suggest, this absence of the dimension of evil is registered in his characteristic *tone*. Flat, dry, unemotional, it gives a convincing voice to disengagement; a language of surfaces, it expresses a world of surfaces. They suggest something else as well, though: that for Percy there is a clear, qualitative difference between the absence of history and this particular absence. The first may not be regretted but the second definitely is: for to be capable of sin, Binx says (and Percy obviously endorses him in this) is to be capable of humanity. The reasons for this difference of perception have to do not with Percy's region but his faith: as a practising Christian, Percy regrets that the sense of evil is no longer operative in the world because, to quote the words of another convert, T. S. Eliot, "the sense of Evil implies the sense of good". Earlier Southern writers did not have to search for sin; it was there, whether they liked it or not, powerfully embodied in the figure of the black. But Percy evidently believes that, if he is not merely to lament sin's disappearance, he is compelled to search for it – that, as the narrator of *Lancelot* explains about half-way through his narrative, "what is needed is a quest for evil".

This quest is, of course, the subject of Percy's fourth novel. Lancelot Andrewes Lamar wakes up from his own personal form of "everyday-ness" – doing everything "moderately" and being "moderately happy" – to the possibility of his wife's adultery. His daughter Siobhan, he learns, has the blood type 1–0: which suggests, quite simply, that she is not his daughter. "There are worse things than bad news", he observes, and in fact this particular piece of bad news prompts, not anger, fear, or feelings of betrayal but something else. "There was a sense of astonishment", he recalls, "of discovery, of a new world opening up, but the new world was totally unknown. Where does one go from here?" The answer, in his case, is into a quest not merely for confirmation of his wife's infidelity but for knowledge, "the Unholy Grail . . . a true sin". "Evil", he argues, "is the only quest appropriate to the age. For everything and everyone's either wonderful or sick and nothing is evil." His search is for evil: and since, he reasons, "the greatest good is to be found in love", it may be there that he will also find "the greatest evil" – it may be there that he will reach into a heart of darkness. His quest fails, however. Lancelot does not see evil: only a botched piece of film on which his wife's negative mingles with her lover's negative, and his daughter Lucy is dimly perceived lying with two other people in "a rough swastikaed triangle" that is diagrammed rather than described. "There is no unholy grail", Lancelot concludes ruefully, "just as there was no Holy Grail";[85] and he turns from his quest to fantasies about what he calls "a new order", a society in which people are judged, not in terms of good and evil, but according to their obedience to a stern, stoic code.

Several points need to be made about Percy's treatment of this quest. In the first place, it is clear that he shares many of his narrator's feelings about "this cocksucking cuntlapping assholelicking fornicating, Happyland U.S.A."[86] However, as this remark indicates, Lancelot's language is so vitriolic that Percy seems also to be parodying his outrage by exaggerating it and, in the process, establishing some distance between himself and his narrator. Lancelot is undoubtedly the least sympathetic of Percy's central characters and the one who is subjected – however implicitly – to the most criticism. Admittedly, his initial decision to search for sin meets with the full approval of his creator. But Percy leaves the reader in little doubt that, once embarked on his search, Lancelot looks for sin in the wrong place: which is to say, in other people's behaviour rather than within himself. All he finds, as a result, is a series of abstract signs, bloodless negatives and blank diagrams. Lancelot cannot discover an appropriate name for evil because he begins with the wrong vocabulary: his failure is a failure of language in the sense that he lacks the equipment necessary to define and therefore know sin. This is evident at every point in the narrative: from his discovery of his own scarlet letter, the blood type I–0 (which leads to all kinds of calculations since, as he puts it, "My blood type and Siobhan's blood type did not compute"), to his puzzled observation of the strange, geometric figures made by his wife and daughter – figures that he then tries to reproduce on the page as if the sign, the pattern possessed some talismanic power, the key to the character of sin. Throughout, Lancelot is like a man attempting to solve an algebraic problem with insufficient formulae

("There was an unknown in the equation",[87] he admits at one point); or, to use a related comparison, he is like a person struggling to describe something for which his culture, the tribe to which he belongs, has never bothered to devise a word. So, in the end, he reverses the experience of Adam: failing to name and know the crucial things, he also fails to know sin and retreats into the innocence of fantasy. Instead of a fortunate fall, he suffers an unfortunate regression into a dream world in which moral complexity and spiritual challenge evidently do not exist.

Which brings us to another significant aspect of Lancelot's story: the fantasy of a new order into which he eventually withdraws. As Lancelot sees it, this order will depend for its success on a certain breed of "honorable men", as noble and powerful as "a Roman legion under Marcus Aurelius Antoninus". These men, he says, will "know each other as gentlemen used to know each other . . . The same way General Lee and General Forrest would know each other at a convention of used-car dealers." They will be recognisable by their obedience to "a stern code, a gentleness towards women and an intolerance of swinishness, a counsel kept, and . . . a readiness to act . . . from perfect sobriety and freedom"; and, apart from them, the only other men will be those categorised as "thieves". Women will also be divided into categories. "The best of women will be what we used to call ladies", Lancelot explains, "like [the] Virgin, Our Lady." "There will be virtuous women . . . and there will be women of the street",[88] he insists; everyone will know just who they are and where they stand. It does not take a great deal of ingenuity, really, to recognise the sources of this fantasy – or, to be more accurate, this exercise in utopian conservatism. The stern code, the division of men and women into categories, the invocation of ideas of chivalry and gentlemanliness, even the references to Marcus Aurelius and the implicit stoicism: all suggest that Lancelot's new order is a thinly disguised, slyly parodic version of the patriarchal South. What Lancelot embraces, in fact, and Percy pokes sly fun at, is the idea of renewing a specifically regional tradition, the roles and ceremonies of an idealised, aristocratic past. The importance of this can hardly be exaggerated. In other books, Percy employs parody to put in question some particular aspect of the Southern inheritance: an inheritance which, having been transmitted to him through his family and his foster father William Alexander Percy[89] in particular, is for him very largely a patriarchal one. In *Lancelot*, however, he goes much further. He uses parody to place a question mark over the entire patriarchal tradition, and to subvert the idea that this tradition might be recoverable or possess some contemporary relevance. Lancelot dreams up his scheme while he is confined in the cell of a New Orleans asylum: which says it all. The idea of resurrecting the structures of the past, Percy thereby suggests, is little short of insane. It implies an avoidance of reality (which includes, for him, the reality of sin) rather than an attempt to come to terms with it; it is, if anything, even more disorienting and soul-destroying than the inanities of "Happyland U.S.A."

Another way of putting all this is to say that, by the end of the book, Lancelot is anticipating his assumption of an heroic role: a mask which, the reader senses, will sit as uneasily on him as every other mask he has tried to wear. With Percy, in fact, that sense of discomfort with traditional roles one finds in Faulkner is taken much further: discomfort now becomes wry despair, because the self is so alienated from the parts written for it that it almost seems pointless trying to learn the lines. Only Lancelot among Percy's central characters even dreams of recovering the role of Southern gentleman: all the others evidently agree that, if there is one thing they cannot do, one possibility which will remain beyond them during their wayfaring, it is that. In this respect, they are rather like some strange, fictional offspring of Horace Benbow or Quentin Compson: a generation further on, that feeling of displacement from the patriarchal model that vexed Faulkner's sad young men has been transformed into a sense of radical separation – the gap has apparently widened into a gulf that nobody apart from Lancelot Lamar bothers to think about bridging. Percy is fond of inserting brief genealogies of his protagonists, which in effect chart this process, this change from comfort with a role, through discomfort and vexation, to total estrangement and alienation. In *The Second Coming*, for instance, the change through the generations in Will Barrett's family is mapped out in terms of changing entertainments: Will's grandfather, we learn, read *Ivanhoe* (because, like Ivanhoe, he had enemies, knew who they were, and hated them), his father read *Lord Jim* (because, like Lord Jim, his principal enemy – the man he hated most – was himself), while Will himself prefers to watch television (because he belongs to a world of stock reactions rather than emotions, from which anything as vividly human as hatred, and anything as individualistic as the notion of a personal enemy, have long ago been expunged). In *The Last Gentleman*, in turn, the differences between Will and his predecessors are expanded upon in this way, in a passage that helps to explain the book's title:

> Over the years his family had turned ironical and lost its gift for action. It was an honorable and violent family, but gradually the violence had . . . turned inward. The great grandfather knew what was what and said so and acted accordingly and did not care what anyone thought . . . The next generation, the grandfather, seemed to know what was what but he was not really so sure. He was brave but he gave much thought to the business of being brave . . . The father was a brave man too and he said he didn't care what others thought, but he did care. More than anything else, he wished to act with honor and to be thought well of by other men. So living for him was a strain. He became

ironical . . . In the end he was killed by his own irony and sadness and by the
strain of living out an ordinary day in a perfect dance of honor . . . As for the
present young man, the last of the line, he did not know what to think. So he
became a watcher and a listener and a wanderer.[90]

Will Barrett's father, we might say, represents the generation from and
of which Faulkner and Tate wrote; indeed, there is more than a little
resemblance between him on the one hand and, on the other, Quentin
Compson or the narrator of "Ode to the Confederate Dead". For all of
them living appears to have been a strain, because their devout wish to
align themselves with the active faith and innocence of the past was
challenged by their desperate belief that such an alignment was very
difficult, if not highly improbable. But they have all gone now, Percy
tells us, replaced by a new generation of men and women who live "in
the sphere of the possible". Unrealised in action, these new people live
not so much in the stream of history as on its margins from where, like
compulsive voyeurs, they watch everything that passes with a glazed
sense of uninvolvement. Their problem, really, is not like their
immediate predecessors, an excess of narrative, but rather its absence, the
suspicion that no stories or ceremonies apply, that there are no more tales
worth telling or parts worth playing. So they spend their time spying on
life; playing the games of their culture, entering its movie, when they feel
required to; and waiting for something to happen – war, perhaps, "or the
end of the world".

If this description of Percy's characters – and, in particular, his
protagonists – sounds familiar, it is because it also defines the typical hero
of the postmodernist novel. Binx Bolling, Will Barrett, Thomas More,
and Lancelot Lamar: all of them fluctuate between a tacit acceptance of
the anonymity of contemporary life, and the absurdly delimited sense of
identity it prescribes, and a dream state in which they do not seem to be
attached to anything or anyone – and least of all to themselves. This
makes them much closer in spirit to, say, Jake Horner, Cabot Wright,
Billy Pilgrim, or Ralph Ellison's invisible man[91] than they are to
Faulkner's and Tate's young men. One could hardly imagine either
Quentin Compson or Tate's Lacey Buchan saying this, for instance; it is
Binx Bolling who is speaking:

> My wallet is full of identity cards, library cards, credit cards. It is a pleasure to
> carry out the duties of a citizen and to receive in return . . . a neat styrene card
> with one's name on it certifying, so to speak, one's right to exist. What
> satisfaction I take in appearing the first day to get my auto tag and brake sticker!
> I subscribe to *Consumer Reports* and as a consequence I own a first-class
> television set, an all but silent air conditioner, and a very long lasting deodorant
> . . . In the evenings I usually watch television or go to the movies . . . The fact
> is I am quite happy in a movie, even a bad movie.[92]

One critic has said of Thomas Pynchon that he portrays a radically dehumanised world, in which people regard and use others as if they were objects and, perhaps even more disconcertingly, tend to see themselves as objects as well. As this passage indicates, exactly the same could be said of Percy. Even his central characters are tempted to surrender to their post-industrial surroundings, and when they do surrender they turn into walking clichés; they become quite as trapped in the prevailing unreality, just as dependent on technology to insulate them from feeling, as any of the other, minor characters on whose lives they eavesdrop with such unfailing facility and humour. Love or hatred for the South is out of the question here; the heroic age is over, and so is the heroic struggle with the machine; all that is left is "niceness", a stifling blandness registered in Percy's work, as in other postmodernist fiction, by references to various tranquillising devices – such as the mass media, pills and drugs, psychotherapy or E.C.T. Binx Bolling may withdraw in the same way Will Barrett commonly does or he may resign himself to the processes of consumerism (become "a consumer receiving an experience-package" to quote from *The Message in the Bottle*); he may disappear into the role of quizzical observer or he may vanish quite as effectively into the namelessness and facelessness of the group. Either way, he achieves a strange kind of unbeing, a peculiar absence of character; and there are millions who are just the same, we are told in *Love in the Ruins*, "destined to haunt the human condition like the Flying Dutchman".

"Men . . . walk as docilely into living death as sheep into a slaughterhouse", observes the narrator of *The Second Coming*; and indeed a substantial slice of every one of Percy's novels is concerned with imaginative analysis of this phenomenon, the "life-which-is-a-living-death" and the docility with which so many people accept it. These people include the protagonists most of the time: but not, so we are asked to suppose, all of it – as was mentioned earlier, Percy tries to move some of *them*, at least, beyond this death-in-life towards moral rebirth and spiritual transcendence. Coming to awareness they also come, Percy wants us to believe, to the threshold of a new existence: a new life involving communion with one other person and, beyond that, with God. It is not really within the brief of this discussion to consider this aspect of Percy's work in any detail. One thing, however, should be noted: there is perhaps a difference between what Percy wants and hopes to do, according to his own accounts of his writing, and what he does do, what is *there* in terms of the meanings made available by the texts. The conclusion of *The Moviegoer*, for instance, is so ambiguous that very few readers agree about it. Some say Binx Bolling does achieve a religious sense; others argue that he simply becomes aware of his moral responsibilities; while others suggest that he does not change at all – that he remains a sadly contracted hero, partly implicated in the consumerist process (in that he has apparently "settled down") and partly separate, out on a limb (in that he is married to someone even more deeply alienated than he is). By contrast, the endings of *The Last Gentleman* and *Love in the Ruins* are far from ambiguous but they rely on some rather strained, heavy-handed symbolism (of, respectively, baptism and rebirth) to do the imaginative work for them; while *Lancelot* depends on the sudden emergence of the fictional narratee, the priest to whom the narrator "confesses", to supply some sense of a positive, the affirmation on which the book closes. In turn, *The Second Coming* ends in this way:

> Will Barrett thought about Allie [the girl he is to marry] . . . her wide gray eyes, her lean muscled boy's arms, her strong quick hands. His heart leapt with a secret joy. What is it I want from her and him, he wondered . . .? Is she a gift and therefore a sign of a giver? Could it be that the Lord is here, masquerading behind this simple silly holy face? Am I crazy to want both, her and Him? No, not want, must have. And will have.[93]

It is as if Percy were talking directly to us here, gesturing towards what he "must have" even if he has to bend experience – imagined experience in his case, of course – twist it until it breaks in order to have it. But what he says fails even as an expression of joyful possibility: because of its assertiveness, its discursiveness, the touch of mawkishness noticeable particularly in the references to Allie – because, in short, it is rhetoric in the Yeatsian sense of will doing the work of the imagination. And in this it is *symptomatic*, it illustrates a general weakness or limitation in Percy's novels. As postmodernist accounts of the abyss they are magnificent; as Christian existentialist attempts to navigate that abyss, however, they will probably convince only those eager to be convinced and willing to take the intention for the effect.

Doubts there may be about this positive, redemptive aspect of Percy's novels, but there can be no doubt that, successfully rendered or not, it owes nothing at all to the author's Southern background. Nor can there be much argument by now about his treatment of those characters who recall aspects of the regional tradition, and who sometimes try to act as mentors to the protagonists. Percy's attitude towards these people is not altogether unsympathetic: which is hardly surprising, given that the model for them is his own foster-father. Percy even wrote an introduction to W. A. Percy's book, *Lanterns on the Levee: Recollections of a Planter's Son*, which makes that sympathy clear. "Is it a bad thing", he asks, "for a man to believe", as his foster-father evidently believed, "that his position in society entails a certain responsibility toward others . . . for a man to care like a father for his servants, spend himself on the poor, the sick, the miserable?"[94] Clearly, Percy feels that it is not, if (and for him it is a large 'if') such beliefs are tenable – provided they can be held to with reasonable certainty, which generally seems to mean provided they are held to by an earlier generation. So there is more than a touch of affection, and even admiration, in his portrait of someone like, say, Emily Cutrer in *The Moviegoer*. Emily – whom Binx Bolling calls "Aunt Emily" although she is actually his great-aunt – speaks for the paternalism, and the stoicism, of a previous age; and she speaks for it most eloquently in a long speech towards the end of the book. She is giving Binx a dressing down for what she sees as his moral indifference, his tendency in "one of life's critical situations" not to "respond in one of the traditional ways" but "simply default. Pass . . . turn on [his] heel and leave." "I did my best for you son", she declares to the young man she now regards as a lost cause:

> "I gave you all I had. More than anything I wanted to pass on to you the one heritage of the men of our family, a certain quality of spirit, a gaiety, a sense of duty, a nobility worn lightly, a sweetness, a gentleness with women – the only good things the South ever had and the only things that really matter in this life".[95]

Her speech is powerful, certainly: so powerful, in fact, that according to Percy himself "people in the South think that's the best part of the book . . . and they give me credit for coinciding with Aunt Emily". The plain truth of the matter is, however, that she and her words are made to seem anachronistic in the context of the narrative as a whole, and that Binx understands her hardly at all. There may be some warmth in Percy's portrait of her, if only because she echoes his own foster-father's faith in "the old ideals, the old strengths" and "the unassailable wintry kingdom of Marcus Aurelius". But it is warmth for something that is regarded as gone: a way of perceiving and dealing with reality that simply does not apply any more, in a culture of credit cards, consumer reports, and movies.

It is probably worth adding that, over the years, Percy's treatment of characters like Aunt Emily – that is, spokesmen for the patriarchal code – has grown markedly less sympathetic. Lancelot Lamar's descriptions of his new order, for instance, often read like pastiches of Aunt Emily's speech: the stern code remains the same in most of its details (a sense of honour, a recognition of duty, gentleness towards women, and so on) but in the later book Percy seems intent on parodying it so as to make it clear just where he stands – in order to leave no room for misinterpretation or misplaced nostalgia. Interestingly enough, there is even something of a difference between the treatment accorded Ed Barrett, Will Barrett's father, in *The Last Gentleman*, published in 1966, and then in *The Second Coming*, which appeared fifteen years later. As he is described in the earlier novel, Ed Barrett, one critic has accurately observed, "has a streak of noblesse oblige" even if he is "incapable of transcending the paltriness around him".[96] He is seen, in fact, as a reasonably sympathetic representative of the Southern stoic tradition: although – as a passage quoted earlier indicates – he evidently found allegiance to that tradition a strain, and so in this connection is rather less impressive than Emily Cutrer. By the time of Percy's fifth novel, however, Ed Barrett has been turned into something of a monster. The stoicism is still there but it is warped; it degenerated into cynicism, the author suggests, because Ed could not deal with – which is to say, could neither handle nor resist – the contemporary problem of death-in-life. "A man is born between an asshole and a pisshole", he is remembered as saying. "He eats, sleeps, shits, fucks, works, gets old, dies. And that's all he does. That's what a man is." Without a strong, tenable faith he "gave in to death", we are told, first trying to kill his son along with himself and then settling for suicide alone. And as a ghostly reminder of the old imperatives he haunts Will Barrett throughout the story, tempting him to give up the struggle: "Go like a man, for Christ's sake", Will seems to hear him saying, "a Roman, here's your sword." Unlike the traditional Southern hero, though, Will does not heed the advice of his father or try to embrace his insubstantial image; on the contrary, he works fiercely and steadily to reject him. "I was never so glad of anything", Will imagines telling him at one point,

> as I was to get away from your doom and your death-dealing and your great honor and great hunts and great hates . . . your great allegiance swearing and your old stories of great deeds which not even you had done but had just heard about, and under it all the death-dealing which nearly killed me and did you.[97]

Ed Barrett's way is seen as "death-dealing" not least because it answers to the needs of a dead and buried culture; it belongs to a world of subterranean ancestral voices. Binx Bolling simply ignored those voices because he did not understand them; Will Barrett, however, understands them only too well. He listens to them carefully and then he defies them ("You gave in to death, old mole, but I will not have it so"); not only that, he explains why he must do so, his reasons for saying "No" to his father. In this respect, *The Second Coming* is even more of an act of exorcism than Percy's other novels, a denial of old Southern tales and talking. In so far as the patriarchal myth concerns either Will Barrett or his creator here it is as a ghost to be laid to rest: a saga of "great honor and great hunts and great hates" that need no longer be told – that is, reimagined and reinvented – because to do so would be to yield to the tyranny of the past.

Perhaps the last word should be given to Percy's black characters, however; since blacks occupy the margins of his stories, just as they do in traditional Southern writing – but occupy them in a distinctly untraditional way. The principal black figures in both *Love in the Ruins* and

Lancelot, for example, are sophisticated and educated, as implicated in the new, computerised world as any of their white friends and acquaintances are. Thus Colley, in *Love in the Ruins*, is referred to by the narrator as "a regular black Leonardo"; an electronic wizard and graduate of Amherst and N.Y.U. medical school, "he lounges around", More tells us,

> like an Amherst man, cocking a quizzical eyebrow and sending out wreaths of maple-sugar smoke, or else he humps off down the hall like a Brooklyn interne, eyes rolled up in his eyebrows, shoes pigeoning in . . .[98]

Similarly, Elgin in *Lancelot*, another technological wizard, seems to have crossed some racial or cultural line – or, as Lancelot Lamar puts it, "sailed in a single jump from Louisiana pickaninny . . . to smart-ass M.I.T. senior, leapfrogging not only the entire South but all of history as well". Just as much as Colley, he has evidently re-created himself in response to the pressure of changed times; and just as much as nearly all of Percy's black characters, he provokes a peculiar kind of uneasiness, the nature of which is suggested by a brief passage in *The Moviegoer*. It occurs when Binx Bolling is trying to describe Aunt Emily's black servant, Mercer: who, according to Binx, seems undecided which role he should play – that of "faithful retainer" required of him by his employer or the one he prefers for himself, of "a remarkable sort of fellow, a man who keeps himself well informed". "This is why I am always uneasy when I talk to him", Binx explains:

> I hate it when his vision of himself dissolves and he sees himself as neither, neither old retainer nor expert in current events. Then his eyes get muddy and his face runs together behind his moustache.[99]

This is very different from the traditional reaction to black characters in Southern writing. There is no sense here of the black man or woman as the bearer of doom, the emblem of an inexorable fate or Original Sin; nor is there much feeling of otherness in the description, the suspicion that what the black figure reminds us of are the unacknowledged forces playing around the closed world of the whites, the subliminal impulses that threaten to subvert white codes by bringing their truth and adequacy into question. "We were like two Jews who have changed their names", says Thomas More of Colley; "there was something between us, a shared secret, an unmentionable common past, an unacknowledged kinship." That captures it exactly: the uneasiness Binx feels springs, like More's, from a feeling of complicity, a common sense of dispossession and loss. Black characters like Mercer, or Colley or Elgin, *mirror* the alienation of the whites who observe them; they are not 'other' but significantly like them, in their displacement, their disconnection from history, and not least their uncertainty about names and roles. The fear they arouse, the sense of dissolution and unbeing they instil, depends directly on the sense that blacks no less than whites are adrift now, and sad – materially comfortable for the most part (Percy clearly believes that all the major civil rights battles have been won), but morally lost. They are strangers in a strange land: not, as they once were, as a result of prejudice and oppression but because – like the people who enslaved and oppressed them – they are *spiritually* or *psychologically* estranged, unknown to the world and themselves.

A sense of being strangers in a strange land is what the South began with, of course: the first white settlers, and those who supported them, found themselves confronted with an unfamiliar territory, and they tried to familiarise it by seeing it in terms of certain inherited – and, it must be said, not entirely irrelevant or inappropriate – myths. The new world across the Atlantic was not merely new to them, it was alien, a foreign wilderness, and they made every effort to domesticate that wilderness; they tried to *write* the South, in a way, by translating their strange surroundings into understandable words, brought from home. Now, however, with writers like Percy that effort has ceased. Neither the patriarchal model nor the populist is operative in Percy's work, except in the form of parody, because in his judgement neither fits or makes sense: which is to say, neither begins to offer a satisfactory means of encoding and understanding reality. The strangeness *he* perceives is the strangeness of moral displacement; the sea across which *he* gazes is figurative; the structure of feeling *he* deploys is variously postmodernist, existentialist, and Catholic; and the news *he* awaits is apocalyptic. "American literature is not having its finest hour", observes the narrator dryly in *Love in the Ruins*:

> The Southern novel yielded to the Jewish masturbatory novel, which in turn gave way to the WASP homosexual novel, which has nearly run its course. The Catholic literary renascence, long awaited, failed to materialize. But old favorites endure, like venerable Harold Robbins and Jacqueline Susann, who continue to write the dirty clean books so beloved by the American housewife. Gore Vidal is the grand old man of American letters.[100]

This has all the characteristic Percy trademarks: a sardonic tone, a crisp, cool prose style, sly knowingness (witness the reference to the "long awaited" Catholic literary renaissance), and a preoccupation with the *detritus* of post-industrial culture. And no less of a trademark, really, is the feeling of everything running down (including, this passage insists, the Southern literary tradition), the sense of waiting for the end. Percy sees himself as very much "a man writing about the end of the world – i.e., the passing of one age and the beginning of another"; and someone writing about this, he has explained,

> must reckon not only like H. G. Wells with changes in the environment but also with changes in man's consciousness which may be quite as radical.[101]

The world alters, systems of perception alter, the novelist must register these alterations: that is the simple message offered here. And to this could be added a rider, a supplementary message announced in Percy's writing as a whole, and in the work of many other postmodernists who just happen to come from below the Mason–Dixon line: that the place where they live has changed beyond recognition and so the codes used to understand it, the vocabulary required to name and know it, will have to undergo a similar change. If these messages are correct, then one thing that Percy and those like him are doing needs to be emphasised. They are finishing a story that began four hundred years ago; they are composing an epitaph – and a not entirely affectionate one, at that – for the idea and arguments of the South.

Postscript

"What the world supplies to myth", writes Roland Barthes,

> is an historical reality, defined, even if this goes back quite a while, by the way in which men have produced or used it; and what myth gives in turn is a *natural* image of reality . . . The world enters language as a dialectical relation between activities, between human actions; it comes out of myth as a harmonious display of essences.[1]

By "myth" Barthes means here what he always does: the complicated network of argument, beliefs, and metaphor that a society constructs in order to support and authenticate its sense of identity. He is referring, in fact, to its ideas of order, its system of meaning. In this sense, at least, it *is* possible to talk about a "myth of the South": if what is understood by this phrase are those versions of experience that are predicated in the language of a community – using "language" here, in turn, to include not only speech and writing but also (and again to quote Barthes) "photography, cinema, reporting, shows, publicity . . . any significant unit or synthesis, whether verbal or visual". "Myth" interpreted in this way is a process rather than a product, a system of communication rather than an object; it is, as one Southerner John Peale Bishop acutely observed, a technique, a way of mediating experience. And it is of its essence that, as Barthes suggests, it should appear natural: in other words, that in converting historical reality into language it should seem to be offering not one particular version of things but things as they really are and presumably always have been. "We reach here the very principle of myth", observes Barthes, "it transforms history into nature." "And just as bourgeois ideology is defined by the abandonment of the name 'bourgeois' ", he observes elsewhere,

> myth is constituted by the loss of the historical quality of things: in it, things lose the memory that they once were made.[2]

271

One or two points need to be made about this notion of myth, before returning to the context of the contemporary South. In the first place, it is worth reminding ourselves that it is precisely the recovery of the memory Barthes is talking about here – that "things . . . once were made" – that distinguishes the good Southern writer from the merely mediocre one. A writer like Faulkner (as I have tried to show) uses the myth in a transitive sense: as a mode of signification, a way of organising experience. But he also employs it in an intransitive way: by drawing our attention to the act of writing and encoding, he requires us to look at the codes, the particular system of language he is using. He writes *about* something and invites us to look *through* the writing to a world beyond it: and he also offers us a critique – which is to say, an examination and a placing – of the process whereby the world has been translated into words. In the second place, it needs pointing out that there is a particular irony implicit in the Southern "myth": which derives from the fact that its characteristic way of transforming history into "nature" involves a claim that it is doing precisely the reverse. Southern myth claims that, far from denying the reality of history, it is locating it at the centre, assigning it a constitutive function. In one sense it is, of course. For the specific codes the region employs make so much of the interplay between past, present, and future. But in another sense it is no more historical than any other mythical form of speech is: because it presents itself, and its particular version of a particular history, as a fundamentally accurate account of the essence of things. Despite the fact that Southern thinking has been shaped by historical circumstances often peculiar to itself and has constantly changed in response to changing pressures, it assumes an air of permanence – an absolute quality and an exemption from the very circumstances that shaped it. In this connection, something that the critic Frank Kermode said is well worth quoting. Discussing Eliade's theory of myth, Kermode remarked that, according to Eliade:

> Myths take place in a quite different order of time – *in illo tempore* . . . *Then* occurred the events decisive as to the way things are; and the only way to get at *illud tempus* is by ritual re-enactment. But here and now, *in hoc tempore*, we are certain only of the dismal linearity of time . . .[3]

It is not difficult to see how, in this way, Southern thinking leans decisively away from the historical and towards the mythical. *Then*, so the regional story goes, in some mythicised version of the past, occurred the events decisive as to the way things are. And the only way to recover their precious essence is by invocation and imitation: the kinds of repetition and re-enactment that so many different Southerners have engaged in over the past few hundred years.

Which brings us to the last point that is worth making about Barthes's idea of myth – and also back to the present state of the region. While considering the character of mythical thinking and its relation to history, Barthes adds this:

> . . . it is human history which converts reality into speech, and it alone rules the life and death of mythical language. Ancient or not, mythology can only have an historical foundation, for myth is a type of speech chosen by history . . .[4]

"There is no fixity in mythical concepts", Barthes adds elsewhere,

> . . . they can come into being, alter, disintegrate, disappear completely. And it is precisely because they are historical that history can very easily suppress them . . .[5]

This, it should be clear, is to return to the present dilemma of the South. As Barthes shows, there are different ways of receiving and using mythical thinking. It is possible to do so cynically, manipulatively: which is what, say, many journalists and politicians do – or anyone who uses such thinking consciously, while trying to disguise the fact. It is possible to do so in a "demystifying" way, the way of the mythologist who offers to decipher the myth, or in a more complex, writerly way, the way of a Faulkner who tries to locate and understand it even while employing it. Most obviously, perhaps, it is possible to do so innocently, with very little awareness that this is what we are doing – thinking mythically, encoding the world: which is what most members of a culture do most of the time. All of these ways, however, apart from that of the "demystifier", lose their thrust, their point, if history acts to "suppress" the myth: that is, if it no longer supplies appropriate material out of which to fashion the traditional codes or an adequate foundation on which to re-create the inherited structures. Even the way of the "demystifier" is deprived of some of its force if the myth it seeks to "demystify" is no longer current. At a certain juncture in the history of any group, Barthes suggests, the forms, the vocabularies evolved by that group to enable them to conceive of and manage the world, disintegrate, disappear; substitutes have to be found. And this, it is at least open to debate, is what is happening now in one particular part of the United States, below the Mason–Dixon line. Writing the South may be about to become a redundant activity, to be replaced by something else: such as – to take the most obvious possibility – writing the Sunbelt.

Writing the South, writing the Sunbelt: at this point, it might be useful to look briefly at two books published in the late 1960s both of which are openly concerned, to the point of obsession, with the problems and possibilities of being a Southerner now. The two books are *The Southern Tradition At Bay* by Richard Weaver, published in 1968, and *North Toward Home* by Willie Morris, which appeared a year earlier. The authors of these two books are not unlike in their initial premises. Both are trying to write the South in a far more deliberate and discursive way than novelists like Welty and Percy. Both are far more argumentative and self-conscious about their Southernness. Both openly confront the present dilemma of their region and relate it eventually to their own personal feelings of discontinuity, inner division. However, this is about as far as the resemblance between the two goes. Having started from similar positions, Weaver and Morris reach virtually opposite conclusions: about the nature of the changes taking place in the historical fabric of the South, their possible impact on its mythical language, and nearly everything else. Coming from backgrounds that were not so very different, possessing the same basic area of interest, these two men seem nevertheless to be talking about two different worlds: shouting from opposite sides of a chasm, an abyss the scope and size of which earlier generations of Southerners would have found it hard to imagine.

As far as *The Southern Tradition At Bay* is concerned, it is perhaps worth saying something first about its author and how the book came to be written. Richard Weaver was born in North Carolina, and began his adult life as a socialist. In fact, in 1932 he formally joined the American Socialist Party. "My disillusionment with the Left", he later recalled (in an essay significantly entitled "Up From Liberalism"), "began with this first practical step." As he saw it, his fellow socialists were mostly innocents and eccentrics, "hopelessly confused about the nature and purpose of socialism". And disappointed by them he began the long journey back to what he was to regard, eventually, as a much sounder philosophy. The first step was taken when he went to Vanderbilt University to do graduate work under the supervision of John Crowe Ransom; there he met many of the Agrarians and became very friendly with some of them, although he was still not quite ready to embrace their beliefs. Then, after a spell of teaching, he moved to Louisiana State University to work on a dissertation that finally bore the rather cumbersome title, "The Confederate South: A Study in the Survival of a Mind and Culture". Weaver's plan, once the dissertation was passed, was to have it published; and, with this in mind, he added an Introduction and and Epilogue. When offered for publication, however, it was firmly rejected, and Weaver put it aside to concentrate on his teaching duties: for in 1944 he became a member of the English faculty at the University of Chicago. In Chicago, he continued his move to the right: writing books and essays that attacked the fragmentation of modern culture, the disappearance of hierarchy, and what he called "the clichés of liberalism". At the same time, his interest in the South revived; and he began writing essays that, in particular, associated the Old South with "the chivalry and spirituality of the Middle Ages".[6] Eventually, under the pressure of these concerns, Weaver returned to the manuscript that had been rejected so many years ago and wrote a new introduction, his plan being to submit it for publication again. Before it could be submitted, however, he died; and it was not until five years after his death that it was finally published under the title *The Southern Tradition At Bay*, with a Foreword by one of his Agrarian friends, Donald Davidson. Posthumously, at least, it gave Weaver the reputation he had always desired: as the most eloquent spokesman, since the Second World War, for the traditional patriarchal idea of his region – the notion, that is, that the Old South was an embodiment of Christian, chivalric values, the last outpost of feudal culture in the Western world.

The bulk of *The Southern Tradition At Bay*, taken from the original dissertation, consists of a detailed, scholarly account of post-bellum writing, and in particular of how Southerners – under the twin pressures of defeat in the Civil War and the Reconstruction – struggled gamely to construct an apologia and preserve their identity. Even here, however, Weaver is aiming at something more than scholarship. As he puts it in his Epilogue:

> In this research . . . I have attempted to find those things . . . which speak for something more than a particular people in a specific situation. The result . . . is not pure history, but a picture of values and sentiments coping with the forces of a revolutionary age, and though failing, hardly expiring.[7]

Weaver's purpose, in short, is the recovery of belief. So he begins his account of the post-war debate with a fairly abstract summary of what he calls "the Southern tradition": which, according to him at least, has "a fourfold root". "A feudal theory of society", "the code of chivalry", "the ancient concept of a gentleman", and "a religiousness" that "leads . . . to the acceptance of life as mystery": these are the four principles, Weaver argues, that existed as determining forces in the Old South. They survived into the post-bellum era, he insists, bloody but unbowed; and they are still "discernible in the peculiar complex of Southern culture today".

At first sight, it may seem strange that in trying to recover the Southern tradition Weaver concentrates on a period when, by his own admission, it was under pressure, even disintegrating. But he has his reasons, he explains:

> "Things reveal themselves passing away", someone remarked to William Butler Yeats, and it is an historical fact that every established order writes its great apologia only after it has been fatally stricken. When the forces of the old and the new come into . . . conflict, then spokesmen appear to formulate the traditional assumptions and to defend what it has always been supposed could never be indicted. At best these win only a forensic victory, for the revolution is in full course, and the body politic dies while they are yet arguing its right to survive.[8]

"Things reveal themselves passing away." It is not difficult to see the personal thrust of this passage; nor is it difficult to discern Weaver's passionate involvement in the arguments he describes. Certainly, he does try to keep some distance, to maintain the scholarly and critical perspectives appropriate to his task. With this aim in mind, he is even willing to admit that the Old South was guilty of weaknesses and excesses ("a highly touchy sense of personal pride", a want of respect for the arts, and so on) and that the post-bellum South tended to romanticise its past. But the distance is never consistently maintained; the perspective frequently blurs; and the voice of the scholar is very often indistinguishable from the voices of his subjects. Sometimes, this loss of detachment is, to say the least, unfortunate. When talking about post-bellum attitudes towards black people, for example, Weaver seems almost to be identifying himself with the clichés of the time. "The Negro was an exceedingly pliable being", he declares at one point, with an "addiction to heathen religious practices"; "the system of slavery", he observes elsewhere,

> like that of military discipline, enforces habits of health and regularity, and when it was suddenly removed, the hitherto unknown ills of syphilis, consumption, and insanity made immediate appearance.[9]

This is the bad side of the coin. On the other, more sympathetic side, there is Weaver's tone of defiance – that familiar regional habit of admiring, and even identifying with, Quixotic gestures – that comes through whenever he is describing some particularly impractical aspect of the Southern apologia. So, when he is about to consider the attempt made by Southerners after the War to justify the Constitutional position of the Confederacy, he explains their motivation in these terms:

> Things which are eternally right in the mind of God may be wickedly perverted in the world, but the perversion must not go unopposed . . . It is . . . part of the duty of chivalry to serve the eternal verities . . . a gentleman may risk destruction but not dishonor . . . the most important thing in life is the cultivation of truth and the preservation of good form, which entail . . . refusing to act from a sense of what will pay.[10]

Again, it is hard to resist the suspicion that Weaver is speaking for himself here, as well as for the likes of Jefferson Davis.

But it is in the Introduction and Epilogue to the book that this personal note rings most clearly. Here, Weaver casts aside the role of scholar – a role that, in any case, he finds it difficult to adapt to – and takes on that of philosopher – or, rather, prophet. "If asked to tell why in these days Southern history is entitled to thoughtful consideration", he declares, "I should list first of all the fact that the South, alone among the sections, has persisted in regarding science as a false messiah." "The precarious state of

our civilization has grown with our control over nature", he goes on,
". . . everywhere crassness, moral obtuseness, and degradation are on the
increase". Far from advancing civilisation, science is helping to destroy
it: thanks to its emphasis on externals, its claims to dominion over the
world, its concentration of power in a few amoral hands, and its
"inexorable standardization". With "the greatest of all wars behind us"
(itself a monument to the destructive tendencies of science), it is now
incumbent upon us, we are told, to see that "the kingdom of civilization
is within", to be achieved by "discipline . . . self-culture and self-
control". If we need an example to follow – and Weaver clearly believes
we do – then one is available in the Southern tradition: above all, in what
is termed its "piety" and "ethics". By "piety", Weaver explains, he
means that attitude towards nature that "comes to us as a warning voice"
announcing "that it is not for us either to know all or control all"; and by
"ethics" he refers to a code of behaviour, religious in origin, that leads
one, via a recognition of "the plurality of personalities in the world", to
"a relatively selfless point of view".[11]
   Developing these notions, Weaver then insists that one, inevitable
measure of civilisation is its "power to create and enforce distinctions".
His argument is simple. Ideas of discipline, he claims, depend on "some
source of discrimination"; knowledge and virtue constitute this source;
and "these two things, it must be said to the vexation of sentimental
optimists, are in their nature aristocracies". We are back, in effect, with a
very familiar regional argument: that without hierarchy all that is
possible is uniformity, anonymity, standardisation. And we are back,
too, with some more specific claims of earlier apologists for the South –
earlier even than the ones Weaver discusses in the core of his book: "that
no man was ever born free", he insists at one point, "and no two men
ever born equal is a more sensible saying than its contrary". To do
Weaver justice, he is well aware of the vast backlog of argument and
imagery on which he is drawing and even alludes to it. While he is
attacking the notion of progress, for instance, he makes a distinction
between the assumptions of the mainstream American culture and what
he calls "the Southern . . . rationale of society": "The North had Tom
Paine", he tells us, "and his postulates assuming the virtuous inclinations
of man; the South had Burke and his doctrine of fallibility and of the
organic nature of society." Similarly, when he goes more deeply into the
idea that society is "a product of organic growth, and that a tested modus
vivendi is to be preferred to the most attractive experiment", he is not
afraid to cite even the most controversial of regional precedents, far and
near. George Fitzhugh is quoted, to the effect that "Philosophy will blow
up any government that is founded on it." And to the words of Fitzhugh
Weaver then adds this:

> . . . today, when the South pleads to be allowed "to work out its own
> problems in its own way", it more often than not has no plans for working
> them out. Its "way" is not to work them out, but to let some mechanism of
> adjustment achieve a balance.[12]

This is an obvious reference to current arguments over desegregation: to
the legal, social, and political upheavals that Weaver once described, in
one of his essays, as having "the look of a second installment of
Reconstruction".

   Which is not to say that Weaver's argument is simply a reworking of
traditional themes. Much of what he has to say will sound familiar to
anyone acquainted with Southern writing. What will probably be
unfamiliar, though, except to readers of George Fitzhugh and Allen
Tate, is the fiercely dogmatic approach Weaver adopts, his eagerness to
place the Southern code in the context of first principles; and, in addition
to this, the note of apocalyptic urgency he sounds, especially in the final
pages of his book. As far as the desire to see things in terms of ultimate
principles is concerned: this leads Weaver to describe the South, and in
particular the region of his own day, in not altogether complimentary
terms. The Old South committed "two great errors", he claims. In the
first place, it failed "to study its position until it arrived at metaphysical
foundations": so it was, and to some extent still is, "in the curious
position of having been right without realizing the grounds of its
rightness". And, in the second, it gradually surrendered the initiative.
"So little has this section shown", remarks Weaver testily, "that one is
prompted to question whether the South ever really believed in itself";
even now, he adds, "it seems to have no faith in its *imprimatur*". Quite
clearly, Weaver believes that he may be able to supply the corrective
here: by establishing a metaphysic of the South's position and so enabling
it to acquire confidence and initiative. Equally clearly, he sees this as an
urgent task, and not least because the errors committed by the region
have multiplied since the end of the nineteenth century. "The South
which entered the twentieth century had largely ceased to be a fighting
South", he observes at the end of his account of the post-bellum
apologists:

> An increasing number of persons showed all the signs of final acceptance of
> defeat: a weariness, a dedication to the less dangerous occupation of money-
> getting, and a willingness to turn collaborationist and cooperate with the victor
> on all points.[13]

Lack of initiative, in fact, turned into something very like abject
surrender; and a reluctance to establish first principles was translated into
a full-scale failure of nerve. "The South", Weaver complains, "possesses
an inheritance which it has imperfectly understood and little used": and

which, he might have added – since it is his purpose to show it – it is understanding and using less with each passing decade.

This brings us to the note of apocalypse that sounds ever more clearly as Weaver continues: that imagination of disaster, the sense of impending doom which is surely the book's *raison d'être*. Weaver knows that he is swimming against the historical tide, and at a moment of acute crisis. What is more he says so, not once but over and over again. "In times of profound revolutionary change", he argues,

> it is not the liberals, the progressives, the social democrats who discern what is at issue . . . It is the men of the old order who see most clearly the implications of the new.[14]

Such a time, he believes, is now, when "civilization is at the crossroads"; and such a man, a spokesman for "the old order", is Weaver himself. His aim is simple, to offer his readers a choice. They can either, he tells them, continue along the present path towards the monolithic state and a standardised culture. Or they can, as he implores them, turn back the historical tide; they can take the path of radical reaction. "The world is seeking as perhaps never before", Weaver declaims,

> for the thing that will lift up our hearts and restore our faith in human communities. . . victims of the confusions and frustrations of our . . . time turn with live interest to that fulfillment represented by the Old South. And it is this that they find: *the last non-materialist civilization in the Western world*. It is this refuge of . . . values . . . whose existence haunts the nation. It is damned for its virtues and praised for its faults . . . But most revealing of all is the fear that it gestates the revolutionary impulse of our future.[15]

Weaver seems to have forgotten for the moment his own, earlier references to the region's failures and errors: but to emphasise this is perhaps to miss the point. Like many before him, he is formulating an idea of the South that is partly a matter of historical fact, partly the product of logical inference – and partly, even, the result of self-conscious mythologising. Weaver says as much elsewhere, and to repeat the point here would be to disturb the flow and so diminish the impact of his oratory; and it is that impact – with its accompanying sense of prophetic urgency – that he is intent upon registering now. In the final pages of his book, especially, Weaver is less concerned with making fine distinctions about what did and did not happen in the past, and much more preoccupied with the facts of the present and future possibilities. That is why, immediately following this passage, he begins to draw up his programme of radical reaction: to describe, at some length, his plan "to save the human spirit by re-creating a non-materialist society".

There is no need to go into the details of Weaver's plan here: except, perhaps, to say that it involves a study of the principles on which the

Southern tradition was supposedly based and an attempt to resurrect them in new guises – a task that "falls upon poets, artists, intellectuals, upon workers in the timeless". "There cannot be a return to the Middle Ages or the Old South", Weaver acknowledges; it should be enough that the values these two cultures embodied should "inform the new order" while being adorned "with the attractions of the hour".[16] In other words, the new society that would evolve out of the programme would be structurally the same as the Old South but different as far as more superficial matters are concerned. Just what those more superficial matters are Weaver does not bother to explain; nor does he investigate the possibility that the spirit and the material shapes of a culture may be more closely linked than he cares to admit. His eye is fixed firmly on a redemptive landscape by this stage, and anything other than this – anything that puts the splendour and symmetry of that landscape in question – is quickly and peremptorily dismissed.

It is impossible not to feel that there is a good deal of wish-fulfilment at work in Weaver's prophecies: when, for instance, he talks about the re-establishment of "the fruitful distinction between the sexes, with the recognition of respective spheres of influence". "The end of the era of 'long-haired men and short-haired women' should bring a renewal of well-being", he adds triumphantly, ". . . and I think that women would have more influence if they did not vote." It is almost as difficult not to believe that certain assumptions Weaver makes, about the chances of this new world coming into being in the first place, are based more on hope than on reason. He claims, for example, that people are eager to accept poets as legislators but he offers virtually no evidence to support this; "the common man", he asserts simply, "is now ready to discard his bastard notions of science and materialism, intellectual hobbies of a hundred years ago".[17] Such things hardly detract from the sense of apocalypse, though. On the contrary, they help to reinforce it. For the desperate nature of Weaver's remedies acts as a gauge of his own mounting despair; the dreams highlight, as it were, the incipient nightmare. It is as if Weaver were admitting that the body politic has grown so cancerous by now that only experimental surgery stands a chance of saving it – measures that are by their nature speculative and risky, involving something not far short of a leap of faith. It is surely no accident that, in the final pages of his book, Weaver quotes two famous lines from Yeats's "The Second Coming", ". . . what rough beast, its hour come round at last, / Slouches towards Bethlehem to be born?"; since in their urgency and ambiguity, their magisterial tone and their candid uncertainty, they seem to distil the essence of his argument. Either the final steps forward have to be taken to nihilism and chaos, Weaver suggests; or, alternatively, several urgent steps backward have to be marched, towards a world whose existence is still said to haunt us. Both movements invite fear, because they involve an encounter with a "beast" of some kind, something strange, sudden, and irrevocable. At that point the resemblance ends, however. One movement, he believes, the movement back, offers a genuine "second coming", the eventual, painful promise of redemption; while the other augurs only destruction, spiritual death.

It is one of the ironies of Weaver's book that it is a celebration of Southern myth written by a Southerner in exile: a man who left his own home early and spent the last twenty years of his life in the North. Weaver was acutely aware of this irony and more than once tried to explain it. In 1950, for instance, he wrote an essay on the Agrarians that attempted to deal with precisely this problem. Many of the Agrarians had left the South, he admitted. But they had done so because the South was ceasing to be Southern. The Snopeses were taking over from the Sartorises, the Agrarian argument was not finding much of an audience in the region, and the Agrarians themselves felt that they could better preserve their heritage if they kept it distant and distinct from what was happening in Southern society at the time. "Thus what has been represented as the flight of the Agrarians", Weaver argues, "may appear on closer examination to be a strategic withdrawal to positions where the contest can be better carried on."[18] From his position in his rented rooms in Chicago, in fact, Weaver saw himself not as an outcast from the South but its true inheritor and re-creator, someone destined to summon the future out of the ashes of the past. Not surprisingly, whenever he considered this, his self-appointed task of rebuilding the patriarchal homeplace, a favourite metaphor or term of reference tended to occur to him. "We all stand today at Appomatox", he declares in *The Southern Tradition At Bay*; "the South . . . fought for . . . long, behind the barricades of revealed Christianity, of humanism, of sentiment . . . Now it can return as to the house of its fathers."[19]

The idea of the homeplace is just as important to that other Southerner in exile, Willie Morris, as the very title of his book indicates. From one point of view, *North Toward Home* is simply another in that long line of books that liberal Southern journalists seem so adept at producing: a line that includes, besides Cash's *Mind of the South*, *Southern Legacy* by Hodding Carter, *The South and the Southerner* by Ralph McGill, *The South and the Nation* by Pat Watters, and *Confessions of a White Racist* by Larry King.[20] Unlike most of these books, however, it is an autobiography: not just a summation of the author's views about the South (as, say, McGill's book is) or an analysis of one crucial and specifically regional aspect of the author's character (as with King's book) but an account of Morris's life from childhood to the time of writing. It is an act of self-exploration that hinges in particular on the relation between the writer's own personal story and what he sees as the story of his region. It is hardly surprising that the book borrows its epigraph from the greatest of all Southern novelists, William Faulkner, and alludes constantly to others, from Twain to Styron. For Morris is aware that what he is trying to do is what so many of them have tried to do before him: to write the South in the sense of struggling to disentangle the ties that bind – or, at least, once bound – him to the place where he was born. Nor is it surprising that, as one critic has observed,[21] the ghostly presence that haunts the book, even in its title, is not Faulkner but Thomas Wolfe; since, whatever else may be said about it, Morris's autobiography charts the same voyage as Wolfe's fiction – a slow journey away from the region towards Europe and the North, a gradual disengagement which ends in the perception that, if the South is to be called home, then he can never go home again.

But this is to simplify things a little. If the book has any controlling conception, it is not so much that the South was Morris's only home and now it is lost, but rather that the meaning of that term "home" can fluctuate, attach itself to different places as one's own beliefs and allegiances alter. Certainly, his first homeplace, and the dearest to him in memory, was in the South of his childhood: in Mississippi, in a small town called Yazoo City. Morris claims that it is located in one of the "magic places of America", and then describes it in some detail several times. Here is at least a small part of this composite portrait:

> . . . out along the highways where the town began there was a raw, desperate, unsettled look . . . But down in the settled places, along the quiet, shady streets . . . were the stately old houses, slightly dark and decaying . . .
> . . . Then it was a lazy town, a lethargic dreamy place . . ., at night full of rumblings and lost ghosts . . .

> I can see the town now on some hot, still, weekday afternoon in midsummer: ten thousand souls and nothing doing. Even the red water truck was a diversion . . . half-naked Negro children followed the truck up the street . . . Over on Broadway, where the old men sat drowsily in straw chairs . . ., whittling to make the time pass, you could laze around on the side-walk – barefoot . . . watching the big cars with out-of-state plates whip by . . . the merchants and lawyers sat in the shade . . ., talking slowly, aimlessly, in the cryptic summer way. The one o'clock whistle at the sawmill would send out its loud bellow, reverberating up the streets to the Yazoo River, hardly making a ripple in the heavy somnolence.[22]

Perhaps the first thing that will strike anyone reading this is how familiar it all is. Yazoo City is situated, Morris tells us, "on the edge of the delta . . . where the hills end and the flat land begins". At the time when he lived there it was "half hills and half delta";[23] and as such it seems to have represented for him a peculiar compound, a strange mixture of the populist and the patriarchal. Not only that, he seems to see it in memory through the filters of those two traditions: in terms that resurrect the codes, the vocabularies that so many Southerners used before him. It is as if he were making a final invocation, rehearsing familiar voices or tunes just one more time before consigning them to the incommunicable past. The most obvious and pervasive voice here is Mark Twain's. The isolation of the town, the lazy atmosphere of a summer afternoon, the children half-naked and barefoot, the old men whittling sticks while younger men yawn and talk, the visitants from the great, outside world passing by (cars in this case, of course, rather than steamboats), above all the brooding presence of the river: all these are, inescapably, elements of that dream which Twain spun out of his memories of Hannibal, Missouri. All, in turn, along with that strange sense of a lost land recovered for one magic moment ("I can see the town now"), were to become part of the populist language, the classic image of the small Southern town that one finds, for example, at the beginning of *The Ballad of the Sad Café* by Carson McCullers and *Other Voices, Other Rooms* by Truman Capote. Twain's is not the only voice, however. The references to "slightly . . . decaying" houses and the "lost ghosts" to be sensed at night ("the Yankees in the sunken gunboat down in the river, the witch in the cemetery . . ."): these seem to invoke and commemorate a quite different idiom, the language and imagery of a patriarchal tradition that found its most memorable articulation in the chronicles of Yoknapatawpha. The point is not that Morris is clearly and consciously borrowing. He may be, or he may not; we have no way of knowing. It is, quite simply, that, by the time Morris came to write about his Southern homeplace, the terms in which it was to be described had become conventional to the point of ossification. They had become potentially intractable: perhaps actually intractable for someone who, as the rest of *North Toward Home* was to show, believed (unlike Weaver) that he could never return to the house of his fathers. One critic has acutely remarked that there is a stylised quality to Morris's book, that it lacks the urgency of earlier Southern exercises in self-exploration. Exactly so, for Morris is forcing himself to write, for much of the time, from within a structure of feeling that he no longer believes to be genuinely his; in order to pay homage to his memories, he is trying to recover – however temporarily – what he patently feels has become, for him, a worn-out, irrecoverable tradition.

Another way of putting all this is to say that the lost land Morris describes, his first home in Yazoo City, is irrevocably lost to him in two senses. In the first and most obvious sense, it is lost to him because he says it is. *North Toward Home* records in detail how Morris developed from small-town boy in the Deep South to cosmopolitan journalist, one of the editors of *Harpers* magazine. From Yazoo City to the University of

Texas, from Texas to Oxford (where Morris was a Rhodes scholar), from Oxford via Texas to New York (which, like Wolfe, he refers to as "the Big Cave"): the life Morris recalls seems positively to invite the use of one of Thomas Wolfe's favourite images for describing *his* life – that of a centrifugal movement, a flight "outward through a series of pressure chambers" (to quote one of Wolfe's biographers) "each widening his horizon and freeing him a little more".[24] And as the movement accelerates, so Morris carefully measures his disengagement from his original homeplace in the South. As far as this disengagement is concerned, a crucial moment occurred, Morris tells us, during a visit to Yazoo City that he paid while at the University of Texas. As he drove back, he recalls, he had "the most overwhelming sense of coming *home*". "I was not merely stunned by the beauty of the countryside", he goes on, "I was surprised to feel so settled inside, as if nothing . . . could destroy my belonging." Back in Yazoo City, he was told by one of the locals, "It's the same old place. It won't ever change much"; and reassured by this he soon settled back into the familiar routines, passing the time with his father, talking to old friends, or just sitting and lazing around. But then something happened, he remembers. A meeting was organised at the school auditorium, in response to the news that the N.A.A.C.P. had selected Yazoo City as one of five places in the state in which to test the recent Supreme Court decision on desegregation. Morris went along, more out of curiosity than anything else; and, within a short time of arriving, listening to the speeches, hearing about plans to set up a White Citizens' Council, he felt "a strange and terrible disgust" welling up within him. "I looked back and saw my father", he says,

> sitting still and gazing straight ahead; on the stage my friends' fathers nodded their heads . . . I felt an urge to get out of there. *Who are these people?* I asked myself. What was I doing there? Was this the place I had grown up in and never wanted to leave? I knew in that instant, in the middle of a mob in the school auditorium, that a mere three years in Texas had taken me irrevocably, even without my recognising it, from home.[25]

It is difficult to exaggerate the importance of this episode. Morris remained close to his family, he assures us, and kept in touch with many of his former friends and neighbours. But the experience in the school auditorium clearly signalled a break, a moment of total disjuncture; from then on, he had to leave the South behind, with all that he loved there and hated, and look for another version of home.

Like many other Southern writers in this vein, though, Morris is intent on something more than autobiography. For he clearly sees his gradual exile from the South and alienation from the Southern inheritance as representative; and he is constantly reminding us how his own flight to the North was and is part of a general movement. At every stage of his transmigration, from small rural town to big city to suburb, he does not hesitate to turn aside for a moment from biography to history, so as to show how his own personal story can be included within a larger drama. As he was leaving the region for other places, he points out, many others were too. Many other young people, besides him, got their first whiff of a larger, international culture at great state universities like the University of Texas; many of them went to New York – or, if not New York, to Los Angeles perhaps or Chicago – in search of wealth and fame; and most of them began retreating to the suburbs in the 1960s just as Morris did, as "the big cities of America" began "falling into extraordinary chaos and decay". Not only that, Morris insists, those who stayed in the South were not rendered immune. Many of them moved too, to "the sprawling and suburbanized cities of the New South – Atlanta, Memphis, New Orleans, Birmingham, Nashville". And even if they did not go out to meet the new culture it came in to meet them. Even Yazoo City, he points out, "developed its own suburbia"; in the city centre the smaller stores were replaced by "the Yankee chains advertised on national television", and only a few of the familiar spots survived. The very portrait of Morris's childhood home, quoted earlier, is prefaced by a cautionary note. "All this was before the advent of a certain middle-class prosperity", Morris warns us, "before the big supermarkets and the neighbourhood 'shopping centers' . . ."[26] Yazoo City has become lost, it seems, even to itself; even those who never made the actual journey northwards appear to have been spiritually translated there.

And then there is the other sense in which *North Toward Home* is the tale of a lost land: formally, that is, in terms of the myths it commemorates. Mention has already been made of the language, and the peculiar feeling of *déjà vu* it radiates; the same holds true for many of the other aspects of the book – its codes, or language in a broader sense. Reading Morris's account of his life, especially his early life, is often like reading a composite narrative; a story full of old tales and talking, not in the way that Faulkner meant, but to the extent that it mixes together traditional gestures and figures and rehearses many familiar events. It is a book that seems to be built upon repetition and re-enactment: rituals that in this case do not so much revitalise the legends as offer them the chance for one last, farewell performance. Given the half-and-half nature of Morris's Southern homeplace, as he describes it, these legends not surprisingly include elements of both the populist and the patriarchal. Morris's father, for example, is described in terms that recall the sturdy rural figures of populist myth. "He was thin and gaunt", Morris says, a hunter and a fisherman . . . He was *country*, in the way that he was tuned to its rhythms and its cycles; he and his Tennessee people were simple, trustworthy, straightforward, and good as grass.[27]

Morris's mother, by contrast, and her family fit more comfortably within the patriarchal framework: they were "of the Deep South", we are told, "emotional, changeable, touched with charisma and given to histrionic flourishes". One member of this family, a certain Henry Foote, a great-great-uncle, enshrines the violence and glamour of the past for his great-great-nephew just as Faulkner's Bayard Sartoris did for *his*: he was "an erratic, courageous bantam of a man", Morris claims, a distinguished and combative politician with a taste for "fervid rhetoric". Another, "grandmother Mamie", born in 1878 and still surviving in 1967, is presented as the "fount of unquestioning lore",[28] and in particular a precious source of stories about the Civil War, just as Faulkner's "Aunt Jenny" Dupre is. There are tales of hunting in "the old primordial wilderness" of the delta that recall the adventures of Ike McCaslin, and anecdotes about the habits of " 'redneck' boys" ("they . . . ran to violence of a general kind, and . . . performed unique acts on an instant's whim") that echo anyone from Twain through Faulkner, Wolfe, and Erskine Caldwell to Flannery O'Connor. There are stories about the "spooked-up and romantic" atmosphere of a small town in the Deep South that might have been written by Welty; and there are references to the omnipresence of blacks ("And always there were the Negroes, the white Southerners' awareness of them – their voices and expressions and gestures . . . they obsessed me"),[29] allusions of a kind so deeply embedded in Southern writing that it seems wrong to identify them with one particular author. None of these stories, allusions, or anecdotes is presented in an overtly self-conscious, narcissistic way – as, say, Truman Capote or Tennessee Williams might present them – nor in the parodic fashion that Walker Percy favours. The manner is more relaxed than this, the tone much easier and mellower. It is as if Morris is recalling and rehearsing a twilight kingdom of remembered fictions, a landscape dwarfed by distance: which, in a manner of speaking, is precisely what he is doing. His book is about disjuncture, loss, and substitution. To be more precise, it is concerned with the process whereby one version of home – one particular, fictive notion of attachment and identity – was gradually replaced by another. So when he returns, in imagination, to the discarded fiction, it is appropriate and inevitable that it should appear as just that: discarded – inoperative and diminished.

Which is not to say that the South no longer haunts or attracts Morris, or that he returns to it only in imagination; on the contrary, his book ends with a detailed account of just one of many trips southward he made, this time in 1965 in the company of his son. It is on this trip, in particular, that he notices the changes that have occurred: the way in which certain familiar landmarks in and around Yazoo City have disappeared or (even worse) been "restored" so that their pictures can appear in travelogues – or the fact that so many of his childhood friends have departed for other places, and that so many of those who remained behind now live in "row after row of split-levels" that seem "not much different from Pleasant-ville or Hawthorne on the Harlem River line". "It was time to get out" of Yazoo City, Morris recalls, and his account of his visit concludes with a car ride he, his son, his mother and grandmother Mamie took to a nearby cemetery where many of his ancestors were buried. It is not difficult to catch the echo of familiar voices again here. Southern writing is, after all, full of scenes in graveyards: scenes in which the protagonist's attempt to commune with the dead becomes a figure for a larger ambition, to achieve vital contact with the past. Tate's "Ode to the Confederate Dead" is only the most obvious example. And yet, for once at least, those voices are echoed with a difference; this is not simply another case of *déjà vu*. They looked "hard enough" for the family gravestones, Morris tells us:

> but we could not find . . . a single one of them . . . We searched in the weeds and stickers on the hill where Mamie thought they had been laid away. "Well, I *thought* they were here somewhere", she said . . . Finally, we found what must have been the plot – the remnants of a fence, the unrecognizable stumps of gravestones, covered now with dark, moist weeds. "I guess they're here somewhere", Mamie said, "but you'd never know it."[30]

At least Tate's protagonist (one is tempted to point out) manages to find and identify the gravestones; having done this he can temporarily re-create a vision of traditional faith. Morris, however, is denied such a vision, and left with very few fragments he could shore against his ruins, even supposing that this is what he wants. The story of the South, no matter how much it may appeal to him at times, can no longer fill his imagination; he no more belongs to it than it belongs to him. And the traditions of the South, all that is implied by Tate's memorable phrase, "the immoderate past" – these no longer survive for him in coherent, recognisable form; he cannot look to them for anchorage and identity. So he has, for good or ill, to accept the path he has taken: the book finishes, in fact, with him returning to New York, feeling as he does so "some easing of a great burden". His journey takes him in the end where he evidently believes nearly all of his generation must go, if not in a literal sense then at least figuratively: which is, as the very last words of his autobiography remind us "north toward home".

Richard Weaver fervently prophesying a return to the house of his fathers from his rented rooms in Chicago, Willie Morris scrabbling about in the graveyard for some memorial to *his* fathers and then returning with relief to his home in New York: these images seem appropriate ones with which to end this account of the present, divided thinking of the region. They provide an appropriate postscript, too, to the larger story: the story told in this book of some of the attempts made over the last few hundred years to write the South. They cannot supply a conclusion, and not merely because – as the greatest of all Southern writers realised – no story is ever finished. There is, in addition to this, the simple fact that *this* story has arrived at a moment of exceptional crisis – exceptional, that is, even for the crisis-ridden South – and we can only speculate, for now, as to the eventual outcome. My own belief, as I hope I have made clear, is that the substantial innovations that have occurred in the historical fabric of the region will lead to equally substantial innovations in its thinking (although not necessarily innovations of the kind that more liberal commentators look for – it is, after all, perfectly possible to embrace the new, post-industrial world *and* be a certain, anti-historicist sort of conservative). However, this *is* only a guess, an inference based on some of the available evidence. Other evidence is ambiguous or seems to point in the opposite direction; and there are still quite a few voices ready to argue in favour of continuity rather than change. One is left, really, with the suspicion that the Southern subculture may survive for some while, as many observers from inside the South and out of it have suggested, and with the related feeling that the business of writing the region may persist indefinitely too, in ways anticipated by people as otherwise different as Eudora Welty and Richard Weaver. Something that Faulkner said about that most autobiographical of his characters, Quentin Compson, is perhaps worth quoting here; for, although Quentin – like his creator – belonged to an earlier generation, the compulsions by which he lived, and the absent presences by which he was haunted, have evidently not lost all of their power. "His very body was an empty hall echoing with sonorous defeated names", Faulkner says of his young protagonist; "he was not a being, an entity, he was a commonwealth. He was a barracks filled with stubborn back-looking ghosts . . ."[31] Like Quentin, many Southerners continue even now to root their identities in the history of their place and then re-create that history in the act of remembering it. The South may be primarily an idea, a matter of "names" waiting to be spoken and "ghosts" seeking resurrection: still, it can hardly be called an idea that has outlived its time – not for everyone, at least, not entirely, not yet.

Notes

PREFACE

1. W.J. Cash, *The Mind of the South* (1941; New York, 1960 edition) p. vii.
2. William Faulkner, *Absalom, Absalom!* (1936; London, 1937 edition), p. 174.

1 VIRGINIA AND THE ARGUMENTS FOR THE SOUTH

1. Wesley Frank Craven, *Dissolution of the Virginia Company: The Failure of a Colonial Experiment* (New York, 1958), p. 24.
2. *The Three Charters of the Virginia Company of London, with Seven Related Documents, 1606–1621*, Jamestown 350th Anniversary Historical Booklets (Richmond, Va., 1957), p. 2; Robert Gray, *A Good Speed to Virginia* (London, 1609), p. 4.
3. William Symonds, *Virginia: A Sermon Preached at White-Chapel* (London, 1609), p. 19. See, e.g., George M. Trevelyan, *English Social History* (London, 1946), p. 119; Godfrey Davies, *The Early Stuarts, 1607–1660* (Oxford, 1937), p. 92; Mildred Campbell, *The English Yeoman Under Elizabeth and the Early Stuarts* (New Haven, Conn., 1942), pp. 64–104.
4. Hugh Latimer, "The First Sermon Preached before King Edward, March 8th, 1549", in *Sermons by Hugh Latimer* edited by George E. Currie (2 vols.; Cambridge, 1844–5), II, 100.
5. Philip Stubbes, *Anatomie of Abuses* (London, 1585), p. 69a. See also, Sir Thomas More, *Utopia*, in *The Complete Works of Sir Thomas More* edited by Edward L. Surtz et al. (New Haven, 1963–), IV, 67; Robert Crowley, *The Way to Wealth*, in *The Select Works of Robert Crowley* edited by J.M. Cowper (London, 1872), p. A3.
6. "Now a Dayes", in *Ballads from MS* edited by Frederick J. Furnivall (2 vols.; London, 1868–73), I, 97, lines 157–60. See also, Thomas Bastard, *Chrestoleros* (London, 1598), Bk iii, Ep. 22.
7. See, e.g., "Vox populi, Vox Dei", in Furnivall, *Ballads from MS*, I, 124, lines 7–9; also, Davies, *Early Stuarts*, p. 271.
8. For a full analysis of this distinction see, Campbell, *English Yeoman*, pp. 20ff.
9. William Stafford, *A Compendious or Briefe Examination of Certayne Ordinary Complaints of Divers of our Countrymen in these our Dayes ...*, New Shakespeare

Society Reprint (London, 1876), series vi, iii, 3b. See also, William Harrison, *Harrison's Description of England in Shakespeare's Youth: Being the Second and Third Books of His "Description of Britain and England"* edited by Frederick J. Furnivall (2 vols.; London, 1876), I, 12–13; Campbell, *English Yeoman*, p. 16.

10. Thomas Fuller, "The Good Yeoman", in *The Holy State and the Profane State* (London, 1642), p. 117.

11. "A Pleasant New Dialogue; or, The Discourse Between The Serving-man and the Husband-man", in *Roxburghe Ballads* edited by William Chappell and Joseph W. Ebsworth (9 vols.; London, 1871–1899), I, 305. See also, *The Kentish Garland* edited by Julia H.L. De Vayne (2 vols., Hertford, 1881), I, 6–7.

12. Fuller, "Good Yeoman", p. 116.

13. Francis Bacon, *Essays Civil and Moral* (1625; London, 1937 edition), p. 205. See also, Latimer, "First Sermon", pp. 100–2; Thomas Overbury, "A Franklin", in *The Overburian Characters* edited by W.J. Paylor (London, 1936), pp. 78–9. For further examples of the qualities traditionally attributed to the yeoman see, Sir John Coke, *The Debate Betweene the Heraldes of Englande and France* (London, 1550), p. 21; Sir John Fortescue, *The Difference Between an Absolute and Limited Monarchy* (London, 1714), p. 90; and the "ballads of yeoman minstrelsy" (a term used by Edmund Chambers, in *English Literature at the Close of the Middle Ages* (Oxford, 1945)), most easily available in Frederick J. Child's *English and Scottish Ballads* edited by Helen C. Sargent and George L. Kittredge (Cambridge, Mass., 1904), nos. 115–54 (see, especially, the summary of Robin Hood's qualities given by Child on p. 255, preceding no. 117).

14. See, e.g., Sir Cornelius Vermuyden, *Discourse Touching the Drayning of the Great Fennes* (London, 1642); also, Robert Powell, *Depopulation Arraigned, Convicted, and Condemned* (London, 1636), p. 7; "Vox Populi, Vox Dei", p. 129, lines 212–13; Latimer, "First Sermon", p. 100. Also of interest here is Arthur Johnson's *The Disappearance of the Small Landowner* (Oxford, 1909), pp. 75ff.

15. Richard Hakluyt, Pamphlet for the Virginia Enterprise, in *The Original Writings and Correspondence of the Two Richard Hakluyts* edited by Eva G.R. Taylor, Hakluyt Society Reprint (2 vols.; London, 1935), I, 340.

16. Sir George Peckham, "Preface", to *The Voyages and Colonising Enterprises of Sir Humphrey Gilbert* edited by David B. Quinn, Hakluyt Society Reprint (2 vols.; London, 1927), I, 462.

17. "M.J.H., His Opinion of the Intended Voyage", in *Voyages of Sir Humphrey Gilbert*, I, 438, lines 12–16.

18. *Discourse Concerning Western Planting* in *Writings and Correspondence*, II, 233.

19. Ibid., p. 234.

20. Ibid., p. 235.

21. See William Bullock, *Virginia Impartially Examined* (London, 1649), p. 44.

22. Royal Proclamation, Dec. 23, 1617.

23. John Donne, "A Sermon Preached to the Virginia Company, 1622", in *The Works of John Donne* edited by H. Alford (6 vols.; London, 1839), VI, 232; Gray, *Good Speed to Virginia*, p. 4.

24. W. Crashawe, "Epistle Dedicatorie" to Alexander Whitaker, in *Good Newes from Virginia* (London, 1617), p. 6.

25. Edward Williams, *Virginia, More Especially the South Part Thereof, Richly and Truly Valued* (1650), in *Tracts and Other Papers Relating Principally to the Origin, Settlement, and Progress of the Colonies in North America* edited by Peter Force (4 vols.; New York, 1947), III, 11. See also, Symonds, *Virginia: A Sermon*, p. 9; Ralph Hamor, *A True Discourse of the Present Estate of Virginia* (London, 1615), p. 51; [Governor William Berkeley], *A True Declaration of the Estate of the Colonie in Virginia*, in Force, *Tracts*, III.

26. Robert Rich, *News from Virginia* (London, 1610), p. 5. For the other quotations here see, Symonds, *Virginia, A Sermon*, p. 26; Robert Johnson, *The New Life of Virginia* (London, 1612), p. 17. See also, Lewis P. Simpson, *The Dispossessed Garden: Pastoral and History in Southern Literature* (Baton Rouge, La., 1975), especially pp. 14–15; J.V. Ridgely, *Nineteenth-Century Southern Literature* (Lexington, Ky., 1980), pp. 3–9.

27. John Hammond, *Leah and Rachel; or, The Two Fruitfull Sisters, Virginia and Maryland* (London, 1656), p. 19. For the other quotations in this paragraph see, Symonds, *Virginia: A Sermon*, pp. 19, 26, 40; Robert Rich, *The New Life of Virginia* (London, 1612), p. 17; Hamor, *True Discourse*, p. 50; Whitaker, *Good Newes*, p. 43; John Rolfe, *A True Relation of the State of Virginia, Lefte . . . in May Last 1616* (New Haven, Conn., 1951 edition), p. 39; Williams, *Virginia*, p. 5.

28. Bullock, *Virginia Impartially Examined*, pp. 34, 51. Cf. Hamor, *True Discourse*, pp. 21–2; Whitaker, *Good Newes*, p. 43; Hammond, *Leah and Rachel*, p. 19.

29. Bullock, *Virginia Impartially Examined*, pp. 14–31.

30. See Wesley Frank Craven, *The Virginia Company of London, 1606–1624*, Jamestown 350th Anniversary Historical Booklets (Richmond, Va., 1957), p. 86; Instructions to Governor Yeardley, Nov. 18, 1618, in *Three Charters of the Virginia Company*, pp. 95–108; Richard Lee Morton, *Colonial Virginia* (2 vols.; Chapel Hill, N.C., 1963), I, 41–2.

31. Bullock, *Virginia Impartially Examined*, p. 44.

32. "The Ruyn of a Ream", in Furnivall, *Ballads From MS*, I, 159, lines 15–18.

33. Quinn, *Colonising Enterprises of Sir Humphrey Gilbert*, I, 188.

34. Ibid., II, 245–78, 313–26.

35. Ibid., p. 277. See also, pp. 249, 276.

36. William Byrd of Westover, Letter to Charles Boyle, Earl of Orrery, July 5, 1726, cited in *The London Diary and Other Writings* edited by Louis Booker Wright and Marion Tinling (New York, 1958), p. 37. See also Simpson, *Dispossessed Garden*, pp. 17–24.

37. On these and related questions see, e.g., John R. Alder, *The South in Revolution, 1767–1789* (1957), vol. III of *The History of the South* edited by Wendell Holmes Stephenson and E. Merton Coulter (10 vols.; Baton Rouge, La., 1947–67), pp. 26–32; Morton, *Colonial Virginia*, I, 144; Thomas J. Wertenbaker, *The Planters of Colonial Virginia* (Princeton, 1922), pp. 84–100 and *The Old South: The Founding of American Civilization* (New York, 1942), pp. 19–30; Louis B. Wright, *The First Gentlemen of Virginia: Intellectual Qualities of the Early Ruling Class* (San Marino, Calif., 1940), pp. 41–2.

38. Robert Beverley II, *The History and Present State of Virginia* (London, 1722), p. 249. See also, p. 247.

39. Rev. Andrew Burnaby, *Travels Through the Middle Settlements in North America in the Years 1759 and 1760* (London, 1798), p. 25. For fuller discussions of the matters considered in these paragraphs see, e.g., Charles M. Andrews, *The Colonial Period of American History* (4 vols.; New York, 1934–8); David Bertelson, *The Lazy South* (New York, 1967); Carl B. Bridenbaugh, *Myths and Realities: Societies in the Colonial South* (Baton Rouge, La., 1952); Philip A. Bruce, *Economic History of Virginia in the Seventeenth Century* (2 vols.; New York, 1896), *Institutional History of Virginia in the Seventeenth Century* (2 vols.; New York, 1910), and *Social Life of Virginia in the Seventeenth Century* (Richmond, Va., 1927); Richard B. Davis, *Literature and Society in Early Virginia, 1608–1840* (Baton Rouge, La., 1973), and *Intellectual Life in the Colonial South, 1585–1763* (3 vols.; Knoxville, Tenn., 1978); Morton, *Colonial Virginia*; Charles S. Sydnor, *Gentlemen Freeholders: Political Practices in Washington's Virginia* (Chapel Hill, N.C., 1952); Wertenbaker, *Planters of Colonial Virginia*; Wright, *First Gentlemen*.

40. William Fitzhugh, *William Fitzhugh and his Chesapeake World, 1676–1701: The*

Fitzhugh Letters and Other Documents edited by Richard B. Davis (Chapel Hill, N.C., 1963), p. 215. To N. Hayward, May 20, 1691.

41. Robert "King" Carter, *Letters of Robert Carter, 1720–1727: The Commercial Interests of a Virginia Gentleman* edited by Louis B. Wright (San Marino, Calif., 1940), pp. 105–6. To John Johnson, June 22, 1721. See also p. 5. To R. Perry, July 13, 1720.

42. Louis Morton, *Robert Carter of Nomini Hall: A Virginia Tobacco Planter Of the Eighteenth Century* (Williamsburg, Va., 1941), pp. 161–85. Compare Eugene Genovese, *The World the Slaveholders Made: Two Essays in Interpretation* (New York, 1969). Concentrating on the nineteenth century, Genovese argues that the "acquisitiveness of Southern planters did not make them bourgeois" (p. 142). In my opinion, this argument carries no more conviction when applied to the ante-bellum period than it does if applied to the colonials.

43. Cited in Wright and Tinling, *London Diary*, pp. 37–8. To Charles Boyle, Earl of Orrery, July 5, 1726; to Mrs Armiger, undated.

44. *Letters*, p. 173. To Dorothy Fitzhugh, April 22, 1686. See also, p. 171. To Henry Fitzhugh, April 22, 1686.

45. Isaac Weld Jr, *Travels through the States of North America ... During the Years 1795, 1796, and 1797* (London, 1799), p. 44. See also, Marquis de Chastellux, *Travels in North America in the Years 1780, 1781, and 1782* (2 vols.; London, 1787), II, 201.

46. Burnaby, *Travels through the Middle Settlements*, p. 27.

47. Landon Carter, *The Diary of Colonel Landon Carter of Sabine Hall, 1752–1778* edited by Jack P. Greene (2 vols.; Charlottesville, Va., 1965), I, 292, 294, 431; II, 589, 633, 635, 1095. See also, William Byrd of Westover, *The Secret Diary of William Byrd of Westover, 1709–1712* edited by Louis B. Wright and Marion Tinling (Richmond, Va., 1941), pp. 281–94; Carter, *Letters*, p. 86. To ————, March 3, 1720. It is also perhaps worth noting that both Byrd and Carter were councillors, magistrates, and leaders of the militia before they were thirty-five: see *Executive Journals of the Council of Colonial Virginia, 1680–1739* edited by H.R. McIlwaine (5 vols.; Richmond, Va., 1925–45), I, 444; II, 221.

48. Chastellux, *Travels*, II, 202. See also, *Journal and Letters of Philip Vickers Fithian: A Plantation Tutor of the Old Dominion* edited by Hunter D. Farish (Williamsburg, Va., 1943), pp. 220–1.

49. Fitzhugh, *Letters*, p. 203. To N. Hayward, Jan. 30, 1686/7. See also, William Byrd of Westover, *History of the Dividing Line Betwixt Virginia and North Carolina*, in *The Prose Works of William Byrd of Westover* edited by Louis B. Wright (Cambridge, Mass., 1966), p. 279.

50. Published in 1622 and 1630 respectively. Both titles constantly recur in lists of library holdings given in Wright, *First Gentlemen*. The qualities mentioned here, courtesy, fortitude, temperance, liberality, hospitality, are discussed by Brathwaite on pp. 155, 68, 305, 65, and 372–3, respectively, of *English Gentleman* and demonstrated by Robert Carter of Nomini Hall, as described in Fithian, *Journal and Letters*, pp. 93, 14, 34–45, 76, and 39, respectively.

51. Beverley, *History of Virginia*, p. 252. See also, *The Journal of John Harrower: An Indentured Servant in the Colony of Virginia, 1773–1776* edited by Edward M. Riley (Williamsburg, Va., 1963), pp. 54–7; Fithian, *Journal and Letters*, pp. 35, 76–7; Carter, *Letters*, p. 78. To R. Smith, Feb. 14, 1720/21; Fitzhugh, *Letters*, pp. 363–4. To F. Hayward, July 21, 1698. Also of interest here is Richard Beale Davis's *Intellectual Life in Jefferson's Virginia, 1790–1830* (Chapel Hill, N.C., 1964), pp. 205–52.

52. Hugh Jones, *The Present State of Virginia* (1724; London, 1865 edition), p. 43.

53. Byrd, *History of Dividing Line*, p. 285. See also Byrd, letter to Charles Boyle, Earl of Orrery, July 5, 1726, cited in *London Diary*, p. 77.

54. Henry Hartwell, J. Blair, and E. Chilton, *The Present State of Virginia, and the College* (London, 1727), pp. 1–2.

55. Wright, *First Gentlemen*, pp. 212–34.
56. Beverley, *History of Virginia*, pp. 283–4. Cf. T. Cooper, *Some Information Respecting America* (London, 1794), p. 21.
57. Fitzhugh, *Letters*, p. 190. To N. Hayward, May 20, 1686. See also, p. 193. To Henry Fitzhugh, Jan. 30, 1686/7.
58. Peacham, *Compleat Gentleman*, p. 11.
59. *Journal of the House of Burgesses of Virginia, 1695–1702* edited by H.R. McIlwaine (Richmond, Va., 1931), p. 188.
60. Byrd, *Secret Diary*, p. 3. Entry for Feb. 12, 1709. For an interesting view of Byrd and his cultural background see, Pierre Marambaud, *William Byrd of Westover, 1674–1744* (Charlottesville, Va., 1971).
61. Clement Eaton, *Freedom of Thought in the Old South* (Durham, N.C., 1940), pp. 3–31; Davis, *Intellectual Life*, pp. 15–23. See also, Daniel J. Boorstin, *The Lost World of Thomas Jefferson* (New York, 1948).
62. Merrill D. Paterson, *The Jeffersonian Image in the American Mind* (New York, 1960).
63. "The republic which Jefferson believed himself to be founding . . . was an enlarged Virginia." Henry Adams, *History of the United States* (9 vols.; New York, 1891–1896), VI, 209. A still further reason is that Jefferson was, on occasion, inconsistent; see, Leo Marx, *The Machine in the Garden: Technology and the Pastoral Ideal in America* (New York, 1964), pp. 135–6. See also, Simpson, *Dispossessed Garden*, pp. 24–33.
64. *The Writings of Thomas Jefferson* edited by H.A Washington (9 vols.; New York, 1853–4), II, 485. To William Wirt, Aug. 5, 1815.
65. *The Papers of Thomas Jefferson* edited by Julian P. Boyd (Princeton, 1950–) II, 682. To Dr Currie, 1787.
66. François Alexandre Frédéric de la Rochefoucauld-Liancourt, *Voyage dans Les États-Unis d'Amérique* (8 vols.; Paris, 1799), V, 32. See also, *Thomas Jefferson's Farm Book* edited by Edwin Morris Betts (Princeton, 1953), pp. 5–47; *Anas*, in *Writings*, IX, 147; *Writings*, VII, 64–5. To Dr J.B. Stuart, May 10, 1817; *Writings*, VI, 381. To Dr Copper, Sept. 10, 1814; *Notes on the State of Virginia* (London, 1787), Query 19.
67. *Writings*, IV, 318. To Dr Priestley, Jan. 27, 1800. See also, Draft of Instructions to the Virginia Delegates in the Continental Congress, July, 1774, published as *A Summary View of the Rights of British America*, in *Papers*, I, 137. For a more detailed discussion of Jefferson's use of the Anglo-Saxon reference see, Gilbert Chinard, *Thomas Jefferson: Apostle of Americanism* (Michigan, 1957).
68. *A Summary View*, p. 122. See also, pp. 86–7.
69. *Papers*, I, 442. To E. Pendleton, Aug. 13, 1776.
70. *Writings*, IV, 527. To John Jay, Feb. 1, 1804. See also, *A Summary View*, pp. 121–2; *Notes on Virginia*, Query 19; *Writings*, VII, 291–2. To Judge Johnson, June 12, 1823.
71. *Notes on Virginia*, Query 19. See also, *The Correspondence of Jefferson and Du Pont de Nemours* edited by Gilbert Chinard (Baltimore, 1931), pp. 163–4. To Dr Du Pont de Nemours, April 15, 1811; *Writings*, I, 403–5. To John Jay, Aug. 23, 1785; II, 332. To James Madison, Dec. 20, 1787; VI, 223–5. To J. Adams, Oct. 28, 1813; *Notes on Virginia*, Query 18.
72. *Papers*, VIII, 682. To James Madison, Oct. 28, 1785. The schemes mentioned here are to be found in *Papers* I, 632, and *Papers* VIII, 682. See also, *Writings*, III, 314. To A. Stuart, Dec. 23, 1791; *Notes on Virginia*, Query 11. Jefferson also seems to have considered self-subsistent farming the best solution for the Indians: see, Address to Captain Hendrick, the Delaware, Mohiccans, etc. in *Writings*, VIII, 226.
73. John Taylor of Caroline, *An Inquiry into the Principles and Policy of the United States* (1814; New Haven, Conn., 1950 edition), p. 274. See also p. 255.
74. See, e.g., *Writings*, III, 557. To —, May 13, 1793; VI, 346. To J.F. Watson, May 17, 1814. Jefferson also doubted that the peasants of France and South America could exercise the right of suffrage: see, *The Letters of Lafayette and Jefferson* edited by

Gilbert Chinard (Baltimore, Md., 1924), pp. 327, 390. To Lafayette, Feb. 14, 1815 and May 14, 1817.

75. *Notes on Virginia*, Query 9.
76. Mason, *The Life of George Mason 1725–1792, Including His Speeches, Public Papers, and Correspondence* edited by Kate Mason Rowland (2 vols.; New York, 1892), II, 33, 326. To G. Mason Jr, Jan. 8, 1783 and to J. Mason, May 20, 1790.
77. Lee, *The Letters of Richard Henry Lee* edited by James C. Ballagh (2 vols.; New York, 1914), II, 438. To George Mason, Oct. 1, 1787.
78. *Writings*, II, 332. To James Madison, Dec. 20, 1787. See also, *Writings*, I, 403. To John Jay, Aug. 23, 1785; *Writings*, VI, 334–5. To H.G. Spafford, March 17, 1814.
79. *Writings*, VII, 64. To Dr J.B. Stuart, May 10, 1817. See also, II, 332. To James Madison, Dec. 20, 1787.
80. For a fuller discussion of these developments, see, e.g., Thomas P. Abernethy, *The South in the New Nation, 1789–1819* (1961), vol. VI in *History of the South* edited by Stephenson and Coulter; Robert V. Cotterill, *The Old South* (Glendale, Calif., 1939); Clement Eaton, *A History of the Old South* (London, 1949), and *The Growth of Southern Civilisation* (London, 1961); Lewis C. Gray, *History of Agriculture in the United States to 1860* (2 vols.; Washington, 1933); Charles S. Sydnor, *The Development of Southern Sectionalism, 1819–1848* (1948), vol. V of *History of the South* edited by Stephenson and Coulter; Francis B. Simkins and Charles P. Roland, *A History of the South* (New York, 1972).
81. Taylor, *An Inquiry*, pp. 259–60. See also, pp. 243, 482 and *American Farmer*, II (Sept. 15, 1820), 194–5.
82. *An Inquiry*, p. 490.
83. *Arator: Being a Series of Agricultural Essays, Practical and Political* (Baltimore, Md., 1817), p. 190. The whole essay, entitled "The Pleasures of Agriculture", from which this quotation is taken is worth reading in this context. In it, Taylor asserts that agriculture encourages the practice of "benevolence" and "liberality"; fosters a love of one's country and of liberty; and offers a fulfilment of the scriptural admonition to "feed the hungry, clothe the naked, and give drink to the thirsty" (pp. 178–9).
84. This process was neatly demonstrated by Jefferson in a letter to Gilmer, June 17, 1816. See, *Correspondence of Thomas Jefferson and Francis Walker Gilmer 1814–1826* edited by Richard B. Davis (Columbia, S.C., 1946), p. 4.
85. *An Inquiry*, p. 184. See also, pp. 142, 206, 256, 259–60, 283, 298, 354, 357, 582, 558–9.
86. Ibid., pp. 87, 89, 239, 255, 259, 266, 279.
87. Ibid., pp. 63, 85, 124, 230, 250, 311–12, 471–2, 485, 487–9, 530, 544.
88. For three interesting discussions of Taylor that adopt rather different approaches see, Charles Beard, *Economic Origins of Jeffersonian Democracy* (New York, 1927); Davis, *Intellectual Life*; E.T. Mudge, *The Social Philosophy of John Taylor of Caroline* (New York, 1939).
89. Cited in William Cabell Bruce, *John Randolph of Roanoke, 1773–1833* (2 vols.; New York, 1922), II, 652. Randolph was converted to Christianity later on in his life – but to the Anglican Church rather than the gloomy Calvinism he associated with the new age and more specifically with New England.
90. *Annals of Congress* (18th Cong., 1st sess.), 11, 2360; *Proceedings and Debates of the Virginia State Convention* (Richmond, Va., 1830), p. 313; Letter to his niece, July 7, 1825, cited in Bruce, *John Randolph*, II, 362; Letter to Josiah Quincy, Oct. 18, 1813, cited in Russell Kirk, *Randolph of Roanoke: A Study in Conservative Thought* (Chicago, 1951), p. 149.
91. Speech on 1822 Apportionment Bill, cited in Bruce, *John Randolph*, II, 222. See also, ibid., II, 221. Letter to Key, Sept. 7, 1818.

92. *Annals of Congress* (18th Cong., 1st sess.), II, 2359–60; *Register of Debates in Congress* (19th Cong., 2nd sess.), II, 125–6; *Annals* (7th Cong., 1st sess.), pp. 367–8; *Proceedings of Virginia State Convention*, pp. 492, 791, 802.

93. Letter to Dr Brockenbough, Feb. 9, 1829, cited in Bruce, *John Randolph*, II, 364–5. See also, Kirk, *Randolph of Roanoke*, p. 21.

94. Letter to George Hay, Jan. 6, 1806, Southern Historical Collection, University of North Carolina, Chapel Hill. See also, *Annals of Congress* (17th Cong., 1st sess.), p. 903; *Register of Debates in Congress* (19th Cong., 1st sess.), p. 117; *Annals* (14th Cong., 1st sess.), p. 1302; Bruce, *John Randolph*, I, 282.

95. Letter to J. Quincy, March 12, 1814, cited in Kirk, *Randolph of Roanoke*, p. 189.

96. Letter to his niece, July 27, 1825, cited in Bruce, *John Randolph*, II, 361. See also letter to Dr Brockenbough, cited in Hugh A. Garland, *The Life of John Randolph of Roanoke* (2 vols.; New York, 1850), II, 343; letter to Quincy, March 12, 1814, cited in Kirk, *Randolph of Roanoke*, p. 189; letter to F.W. Gilmer, March 11, 1825, cited in Bruce, *John Randolph*, II, 361; John Randolph, *Letters of John Randolph to a Young Relative* (Philadelphia, Pa., 1834), p. 233.

97. Letter to his niece, Christmas Day, 1828, cited in Bruce, *John Randolph*, II, 363. See also, ibid., II, 626.

98. Letter to Dr Brockenbough, 1827, cited in Bruce, *John Randolph*, II, 5. See also, I, 626. Speech during the Virginia Convention, 1829–30.

99. *Register of Debates in Congress* (19th Cong., 2nd sess.), II, 126.

100. *Annals of Congress* (18th Cong., 1st sess.), ii, 2359. Randolph went so far as to anticipate "civil war" between the sections on either side of this line. Letter to W. Wallace, March 17, 1832. Randolph MSS, Duke University Library, Durham, North Carolina.

2 HOLDING THE LINE IN THE OLD SOUTH

1. "The First Set of the Fundamental Constitutions of South Carolina, as Compiled by Mr John Locke", in *Historical Collections of South Carolina* edited by B.R. Carroll (2 vols.; New York, 1836), II, 362–8.

2. Ibid., p. 368. See also, pp. 362, 389.

3. E. Merton Coulter, *A Short History of Georgia* (Chapel Hill, N.C., 1933), p. 20.

4. For this and the following details see, Francis Moore, *A Voyage to Georgia* (London, 1744), pp. 3–10.

5. Edward Sapir, *Selected Writings in Language, Culture and Personality* edited by David G. Mandelbaum (Berkeley, Calif., 1949), p. 162. See also, Williams, *Virginia Richly and Truly Valued*, p. 19.

6. Benjamin Lee Whorf, *Language, Thought and Reality: Selected Writings of Benjamin Lee Whorf* edited by John B. Carroll (Cambridge, Mass., 1950), p. 213.

7. On these and related developments see, Monroe Lee Billington, *The American South: A Brief History* (New York, 1971), pp. 96ff.; Avery O. Craven, *The Growth of Southern Nationalism, 1846–1861* (1953), vol. VI in *History of the South* edited by Stephenson and Coulter, *The Coming of the Civil War* (Chicago, 1957), pp. 36–66, and *Civil War in the Making, 1815–1860* (Baton Rouge, La., 1961), pp. 50ff.; William and Bruce Catton, *Two Roads to Sumter* (New York, 1963), p. 70; Simkins and Roland, *History of the South*, pp. 167–78; Sydnor, *Southern Sectionalism*, pp. 104ff. For contemporary observations on the depression see, Capt. Basil Hall, *Travels in North America in the Years 1827 and 1828* (3 vols.; London, 1833), I, 12, 41, 238; Capt. Robert Barclay-Allardice, *Agricultural Tour in the United States* (London, 1842), p. 99; George W. Featherstonhaugh, *Excursion Through the Slave States* (2 vols.; London, 1844), II, 129; Alexander Mackay, *Travels in the United States in 1846–1847* (3 vols.;

London, 1849), III, 69; William Chambers, *Things as they are in America* (London, 1854), p. 269.

8. *Register of Debates in Congress* (21st. Cong., 1st sess.), p. 33. See also John Caldwell Calhoun, Speech on the Tariff Bill, in *The Works of John C. Calhoun* edited by Richard K. Cralle (6 vols.; New York, 1958 edition), IV, 184; Charles Mackay, *Life and Liberty in America* (2 vols.; London, 1859), II, 37. For contemporary observations on the growth and movement of population see, William N. Blane, *An Excursion through the United States and Canada* (London, 1824), pp. 202–3; Sir Charles Lyell, *A Second Visit to the United States of America* (2 vols.; London, 1845), II, 60, 63, 109.

9. For these and related details see, Eaton, *Freedom of Thought*, pp. 162–217; Sydnor, *Southern Sectionalism*, pp. 178–9.

10. Speech on the Slave Question, in *Works*, IV, 348.

11. *Correspondence of John C. Calhoun* edited by J. Franklin Jameson. Annual Report of the American Historical Association, 1899 (2 vols.; Washington, 1900), II, 325. To T.G. Holland and others, July 25, 1833. See also, "A Disquisition on Government", in *Works*, I, 5; Speech on the Oregon Bill, in *Works*, IV, 245; *Correspondence*, II, 753. To Mrs T.G. Clemson, April 28, 1848; Remarks on the States Rights Resolutions, in *Works*, III, 148; *Correspondence*, II, 210. To S.L. Gouvernour, Feb. 13, 1832; II, 317. To C. Van Deventer, March 31, 1832; II, 443. To J.H. Hammond, Jan. 25, 1840.

12. "Disquisition on Government", p. 49. See also, pp. 15, 50; "A Discourse on the Constitution and Government of the United States", in *Works*, I, 131; *Correspondence*, II, 758, 767. To Mrs T.G. Clemson, June 23, 1848, and June 15, 1849.

13. "Disquisition on Government", pp. 1–2. See also, pp. 7–8.

14. Remarks on the States Rights Resolutions, p. 180. See also, Speech on the Bill granting Pre-emption Rights, in *Works*, III, 135.

15. Speech on the Abolition Petitions, in *Works*, II, 632.

16. Mark Twain, *The Adventures of Huckleberry Finn* (1885; London, 1968 edition), p. 222.

17. Frances Anne Kemble, *Journal of A Residence on a Georgian Plantation in 1838–1839* (1839; London, 1961 edition), pp. 110–111.

18. For contemporary observations on the impact of slavery on white society see, Harriet Martineau, *Society in America* (3 vols.; London, 1837), II, 311; James S. Buckingham, *The Slave States of America* (2 vols.; London, 1842), II, 537; Frederick Law Olmsted, *A Journey to the Seaboard Slave States* (2 vols.; London, 1856), II, 153; James Stirling, *Letters from the Slave States* (London, 1857), p. 47; Benjamin H. Latrobe, *The Journal of Latrobe* (New York, 1905), p. 34. See also W.J. Cash's account of the South's "tragic descent into unreality" (p. 50) in *Mind of the South*.

19. Speech on the Oregon Bill, in *Works*, IV, 507–8. See also, *Correspondence*, II, 671. To J.H. Hammond, Aug. 30, 1845. For a fuller discussion of how the paternalist spirit could impinge on the relationships between whites see, Eugene D. Genovese, *Roll, Jordan, Roll: The World the Slaves Made* (1974; New York, 1976 edition), pp. 91ff.

20. *Correspondence*, II, 374. To D. Green, July 27, 1837. See also, II, 319. To J.E. Calhoun, April 28, 1832; II, 494. To J. Van Buren and others, 29 Sept., 1841; Address to the People of the United States, in *Works*, VI, 200; Speech on the Bill to Regulate Public Deposits, in *Works*, II, 553–4.

21. [John C. Calhoun], *Life of John C. Calhoun, 1811–1843* (New York, 1843), p. 74. See also, Address on Taking the Chair of the South-western Convention, in *Works*, VI, 280; T.C. Grattan, *Civilised America* (2 vols.; London, 1859), I, 182. For a thoroughgoing discussion of Calhoun see, Charles M. Wiltse, *John C. Calhoun: Nationalist, 1782–1828* (New York, 1944), *John C. Calhoun: Nullifier, 1829–1839* (New York, 1949), and *John C. Calhoun: Sectionalist, 1840–1850* (New York, 1951). For two

very different views see, Margaret L. Coit, *John C. Calhoun: American Portrait* (London, 1950), and Gerald M. Caspers, *John C. Calhoun, Opportunist: A Re-appraisal* (Gainesville, Fla., 1964).

22. *Russell's Magazine*, I (May, 1857), 178, cited in John Hope Franklin, *The Militant South* (Cambridge, Mass., 1968), p. 222.
23. Olmsted, *Seaboard Slave States*, II, 136. For a fuller discussion of the developments mentioned here see, Sydnor, *Southern Sectionalism*, pp. 257–93.
24. Speech in the Senate, *Congressional Globe* (35th Cong., 2nd sess.), p. 1568.
25. John Joseph Craven, *The Prison Life of Jefferson Davis* (London, 1866), p. 88.
26. James D.B. De Bow, *The Industrial Resources of the Southern and Western States* (3 vols.; New Orleans, 1852), II, 197. See also, III, 35.
27. Ibid., III, 67.
28. Ibid., I, 77.
29. Cited in John W. Du Bose, *The Life and Times of William Lowndes Yancey* (2 vols.; New York, 1942), I, 301.
30. Speech in the Senate, *Congressional Globe* (31st Cong., 1st sess.), p. 1643. See also John Pendleton Kennedy, *Swallow Barn; or, A Sojourn in the Old Dominion* (1832; New York, 1872 edition), pp. 445–6.
31. *The Correspondence of Robert Toombs, Alexander H. Stephens, and Howell Cobb* edited by Ulrich B. Phillips. Annual Report of the American Historical Association, 1912 (Washington, 1913), p. 7. To J.H. Smith, May 8, 1860.
32. *Congressional Globe* (36th Cong., 2nd sess.), pp. 328–30. See also, pp. 77–8.
33. Frederick L. Olmsted, *A Journey in the Back Country* (2 vols.; 1856; New York, 1904 edition), I, 63. See also, Buckingham, *Slave States*, II, 8; also Fredrika Bremer, *The Homes of the New World* translated by M. Howitt (2 vols.; London, 1853), I, 282.
34. James H. Hammond, Speech in the Senate, *Annals of Congress* (24th Cong., 1st sess.), p. 2456. For a fuller discussion of the issues discussed here see, Genovese, *Roll, Jordan, Roll*, pp. 25–49; Charles G. Sellers, "The Travail of Slavery", in *The Southerner as American* edited by C.G. Sellers (Chapel Hill, N.C., 1960); Kenneth Stampp, *The Peculiar Institution* (London, 1964), p. 312.
35. Joseph Glover Baldwin, *The Flush Times of Alabama and Mississippi* (New York, 1853), pp. 79–80; Tyrone Power, *Impressions of America During the Years 1833, 1834, and 1835* (2 vols.; London, 1836), II, 235–6. See also, George Lewis, *Impressions of America and the American Churches* (Edinburgh, 1845), p. 119; Mackay, *Travels*, III, 35. Also, E.S. Abdy, *Journal of a Residence and Tour in the United States of America* (3 vols.; London, 1835), II, 218, 354; Achille Murat, *A Moral and Political Sketch of the United States* (London, 1833), p. 352; Frances Trollope, *Domestic Manners of the Americans* (2 vols.; London, 1832), II, 42; Bishop Whipple, *Bishop Whipple's Southern Diary* edited by L.B. Shippee (Minneapolis, Minn., 1937), pp. 43–4.
36. On this and related points see, Howard R. Floan, *The South in Northern Eyes, 1831–1861* (New York, 1958).
37. Dorothy Lee, "Lineal and nonlineal codifications of reality", in *Explorations in Communication* edited by Edmund Carpenter and Marshall McLuhan (Boston, Mass., 1960), p. 136.
38. Cited in Jay B. Hubbell, *The South in American Literature* (Durham, N.C., 1954), p. 582. All quotations from Simms's correspondence are either from Hubbell's book or from *The Letters of William Gilmore Simms* edited by Mary C. Simms Oliphant, Alfred T. Odell, and T.C. Duncan Greaves (Columbia, S.C., 1952–6). Biographical information is drawn from J.V. Ridgely, *William Gilmore Simms* (New York, 1962). One discussion of Simms I have found especially useful is Simone Vauthier, "Of Time and the South: The Fiction of William Gilmore Simms", *Southern Literary Journal* (Fall, 1972).

39. Cited in Hubbell, *South in American Literature*, p. 585.
40. Ibid., p. 580.
41. William Gilmore Simms, "The Epochs and Events of American History", in *Views and Reviews in American Literature, History, and Fiction* (1845; Cambridge, Mass., 1962 edition), p. 32.
42. Ridgely, *Nineteenth-Century Southern Literature*, p. 68. See also, William Gilmore Simms, *Guy Rivers, The Outlaw: A Tale of Georgia* (3 vols.; New York, 1835), III, 71.
43. Simms, *The Partisan: A Tale of Revolution* (2 vols.; New York, 1835), I, 122.
44. *Eutaw; or, A Sequel to the Forayers* (New York, 1856), p. 12. See also, *Katharine Walton; or, The Rebel of Dorchester* (Philadelphia, 1851), p. 59; *The Forayers; or, The Raid of the Dog-Days* (New York, 1855), pp. 540–53.
45. *The Kinsmen; or, The Black Riders of the Congaree* (2 vols.; Philadelphia, Pa., 1841), I, 209–10.
46. *Katharine Walton*, p. 86.
47. *The Sword and the Distaff; or, "Fair, Fat, and Forty"* (1852; Philadelphia, Pa., 1853 edition), p. 53.
48. *The Partisan*, I, 121.
49. *Katharine Walton*, p. 80. See also, pp. 33, 110.
50. *The Forayers*, p. 86. See also, *The Partisan*, II, 10.
51. *The Partisan*, I, 100. See also, William R. Taylor, *Cavalier and Yankee: The Old South and American National Character* (London, 1963). *passim.*
52. *The Forayers*, pp. 140–1.
53. Ibid., p. 291.
54. Ibid., p. 294. See also, pp. 347–8, 381.
55. Ibid., p. 408. See also, p. 293.
56. *The Sword and the Distaff*, p. 123. See also, pp. 54, 111, 195, 210; *The Partisan*, I, 21, 115. Also, Taylor, *Cavalier and Yankee*, pp. 287–91.
57. *The Sword and the Distaff*, p. 213.
58. Ibid., pp. 327–8.
59. Ibid., p. 330. See also, p. 580.
60. William Alexander Caruthers, *The Kentuckian in New York; or, The Adventures of Three Southerners* (2 vols.; New York, 1834), II, 193–4.
61. James Kirke Paulding, *The Banks of the Ohio; or, Westward Ho!* (2 vols.; 1832; London, 1833 edition), I, 15–16. See also, I, 14, 28–9. Other stories that use the solution of westward emigration include, William Alexander Caruthers, *The Knights of the Horse-Shoe: A Traditionary Tale of the Cocked Hat Gentry in the Old Dominion* (2 vols.; Wetumpka, Ala., 1845); William Gilmore Simms, "Oakatibbe; or, The Choctaw Sampson", in *The Wigwam and the Cabin* (2 vols.; New York, 1845–1846).
62. *Westward Ho!*, I, 149. See also, II, 39, 172.
63. Caruthers, *The Kentuckian in New York*, I, 108. Among the discussions of Caruthers I have found particularly useful are Curtis Carroll Davis, *Chronicler of the Cavaliers: A Life of the Virginia Novelist, Dr. William A. Caruthers* (Richmond, Va., 1953), and Taylor, *Cavalier and Yankee*, pp. 205–24.
64. *The Cavaliers of Virginia; or, The Recluse of Jamestown* (2 vols.; New York, 1835), I, 16. See also, I, 76, 95, 99; II, 161. Much of this analysis draws on Taylor, *Cavalier and Yankee*, although Taylor argues that Caruthers did *not* have any "separate and distinct Southern destiny" in mind (p. 216). My belief, however, is that Caruthers was primarily concerned with that destiny: that, like Paulding, Tucker, and Simms, he was preoccupied with the decline of the region – and its possible recovery.
65. *The Cavaliers of Virginia*, I, 118. See also, I, 33, 137; II, 245.
66. Georg Lukács, *The Historical Novel* translated by Hannah and Stanley Mitchell (1962; London, 1969 edition), p. 36.

67. *The Cavaliers of Virginia*, II, 179. See also, I, 77; II, 120, 245.

68. Cited in Hubbell, *The South in American Literature*, pp. 424–5.

69. *The Partisan Leader: A Tale of the Future* (1836; Richmond, Va., 1862 edition), p. 36.

70. Ibid., pp. 74–5. See also, pp. 73, 144. Tucker is relying here, to some extent, on the image of Van Buren fostered by his political opponents: see Oliver P. Chitwood and Frank L. Owsley, *A Short History of the American People* (2 vols.; New York, 1943), I, 472.

71. *Annals of Congress* (16th Cong., 1st sess.), 414. See also, Anne Scott, *The Southern Lady: From Pedestal to Politics* (Chicago, 1970).

72. *The Partisan Leader*, p. 69.

73. Ibid., p. 136.

74. Ibid., p. 23. See also, pp. 141, 194. For another example of the Revolutionary analogy, see Laura A. White, *Robert Barnwell Rhett: The Father of Secession* (New York, 1930), p. 24.

75. See, e.g., Harriet Beecher Stowe, *Uncle Tom's Cabin; or, Life among the Lowly* (New York, 1852) and G.P.R. James *The Old Dominion* (3 vols.; London, 1856). For a fairly comprehensive discussion of Southern and Northern novels dealing with the aristocratic Old South see, Francis P. Gaines, *The Southern Plantation: A Study in the Development and Accuracy of a Tradition* (New York, 1924). An interesting recent account of the Cavalier myth, and its relation to Victorian culture is to be found in Daniel J. Singal, *The War Within: From Victorian to Modernist Thought in the South, 1919–1945* (Chapel Hill, N.C., 1982), pp. 11–36.

76. Baldwin, *Flush Times*, pp. 88–9.

77. For this and other aspects of Southwestern humour see, e.g., Walter Blair, *Native American Humor 1800–1900* (New York, 1937), and *Horse Sense in American Humor* (Chicago, 1942); Kenneth S. Lynn, *Mark Twain and Southwestern Humor* (Boston, Mass., 1959); Constance Rourke, *American Humor: A Study of the National Character* (New York, 1931). Lynn's controversial thesis concerning this humour is sometimes taken a little too easily on trust: see, e.g. Singal, *War Within*, p. 19.

78. *Flush Times*, pp. 92–3. See also, pp. 100–3.

79. Ibid., pp. 228–9.

80. Johnson Jones Hooper, *Some Adventures of Captain Simon Suggs, Late of the Tallapoosa Volunteers* (1845; Philadelphia, Pa., 1851 edition), pp. 53–4.

81. George Washington Harris, *Sut Lovingood: Yarns Spun by a "Nat'ral Born Durn'd Fool"* (New York, 1867), p. 67. See also, p. 172.

82. Ibid., pp. 106–7. See also, p. 19.

83. William Tappan Thompson, *The Chronicles of Pineville; Embracing Sketches of Georgia Scenes, Incidents, and Characters* (Philadelphia, Pa., 1847), p. 6.

84. *Major Jones's Sketches of Travel; Comprising the Scenes, Incidents, and Adventures of His Tour from Georgia to Canada* (Philadelphia, Pa., 1848), p. 22.

85. Ibid., p. 92. See also, p. 46; *Major Jones's Courtship; Detailed with Humorous Scenes, Incidents, and Adventures* (1843; Philadelphia, Pa., 1844 edition), pp. 12, 153. Major Jones also appears in some of the *Chronicles of Pineville* stories.

86. See, e.g., R.B. Nye and J.E. Morpurgo, *A History of the United States* (London, 1964), pp. 384–5.

87. Augustus Baldwin Longstreet, *Georgia Scenes: Characters, Incidents, etc., in the First Half-Century of the Republic* (1835; New York, 1848 edition), p. 53.

88. Ibid., p. 14. See also, p. 12.

89. Ibid., p. 15. See also, pp. 14, 17.

90. Ibid., p. 105. See also, pp. 82, 101.

91. See, e.g., Raymond Williams, *Culture and Society, 1780–1850* (London, 1958), pp. xiv–xv.

92. T.W. Lane, "The Thimble Game", in *Tall Tales of the South-West* edited by Franklin

J. Meine (New York, 1930), p. 374. See also, H.C. Jones, "McAlpin's Trip to Charleston", in *A Quarter Race in Kentucky; Illustrative of Scenes, Characters and Incidents throughout the "Universal Yankee Nation"* edited by William T. Porter (Philadelphia, Pa., 1846); " A Missourian", "Swallowing an Oyster Alive", in *The Big Bear of Arkansas; and Other Sketches Illustrative of Character and Incident in the South-West* edited by William T. Porter (Philadelphia, Pa., 1845).

93. Cited in Hubbell, *The South in American Literature*, p. 668. See also Porter, Preface to *The Big Bear of Arkansas*, p. viii; Baldwin, *Flush Times*, p. 1; Thompson, Preface to *Chronicles of Pineville*, p. 6.

3 THE NEW SOUTH, THE LOST CAUSE, AND THE RECOVERED DREAM

1. Eliza Frances Andrews, *The War-Time Journal of A Georgia Girl, 1864–1865* (New York, 1938), p. 371. Entry for August 18, 1865.

2. Among the few books I have found useful are Thomas J. Pressley, *Americans Interpret Their Civil War* (1954; New York 1965 edition), and Bell I. Wiley, *The Life of Johnny Reb: The Common Soldier of the Confederacy* (New York, 1945). Of related interest are David Aaron, *The Unwritten War* (New York, 1973); Robert A. Lively, *Fiction Fights to Civil War* (Chapel Hill, N.C., 1957); Edmund Wilson, *Patriotic Gore: Studies in the Literature of the Civil War* (New York, 1962).

3. The Reverend Dr Palmer, cited in John Esten Cooke, *A Life of General Robert E. Lee* (New York, 1871), p. 529.

4. Cited in Pressley, *Americans Interpret Their Civil War*, pp. 103–4. See also, Comer Vann Woodward, *The Origins of the New South, 1877–1913* (1951) vol. IX of *History of the South* edited by Stephenson and Coulter, pp. 51ff.

5. Alfred Roman, *The Military Operations of General Beauregard in the War Between the States, 1861 to 1865* (2 vols; New York, 1886), I, 1.

6. John Esten Cooke, *Wearing of the Gray; Being Personal Portraits, Scenes, and Adventures of the War* (New York, 1867), p. 17. See also, Edward A. Pollard, *The First Year of the War in America* (New York, 1863), p. 180; John Esten Cooke, *Mohun or, The Last Days of Lee and his Paladins* (New York, 1869), pp. 117, 204.

7. Cooke, *Wearing of the Gray*, pp. 17–18. See also, pp. 19, 24, 26, 37–8, 174; Cooke, *Mohun*, pp. 14, 107, 204; Edward A. Pollard, *Lee and His Lieutenants: Comprising the Early Life, Public Services, and Campaigns of R.E. Lee and his Companions* (New York, 1867), pp. 421–39.

8. Pollard, *Lee and his Lieutenants*, p. 738.

9. Cooke, *Wearing of the Gray*, p. 62.

10. Robert L. Dabney, *Life of Lieutenant-General Thomas J. Jackson*, (2 vols.; London, 1864–6), I, 108–9. See also, p. 40.

11. Roman, *Military Operations of General Beauregard*, I, 213; Edward A. Pollard, *The Second Year of the War* (New York, 1864), p. 57, and *Lee and his Lieutenants*, p. 586; William M. Polk, *Leonidas Polk: Bishop and General* (2 vols.; New York, 1965), I, 389; James A. Wyeth, *Life of General Nathan Bedford Forrest* (New York, 1899), pp. 3, 15, 49–51, 625–7.

12. Pollard, *Lee and his Lieutenants*, p. 55.

13. John W. Daniel, *Robert E. Lee: An Oration* (Savannah, Ga., 1883), p. 1. See also, Thomas Nelson Page, *General Lee, Man and Soldier*, (New York, 1909), p. 5; Fitzhugh Lee, *General Lee of the Confederate Army* (New York, 1894), p. 2; Armistead L. Long, *Memoirs of Robert E. Lee: His Military and Personal History* (London, 1886), p. 17.

14. John H. Chamberlayne, *Address on the Character of General Robert E. Lee* (New York, 1878), p. 2. See also John Esten Cooke, *A Life of General Robert E. Lee* (New York, 1870), p. 529; Archer Anderson, *Robert E. Lee: An Address* (Richmond, Va., 1890), p. 45.
15. Cooke, *Lee*, p. 527. See also, pp. 37, 488, 511; Robert Stiles, *Four Years Under Marse Robert* (New York, 1903), p. 22; Page, *Lee*, p. 153; Daniel, *Lee: An Oration*, p. 38; Cooke, *Mohun*, p. 14; John W. Jones, *Personal Reminiscences, Anecdotes and Letters of General Robert E. Lee* (New York, 1875), p. 69; Long, *Memoirs of Lee*, p. 131.
16. Page, *Lee*, p. 56. See also, p. 54; Cooke, *Lee*, pp. 2, 14, 37, 468; Jones, *Reminiscences of Lee*, pp. 169, 283; Anderson, *Lee: An Address*, pp. 11, 12; Capt. Robert E. Lee, *Recollections and Letters of Robert E. Lee*, (New York, 1904), pp. 8–9; Walter H. Taylor, *Four Years With General Lee* (New York, 1878), p. 76; Daniel, *Lee: An Oration*, p. 47.
17. Lee, *Recollections of Lee*, p. 106. See also, Taylor, *Four Years With Lee*, p. 77.
18. Taylor, *Four Years With Lee*, pp. 192–3. See also, John D. McCabe Jr, *Life and Campaigns of General Robert E. Lee* (Atlanta, Ga., 1866), p. 637.
19. Pollard, *Lee and his Lieutenants*, pp. 35–6. Curiously, several later Southern writers tended to equate this carefully nurtured, idealised image of Lee with Lee himself. Robert Penn Warren, for example, asked, "Who cares about Lee? Now there's a man who's smooth as an egg. Turn him around, this primordial perfection: you see, he has no story." ("An Interview with Flannery O'Connor and Robert Penn Warren, held at the Vanderbilt Literary Symposium, 23 April, 1959." Photocopy in the University of North Carolina Library, Chapel Hill). Similarly, John Peale Bishop warned Tate, who was planning a biography of Lee, that "With Lee, you have a most difficult subject. There seems to be no drama, no conflict in the man." Tate's reply to this was, "You are right about the problem of Lee"; and eventually he gave the project up (*The Republic of Letters in America: The Correspondence of John Peale Bishop and Allen Tate* edited by Thomas D. Young and John J. Hindle (Lexington, Ky., 1981), p. 38. To Tate, June 24, 1931, p. 64. To Bishop, Oct. 19, 1932). It is difficult to see how any human being could be described as perfect, without conflict; and it is odd to find writers with normally such a powerful sense of human fallibility and weakness entertaining such an idea. See also, Thomas L. Connelly, *The Marble Man: Robert E. Lee and His Image in American Society* (Baton Rouge, La., 1977).
20. General J.B. Gordon, *Reminiscences of the Civil War* (New York, 1904), p. 37. See also, Cooke, *Lee*, p. 526; Anderson, *Lee: An Address*, pp. 18–19; Fitzhugh Lee, *Lee*, pp. 79, 82.
21. Carlton McCarthy, *Detailed Minutiae of Soldier Life in the Army of Northern Virginia, 1861–1865* (Richmond, Va., 1882), pp. 1–2.
22. James A. Wyeth, *With Sabre and Scalpel: The Autobiography of a Soldier and Surgeon* (New York, 1914), pp. xiv–xvi.
23. Randolph H. McKim, *A Soldier's Recollections: Leaves from the Diary of a Young Confederate* (London, 1910), p. 272. See also, James Dinkins, *Personal Recollections and Experiences in the Confederate Army* (Cincinnati, 1897), p. 86; Isaac Hermann, *Memoirs of a Veteran Who Served as a Private in the 60's in the War Between the States: Personal Incidents, Experiences, and Observations* (Atlanta, Ga., 1911), p. 8; McCarthy, *Soldier Life*, p. 3.
24. George C. Eggleston, *A Rebel's Recollections* (New York, 1878), pp. 31–2. See also, McCarthy, *Soldier Life*, p. 39.
25. McCarthy, *Soldier Life*, pp. 6–7. See also, pp. 6, 9, 213; Dinkins, *Personal Recollections*, pp. 150, 237; Arthur P. Ford, *Life in the Confederate Army; Being Personal Experiences of a Private Soldier in the Confederate Army* (New York, 1905),

pp. 44, 101; Harry Gilmore, *Four Years in the Saddle* (London, 1866), pp. 51, 173, 220; Hermann, *Memoirs of a Veteran*, pp. 195, 223–5, 227, 234; William G. Stevenson, *Thirteen Months in the Rebel Army* (New York, 1862), pp. 69–70, 71, 72–3; Marcus B. Toney, *The Privations of a Private: The Campaign under General R.E. Lee; the Campaign under General Stonewall Jackson; Bragg's Invasion of Kentucky* (Nashville, Tenn., 1905), p. 42; Samuel R. Watkins, *"Co. Aytch", Maury Grays, First Tennessee Regiment; or, A Side-Show of the Big Show* (Nashville, Tenn., 1882), pp. 113, 147–8.

26. Richard Taylor, *Destruction and Reconstruction: Personal Experiences of the Late War in the United States* (London, 1879), p. 15.
27. Ibid. See also, Cooke, *Wearing of the Gray*, pp. 37–8; John W. Munson, *Reminiscences of a Mosby Guerilla* (London, 1906), pp. vii, 9, 127.
28. Gordon, *Reminiscences*, p. 18. See also, pp. 217–18, 381; Stiles, *Marse Robert*, p. 51; Edward P. Alexander, *The Civil War: A Critical Narrative* (London, 1908), p. viii; Anderson, *Lee: An Address*, p. 18; Mckim, *Soldier's Recollections*, p. 160.
29. Pollard, *First Year of War*, p. 210. See also, Dinkins, *Personal Recollections*, pp. 41, 79; Taylor, *Personal Experiences*, p. 75; Gilmore, *Four Years in the Saddle*, p. 276.
30. Munson, *Reminiscences*, p. 127. Cf. Anderson, *Lee: An Address*, p. 12.
31. David Donald, "The Southerner as Fighting Man", in Sellers, *Southerner as American*, pp. 73, 83–5.
32. Bishop and Tate, *Correspondence*, p. 38. To Tate, June 24, 1931.
33. McKim, *Soldiers Recollections*, p. 290.
34. Robert Somers, *The Southern States Since the War, 1870–1871* (London, 1871), p. 114. Other quotations from, Sidney Andrews, *The South Since the War; As Shown by Fourteen Weeks of Observation and Travel in Georgia and the Carolinas* (Boston, Mass., 1866), p. 1; Edward King, *The Southern States of North America* (London, 1875), p. 451. See also Sir John Henry Kennaway, *On Sherman's Track; or, The South After the War* (London, 1867), pp. 178–9; William Reid, *A Southern Tour* (Cincinnati, 1866), p. 224; George Rose, *The Great Country; or, Impressions of America* (London, 1868), p. 17; John T. Trowbridge, *The South: A Tour of its Battle-Fields and Ruined Cities* (Hartford, Conn., 1866), p. 567; Foster B. Zincke, *Last Winter in the United States* (London, 1868), p. 93.
35. On these and related developments see, Thomas D. Clark and Henry W. Grady, *The South Since Appomatox* (New York, 1967); J.S. Ezell, *The South Since 1865* (New York, 1963); Vann Woodward, *Origins of the New South*.
36. For fuller discussions of some of the issues raised here see, Bruce Clayton, *The Savage Ideal: Intolerance and Intellectual Leadership in the South, 1890–1914* (Baltimore, Md., 1972); Gaines, *Southern Plantation*; Paul M. Gaston, *The New South Creed: A Study in Southern Mythmaking* (New York, 1970); Wayne Mixon, *Southern Writers and the New South Movement, 1865–1913* (Chapel Hill, N.C., 1980).
37. Mixon, *Southern Writers and the New South Movement*, p. 8.
38. Compare, e.g., Lucinda H. Mackethan, *The Dream of Arcady: Place and Time in Southern Literature* (Baton Rouge, La., 1980), p. 10 and Mixon, *Southern Writers and the New South Movement*, p. 31.
39. Francis Hopkinson Smith, *Colonel Carter of Cartersville* (London, 1891), pp. 61–2. See also, Joel Chandler Harris, *Told by Uncle Remus: New Stories of the Old Plantation* (London, 1905), p. 59; Thomas Nelson Page, "Marse Chan: A Tale of Old Virginia", in *In Ole Virginia; or, Marse Chan and Other Stories* (1887; London, 1889 edition), p. 10.
40. Preface to Thomas Nelson Page, *Red Rock: A Chronicle of Reconstruction* (London, 1898).
41. See, e.g., Page, "Marse Chan", p. 38.

42. See, e.g. Smith, *Colonel Carter*, p. 134; Joel Chandler Harris, *The Chronicles of Aunt Minervy Ann* (London, 1899), p. 73.

43. Joel Chandler Harris, *Gabriel Tolliver: A Story of Reconstruction* (London, 1902), p. 18.

44. Thomas Nelson Page, *On Newfound River* (London, 1891), p. 2.

45. See, e.g., Marion Harland, *His Great Self* (London, 1892), pp. 35–6; Smith, *Colonel Carter*, pp. 62–83.

46. John Esten Cooke, *Fairfax; or, The Master of Greenway Court* (New York, 1868), p. 132. See also, Harland, *His Great Self*, p. 11; Virginia F. Boyle, *Serena* (New York, 1905), p. 88. For other examples of the character types mentioned here see, James Lane Allen, *The Choir Invisible* (New York, 1898), pp. 193–4; John Esten Cooke, *Justin Harley: A Romance of Old Virginia* (Philadelphia, Pa., 1875), pp. 24, 156; Joel Chandler Harris, *Uncle Remus; or Mr. Fox, Mr. Rabbit, and Mr. Terrapin* (London, 1883), pp. 204, 240, and *Uncle Remus and His Friends* (London, 1892), p. 255; Thomas Nelson Page, "Polly: A Christmas Recollection", in *In Ole Virginia*, pp. 198, 205.

47. See, e.g., Mary Johnston, *Prisoners of Hope* (London, 1899), pp. 53, 92; Page, "Unc' Edingburg's Drowndin': a Plantation Echo", in *In Ole Virginia*, pp. 41ff., and *Red Rock*, p. 35.

48. Joel Chandler Harris, "Ananias", in *Balaam and His Master and Other Sketches and Stories* (London, 1891), pp. 127, 128.

49. Page, *Red Rock*, p. 178.

50. John Esten Cooke, *The Virginia Bohemians* (New York, 1880), p. 48. See also, James Lane Allen, "Two Gentlemen of Kentucky", in *Flute and Violin, and Other Kentucky Tales and Romances* (New York, 1900), p. 112; Joel Chandler Harris, "The Old Bascom Place", in *Balaam and His Master*, p. 293; Thomas Nelson Page, "Ole 'Stracted", in *In Ole Virginia*, p. 154; Smith, *Colonel Carter*, p. 60.

51. Sidney Lanier, *The Centennial Edition of the Works of Sidney Lanier* edited by Charles R. Anderson and Aubrey H. Starke (10 vols; Baltimore, Md., 1945), I, 3–4. The most useful discussions of Lanier are to be found in Jack A. De Bellis, *Sidney Lanier* (New York, 1972); Mackethan, *The Dream of Arcady*; Mixon, *Southern Writers and the New South Movement*; Louis D. Rubin, *William Elliott Shoots a Bear: Essays on the Southern Literary Imagination* (Baton Rouge, La., 1975).

52. Lanier, *Works*, I, 24–5.

53. Ibid., I, 194–6.

54. Mathew B. Hammond, *The Cotton Industry: An Essay in American Economic History* (New York, 1897), p. 149. For fuller discussions of the developments mentioned here see, e.g., Alex M. Arnett, *The Populist Movement in Georgia* (New York, 1922); John D. Hicks, *The Populist Revolt: A History of the Farmer's Alliance and the People's Party* (Minneapolis, Minn., 1931); Frederick A. Shannon, *The Farmer's Last Frontier: Agriculture 1860–1897* (New York, 1945); Vann Woodward, *Origins of the New South*.

55. See, e.g., Richard Hofstadter, *The Age of Reform: From Bryan to F.D.R.* (New York, 1955).

56. Lanier, *Works*, VIII, 224. To Paul H. Hayne, April 17, 1872.

57. Ibid., I, 34–9.

58. Cited in Aubrey H. Starke, *Sidney Lanier: A Biographical and Critical Study* (1933; New York, 1964 edition), p. 189.

59. Lanier, *Works*, I, 46–56, 119–22.

60. Ibid., V, 334–58.

61. See Starke's discussion of this essay in *Sidney Lanier*, pp. 152–3, 394–6.

62. Richard Malcolm Johnston, Preface to *The Primes and Their Neighbours: Ten Tales*

of Middle Georgia (New York, 1891). See also, Dedication to *Dukesborough Tales* (New York, 1871).

63. Ellen Glasgow, *The Miller of Old Church* (New York, 1911), p. 48. See also, *The Woman Within* (New York, 1955), pp. 180–1.

64. Ellen Glasgow, *The Builders* (New York, 1919), p. 112.

65. Cited in Dixon Wecter, *Sam Clemens of Hannibal* (Boston, 1952), p. 67. Of the many discussions of Twain, the ones I have found most useful as far as the Southern dimension is concerned are, Arthur G. Pettit, *Mark Twain and the South* (Lexington, Ky., 1974), and Arlin Turner, "Mark Twain and the South: An Affair of Love and Anger", *Southern Review*, IV (April, 1968), 493–519.

66. Henry Nash Smith, *Mark Twain: The Development of a Writer* (Cambridge, Mass., 1962).

67. *Mark Twain–Howells Letters* edited by H.N. Smith and W.M. Gibson (2 vols.; Cambridge, Mass, 1960), II, 534. To Howells, July 21, 1885. See also, *The Autobiography of Mark Twain* edited by Charles Neider (New York, 1959), p. 121.

68. *Twain–Howells Letters*, I, 34. To Howells, Oct. 24, 1874.

69. Ibid., I, 417. To Howells, Oct. 30, 1882.

70. *Life on the Mississippi* (1883; New York, 1961 edition), pp. 67–8.

71. Tony Tanner, *The Reign of Wonder* (Cambridge, 1965), p. 120.

72. *Life on the Mississippi*, p. 142. See also, pp. 144, 237, 266, 331.

73. Brander Mathews, cited in Walter Blair, *Mark Twain and Huck Finn* (Berkeley, Calif., 1960), p. 51.

74. Preface to *The Adventures of Tom Sawyer* (1876; London, 1968 edition), p. 23. See also, *Twain–Howells Letters*, I, 91, 110; Blair, *Mark Twain and Huck Finn*, p. 51.

75. *Tom Sawyer*, p. 101. See also, p. 140.

76. Ibid., p. 29. See also, pp. 34, 41, 47, 66, 70.

77. On this relationship see, in particular, Clara Clemens, *My Father Mark Twain* (New York, 1931), pp. 13–23, and Justin Kaplan, *Mr. Clemens and Mark Twain: A Biography* (New York, 1966), pp. 76–93.

78. Bernard De Voto (*Mark Twain's America* (Boston, 1932)) claims that Twain did not return to the manuscript until 1882; whereas Smith (*Mark Twain*) and Blair (*Mark Twain and Huck Finn*), who are probably more reliable on this as on other matters, say that the rest of the book was written between 1879 and 1883.

79. See Kaplan, *Mr. Clemens and Mark Twain*, p. 198; also, Blair, *Mark Twain and Huck Finn*.

80. See, e.g., Blair, *Mark Twain and Huck Finn*; Lynn, *Mark Twain and Southwestern Humour*. For a different view see, David E. Sloane, *Mark Twain as a Literary Comedian* (Baton Rouge, La., 1979).

81. *The Adventures of Huckleberry Finn* (1885; London, 1968 edition), pp. 222–3.

82. For an account of the image of the Southern poor white in literature see, Shields McIlwaine, *The Southern Poor-White: From Lubberland to Tobacco Road* (Norman, Okla., 1939), and Sylvia Jenkins Cook, *From Tobacco Road to Route 66: The Southern Poor White in Fiction* (Chapel Hill, N.C., 1976).

83. See, e.g., *Huckleberry Finn*, 284–5, 291–2, 317–18, 385.

84. Or by some variant on this formula such as "individual freedom" versus "the restraints imposed by convention" (Edgar Branch, *The Literary Apprenticeship of Mark Twain* (Urbana, Ill., 1950)) or "moral intuition" versus "the mores of the folk" (Gladys Bellamy, *Mark Twain as Literary Artist* (Norman, Okla., 1950)). See, e.g., the discussions in Smith, *Mark Twain* and Tanner, *Reign of Wonder*.

85. See *Mark Twain's "Which Was the Dream" and Other Symbolic Writings of the Later Years* edited by John S. Tuckey (Berkeley, Calif., 1967).

86. See Henry James on this, in *Hawthorne* (1879; Ithaca, N.Y., 1956 edition), p. 114.

87. *Huckleberry Finn*, p. 299.
88. Cited in Michael Hamburger, *The Truth of Poetry* (London, 1969) p. 36. Compare the notion of the Czech linguist Jan Mukarovsky that "The function of poetic language consists in the maximum of foregrounding of the utterance . . . in order to place in the foreground the act of expression, the act of speech itself." (Jan Mukarovsky, "Standard language and poetic language", in *A Prague School Reader on Aesthetics, Literary Structure and Style* selected and translated by Paul L. Garvin (Washington, D.C., 1964), pp. 43–4); or the Russian formalist Roman Jakobson's notion that "the distinctive feature of poetry" is that "a word is perceived as a word and not merely a proxy for the denoted object or an outburst of emotion, that words . . . acquire weight and value of their own". Cited in Victor Erlich, *Russian Formalism: History–Doctrine* (1955; The Hague, 1965 edition), p. 183.
89. This comes, of course, from Chaucer's description of the Knight in the Prologue to *The Canterbury Tales*, line 46. See also, line 72.
90. Ernest Hemingway, *The Green Hills of Africa* (New York, 1935), p. 22. For two interesting, if ultimately unconvincing, attempts to argue against this verdict see, T.S. Eliot, Introduction to New York, 1950 edition of *Huckleberry Finn*, p. xvi, and William M. Gibson, *The Art of Mark Twain* (New York, 1976), pp. 101–2.
91. *Autobiography*, p. 273.
92. *A Connecticut Yankee in King Arthur's Court* (1889; London, 1957 edition), p. 59. See also, p. 4.
93. Twain referred to Arthurian England as Hank Morgan's "lost land" in his Notebooks. See H.N. Smith, *Mark Twain*, p. 156. See also, *Life on the Mississippi*, p. 94.
94. *Connecticut Yankee*, p. 228. See also, p. 227.
95. Ibid., p. 8.
96. Ibid., p. 71. Cf. *Autobiography*, pp. 12–13.
97. *Connecticut Yankee*, p. 317.
98. See *Mark Twain's Hannibal, Huck & Tom* edited by Walter Blair (Berkeley, Calif., 1969), and *The Adventures of Tom Sawyer, Tom Sawyer Abroad, and Tom Sawyer, Detective* edited by John C. Gerber, Paul Baender, and Tony Fiskins (Berkeley, Calif., 1980), vol. IV. of *The Works of Mark Twain*.
99. *The Tragedy of Pudd'nhead Wilson* (1894; New York, 1964 edition), p. 46.
100. F.R. Leavis "Pudd'nhead Wilson", in *Anna Karenina and Other Essays* (London, 1967), pp. 126. See also, p. 130; *Pudd'nhead Wilson*, pp. 21, 22.
101. *Pudd'nhead Wilson*, p. 29.
102. Ibid., p. 109. Cf. Page, "Unc'Edingburg's Drowndin'", p. 47; Smith, *Colonel Carter*, p. 60.
103. *Pudd'nhead Wilson*, p. 166. See also, p. 100.
104. Cited in Hubbell, *The South in American Literature*, p. 822.
105. The two quotations are from the last line of "East Coker" and the second line of "The Dry Salvages", respectively.

4 A CLIMATE OF FEAR: THE SOUTH BETWEEN THE WARS AND THE NASHVILLE AGRARIANS

1. Bishop and Tate, *Correspondence*, p. 34. To Bishop, June 31, 1931. See also, p. 77. To Bishop, April 7, 1933.
2. Allen Tate, *Essays of Four Decades* (New York, 1968), p. 545.
3. The material is far too voluminous to cite here. The most useful introduction to the developments and problems of the period is provided by George B. Tindall, *The*

Emergence of the New South 1913–1945 (1967), vol. x of *History of the South* edited by Stephenson and Coulter. Other books of particular interest in connection with the issues raised here are Dewey W. Grantham, *The Regional Imagination: The South and Recent American History* (Nashville, Tenn., 1979); Allan P. Sindler (ed.), *Change in the Contemporary South* (Durham, N.C., 1963); Louis D. Rubin, Jr (ed.), *The Lasting South: Fourteen Southerners Look at Their Home* (Chicago, 1957).

4. Ralph Linton, "The Distinctive Aspects of Acculturation", in *Acculturation in Seven American Tribes* edited by R. Linton (New York, 1940), p. 517. See also, Tate, *Essays*, p. 545.

5. William Ogburn, *Social Change* (New York, 1922), p. 203.

6. Lucien Goldmann, *The Hidden God* translated by Philip Thody (London, 1956), p. 49.

7. Bishop and Tate, *Correspondence*, p. 36. To Bishop, June 31, 1931. The material on the Agrarians is quite extensive. Reference to some of the approaches adopted by critics and commentators will be made later. However, it is worth noting here that useful books on the Agrarians, and books containing helpful discussions of the Agrarian movement include, John M. Bradbury, *The Fugitives: A Critical Account* (Chapel Hill, N.C., 1958); Louise Cowan, *The Fugitive Group: A Literary History* (Baton Rouge, La., 1959); F. Garvin Davenport, *The Myth of Southern History: Historical Consciousness in Twentieth Century Southern Literature* (Nashville, Tenn., 1980); William C. Havard and Walter Sullivan (eds.), *A Band of Prophets: The Vanderbilt Agrarians After Fifty Years* (Baton Rouge, La., 1982); Alexander Karanikas, *Tillers of a Myth: Southern Agrarians as Social and Literary Critics* (Madison, Wisc., 1966); Richard H. King, *A Southern Renaissance: The Cultural Awakening of the South, 1934–1955* (New York, 1980); Louis D. Rubin, Jr, *The Wary Fugitives: Four Poets and the South* (Baton Rouge, La., 1978); Singal, *War Within*; John L. Stewart, *The Burden of Time: The Fugitives and Agrarians* (Princeton, 1965); Thomas D. Young, *Gentleman in a Dustcoat: A Biography of John Crowe Ransom* (Baton Rouge, La., 1976), and *Waking Their Neighbors Up: The Nashville Agrarians Rediscovered* (Athens, Ga., 1982). Also well worth mentioning is Virginia Rock, "The Making and Meaning of *I'll Take My Stand*: A Study of Utopian Conservatism, 1925–1939" (Ph.D. diss., University of Minnesota, 1961).

8. Allen Tate, "The Fugitive, 1922–1925: A Personal Recollection Twenty Years After", *Princeton University Library Chronicle*, III (April, 1942), 84. See also, Donald Davidson, "*I'll Take My Stand.* A History", *Southern Writers in the Modern World* (Athens, Ga., 1958), pp. 29–30.

9. See Rubin, *Wary Fugitives*, p. 37.

10. Cited in Young, *Gentleman in a Dustcoat*, p. 206. See also, *The Literary Correspondence of Donald Davidson and Allen Tate*, edited by John T. Fain and Thomas D. Young (Athens, Ga., 1974), p. 104. To Davidson, April 17, 1924.

11. Cited in Young, *Gentleman in a Dustcoat*, p. 204. See also, p. 205.

12. Cited in Rock, "Making and Meaning of *I'll Take My Stand*", p. 252.

13. "Appendix B" to Davidson and Tate, *Correspondence*, p. 406. "To the Contributors to the Southern Symposium", July 24, 1930.

14. Davidson and Tate, *Correspondence*, p. 158. To Davidson, March 3, 1926.

15. Ibid., p. 181. To Davidson, Dec. 29, 1926. See also, Rubin, *Wary Fugitives*, p. 181.

16. Davidson and Tate, *Correspondence*, pp. 186–7. To Tate, Feb. 15, 1927.

17. Ibid., p. 188. To Davidson, Feb. 20, 1927.

18. Ibid., p. 195. To Davidson, March 17, 1927.

19. Ibid., p. 193. To Tate, March 4, 1927. See also, p. 191. To Davidson, March 1, 1927.

20. Ibid., p. 199. To Davidson, May 5, 1927.

21. Ibid., p. 201. To Tate, May 9, 1927.

22. Davidson and Tate, *Correspondence*, p. 227. To Tate, July 29, 1929. See also, p. 202. To Tate, May 9, 1927; p. 223. To Davidson, Feb. 16, 1929.
23. Ibid., p. 230. To Davidson, Aug. 10, 1929.
24. Ibid. See also, p. 229. Davidson's remark concerning Europe is cited in Michael O'Brien, *The Idea of the American South 1920–1941* (Baltimore, Md., 1979), p. 186.
25. Davidson and Tate, *Correspondence*, p. 241. To Davidson, Nov. 9, 1929. See also, p. 234. To Tate, Aug. 20, 1929.
26. Ibid., p. 251. To Tate, July 21, 1930. See also, Robert Penn Warren, "The Briar Patch", in *I'll Take My Stand: The South and the Agrarian Tradition* (1930; New York, 1962 edition), p. 264.
27. See, Robert B. Heilman, "Spokesman and Seer: The Agrarian Movement and European Culture", in *Band of Prophets*, pp. 93–116; Rubin, *Wary Fugitives*; Young, *Waking Their Neighbors Up*.
28. See, R. Alan Lawson, *The Failure of Independent Liberalism* (New York, 1971); O'Brien, *Idea of the American South*; Richard H. Pell, *Radical Visions and American Dreams: Culture and Social Thought During the Depression Years* (New York, 1973).
29. Lewis P. Simpson, "The Southern Republic of Letters and *I'll Take My Stand*", in *Band of Prophets*, p. 70. See also, "Introduction" to *Band of Prophets*, pp. 8–9; Young, *Waking Their Neighbours Up*, p. 24.
30. See, e.g., Ransom's poem, "Antique Harvesters", first published in 1925, and Lytle's novels, *A Name for Evil* (New York, 1947) and *The Velvet Horn* (New York, 1956). Compare, Herbert Agar and Allen Tate (eds.), *Who Owns America? A New Declaration of Independence* (Boston, 1936); Andrew Nelson Lytle, "The Backwoods Progression", *American Review*, I (September, 1933), 409–34, and "John Taylor and the Political Economy of Agriculture", *American Review*, III (September, 1934), 432–47, 630–40.
31. See, e.g., John Crowe Ransom, "Forms and Citizens" and "Poets Without Laurels", in *The World's Body* (New York, 1938). Compare, "Land! An Answer to the Unemployment Problem", *Harper's Magazine*, CLXV (July, 1932), 217–18, 219, 222; "Happy Farmers", *American Review*, I (October, 1933), 513–35.
32. Davidson and Tate, *Correspondence*, p. 280. To Davidson, Dec. 10, 1932. See also, Donald Davidson, "Southern Literature: A Partisan View", in William T. Couch (ed.), *Culture in the South* (Chapel Hill, N.C., 1934), p. 208.
33. Stark Young, "Not in Memoriam, But in Defense", p. 358. See also, p. 350; Andrew Nelson Lytle, "The Hind Tit", p. 217. The essays cited here, and hereafter in this chapter, are from *I'll Take My Stand* unless otherwise stated; all references are to the 1962 edition.
34. King, *Southern Renaissance*, p. 303.
35. Frank Owsley, "The Irrepressible Conflict", pp. 70, 71. See also, Young, "Not in Memoriam, But in Defense", pp. 336, 337.
36. Lytle, "Backwoods Progression", p. 411. See also, "Foreword" to *A Novel, A Novella, and Four Stories* (New York, 1958), p. xvii.
37. Andrew Nelson Lytle, *Bedford Forrest and His Critter Company* (1931; London, 1939 edition), p. 16. See also, pp. 9, 36, 44, 71, 194.
38. Ibid., pp. 35–6. See also, pp. 357, 373, 390.
39. Herman Clarence Nixon, "Whither Southern Economy?", p. 188.
40. John Crowe Ransom, "Reconstructed but Unregenerate", pp. 13–14.
41. Allen Tate, *Jefferson Davis: His Rise and Fall* (New York, 1929), pp. 301–2. See also, Ransom, "Reconstructed but Unregenerate", p. 12.
42. Ransom, "Reconstructed but Unregenerate", p. 3. See also, Davidson and Tate, *Correspondence*, pp. 279–80. To Davidson, Dec. 10, 1932. If anything, Tate was a Francophile rather than an Anglophile: which, according to O'Brien, was why he

"felt that France should be taken as a model for the South" (*Idea of the American South*, p. 154).

43. Ransom, "Reconstructed but Unregenerate", p. 22. See also, pp. 13, 14, 21.
44. Allen Tate, "Remarks on the Southern Religion", p. 168. See also, p. 166.
45. Ibid., p. 175. See also, p. 174.
46. Andrew Nelson Lytle, "The Working Novelist and the Mythmaking Process", in *The Hero with the Private Parts* (Baton Rouge, La., 1966), pp. 178–9.
47. Robert Penn Warren, *A Place To Come To* (New York, 1977), p. 76.
48. Roland Barthes, *S/Z* translated by Richard Miller (New York, 1974), p. 4.
49. Ransom, "Reconstructed but Unregenerate", p. 23.
50. Young, *Waking Their Neighbours Up*, p. 67. See also, Owsley, "Irrepressible Conflict", p. 62; Rubin, *Wary Fugitives*, p. 232.
51. Marx, *The Machine in the Garden*, p. 242.
52. Pierre Macherey, *A Theory of Literary Production* translated by Geoffrey Wall (London, 1978), p. 85. See also, p. 86.
53. *Light in August* (New York, 1932), p. 270.
54. Useful discussions of the apologists for slavery are to be found in William S. Jenkins, *Pro-Slavery Thought in the Old South* (Chapel Hill, N.C., 1935); Wilson, *Patriotic Gore*; Harvey Wish, *George Fitzhugh, Propagandist of the Old South* (Baton Rouge, La., 1943).
55. See, Owsley, "Irrepressible Conflict", pp. 81–2; Davidson and Tate, *Correspondence*, p. 232. To Davidson, Aug. 10, 1929.
56. James Henry Hammond, "Hammond's Letters on Slavery", in *The Pro-Slavery Argument: As Maintained by the Most Distinguished Writers of the Southern States* (Charleston, S.C., 1852), p. 149.
57. Ransom, "Reconstructed but Unregenerate", p. 14.
58. Cited in Jenkins, *Pro-Slavery Thought*, p. 87.
59. Hammond, "Letters on Slavery", p. 104.
60. Appendix to *Congressional Globe* (75th Cong., 1st. sess.), p. 1460. See also, Donald Davidson, "A Mirror for Artists", p. 53; Nixon, "Whither Southern Economy?", p. 198.
61. Tate, "Remarks on Southern Religion", p. 159. See also, Chancellor Harper, "Harper on Slavery", in *Pro-Slavery Argument*, p. 9.
62. John Gould Fletcher, "Education, Past and Present", p. 94. See also, Warren, "Briar Patch", p. 257; William Gilmore Simms, "The Morals of Slavery", in *Pro-Slavery Argument*, p. 233.
63. See, e.g., *Pro-Slavery Argument*, pp. 110–11, 162–3, 257; *I'll Take My Stand*, pp. 13, 34, 111, 167, 282, 308, 344.
64. Ransom, "Reconstructed but Unregenerate", p. 5.
65. Edmund Ruffin, *The Political Economy of Slavery; or, The Institution Considered in Regard to its Influence on Public Wealth and the General Welfare* (Virginia, 1858), p. 28.
66. George Fitzhugh to Holmes, April 11, 1855, cited in Wish, *George Fitzhugh*, p. 118.
67. Simms, "Morals of Slavery", p. 257. See also, Davidson, "Mirror for Artists", pp. 34, 49, 53; Fletcher, "Education, Past and Present", p. 110; Henry Blue Kline, "William Remington: A Study in Individualism", p. 321; Harper, "Harper on Slavery", p. 52.
68. *Annals of Congress* (16th Cong., 1st. sess.), p 269. See also, Harper, "Harper on Slavery", pp. 6, 7, 52; Hammond, "Letters on Slavery", p. 110; *Annals of Congress* (6th Cong., 1st sess.), p. 230.
69. George Fitzhugh, *Cannibals All!; or, Slaves Without Masters* (1857; Cambridge, Mass., 1960 edition), p. 187. See also pp. 142, 175, 205.
70. George Fitzhugh, *Sociology for the South; or, The Failure of Free Society* (Richmond, Va., 1854), p. 229. See also, p. 11.

71. Lyle H. Lanier, "A Critique of the Philosophy of Progress", p. 130. See also, pp. 122, 146; Nixon, "Whither Southern Economy?", p. 188.
72. *Annals of Congress* (16th Cong., 1st sess.), p. 35. See also, Young, "Not in Memoriam, but in Defense", p. 334; Fitzhugh, *Sociology for the South*, pp. 65, 70; Ransom, "Reconstructed but Unregenerate", p. 10.
73. Cited in Singal, *War Within*, p. 204.
74. Hammond, "Letters on Slavery", pp. 162–3; Ransom, "Reconstructed but Unregenerate", pp. 7–8.
75. Lanier, "Critique of Philosophy of Progress", p. 125. See also, Ransom, "Reconstructed but Unregenerate", p. 5; Fitzhugh, *Sociology for the South*, p. 226. For examples of the rhetoric mentioned here, see, e.g., *Pro-Slavery Argument*, pp. 110–11, 149; *I'll Take My Stand*, pp. 4, 5, 17, 19, 24, 53, 69.
76. Henry Hughes, *A Treatise on Sociology, Theoretical and Practical* (Philadelphia, Pa., 1854), p. 292. See also, Simpson, *Dispossessed Garden*, p. 2. For a similarly idyllic description of plantation life by another apologist for slavery see, William J. Grayson, "The Hireling and the Slave", in *The Hireling and the Slave, Chicora, and Other Poems* (Charleston, S.C., 1856), pp. 50ff.
77. Owsley, "Irrepressible Conflict", pp. 69, 71.
78. Young, "Not in Memoriam, but in Defense", p. 347.
79. Ransom, "Reconstructed but Unregenerate", p. 20. See also, pp. 8–9, 13; Simms, "Morals of Slavery", p. 257; Thomas R. Dew, "Review of the Debate in the Virginia Legislature", in *Pro-Slavery Argument*, p. 490.
80. Fitzhugh, *Cannibals All!*, p. 133. See also, Fletcher, "Education, Past and Present", p. 95. For further examples of this portrait of Northern and/or urban society see, e.g., Fitzhugh, *Sociology for the South*, pp. 227–8; Ruffin, *Political Economy of Slavery*, p. 25; Lytle, "Hind Tit", p. 238; Kline, "William Remington", pp. 307–9.
81. Robert Barnwell Rhett, cited in *Rhett: Father of Secession*, p. 24. Some of the apologists for slavery tried to make an explicit, categorical distinction between the American Revolution and the constitutional developments that followed it. The first, they argued, anticipated the South's own struggle for its independence against an oppressive "colonial" power; while the second was an artificial accretion, representing an attempt to turn a fight for local autonomy into a crusade for certain abstract principles. See, e.g., Fitzhugh, *Sociology for the South*, pp. 173–83.
82. Lewis P. Simpson, *The Man of Letters in New England and the South: Essays on the History of the Literary Vocation in America* (Baton Rouge, La., 1973), p. 248. See also, Simms, "Morals of Slavery", p. 179; Bishop and Tate, *Correspondence*, p. 48. To Tate, Aug. 25, 1931.
83. Davidson and Tate, *Correspondence*, p 280. To Davidson, Dec. 10, 1932.
84. Ibid., p. 370. To Davidson, Jan. 14, 1953. See also, p. 328. To Davidson, Dec. 4, 1932; Tate, "Remarks on Southern Religion", p. 173.
85. John Crowe Ransom, "Art and the Human Economy", *Kenyon Review*, VII (Autumn, 1945), 686. See also, Davidson and Tate, *Correspondence*, p. 344. To Tate, Oct. 3, 1945.
86. Ransom, "Art and the Human Economy", pp. 686–7.
87. Ibid., p. 686. See also, p. 685.
88. Discussion between Lyle Lanier, Andrew Lytle, and Robert Penn Warren, "The Agrarian-Industrial Metaphor: Culture, Economics, and Society in a Technological Age", in *Band of Prophets*, p. 164.
89. Stark Young, *The Pavilion: Of People and Times Remembered, Of Stories and Places* (New York, 1951), p. 187. See also, *The Flower in Drama: A Book of Papers on the Theatre* (New York, 1923), p. 11. One of Young's collections of essays on the theatre is actually called *Glamour* (New York, 1925); and the narrator of Young's first novel,

Heaven Trees (New York, 1926) – which is set in the old South – actually begins the story by saying, "It all seems romance to me so far back in the fifties, like a gentle elegy of remembered things, never quite real almost ..." (p. 1). For a further discussion of the link between Young's drama criticism and his interest in the Southern tradition see, Eric Bentley, "An American Theatre Critic! (or, the China in the Bull Shop)", *Kenyon Review*, XII (Winter, 1950), pp. 142, 145. See also Virginia Rock, "The Twelve Southerners: Biographical Essays", appendix to 1962 edition of *I'll Take My Stand*, p. 373.

90. Cited in O'Brien, *Idea of the American South*, p. 112. See also, Rock, "Twelve Southerners", p. 370.

91. Davidson and Tate, *Correspondence*, pp. 323–4. To Tate, Feb. 23, 1940.

92. Lytle, "Hind Tit", p. 221. For a useful and stimulating discussion of the Agrarians in their New Critical phase, see King, *Southern Renaissance*, pp. 63–76. See also, Karanikas, *Tillers of a Myth*.

93. Allen Tate, *The Fathers* (New York, 1938), p. 186. Another edition of this novel appeared in 1977, with a revised ending. According to Tate, the aim of this revision was to give the novel two heroes: Major Buchan and George Posey. See, *The Fathers and Other Fiction* (Baton Rouge, La., 1977), p. xxii.

5 OUT OF THE SOUTH: THE FICTION OF WILLIAM FAULKNER

1. Gary Lee Stonum, *Faulkner's Career: An Internal Literary History* (Ithaca, N.Y., 1979), p. 19. See also Malcolm Cowley, "Introduction", to *The Portable Faulkner* (New York, 1946), p. 8; John T. Irwin, *Doubling and Incest | Repetition and Revenge: A Speculative Reading of Faulkner* (Baltimore, Md., 1975), p. 157; Estella Schoenberg, *Old Tales and Talking: Quentin Compson in William Faulkner's "Absalom, Absalom!" and Related Works* (Jackson, Miss., 1975), p. 120; Joanne V. Creighton, *William Faulkner's Craft of Revision* (Detroit, 1977), p. 12; Lyall H. Powers, *Faulkner's Yoknapatawpha Comedy* (Ann Arbor, Mich., 1980), p. 256.

2. *Lion in the Garden: Interviews with William Faulkner 1926–1962* edited by James B. Meriwether and Michael Millgate (New York, 1968), p. 217. See also, Cowley, "Introduction", p. 5.

3. *Lion in the Garden*, p. 255.

4. *The Faulkner–Cowley File* edited by Malcolm Cowley (London, 1966), p. 90. Faulkner to Cowley, Feb. 18, 1946. See also, *Absalom, Absalom!*, p. 261; Irwin, *Doubling and Incest*, p. 8.

5. *The Unvanquished* (1938; London, 1955 edition), p. 36.

6. *The Mansion* (1959; London, 1961 edition), p. 92. See also, *Faulkner in the University: Class Conferences at the University of Virginia 1957–1958* edited by Frederick L. Gwynn and Joseph L. Blotner (Charlottesville, Va., 1959), p. 61.

7. *Faulkner in the University*, p. 3. See also, *Faulkner at West Point* edited by Joseph L. Fant and Robert Ashley (New York, 1964), p. 90. An interesting discussion of Faulkner's attitude towards the novelist's "tools" is to be found in Joseph W. Reed, Jr, *Faulkner's Narrative* (New Haven, Conn. 1973).

8. *Cours de linguistique générale* edited by Charles Bally, Albert Sechehaye with Albert Riedlinger (1915) was translated by Wade Baskin as *Course in General Linguistics* (New York, 1959), and it is on this translation that my discussion of Saussure draws.

9. Claude Lévi–Strauss, *Structural Anthropology* translated by Claire Jacobson and Brooke Grundfest Schoepf (London, 1968), p. 203.

10. Ibid., p. 212.

11. *Faulkner at Nagano* edited by Robert A. Jelliffe (1956; New York, 1973 edition), p. 26. See also David Minter, *William Faulkner: His Life and Work* (Baltimore, Md., 1980), p. 76: *Absalom, Absalom!*, p. 378; "Mississippi", in *Essays, Speeches, and Public Letters by William Faulkner* edited by James B. Meriwether (London, 1967), p. 36.

12. *Intruder in the Dust* (1948; London, 1960 edition), p. 149. See also, *Lion in the Garden*, p. 72.

13. "An Introduction to *The Sound and the Fury*", edited by James B. Meriwether, *Mississippi Quarterly*, XXVI (Summer, 1973), 411.

14. Eugene Walter, *Untidy Pilgrim* (New York, 1954), p. 21.

15. Elizabeth Spencer, *Fire in the Morning* (New York, 1948), p. 163. See also, p. 17.

16. Eudora Welty, "Place in Fiction", in *Three Papers on Fiction* (Northampton, Mass., 1962). For a fuller discussion of the sense of place see, Simpson, *Dispossessed Garden*. For other examples of just how strong this sense is in minor Southern writing see, Clifford Dowdey, *Gamble's Hundred* (Boston, 1939), p. 8; John Bell Clayton, *Wait, Son, October is Near* (New York, 1953), p 29; Ovid Williams Pierce, *The Plantation* (New York, 1953), p. 12.

17. *Soldier's Pay* (1926; London, 1938 edition), pp. 92–3. See also, *Pylon* (1935; London, 1955 edition), p. 35; *Flags in the Dust* (1973; New York, 1974 edition), p. 127; *Sanctuary* (1931; London, 1953 edition), p. 89.

18. *The Town* (1957; London, 1965 edition), p. 7. See also, "The Tall Men", in *Collected Stories of William Faulkner* (1950; New York, 1977 edition), p. 49; "Shall Not Perish", ibid., p. 114.

19. John Crowe Ransom, "Antique Harvesters", in *Selected Poems* (New York, 1963), p. 71, line 43. See also, line 3; also, Robert Creeley, "To Define", in *A Quick Graph: Collected Notes and Essays* edited by Donald Allen (San Francisco, 1970), p. 23.

20. *Light in August*, p. 8. See also, *Absalom, Absalom!*, p. 361; *Requiem for a Nun* (1951; London, 1953 edition), pp. 202, 231. The girl who scratches her name on the window pane is also referred to in *Intruder in the Dust*, p. 50.

21. Walter Sullivan, *Sojourn of a Stranger* (New York, 1957), p. 234. See also, William Goyen, *The House of Breath* (New York, 1959), p. 27; Tate, *Essays*, p. 545.

22. Madison Jones, *A Buried Land* (New York, 1963), p. 295. See also, p. 94.

23. William Humphrey, *The Ordways* (New York, 1965), p. 36. For a fuller discussion of the sense of the past see, Thomas D. Young, *The Past in the Present: A Thematic Study of Modern Southern Fiction* (Baton Rouge, La., 1981). For other examples of how the past is used in minor Southern writing see, Isa Glenn, *A Short History of Julia* (New York, 1930), pp. 3, 8, 11, 184; Edward Kimbrough, *Night Fire* (New York, 1946), pp. 21, 79, 299; William Hoffman, *The Trumpet Unblown* (New York, 1955), pp. 84, 183.

24. *The Town* (1957; London, 1958 edition), pp. 272–3. See also, *Requiem for a Nun*, p. 85; *Absalom, Absalom!*, p. 213; *Light in August*, p. 91.

25. See, e.g., Allen Tate, "Ode to the Confederate Dead", in *The Swimmers and Other Poems* (New York, 1970), p. 18, lines 44–51. See also, *Absalom, Absalom!*, p. 377. Also of interest in this context are, Tate, *The Fathers*, p. 21; Robert Penn Warren, "I Am Dreaming of A White Christmas: The Natural History of a Vision", in *Selected Poems, 1923–1975* (New York, 1976), p. 34, section 12.

26. *Intruder in the Dust*, pp. 187–8. See also, *Soldier's Pay*, p. 128.

27. R.G. Collingwood, *The Idea of History* (1946; New York, 1962 edition), p. 243. See also, *Sanctuary: The Original Text* edited by Noel Polk (London, 1981), p. 142.

28. Collingwood, *Idea of History*, p. 215. See also, p. 242.

29. Ibid., p. 242.

30. *Absalom, Absalom!*, p. 303. See also, Schoenberg, *Old Tales and Talking*, p. 135.

31. *Absalom, Absalom!*, p. 247. See also, pp. 30, 45, 49, 79, 254. In the light of the later discussion of *The Sound and the Fury* and, more generally, Faulkner's attitude to

language, it is perhaps worth noting that, as Mr Compson tells it, all the people of Jefferson knew of Sutpen at first was his *name*: which "went back and forth" among them in "steady strophe and antistrophe: *Sutpen, Sutpen, Sutpen*" (p. 32). In a sense, the entire book could be seen as an attempt to build on this initial act of naming.

32. Cited in Tony Tanner, *City of Words: American Fiction 1950–1970* (London, 1971), p. 34.

33. Cited in Minter, *William Faulkner*, p. 34.

34. See C. Vann Woodward, "The Search for Southern Identity", in *The Burden of Southern History* (Baton Rouge, La., 1966).

35. Madison Jones, *Forest of the Night*, p. 94. See also, Andrew Nelson Lytle, "The Son of Man: He Will Prevail", in *Hero with the Private Parts*, p. 127; Sullivan, *Sojourn of a Stranger*, p. 58: Barbara Giles, *The Gentle Bush* (New York, 1947), p. 471. Bishop's novel was first published in 1935, and Lytle's in 1947.

36. Cormac McCarthy, *Child of God* (1973; London, 1975 edition), p. 135. See also, p. 4.

37. Ibid., p. 194. For a fuller discussion of the sense of evil see, Vann Woodward, *Burden of Southern History*. Also of interest is the chapter on "Myth" in Walter Sullivan, *A Requiem for the Renascence: The State of Fiction in the Modern South* (Athens, Ga., 1976). For illustrations of how the sense of evil affects minor Southern fiction see, Vurrell Yentzen, *A Feast for the Forgiven* (New York, 1954), pp. 235–6, 243; Ann Hebson, *A Fine and Private Place* (New York, 1958), p. 184; George Garrett, *The House on Mulberry Tree* (New York, 1959), pp. 9, 246. Madison Jones in what is surely his best novel, *A Cry of Absence* (New York, 1971), offers a particularly subtle example of the way evil can grow out of apparent good. Here, in fact, Jones comes close to achieving that active, exploratory, and critical approach to the problem and consciousness of evil that characterises the best Southern writing. For instances of this kind of writing see the novels by Bishop and Lytle cited earlier; also, the subtle dialectic between "the human filth" and "the human hope" to be found in so much of Robert Penn Warren's work. (The phrases quoted here are from his *Audubon: A Vision*, in *Selected Poems*, p. 92, section II, line 6. See also, *Meet Me in the Green Glen* (New York, 1972), p. 370, and *Brother to Dragons: A Tale in Verse and Voices (A New Version)* (New York, 1979), p. 118.)

38. *Go Down, Moses* (1942; London, 1960 edition), p. 91. See also, *Sanctuary*, p. 176. The best book on Faulkner's treatment of blacks is still Charles H. Nilon, *Faulkner and the Negro* (New York, 1965). But see also, Thadious M. Davis, *Faulkner's "Negro": Art and the Southern Context* (Baton Rouge, La., 1983).

39. *Intruder in the Dust*, p. 13. See also, *Soldier's Pay*, p. 119; *Flags in the Dust*, p. 127; *The Unvanquished*, p. 60; Jean-Paul Sartre, *Baudelaire* (Paris, 1947), p. 201 (my translation).

40. *Sanctuary*, p. 17. See also, *The Sound and the Fury* (1929; London, 1964 edition), pp. 90, 118; *Light in August*, pp. 93, 143; *Sanctuary*, p. 133; *The Town*, p. 45; *Go Down, Moses*, p. 240.

41. For interesting discussions of Faulkner's treatment of women that reach slightly different conclusions see, Sally R. Page, *Faulkner's Women: Characterization and Meaning* (Deland, Fla., 1972); David Williams, *Faulkner's Women: The Myth and the Muse* (Montreal, 1977).

42. Cash, *Mind of the South*, p. 89.

43. *Absalom, Absalom!*, p. 109. See also, p. 114. On Mr Compson see, e.g., *Faulkner in the University*, p. 3; also, Michael Millgate, *The Achievement of William Faulkner* (London, 1966), p. 95, and André Bleikasten, *The Most Splendid Failure: Faulkner's "The Sound and the Fury"* (Bloomington, Ind., 1976), pp. 109–14.

44. *The Sound and the Fury*, p. 86.

45. *Sanctuary*, pp. 177–8. See also, pp. 73, 133; *Sanctuary: The Original Text*, p. 16. For

discussions of *Sanctuary* that see it in terms of a vision of evil see, e.g., Cleanth Brooks, *William Faulkner: The Yoknapatawpha Country* (New Haven, Conn., 1963); Olga Vickery, *The Novels of William Faulkner* (Baton Rouge, La., 1964). See also, Albert Guerard, Jr, "The Misogynous Vision as High Art: Faulkner's *Sanctuary*", *Southern Review*, XII (1976), 215–31.

46. Perhaps it is worth mentioning, however, that none of these writers – and in fact no other Southern writer – approaches Faulkner in the sheer range and depth of his self-consciousness. No one goes quite so far as him in explaining and exploring the region's myths, while at the same time allowing those myths to shape the structure and thicken the texture of his stories.

47. James Branch Cabell, *Beyond Life: Dizain des Demiurges* (1919), in *The Works of James Branch Cabell* (18 vols.; New York, 1927–30), I, 269. See also, Hamilton Basso, *In Their Own Image* (New York, 1935), p. 142; Kimbrough, *Night Fire*, pp. 37–8, 79.

48. Peter Taylor, *A Woman of Means* (New York, 1950), pp. 35, 38. See also, "Two Ladies in Retirement", in *The Widows of Thornton* (New York, 1954), p. 187.

49. Shelby Foote, *Tournament* (New York, 1949), p. 212. See also, pp. xiii, xiv, 18, 19, 75. It is perhaps worth noting that Foote comes in for special mention in *Faulkner at the University* and that *Tournament* was one of the relatively few post-Second World War novels kept in Faulkner's Oxford library. See Joseph Blotner, *William Faulkner's Library: A Catalogue* (Charlottesville, Va., 1964), p. 31. For other examples of the treatment of the heroic sense in Southern writing see, Green Peyton, *Rain on the Mountain* (New York, 1934), pp. 26, 33, 96, 106, 216; Caroline Ivey, *The Family* (New York, 1952), pp. 36, 314; William Humphrey, *Home from the Hill* (New York, 1958), pp. 10–12, 191.

50. *Absalom, Absalom!*, p. 46. See also, pp. 8, 69, 72–3, 179, 217.

51. Ibid., pp. 9–10. See also, p. 11.

52. Ibid., p. 96. See also, p. 174; *Mosquitoes* (1927; London, 1964 edition), p. 209.

53. *As I Lay Dying* (1930; London, 1963 edition), p. 164. See also, p. 136; *Flags in the Dust*, p. 8.

54. *Intruder in the Dust*, p. 84. See also, p. 236.

55. Cited in William L. Andrews, *The Literary Career of Charles W. Chesnutt* (Baton Rouge, La., 1980), p. 276.

56. Cited in Tanner, *City of Words*, p. 432.

57. *The Unvanquished*, p. 132.

58. Ibid., p. 156.

59. Ibid., p. 163.

60. *Lion in the Garden*, pp. 70–1.

61. Ibid., p. 71.

62. Cash, *Mind of the South*, p. 53.

63. *Mosquitoes*, p. 156.

64. Ibid., p. 175.

65. "Introduction to *The Sound and the Fury*", *Mississippi Quarterly*, p. 415. See also, *Sanctuary*, p. 261; *Soldier's Pay*, p. 52.

66. *Pylon*, p. 81. See also, *Mosquitoes*, p. 175; *The Wild Palms* (1939; London, 1961 edition), p. 20.

67. *The Mansion*, pp. 192, 222, See also, "An Introduction to *The Sound and the Fury*" edited by James B. Meriwether, *Southern Review*, VIII (Autumn, 1972), 710; *Soldier's Pay*, p. 207; *Mosquitoes*, p. 96.

68. *Notes Toward a Supreme Fiction*, "It Must Be Abstract", poem 1, line 3.

69. "Nympholepsy", in *Uncollected Stories of William Faulkner* edited by Joseph Blotner (London, 1980), p. 335. See also, pp. 332, 333, 334, 336; Cleanth Brooks, *William Faulkner: Toward Yoknapatawpha and Beyond* (New Haven, Conn., 1978), p. 51. For

"L'Apres-Midi d'un Faune" and "The Hill" see, *William Faulkner: Early Prose and Poetry* (1962; London, 1963 edition), pp. 39–40, 90–2. Also of interest in this respect is *Mayday*, an allegory written as a gift for Helen Baird and dated 27 January, 1926. This was published in a facsimile edition, edited by Carvel Collins, by the University of Notre Dame Press in 1977: see especially, pp. 48, 51.

70. *The Town*, p. 9.

71. *Soldier's Pay*, p. 175.

72. *Mosquitoes*, p. 265. See also, pp. 23, 89, 137, 138, 253.

73. *Flags in the Dust*, pp. 190–1. See also, p. 398; *Go Down, Moses*, p. 226; *The Mansion*, p. 216. In *Sartoris* (1929; London, 1964 edition), "quietness" is substituted for "quietude": see pp. 134, 261.

74. *Faulkner in the University*, p. 61. See also p. 77; *Faulkner at Nagano*, p. 106.

75. Cited in Joseph Blotner, *Faulkner: A Biography* (New York, 1974), p. 1522. On the genesis of *The Sound and the Fury* and its tangled relationship to Faulkner's own life, see pp. 560–633 of Blotner's biography. Also, Judith B. Wittenberg, *Faulkner: The Transfiguration of Biography* (Lincoln, Nebraska, 1979), pp. 75–87; Minter, *William Faulkner*, pp. 91–107.

76. Cited in Minter, *William Faulkner*, p. 95.

77. *Lion in the Garden*, p. 245. Cf. p. 222; *Faulkner in the University*, p. 31. For an account of the book's genesis that is slightly different in its emphases see, *Faulkner at Nagano*, pp. 103–5.

78. *Faulkner in the University*, p. 6.

79. "Introduction to *The Sound and the Fury*", *Southern Review*, p. 709. See also, *Mosquitoes*, p. 208; "Introduction to *The Sound and the Fury*", *Mississippi Quarterly*, p. 415.

80. However, it is not unique. Although she is a very different figure, or rather a very different kind of absent presence, Addie Bundren is just as complex and paradoxical: as fierce in her demands as Drusilla Hawk, as committed to motion as Faulkner's nymphs, and as close to the earth, "clinging to it", as Eula Varner or Lena Grove.

81. "Caddy ... is first and foremost an image". Bleikasten, *The Most Splendid Failure*, p. 65.

82. *The Sound and the Fury*, pp. 52–3. For a rather different notion of the language of this section see, Cecil L. Moffitt, "A Rhetoric for Benjy", *Southern Literary Journal*, II (Fall, 1970), 32–46.

83. *The Sound and the Fury*, p. 159. See also, Henry James, *The Art of the Novel* edited by R.P. Blackmur (New York, 1942), p. 42.

84. *The Sound and the Fury*, p. 91. See also, pp. 82, 102, 113, 151.

85. For an interesting discussion of the possible link between Quentin's aristocratic pose, the declining culture to which he tries to attach himself, and his preoccupation with incest see, Bleikasten, *The Most Splendid Failure*, pp. 115, 227. A recent book on Faulkner argues that he never completely disengaged himself from the patrician values and aristocratic attitudes of the South: see Walter Taylor, *Faulkner's Search for a South* (Urbana, Ill., 1983).

86. See, e.g., Bleikasten, *The Most Splendid Failure*, p. 147, Stephen M. Ross, "Jason Compson and Sut Lovingood: Southwestern Humor as Stream of Consciousness", *Studies in the Novel*, VIII (1976), 278–90.

87. *Lion in the Garden*, p. 225.

88. *The Sound and the Fury*, pp. 163, 174.

89. Ibid., p. 236. See also, Wayne Booth, *The Rhetoric of Fiction* (Chicago, 1961).

90. An essay that does not forget this, but then tends to overstate the negative case, is John V. Hagopian's "Nihilism in *The Sound and the Fury*", *Modern Fiction Studies*, XIII (Spring, 1967), 45–55.

91. *The Sound and the Fury*, p. 284. See also, p. 264. For a detailed examination of the book's ending see, Beverly Gross, "Form and Fulfillment in *The Sound and the Fury*", *Modern Language Quarterly*, XXIX (December, 1968), 439–49.

92. The tendency to identify Faulkner with a specifically international modernist movement, and to deprecate or at least play down his regionalism, dates back at least as far as 1929. See Winfield Townley Scott's review of *The Sound and the Fury* (Providence *Sunday Journal*, Oct. 20, 1929), in *William Faulkner: The Critical Heritage* edited by John Bassett (London, 1975). See also, Millgate, *Achievement of William Faulkner*, and Donald M. Kartiganer, *The Fragile Thread: The Meaning of Form in Faulkner's Novels* (Amherst, Mass., 1979) for, respectively, one of the most effective and one of the more recent examples of this tendency.

93. *Lion in the Garden*, pp. 30–1.

6 THE SOUTHERNER AS AMPHIBIAN: THE REGION SINCE THE WAR

1. Jonathan Yardley, "The Last Good One?" *New Republic*, CLXII (May 9, 1970), 36.
2. Sullivan, *Requiem for the Renascence*, p. 19. See also, "Twentieth-Century Southern Literature", Louis D. Rubin, Jr and C. Hugh Holman (eds.), *Southern Literary Study: Problems and Possibilities* (Chapel Hill, N.C., 1975), p. 141; Young, *Past in the Present*, p. xvi.
3. Simpson, *Dispossessed Garden*, p. 71. See also, Rubin and Holman, "Twentieth-Century Southern Literature", p. 139. For other contributions to this debate see, e.g., Louis D. Rubin, Jr, "The Boll Weevil, the Iron Horse, and the End of the Line: Thoughts on the South", in *A Gallery of Southerners* (Baton Rouge, La., 1982), pp. 197–222; Walter Sullivan, "In Time of the Breaking of Nations: The Decline of Southern Fiction", in *Death by Melancholy: Essays on Modern Southern Fiction* (Baton Rouge, La., 1972), pp. 87–96; Floyd C. Watkins, *The Death of Art: Black and White in the Recent Southern Novel* (Athens, Ga. 1970).
4. Simpson, *Dispossessed Garden*, p. 89. See also Rubin and Holman (eds.), "Twentieth-Century Southern Literature", p. 141.
5. Jack Temple Kirby, *Media-Made Dixie: The South in the American Imagination* (Baton Rouge, La., 1978), p. 161. See also, Numan V. Bartley and Hugh D. Graham, *Southern Politics and the Second Reconstruction* (Baltimore, Md., 1975), p. 19.
6. John C. McKinney and Linda Brookover Bourque, "The Changing South: National Incorporation of a Region", *American Sociological Review*, XXXVI (June, 1971), 399. See also, p. 401.
7. Ibid., p. 407. See also, pp. 403, 406.
8. Margaret L. Andersen, "Race Beliefs in the New South: From Caste to Class", in Merle Black and John Shelton Reed (eds.), *Perspectives on the American South*, volume 2 (New York, 1984), p. 251. See also, *The New York Times*, Nov. 4, 1984, p. E4.
9. William C. Havard, "The South: A Shifting Perspective", in *The Changing Politics of the South* edited by William C. Havard (Baton Rouge, La., 1972), p. 17. See also, pp. 15–16.
10. Monroe Lee Billington, *The Political South in the Twentieth Century* (New York, 1975), pp. xiii, 179. See also, Bartley and Graham, *Southern Politics and the Second Reconstruction*, p. 22; Havard, "The South: A Shifting Perspective", pp. 20–1.
11. George Christian, former White House press secretary for Lyndon B. Johnson, cited in *The Washington Post*, Nov. 8, 1984, p. A47. See also, *The New York Times*, Nov. 11, 1984, p. 30; *Time*, Nov. 19, 1984, p. 12.

12. *The New York Times*, Nov. 11, 1984, p. 30. See also, Jack Temple Kirby, "The South as Pernicious Abstraction", in Black and Reed (eds.), *Perspectives on the South*, p. 175; William C. Havard, "From Past to Future: An Overview of Southern Politics", in Havard (ed.), *Changing Politics of the South*, pp. 691, 706.

13. Kirby, *Media-Made Dixie*, pp. 159–60. See also, Marshall Frady, "Gone with the Wind", *Newsweek*, July 28, 1975, p. 11.

14. McKinney and Bourque, "Changing South", p. 408.

15. Robert Coles, *Flannery O'Connor's South* (Baton Rouge, La., 1980), p. 72. See also, p. 137; Andersen, "Race Beliefs in the New South", p. 251. Also, Harold Grasmick, "Social Change and Modernism in the American South", *American Behavioral Scientist*, XVI (July-August, 1973), 913–33.

16. W. Carey McWilliams, "The Meaning of the Election", in Gerald Pomper (ed.), *The Election of 1976: Reports and Interpretations* (New York, 1977), p. 151. See also, Kirby, *Media-Made Dixie*, pp. 170–4.

17. John Shelton Reed, *The Enduring South: Subcultural Persistence in Mass Society* (Lexington, Mass., 1972). See also, Bartley and Graham, *Southern Politics and the Second Reconstruction*, p. 200. Also, Havard, "The South: A Shifting Perspective", pp. 24–5.

18. Edwin M. Yoder, "W.J. Cash After A Quarter Century", in Willie Morris (ed.), *The South Today: 100 Years After Appomatox* (New York, 1965), p. 92. See also, Andersen, "Race Beliefs in the New South", p. 259.

19. Ralph McGill, *The South and the Southerner* (Boston, 1963), p. 16. See also, C. Vann Woodward, "From the First Reconstruction to the Second", in Morris (ed.), *South Today*, p. 14.

20. See Reed, *Enduring South*, especially chapters IV–VI. See also, John Shelton Reed, *The Enduring South: An Ethnic Approach to Regional Culture* (Baton Rouge, La., 1982).

21. *Atlanta Constitution*, April 11, 1984, p. A1.

22. Colette Dowling, *The Cinderella Complex: Women's Hidden Fear of Independence* (New York, 1982), p. 87. See also, Anne Goodwyn Jones, *Tomorrow is Another Day: The Woman Writer in the South, 1859–1936* (Baton Rouge, La., 1981), pp. 11, 93. Also, Winthrop Jordan, *White Over Black: American Attitudes Toward the Negro* (Chapel Hill, N.C., 1968), p. 474.

23. Cherry Good, "In Search of the Southern Lady", University of Essex Research Project, 1984, p. 16.

24. Andersen, "Race Beliefs in the New South", p. 256. See also, pp. 251, 259; Denis R. Hogan and David L. Featherman, "Racial Stratification and Socioeconomic Change in the American North and South", *American Journal of Sociology*, LXXXII (July, 1977), 100–26; Guy Hunter (ed.), *Industrialization and Race Relations* (New York, 1965); W. Clark Roof, Thomas Van Valey, and Daphne Spain, "Residential Segregation in Southern Cities: 1970", *Social Forces*, LV (September, 1976), 59–71.

25. Raymond D. Gastil, "Homicide and a Regional Culture of Violence", *American Sociological Review*, XXXVI (June, 1971), p. 416. See also, W.G. Doerner, "Index of Southerness Revisited: The Influence of Wherefrom Upon Whodunnit", *Criminology*, XVI (1978), 47–56; H.S. Erlanger, "Is There a 'Subculture of Violence' in the South?", *Journal of Criminal Law and Criminology*, LXVI (1975), 483–90: J.F. O'Connor and A. Lizotte, "The 'Southern Subculture of Violence' Thesis and Patterns of Gun Ownership", *Social Problems*, XXV (1978), 420–9.

26. J. Sherwood Williams *et al.*, "Southern Subculture and Urban Pistol Owners", in Black and Reed (eds.), *Perspectives on the South*, p. 269. The authors of this essay add that "the considerably more complex issue of what 'southerness' means, in this

connection, is a logical next step for research" (p. 270). See also, A.D. Newton and
F.E. Zimring, Jr, *Firearms and Violence in America* (Washington, D.C., 1970). On the
larger issues raised by this debate see, in particular, Dickson D. Bruce, Jr, *Violence
and Culture in the Antebellum South* (Austin, Tex., 1979); Bertram Wyatt-Brown,
Southern Honor: Ethics and Behavior in the Old South (New York, 1982), especially pp.
17, 22, 34.

27. Willie Morris, *Good Old Boy: A Delta Boyhood* (London, 1974), p. 143.
28. Eudora Welty, *One Writer's Beginnings* (Cambridge, Mass., 1984), p. 104.
29. Alice Walker, *Meridian* (1976; London, 1983 edition), p. 14. See also, Ellen
    Gilchrist, *The Annunciation* (1983; London, 1984 edition), p. 15.
30. Peter Gould and Rodney White, *Mental Maps* (Baltimore, Md., 1974), pp. 93–118.
    See also, Louis Wirth, "The Problem of Minority Groups", in Ralph Linton (ed.),
    The Science of Man in the World Crisis (New York, 1945), p. 2.
31. Robert M. Pierce, "Jimmy Carter and the New South: The View From New
    York", in Black and Reed, *Perspectives on the South*, pp. 181–94.
32. James Orrick, cited in Yoder, "W.J. Cash After a Quarter Century", p. 97. See also
    Reed, *Enduring South*.
33. Billington, *Political South in the Twentieth Century*, p. 183. See also, *Time*, Nov. 19,
    1984, pp. 12, 27, 29, 39.
34. The debate about whether the South has changed definitively since the Second
    World War is a fierce and continuing one. Among those who argue that it has
    changed in some conclusive way (apart from works cited in this or previous
    chapters) are Harry Ashmore, *An Epitaph For Dixie* (New York, 1958); Selz C.
    Mayo, "Social Change, Social Movements, and the Disappearing Sectional
    South", *Social Forces*, XLIII (October, 1964), 1–10; George E. Mowry, *Another Look
    at the Twentieth-Century South* (Baton Rouge, La., 1973); Leonard Reissman,
    "Social Developments and the American South", *Journal of Social Issues*, XXII
    (January, 1966), 101–16; John Westbrook, "Twilight of Southern Regionalism",
    Southwest Review, XLII (Summer, 1957), 231–4. Among those who argue for
    continuity (again, apart from works cited elsewhere) are Carl N. Degler, *Place Over
    Time: The Continuity of Southern Distinctiveness* (Baton Rouge, La., 1977); Leslie W.
    Dunbar, "The Changing Mind of the South: An Exposed Nerve", in Avery O.
    Leiserson (ed.), *The American South in the 1960's* (New York, 1964); Francis B.
    Simkins, *The Everlasting South* (Baton Rouge, La., 1963); George M. Tindall,
    "Mythology: A New Frontier in Southern History", in Frank E. Vandiver (ed.),
    The Idea of the South: Pursuit of A Central Theme (Chicago, 1964), pp. 1–15; *Why the
    South Will Survive: Fifteen Southerners Look at their Region a Half Century after "I'll
    Take My Stand"* (Athens, Ga., 1981). Of course, many observers offer a mixed
    verdict. Among the most interesting of these (apart from works cited elsewhere) are
    James McBride Dabbs who, in *Who Speaks for the South?* (New York, 1964), argues
    that the black may become the essential Southerner; and Lewis M. Killian who, in
    White Southerners (New York, 1970) expresses the hope that a South that is closer to,
    and yet still different from, the rest of the nation may be capable of showing other
    Americans the way to racial harmony.
35. William Styron, *Sophie's Choice* (1979; London, 1980 edition), p. 158. See also, p.
    156.
36. Lee Smith, *Fancy Strut* (New York, 1975), p. 9.
37. Sylvia Wilkinson, *Bone of my Bones* (New York, 1982), p. 256.
38. Ibid., p. 255.
39. Styron, *Sophie's Choice*, p. 249. See also, p. 204.
40. Ibid., p. 401. See also, pp. 149, 315, 330, 331.

41. Barry Hannah, *Ray* (1980; New York, 1981 edition), p. 81. See also, pp. 41, 97, 98; R. Vanarsdall, "The Spirits Will Win Through: An Interview with Barry Hannah", *Southern Review*, XIX (April, 1983), pp. 322, 326, 328.

42. Hannah, *Ray*, p. 103.

43. Cited in Daniel Snowman and Malcolm Bradbury, "The Sixties and Seventies", in *Introduction to American Studies* edited by Malcolm Bradbury and Howard Temperley (London, 1981), p. 281. See also, Donald Barthelme, "See the Moon?", in *Unspeakable Practice, Unnatural Acts* (1968; London, 1969 edition), p. 153.

44. Vanarsdall, "The Spirits Will Win Through", p. 336. See also, p. 331.

45. Barbara King, "Walker Percy Prevails", *Southern Voices*, I (May–June, 1974), 23.

46. "A Still Moment", in *The Collected Stories of Eudora Welty* (1980; London, 1981 edition), p. 198. See also, p. 195.

47. "The Radiance of Jane Austen", in *The Eye of the Story: Selected Essays and Reviews* (New York, 1978). Some particularly useful discussions of Welty are to be found in Ruth M. Vande Kieft, *Eudora Welty* (New York, 1962); Michael J. Kreyling, *Eudora Welty's Achievement of Order* (Baton Rouge, La., 1980); Peggy W. Prenshaw (ed.), *Eudora Welty: Critical Essays* (Jackson, Miss., 1979).

48. Charles T. Bunting, " 'The Interior World': An Interview with Eudora Welty", *Southern Review*, VIII (October, 1972), 721. See also, Linda Kuehl, "The Art of Fiction XLVII: Eudora Welty", *Paris Review*, LV (Fall, 1972), 84; Kreyling, *Eudora Welty's Achievement of Order*, p. 76.

49. *Delta Wedding* (1946; London, 1982 edition), p. 221. See also, pp. 8, 222.

50. "Is Phoenix Jackson's Grandson Really Dead?", in *Eye of the Story*, p. 160.

51. *Delta Wedding*, p. 35. For a few useful comments on Welty's treatment of black characters elsewhere see, Elizabeth Evans, *Eudora Welty* (New York, 1981), pp. 133ff.

52. *The Robber Bridegroom* (1942; London, 1982 edition), pp. 126, 185.

53. Ibid., p. 126. See also, p. 134; *Fairy Tale of the Natchez Trace* (Jackson, Miss., 1975).

54. *Robber Bridegroom*, p. 104. See also, "Place in Fiction", p. 3. Cf. François–René de Chateaubriand, *Atala* (1801) translated by Walter J. Cobb (New York, 1962), pp. 15–18.

55. *Robber Bridegroom*, pp. 142–4. See also, p. 87.

56. *Absalom, Absalom!*, p. 261.

57. Kuehl, "Art of Fiction", p. 77. See also, p. 85. For useful discussions of *Losing Battles* other than those included in the books cited earlier see, Louis D. Rubin, Jr, "Everything Brought Out into the Open: Eudora Welty's *Losing Battles*", in *William Elliott Shoots a Bear*, pp. 213–25; Sheila Stroup, "We're All Part Of It Together: Eudora Welty's Hopeful Vision in *Losing Battles*", *Southern Literary Journal*, XV (Spring, 1983), 42–58.

58. *Losing Battles* (1970; New York, 1978 edition), pp. 340–1. See also, pp. 54, 210, 236, 259, 372.

59. Kuehl, "Art of Fiction", p. 80.

60. *Losing Battles*, p. 169. See also, pp. 303, 347, 412.

61. Ibid., p. 288. See also, pp. 286, 287.

62. Ibid., p. 331. See also, p. 227.

63. Ibid., p. 274. See also, pp. 267, 268, 272, 274, 286.

64. Ibid., p. 9. See also, *One Time, One Place: Mississippi in the Depression. A Snapshot Album, with an Introduction by Eudora Welty* (New York, 1971), pp. 6–7.

65. See, e.g., "Lily Daw and the Three Ladies", "Livvie", "June Recital", and "The Burning", in *Collected Stories*.

66. *The Optimist's Daughter* (New York, 1972), p. 34. This novel first appeared, in a different form, in the *New Yorker* in 1969.

67. "The Delta Factor", in *The Message in the Bottle* (New York, 1975), p. 19. See also, pp. 7, 20; "The Sustaining Stream", *Time*, Feb. 1, 1963, p. 82; Carleton Cremeens, "Walker Percy, the Man and the Novelist: An Interview", *Southern Review*, IV (April, 1968), 280.

68. "Notes for a Novel about the End of the World", in *Message in the Bottle*, p. 112.

69. Cremeens, "Walker Percy: An Interview", p. 285. See also, p. 280; "Notes for a Novel about the End of the World", p. 116.

70. "Delta Factor", p. 11. See also John Carr, "Rotation and Repetition: Walker Percy", in John Carr (ed.), *Kite-Flying and Other Irrational Acts: Conversations with Twelve Southern Writers* (Baton Rouge, La., 1972), p. 54; "The Message in the Bottle", in *Message in the Bottle*, p. 143.

71. "Message in the Bottle", p. 143. See also, Cremeens, "Walker Percy: An Interview", p. 284; "The Loss of the Creature", in *Message in the Bottle*, p. 60; "Delta Factor", p. 3.

72. *The Moviegoer* (1961; London, 1966 edition), p. 17.

73. The terms "carnal" and "angelic knowledge", and "bestialism" and "angelism" are to be found in, respectively, *The Last Gentleman* (1966; New York, 1968 edition), p. 136 and *Love in the Ruins* (1971; London, 1972 edition), p. 27. See also, "Delta Factor", p. 44.

74. *Lancelot* (London, 1977), p. 52.

75. *The Second Coming* (1980; London, 1981 edition), p. 3. See also, pp. 16, 186.

76. "Message in the Bottle", p. 146. For the existentialist aspects of Percy's fiction see, e.g., the essays (especially those by Janet Hobbs and Lewis A. Lawson) in Panthea Reid Broughton (ed.), *The Art of Walker Percy: Stratagems for Being* (Baton Rouge, La., 1979); Martin Luschei, *The Sovereign Wayfarer: Walker Percy's Diagnosis of the Malaise* (Baton Rouge, La., 1972); see also Carr, "Rotation and Repetition".

77. *Second Coming*, p. 19. See also, *Moviegoer*, p. 11.

78. *Love in the Ruins*, p. 9. See also, p. 3.

79. *Lancelot*, p. 120. See also, *Last Gentleman*, pp. 49, 152, 207; *Love in the Ruins*, pp. 181, 279; *Moviegoer*, p. 105.

80. Gilles Deleuze, *Logique du sens* (Paris, 1972), pp. 164–5. My translation. For an interesting discussion of the uses of irony in recent fiction see, Josephine Hendin, *Vulnerable People: A View of American Fiction Since 1945* (1978; New York, 1979 edition), pp. 11ff.

81. *Moviegoer*, p. 113. See also, p. 72; *Lancelot*, pp. 23, 105.

82. *Moviegoer*, p. 21. See also, *Second Coming*, pp. 7, 79, 80. For an interesting discussion of point-of-view in Percy's first novel see, Tony Tanner, *Reign of Wonder* pp. 349–56. This total, blank immersion in the present is something that Binx Bolling shares with a number of other narrators in postmodernist fiction: cf. Maria Wyeth in Joan Didion's *Play It As It Lays* (New York, 1970).

83. *Last Gentleman*, p. 122. See also, *Moviegoer*, pp. 12, 150; *Second Coming*, p. 51; *Lancelot*, p. 231.

84. *Moviegoer*, p. 171. See also, *Lancelot*, pp. 21, 138; T.S. Eliot, "Baudelaire", in *Selected Essays* (London, 1934), p. 389.

85. *Lancelot*, p. 253. See also, pp. 24, 42, 131, 138, 156. For a fuller discussion of the moral and spiritual implications of Lancelot's quest see, William J. Dowie, "*Lancelot* and the Search for Sin", in Broughton (ed.) *Art of Walker Percy*, pp. 245–59.

86. *Lancelot*, p. 158.

87. Ibid., p. 28. See also, p. 29. There can be little doubt that Percy wants us to see Lancelot's failure as characteristic of his time, since the language he deploys, and the techniques he relies on, in his attempt to name and know evil, are mostly borrowed from the world of microcomputers, video equipment, and advanced technology.

88. Ibid., p. 178. See also, pp. 157, 158.
89. For Percy's use of his family background in his fiction see, Jim Van Cleave, "Versions of Percy", *Southern Review*, VI (October, 1970), 990–1010; Lewis A. Lawson, "Walker Percy's Southern Stoic", *Southern Literary Journal*, III (Fall, 1970), 5–31.
90. *Last Gentleman*, p. 16. Cf. *Second Coming*, p. 146.
91. These characters are to be found in, respectively, John Barth, *The End of the Road* (1958); James Purdy, *Cabot Wright Begins* (1965); Kurt Vonnegut, *Slaughterhouse-Five, or, The Children's Crusade* (1969); Ralph Ellison, *Invisible Man* (1952).
92. *Moviegoer*, pp. 11–12. See also, "Loss of the Creature", p. 57; *Love in the Ruins*, p. 34. The critic mentioned here is Tony Tanner: see *City of Words*, p. 159.
93. *Second Coming*, p. 360. See also, pp. 271, 272. Another weakness of these closing pages is the florid – not to say, sentimental and embarrassing – nature of the conversations between Will and Alison (see, e.g., pp. 339, 341, 355). These might be defended on the grounds that Alison has the naïveté of a child and Will is in love. However, this hardly helps to establish their relationship as a valid, adequate, and lasting alternative to the "life-which-is-a-living-death". For differing interpretations of the ending of *Moviegoer* see, e.g., Young, *Past in the Present*, pp. 137–66; Robert Coles, "Walker Percy", *New Yorker*, Oct. 2, 1978, pp. 86ff.; Jerry H. Bryant, *The Open Decision: The Contemporary American Novel and its Intellectual Background* (New York, 1970), pp. 273–7.
94. Introduction to William Alexander Percy, *Lanterns on the Levee: Recollections of a Planter's Son* (1930; Baton Rouge, La., 1973 edition), p. 4.
95. *Moviegoer*, p. 190. See also, Carr, "Rotation and Repetition", p. 48; W.A. Percy, *Lanterns on the Levee*, chapter XXIV.
96. Lewis A. Lawson, "The Fall of the House of Lamar", in Broughton (ed.) *Art of Walker Percy*, p. 244.
97. *Second Coming*, p. 72. See also, pp. 176, 273, 337.
98. *Love in the Ruins*, p. 108. See also, *Lancelot*, p. 92.
99. *Moviegoer*, p. 25. See also, *Love in the Ruins*, p. 108. For some interesting remarks by Percy on his attitude to treatment of blacks and the issue of race in fiction see, Creemens, "Walker Percy: An Interview", pp. 272ff. Percy also tends to disagree with Welty on this point: see particularly, p. 272. Also of interest here, in connection with this last point (i.e. the comparison between Welty and Percy) is William F. Buckley, Jr, "The Southern Imagination": interview with Eudora Welty and Walker Percy on *Firing Line*, television broadcast of Dec. 24, 1972, *Mississippi Quarterly*, XXVI (Fall, 1973), 493–516.
100. *Love in the Ruins*, p. 19. For a very different view of Percy and the South see, Rubin, "The Boll Weevil, the Iron Horse, and the End of the Line", pp. 206ff. Discussions of postmodernism with specific reference to the American novel are already fairly numerous. Among the most interesting and useful are Hendin, *Vulnerable People*; Jerome Klinkowitz, *Literary Disruptions: The Making of a Post-Contemporary American Fiction* (1975; Urbana, Ill., 1980 edition); Raymond M. Olderman, *Beyond the Waste Land: A Study of the American Novel in the Nineteen-Sixties* (New Haven, Conn., 1972); Robert Scholes, *The Fabulators* (New York, 1967); Tanner, *City of Words*.
101. "Notes for a Novel about the End of the World", p. 114.

POSTSCRIPT

1. Roland Barthes, *Mythologies* selected and translated by Annette Lavers (London, 1972), p. 142. See also, p. 110; John Peale Bishop, "The South and Tradition", in *The*

Collected Essays of John Peale Bishop edited by Edmund Wilson (New York, 1948), p. 8.

2. Barthes, *Mythologies*, p. 142. See also, p. 129.
3. Frank Kermode, *Continuities* (London, 1968), p. 40. For a very different view of the Southern relationship to history see, C. Hugh Holman, *The Immoderate Past: The Southern Writer and Southern History* (Athens, Ga., 1977), especially chapter 1.
4. Barthes, *Mythologies*, p. 110.
5. Ibid., p. 120. See also, p. 128.
6. Richard Weaver, *Ideas Have Consequences* (Chicago, 1948), p. 187. See also, "Up From Liberalism", in *Life Without Prejudice and Other Essays* (Chicago, 1965). Also, "Lee the Philosopher", *Georgia Review*, 11 (Fall, 1948), 297–303; "The Tennessee Agrarians", *Shenandoah*, III (Summer, 1952), 3–10; "Contemporary Southern Literature", *Texas Quarterly*, II (Summer, 1959), 126–44; "The Regime of the South". *National Review*, March 14, 1959, pp. 587–99; "The Southern Phoenix", *Georgia Review*, XVII (Spring, 1963), 6–17. The most useful discussions of Weaver are M.E. Bradford, "The Agrarianism of Richard Weaver", *Modern Age*, XIV (Summer, 1970), 249–56; George Core, "One View of the Castle: Richard Weaver and the Incarnate World of the South", in *The Poetry of Community: Essays on the Southern Sensibility of History and Literature* edited by Lewis P. Simpson (Atlanta, Ga., 1972); Fred Hobson, *Tell About the South: The Southern Rage to Explain* (Baton Rouge, La., 1983), pp. 323–35. The Foreword to *The Southern Tradition At Bay*, by Donald Davidson, and the Preface by Bradford and Core are also very helpful.
7. Richard Weaver, *The Southern Tradition At Bay: A History of Postbellum Thought* edited by George Core and M.E. Bradford (New Rochelle, N.Y., 1968), p. 388. See also, pp. 47–8.
8. Ibid., p. 112.
9. Ibid., p. 268. See also, pp. 61, 261–2.
10. Ibid., p. 115.
11. Ibid., p. 34. See also, pp. 30, 31, 32. For Weaver's attempt to come to terms with the fact that the Old South was a slave-holding society see, p. 35.
12. Ibid., p. 42. See also, pp. 36, 39; "The South and the American Union", in Rubin (ed.), *Lasting South*, p. 66.
13. *Southern Tradition At Bay*, p. 387. See also, p. 388, 389, 390.
14. Ibid., pp. 43–4.
15. Ibid., p. 391.
16. Ibid., pp. 394–5. See also, p. 392.
17. Ibid., p. 392. See also, p. 394. There is also a touch of desperate casuistry in Weaver's claim that, by appealing to the same impulses as the fascist state does (the desire for "holiness and heroism", for instance), his new order will act as a safety-valve in a way that a social democracy never could and so supply a bulwark against fascism as well as communism. See pp. 395–6.
18. "Agrarianism in Exile", *Sewanee Review*, LVIII (Autumn, 1950), 602.
19. *Southern Tradition At Bay*, p. 392. See also, p. 393.
20. Hodding Carter, *Southern Legacy* (Baton Rouge, La., 1950); Pat Watters, *The South and the Nation* (New York, 1969); Larry King, *Confessions of a White Racist* (New York, 1971).
21. Hobson, *Tell About the South*, p. 305. The figure of Thomas Wolfe seems to hover behind a good deal of recent Southern fiction: for example, Gilchrist, *Annunciation*, Barry Hannah, *Geronimo Rex* (New York, 1972), Styron, *Sophie's Choice*. Perhaps the major reason for this is that Wolfe was so openly concerned with the process of disengagement from the South.
22. Willie Morris, *North Toward Home* (1967; London, 1968 edition), pp. 6–7, 108–9. See also, p. 3.

23. Ibid., p. 4. See also, Carson McCullers, *The Ballad of the Sad Café* (1951; London, 1963 edition), pp. 7–8; Truman Capote, *Other Voices, Other Rooms* (New York, 1948), pp. 17–18; Hobson, *Tell About the South*, p. 306
24. Andrew Turnbull, *Thomas Wolfe* (New York, 1967), p. 78.
25. Morris, *North Toward Home*, pp. 179–80. See also, pp. 176, 177.
26. Ibid., p. 6. See also, pp. 422, 435. See also, Morris, *Good Old Boy*, pp. 141–2.
27. Morris, *North Toward Home*, p. 9.
28. Ibid., p. 57. See also, pp. 9, 10, 11.
29. Ibid., p. 376.
30. Ibid., pp. 436–7. See also, p. 435; Tate, "Ode to the Confederate Dead", p. 18, line 44.
31. Faulkner, *Absalom, Absalom!*, p. 12.

Index